FROM UNIFORMITY TO UNITY

1662—1962

FROM UNIFORMITY TO UNITY

1662–1962

EDITED BY

GEOFFREY F. NUTTALL

AND

OWEN CHADWICK

LONDON
S·P·C·K
1962

First published in 1962
by S.P.C.K.
Holy Trinity Church
Marylebone Road
London N.W.1

Made and printed in Great Britain by
William Clowes and Sons, Limited
London and Beccles

PUBLISHER'S NOTE

This volume has been prepared under the auspices of a Committee of the Three Denominations (Baptist, Congregational, and Presbyterian) and of the Society for Promoting Christian Knowledge, with the support of the Church Historical Society.

CONTENTS

ABBREVIATIONS

Al. Cant.	*Alumni Cantabrigienses.*
Al. Ox.	*Alumni Oxonienses.*
Bate	F. Bate, *The Declaration of Indulgence 1672*, 1908.
Bosher	R. S. Bosher, *The Making of the Restoration Settlement*, 1951.
Burnet, *HOT*	G. Burnet, *History of My Own Time*, ed. O. Airy, 1897–1900 (references to folio edn of 1724–34 in brackets).
Calamy, *Abridgement*	Edmund Calamy, *Abridgement of Mr Baxter's History*, 2nd edn, 1713.
CJ	*Journal of the House of Commons.*
Clarendon, *Corresp.*	Henry Hyde, *The Correspondence of Henry Hyde, Earl of Clarendon . . . with the Diary of Lord Clarendon from 1687 to 1690*, ed. S. W. Singer, 1828.
CR	A. G. Matthews, *Calamy Revised*, Oxford, 1934.
CSPD	*Calendar of State Papers, Domestic.*
CSP Ven.	*Calendar of State Papers . . . Venice.*
DNB	*Dictionary of National Biography.*
D.W.L.	Dr Williams's Library.
Ec. HR	*Economic History Review.*
EHD viii	*English Historical Documents 1660–1714*, ed. Andrew Browning, 1953.
EHR	*English Historical Review.*
HEM	*History of the Ecumenical Movement*, ed. R. Rouse and S. C. Neill, 1954.
H.M.C.	Historical Manuscripts Commission.
JEH	*Journal of Ecclesiastical History.*
LJ	*Journal of the House of Lords.*
Morrice MS.	Dr Williams's Library Roger Morrice MS. Entry Books (P, Q, R) being a diary of public events from 1679 to 1693.

Pepys, *Diary*	Samuel Pepys, *Diary*, ed. H. B. Wheatley, 1905.
Powicke i	F. J. Powicke, *Life of the Reverend Richard Baxter*, 1924.
Powicke ii	F. J. Powicke, *The Reverend Richard Baxter under the Cross*, 1927.
RB	*Reliquiae Baxterianae*, ed. Matthew Sylvester, 1696 (quoted by book, part, and paragraph).
TRHS	*Transactions* of the Royal Historical Society.
VCH	*Victoria County History*.
WR	A. G. Matthews, *Walker Revised*, Oxford, 1948.

INTRODUCTION

OWEN CHADWICK

IN 1957 a committee of representatives appointed by each of the Three Denominations (Presbyterian, Congregational, Baptist) began to plan a volume of essays, to be published in 1962 as part of a commemoration of 1662. At almost the same moment, and independently, the Society for Promoting Christian Knowledge began to plan a volume of essays to commemorate the restoration of the Church of England and the revision of the Book of Common Prayer, in consultation with Dr Norman Sykes (who agreed to act as editor) and other members of the Publications Committee of the Church Historical Society. The two companies became aware of the overlap when each asked a writer of the other group to contribute an essay. In 1958 they determined to unite. This was approved by the committee of the Three Denominations and welcomed by the then Archbishop of Canterbury, to whom the S.P.C.K. proposal had been made known when the bishops were considering preparations for marking the tercentenary. One editor was selected from each group, originally Dr Norman Sykes and Dr Geoffrey Nuttall. Before his premature death Dr Sykes was able to contribute much with Dr Nuttall to the general plan of the book and choice of contributors. This volume aims to study the reasons and circumstances of the religious separation of 1662, the consequent failure of plans to reunite or "comprehend" the divided bodies, and the subsequent changes in relationship between the Church of England and the Free Churches.

The title might well raise a smile, perhaps a satirical smile, in those who know what breaches of uniformity existed in 1662 and what painful disunity exists in 1962. The title must be taken rather as a symbol than as a literal description. Yet as a symbol it is meaningful. One of the notable changes in the English religious atmosphere since 1910 has been the growth of mutual understanding and the decline of mutual recrimination. Even here it is unhistorical to exaggerate the gain. In July 1688 (admittedly in the special circumstances of that year of revolution) Archbishop Sancroft, whose frame was not composed without a certain conscientious rigidity, sent to the bishops a list of articles upon which they were more fully to insist in their addresses to the clergy and people. The clergy were exhorted to have "a very tender regard to our brethren the Protestant Dissenters; that upon occasion offered, they visit them at their houses, and receive them kindly at their own, and treat them fairly wherever they meet them, discoursing calmly and civilly with them; persuading them (if it may be) to a full compliance with our Church, or at least that 'whereto we have already attained, we may all walk by the same rule, and mind the same thing' ".[1] And yet there is a subtle touch of patronage, even about these eirenical phrases of the archbishop, which seems altogether lacking in the corresponding exchanges of recent years. If no one can say that "unity" (in the sense in which most Anglicans and most Free Churchmen understand it) has been achieved or appears near to being achieved, at least there is more "unity" of some sort than at any point of English history since 1662. The work of the British Council of Churches is evidence enough; and even more unusual in the light of history is the existence of agreed syllabuses for religious education in the national schools since (and before) 1944. A hundred years ago, the year 1662 was commemorated, not only by humane writers like Stoughton, but with acrimonious pamphlets and uncharitable speeches. If there are bitter utterances in 1962, they are not the utterances of responsible churchmen upon either side.

Throughout Christendom, the Middle Ages left a religious axiom among its legacies, that Church and State were coextensive, that a man could not be a loyal citizen of the State unless he was a member of the Church of that State. The

[1] G. D'Oyly, *The Life of William Sancroft* (1821), i. 324.

Reformation, inheriting this axiom, attempted to found a series of reformed States where all forms of religious dissent were excluded under secular penalties. For a time, and in some countries, the attempt was almost as successful as in the Spain of the Counter-Reformation.

But not for long. The printing press had permitted the spread of Protestantism, and it permitted the divisions of Protestantism. No strongly or widely held body of opinion could now be suppressed indefinitely. All the censorship in the world (and the censorship of the sixteenth and seventeenth centuries was clumsy and cumbersome) could not prevent the dissemination of ideas critical of the European régimes in Church and State.

The Protestants told men to go to their Bibles. They translated the Bible into the vernacular, printed editions handy for the pocket, expounded it from the pulpit, used it in the liturgy. By 1650, the ideal of Erasmus that every ploughboy should read the Bible for himself was far from being realized. But an elementary knowledge of the life of George Fox, or of John Bunyan, shows how some of the people, the potmen and the tinkers and the bagmen and the rude "mechanicks", were immersed in Biblical language, men of one book, their encyclopaedia of secular knowledge and their guide to conduct as well as their source of divine truth. The Reformation had appealed to the Bible, had opened the gates to the stream of Pauline and evangelical ideas; and a hundred years later was finding it difficult enough to keep the flood within the banks which the first Reformers had intended. They had released a power which they could hardly contain by law-courts and censorship and banishments.

Across Europe, in the sixteenth century, ran the disagreement between the Protestant right and the Protestant left, between Wittenberg and Zürich, conservative and radical, Lutheran and Reformed. In France, Holland, and Scotland, the Swiss way rapidly became the accepted norm of reformation, "the pattern of the best reformed Churches". In

Scandinavia and in central and north-east Germany, though more slowly, the Lutheran way maintained its ground against the inroad of Swiss ideas. But by 1555, still more by 1600, Germany was divided, not only into Roman Catholic and Protestant, but into Roman Catholic, Lutheran, and Reformed. Should the old customs, so far as possible, be maintained in Protestant Churches if those customs were harmless? Was it necessary to have the authority of Scripture for whatever was done in worship? What was the legitimate place of the civil power in the administration of the Church? Was the doctrine of absolute predestination (to life or death by divine decree from all eternity, irrespective of conduct) a necessary corollary, or was it indeed the foundation of the doctrine of justification by faith alone? What was the nature or mode of the objective gift in the two Gospel sacraments? Was there continuity with the tradition of the Church of the Middle Ages, or had the Reformation made a clean break? Was it the same house repaired, or a reconstructed house upon old foundations?

Elizabethan England resembled Germany in being divided into three main religious groups. But whereas Protestant disunity in Germany could easily rest amidst the almost independent German states, the England of Elizabeth uniquely attempted to find room, within the borders of a single state, for the conservative (provided he were not too conservative), and the radical (provided he were not too radical).

With one eye upon Catholic squires in Lancashire and the other upon Puritan merchants in London and East Anglia, the Queen and her advisers tried to maintain sufficient continuity of structure and worshipping life to satisfy the Catholic, and sufficient reformation to satisfy the Calvinist. The leaders of the Church of England claimed that in all essentials the Church was following the pattern of the best reformed Churches. On the other hand, when there was a question whether the Queen might marry a French Catholic, the Duke of Anjou, Mr Francis Walsingham told the French agent (25 May 1571) that the Duke should "examine whether he might not with good devotion use the form of prayer appointed throughout her realm, the same being in effect nothing but that which the Church of Rome uses, saving that it is in the English tongue, which, if he pleased, might be translated into French; and further, that the usage of the Divine service in England did not properly compel any man to alter his opinion in the great matters being now in controversy in the Church"; while on 3 November 1635 Bishop Montague of Chichester is said to have told the Pope's agent Panzani that he was ready to subscribe all the Pope's articles unless it be transubstantiation.[1] Politicians, for their purposes, have been known to minimize differences of religious belief and practice.

These extremes could have been held together only by a comprehensiveness of doctrine and tolerance of practice impossible in that age. There was never any question of putting Walsingham's diplomatic conservatism into ecclesiastical usage; nor that the Church of England was a reformed Church, and at first a Church whose divines looked mainly to Zürich, though sometimes to Geneva, for guidance in their divinity; nor that to controvert Popery was one of the duties which exercised their intellects.

A Reformed divinity, with a traditional structure of bishops and law-courts and a liturgy as traditional-sounding as the conservative Lutheran liturgies—the nearest parallel to the Elizabethan endeavour is not a Church containing Roman Catholic and Protestant, but a Church containing Lutheran and Calvinist harmoniously. It ought theoretically to have been possible to declare that these differences between Protestants were sometimes disputes of the lecture-room, sometimes legitimate disagreement among Christians, sometimes (as with consubstantiation) cases where unity and mutual forbearance should triumph over contradictions

[1] *CSP Foreign 1569–71*, no. 1,729: *Memoirs of Gregorio Panzani*, ed. Joseph Berington (1793), 237.

imposed as much by the conscience as the intellect. It ought theoretically to have been possible to marry Lutheran and Reformed; by 1614, when David Pareus of Heidelberg published his *Irenicum*, some Reformed theologians were pleading for the marriage, and in England Richard Hooker had come near to reaching the same plea before 1593. But it was not easy to convert the pleas of a few theorists and academics into religious practice. No German state, where the two main reforming ideals were intermingled, succeeded in achieving the marriage before the second half of the seventeenth century, and then it was not comfortable.

England was the one state where the government persevered over a long period in attempting something like this unity between the conservative Protestants and the Reformed. Given time and a favourable breeze in politics, the ship might have sailed into harbour. From 1603, and especially from 1625, the political winds were not friendly; and by the time that the ecumenical ideals of the middle seventeenth century were making their impact, by the time that *toleration* and *comprehension* were beginning to be advocated as good and not always repudiated as wicked, the civil wars had destroyed almost all hope of uniting "Anglican" and "Presbyterian" in a single, organic, national Church. The divisions of the Church of England helped to divide the State; and the division of England into armed camps helped to divide the Church, even after the King had come into his own. Political schism and ecclesiastical schism were bedfellows. It could not be otherwise when most men believed that citizen and churchman were synonymous.

The idea of comprehension was not an idea to command heartfelt discipleship. Men will contend for the truth, for in their consciences they know that they must. They could rarely contend for the freedom of other men to be wrong. They could devote themselves to a creed, not to a proposition which affirmed that their creed might be denied with impunity. The last man to be executed for heresy in

England, Edward Wightman, was burnt in 1612, and burning was ended because the authorities believed this form of punishment to be inexpedient, not because they believed penalties for heresy to be wrong. Comprehension seemed to be a negative, an expedient, a political device. It were better that all men should agree upon the truth and accept it. If they were going to allow rival opinion, they would allow it because the State needed it, or because it was advantageous to unite the Protestants against the Papists, and not because it might be true. They believed that the truth was sufficiently known.

The defence of a known and imperative truth elicits the highest decision of the conscience. Comprehension was charitable expediency; and expediency, however charitable, is a judgement of the reason and cannot easily stand against the judgement of the conscience. Catholic France accepted the Edict of Nantes of 1598, which at last gave toleration to French Protestants, not because Catholic France affirmed toleration to be merely right, but because without the Edict France must be destroyed.

No endeavour for Christian unity can succeed unless it can persuade men that this recommended comprehension possesses a moral imperative comparable in degree with the moral duty of loyalty to truth.

From 1567, still more from 1581, there existed little groups of "Separatists", especially in London: the origins of those communions later to be called Baptist or Congregational or Independent. These religious groups possessed one common characteristic. Their members, with few exceptions, believed that the magistrate (the State) had no concern with religion, that his duty was to hold the ring to secure the independent life of independent and autonomous congregations. The generous toleration of most groups under the Commonwealth nearly approached their idea of state action in religion. Cromwell's rule allowed them to flourish and take deep roots in the land. By 1660 they had come to stay within the national life.

There could be little question, in 1660, of reuniting them to the Establishment. They were opposed in conscience to union with an Establishment and to the use of a formal liturgy. Here is John Bunyan's description of his examination before the justices at Bedford in November 1660.[1]

> *Justice Keelin:* Do you come to church, you know what I mean; to the parish church to hear Divine Service?
>
> *Bunyan:* I answered, No, I did not.
>
> *Keelin:* He asked me, Why?
>
> *Bunyan:* I said, Because I did not find it commanded in the Word of God.
>
> *Keelin:* He said, We were commanded to pray.
>
> *Bunyan:* I said, But not by the Common Prayer-Book.
>
> *Keelin:* He said, How then?
>
> *Bunyan:* I said, With the Spirit. As the apostle saith, "I will pray with the Spirit and with the understanding". (1 Cor. XIV. 15)
>
> *Keelin:* He said, We might pray with the Spirit, and with the understanding, and with the Common Prayer-Book also.
>
> *Bunyan:* I said, The prayers in the Common Prayer-Book were such as was made by other men, and not by the motions of the Holy Ghost, within our hearts; and as I said, the apostle saith, he will pray with the Spirit, and with the understanding; not with the Spirit and the Common Prayer-Book.

No concession by a restored Church could have satisfied this conscience. Either he must be given freedom, or he must be suppressed. It took the State a further quarter of a century to learn that he could not be suppressed and must therefore be given freedom.

The Independent of the twentieth century is not always so sure of his ground as Bunyan. The action of the State in religion since 1851 has been different from the action of the

[1] John Bunyan, *A Relation of my Imprisonment in the Month of November 1660* (1905 edn of 1765 first edition), 199 f.

State before 1689, and Establishment has been valued by some Congregationalists and Baptists as a sign of a national profession of Christian faith. But it would be naïve and sentimental to overlook the profound historical force of the kind of conscience represented by Bunyan. If anyone thinks that an organic unity between Church of England and Independency is likely to be easy or rapid, let him read the evidence[1] submitted in 1931 by the Congregationalist Bernard Manning to the Archbishops' Commission on the Relations between Church and State. "We never for one moment [he is writing of the legal relation between the Church of England and the State] regret the choice which our ecclesiastical fathers made and which we daily confirm." All his evidence, from which this characteristic utterance is selected, should be read, for one especial reason—Bernard Manning understood the Church of England, and loved its common prayers, more deeply than many Anglicans.

The question in 1660–2 could not be of freedom, for freedom and disunity seemed to be identical. The question was of comprehension; of what arrangements could be made, in order or liturgy, to satisfy the Presbyterian leaders.

Uniformity was always practical in intention. Theorists might recognize that different liturgies were used in Wittenberg or Nuremberg or Strasburg and that the differences no more invalidated the rites than the differences between Greek and Latin liturgies in the ancient Church. Dutch or French liturgies had been permitted to residents in London. But experience taught that in a single city or state, variety and change bred dispute; and the 1662 Act of Uniformity charged the absence of a uniform liturgy, during the past years, with leading "into factions and schisms, to the great decay and scandal of the reformed religion of the Church of England, and to the hazard of many souls". "Nothing", recorded the Act as an axiom, "conduces more to the settling

[1] Printed in *Essays in Orthodox Dissent* (1939), 196 ff.

of the peace of this nation (which is desired of all good men), nor to the honour of our religion, and the propagation thereof, than an universal agreement in the public worship of Almighty God."[1]

The Presbyterians might have been reconciled, so far as outward liturgy and order went. There was more flexibility in their tradition than subsequently appeared when they had become dissenters. Episcopalian and Presbyterian (though the terms are almost anachronistic under Queen Elizabeth) had worked side by side in a single Church between 1558 and 1642, the Presbyterians mostly conforming to the established discipline even when they were protesting against it. They had tried to introduce a partial and unofficial system of presbyteries in the hope that as this grew within the episcopalian system it would slowly win the approval of the State; and they had used the system of parish lectureships to achieve a certain independence of the parochial control exercised through patronage and the law of benefices. Conversely, King James I of England in 1610 introduced bishops into Scotland, in order that this partial and modified episcopacy might slowly win its way and in the end Scotland might have a common order with England. The incompatibility had issued in vehement pamphlet war and physical repression of presbyteries, first under Archbishop Whitgift (1583–1604) and then under Archbishop Laud (1633–45); and finally, when the Civil War came, in the formal agreement of the Solemn League and Covenant in 1643 to make the English Church Presbyterian. Despite all these discomforts, most of the ministers who accepted Presbyterian principles never ceased, before 1662, to regard themselves as members of the Church of England. There was more flexibility than sometimes appeared in their demands to abolish the surplice or the sign of the cross in baptism. Perhaps most of them would have continued to serve the

[1] H. Gee and W. J. Hardy, *Documents Illustrative of English Church History* (1921), 601 ff.

Church of England after 1662 if they had not been compelled, first, to declare their "unfeigned assent and consent to all and everything" contained in the Book of Common Prayer; and secondly, still more, if those ordained by presbyteries under the Commonwealth and Protectorate had not been compelled to receive episcopal ordination before St Bartholomew's Day 1662. By this second provision they were being asked, or appeared to be asked, to renounce their previous ministry, which might have been already exercised for many years in English parishes.

The Anglicans had no notion, in modern terms, that the Civil War and Commonwealth had thrust anomaly upon the Church of England; still less had they any notion that an interim period of anomaly might be permitted for the sake of remedying past disorder with gentleness. They had no such notion, in the main, because King Charles I had been executed. The Presbyterians had not killed the King; most of them had disapproved the act as vehemently as many Episcopalians. In 1662, however, the maintenance of the old Church was a part of the citizen's loyalty and affection for the constitution.

Policy and history were more momentous than theology for the decision of 1662. But it does not follow that theology may be overlooked. It is worth asking how far the debate then turned upon the notion of "validity" in sacraments, the notion which after the Oxford Movement was to transform the conditions of the argument. The answer is, hardly at all, in those words. But if High Churchmen of that age like Bramhall or Thorndike had been asked what led them not to compromise, they would have replied in terms like the following:

Our paramount duty is to the Catholic Church; our subordinate and derivative duty is to the Church of England as the representative of the Catholic Church in this country.

The Catholic Church is known by its faithfulness to the primitive model. The Church of England has no choice but to follow that model, must seek to apply the principle rigorously and exactly.[1] "I am satisfied", wrote Thorndike in 1660, "that the differences, upon which we are divided, cannot be justly settled upon any terms, which any part of the *Whole* Church shall have just cause to refuse, as inconsistent with the unity of the *Whole* Church."[2] He has an ominous phrase about men "ordained by Presbyters against Bishops"[3]—how shall we recognize as ordained men who were ordained for the purpose of setting up altar against altar? The Church of England is to be re-established by law; and if some pretend tenderness of conscience against that law, some might pretend tenderness of conscience against any law. "Supposing the Unity of the Church ordained by God; to forbear those Laws which it requireth, because tenderness of conscience may be alleged against them, is to offend the whole rather than a part. For the same might have been alleged against any Law of God's Church."[4]

The argument is put rigidly, partly because the circumstances of the day encouraged rigour, and partly because Thorndike was notorious for his inability to write persuasively. But it represents a contention which has survived the centuries and must still be reckoned with. Any act which divides the Church of England from the universal Church of the centuries is to be eschewed, even if that act offers temporary or local advantage; and the test of universality, in this sad, divided state of Christendom, may be found in appeal to the ancient and undivided Church of the first centuries. The question whether there are sufficient ambiguities or exceptions in the episcopal practice of the ancient

[1] Cf. A. W. Haddan, *Life of Herbert Thorndike* (1856), 218.

[2] *The Due Way of Composing the Differences on Foot*, in *Works*, ed. A. W. Haddan, v. (1854), 29.

[3] Ibid., v. 63.

[4] *Just Weights and Measures* (1662), 23.

Church to warrant modern exceptions, Thorndike answered with a vigorous negative. The question whether these objections against an act in breach of Catholicity apply with equal force to a temporary, an interim, exception to episcopacy as a charitable remedy for an anomalous predicament, he made no attempt to consider.[1]

These, then, were the conditions of the problem, stripped to essentials, in 1662, and despite the absence of the political struggle which helped to create the calamity of St Bartholomew's Day, they are the same conditions still—the desirability of agreement in worship; the hypothetical possibility of comprehension; the refusal of Presbyterians (and later of Methodists) to accept any act which might be interpreted as confessing their present ministry to be inefficacious or "invalid"; the refusal of Episcopalians to countenance any act which they would regard as a "breach in Catholic order"; the conviction of Independents that in the last resort no mere comprehension will satisfy by its limitations, since each congregation of Christians must retain its liberty. Much has altered, in three hundred years, but not the foundations of the problem.

The first half of this book studies the setting of the problem, from 1660 to 1689—the mode and consequences of the Restoration of Charles II; the division of 1662 and the first Nonconformists; the later attempts to secure either comprehension or indulgence until the Toleration Act of 1689; and the slow movement of the Presbyterians towards accepting an outlook like that of the Independents, in that, once separated, they were drawn towards other separatists, subjected to a common disability by the law.

From 1689 to 1828, when the Test and Corporation Acts

[1] Such a consideration of anomaly naturally arose among the Laudian exiles upon the Continent during the Commonwealth, on the question whether they should communicate with the Huguenot churches. See e.g. John Cosin's *Letter to Mr Cordel at Blois* (1650) in *Works* (1851 edn), iv. 401.

were repealed, the predicament of Dissent altered little. The Presbyterian interest weakened as their congregations fell away into Unitarianism. The rise of the Methodists added many to the number whose prime allegiance was not devoted to the Church of England. But because the Methodists were separating for reasons chiefly pastoral, because John Wesley had professed himself a son of the Church of England, and because many of them were linked by sympathy and theology to the evangelicals of their movement who remained within the Established Church, a majority retained a sense of link between themselves and the Establishment not unlike that felt by the original Presbyterians after 1662. Yet on many important points they shared a common outlook with the older Dissenters. In time, they began to help the Anglicans and old Dissent towards a better understanding.

From the repeal of the Test Act in 1828 to the Burial Laws Amendment Act of 1880, or perhaps to Mr Balfour's Education Act of 1902, the strife of Church and Dissent reached its most acrimonious point. Little by little the Church of England was being stripped of its exclusive privileges, in marriage, education, taxation, burials; and the process was the more painful because the disputes could not be settled quietly but became the cry of the hustings and the battles of the House of Commons. Upon the religious plane the Oxford Movement, and the growing strength of high churchmanship, broadened the gulf between Anglican opinion and Dissenting opinion. The Free Churchmen were themselves not uncritical of the Reformation; but they could not view with equanimity the new attitudes to the Reformers found in Hurrell Froude's *Remains* (1838–9) and in some disciples of the Tractarians thereafter, and as early as 1843 (for example) publicly declared their anxiety about this new development within the Church of England. It would be unrealistic not to recognize that in this respect the nineteenth century made the problem of unity more thorny, and partly because of the bitternesses of political strife. But it would be wrong to judge all the parochial relations of the two bodies by the conflicts of politics; and even in Parliament, it was momentous that Mr Gladstone, more responsible than any other single person for the stripping of privileges, was the only Prime Minister of the century to be a devout disciple of the Oxford Movement.

If the process was painful, it was also purging. The entry of Dissenters into the University, and the subsequent appearance of distinguished scholars, was necessary to the new atmosphere after 1910. The virtual disappearance of the grievances meant that the less religious and less theological grounds for division, the political and social suspicions, were evaporating. The separation could be treated on its merits as a Christian question, and ceased to be cluttered and confused with Liberal politics or class divisions or educational claims.

One other great change was appearing before 1910—liturgical variety. All the communions concerned, faced with the needs of industrial evangelism and the sense that their traditional worship was not always commanding the allegiance of industrial man, permitted a hitherto unknown diversity in worship. Beyond all other denominations the Church of England permitted a new diversity, and sometimes a new diversity appeared whether permitted or not. Nor were some of these varieties likely to encourage the traditional Dissenter to look upon them with favour. Nevertheless the old questions of uniformity and comprehensiveness assumed a new, and less insoluble, form. Not everyone was as convinced that "an universal agreement in the public worship of Almighty God" would invariably be so conducive to "the propagation" of "our religion" as the drafters of the 1662 Act of Uniformity had declared.

The year 1910 is the year of the Edinburgh Conference, commonly taken to mark the formal beginning of the modern Ecumenical Movement. The two last chapters of this book describe the new conditions which prevailed after 1910; the ecumenical organizations in which Anglicans and English Free Churchmen were from the first among the leaders; the maturity of the younger Churches of India and Africa, who were confronted with vast non-Christian populations and could not understand why the melancholy history of European controversy was relevant; the venture in South India to unite episcopal with non-episcopal; the co-operation of Anglican and Free Churchmen in religious education, in divine studies, in historical inquiry (of which this volume may be taken as a modest portent), and in exercising Christian influence upon social and moral questions of national import; and the suggestions put forward from various quarters to translate these sympathies and aspirations into a unity which the participants would recognize, at once as Scriptural and as Catholic.

I

THE RESTORATION OF THE CHURCH OF ENGLAND

ANNE WHITEMAN

IN August 1662 Matthew Newcomen preached his farewell sermon to the congregation in the small Essex town of Dedham, which had been privileged to have first the famous Puritan preacher John Rogers and then himself as their lecturer. "My third Advice is this, and I beseech you take it in love, for it is out of love that it is given you", he told his hearers,

> if you should perceive at this time, a difference in opinion and practice among us, that are the Ministers of the Gospell in this Nation; standing, and sticking, at things that others can digest, and doe; and others doing things, that some of their Brethren cannot come up unto. Be not offended, thus it hath alwayes been from the beginning, it is no new thing. Thus it was in King *Edwards* dayes. If there be any of God's Servants that are Learned, and Holy, and Faithfull, that do now for the enjoyment of their Ministry, yield a conformity, to all that is injoyned, I doubt not, but many of them are grieved, that they cannot have the exercise of their Ministry without this: and we who cannot come up to this, are grieved, that we cannot come up to it; the one, and the other, have griefe enough; adde not your censures to this griefe, that is already upon them. It hath been all along, a Mercifull Providence of God, that when some of his servants could not satisfy their consciences, and come up to the things that have been imposed upon them, without injuring their Consciences; yet others have had a greater freedom given them, that they could yield; and if not so, What would have become of the people of God? Therefore, in those things, acknowledg there may be some providence of God, for good to you in it.[1]

It was indeed no new thing that differences should exist among Protestants in England; what was new in 1662, and

[1] *Mr Matthew Newcomen His Farewel Sermon, Preached at Dedham in Essex, Aug. 20. 1662*, reprinted in *The Second and last Collection of the late London-Ministers Farewell-Sermons* (1663), 163 (spelling and punctuation slightly modified); see *RB* I.ii.§168 for complaints about the publication of these sermons. For Newcomen and Rogers, see *DNB*.

what needs explanation if the genesis of Church and Dissent is to be traced, is that a dichotomy then became permanent and officially recognized. Certainly in some respects the controversies which were to divide them go back, as Newcomen suggested, into the sixteenth century, for from one point of view the ejections are as much the result of problems which the Reformation left unresolved, and the discussions of such years as 1559 and 1604 compromised over or chose to ignore, as of the upheavals of the Civil War or the negotiations of the Restoration itself. But the birth of Dissent must also be regarded as the direct consequence of the "Puritan Revolution", a revolution which failed and, bringing in its wake political bitterness and a new rigidity in theological thinking and ecclesiastical policy, made it very difficult, if not impossible, to re-establish a comprehensive Church when the King came back in 1660. The story of the restoration of the Church of England and the ejections of the Nonconformists is well known; it has often been told by both Anglicans and Dissenters. But it is only in recent years that the researches of such scholars as Mr A. G. Matthews, Dr R. S. Bosher, and the late Dean of Winchester have given it a new precision, and enabled some of the associated problems to be viewed in better perspective. If the recapitulation of the same events in this chapter leans heavily on their accounts, it is because their work has done so much to exhaust the available sources, and it is difficult, for the most part, to dispute their interpretation of the facts.

On the eve of the Great Rebellion, the Church of England could with some truth be said to comprehend all Englishmen except Roman Catholics: unlike, for example, the Dutch Reformed Church, bitterly divided between Gomarists and the proscribed Arminians. But it was neither united nor homogeneous; easily discernible in it were the "Arminian" right wing, the "Calvinist" left wing, and a centre group, the extremes differing widely on much the same questions as were to cause the split in 1662, and each section within itself deeply fissured.[1] But the still conventionally accepted idea of uniformity and the general horror of schism,[2] together with the hope enjoyed by each wing that its views would ultimately prevail, kept the divergent parts together, though at times loosely, within one established Church. Such bodies of separatists as existed were as yet without much ecclesiastical or political significance, however startling was to be their irruption into national life once, with the coming of the Long Parliament, old bonds were broken and long-standing conventions set aside.

The chief characteristics of each wing need only brief recapitulation here. The right, dominated in the 1630s by Archbishop Laud, emphasized strict liturgical observance according to the Prayer Book, a heightened respect for the sacraments, scrupulous use of ceremonial and due decorum in the performance of services, and, above all, the government of the Church by bishops, who were to work closely under active archiepiscopal and royal supervision. A growing number—though probably never very many in the whole country—were spiritually and temperamentally satisfied by its ordered, formal piety and sense of continuity with the past, and found themselves, in addition, more convinced by Arminian than Calvinist teaching on grace. The tradition behind it was primarily that given coherence by Hooker: the legacy of the first centuries of Christianity as well as that

[1] Cf. the threefold grouping in *Complaints concerning Corruptions and Grievances in Church-Government . . . by certain peaceably affected Presbyters, of the Church of England* . . . (1660), 2, and the fourfold division into Erastians, Episcopalians, Presbyterians, and Independents in *RB* I.ii.§§1–6. For an analysis of the differences within Puritanism, see G. F. Nuttall, *The Holy Spirit in Puritan Faith and Experience* (Oxford, 1947), 8–14.

[2] On the strength and continuity of this belief in unity, and its relevance to the post-Restoration habit of occasional conformity, see Norman Sykes, *The Church of England & Non-Episcopal Churches in the Sixteenth & Seventeenth Centuries* (*Theology* Occasional Papers, N.S., no. 11, 1948), esp. 39–42.

of the Reformation.[1] It is scarcely surprising that to its critics it seemed popish in ceremonies, Catholic in doctrine, and dangerously subservient to a dynasty whose Protestant reliability was easily and frequently questioned. In reality members of the right wing were almost without exception highly critical of Roman Catholicism,[2] and proudly conscious that they belonged to a reformed Church; but they also insisted that the Church of England was itself unique, a Church more perfect and nearer the primitive original than any other on earth. "... I doe not believe that the whole world hath any church that cometh nearer to apostolical truth, both in doctrine and discipline", Archbishop John Bramhall firmly asserted in his will.[3] Naturally this claim was by no means acceptable to men of the left, nor, we may surmise, to many in the centre.

The left wing still had a programme barely changed in essentials since the age of Elizabeth: to carry the Reformation through to what might seem its logical conclusions with regard to church government, doctrine, and ceremonies, so that everything reminiscent of popery was totally extirpated.[4] The episcopal organization of the Church, with all its ramifications, was relentlessly criticized, and emphasis placed by contrast on a preaching, evangelical ministry,[5]

[1] Jeremy Taylor's preface to his *Collection of Offices* (1658) well illustrates this mingling of historical tradition with biblical authority (*Works* [ed. R. Heber and C. P. Eden, 1861–5], viii.573).

[2] Cf. P. E. More and F. L. Cross (ed.), *Anglicanism* (1935), 53–72.

[3] Quoted in *Rawdon Papers* (ed. Edward Berwick, 1819), 4; cf. More and Cross, op. cit., 8 f.

[4] The pamphlet *Complaints concerning Corruptions and Grievances in Church-Government* (1660), 1 f, and J. Gailhard's *The Controversie between Episcopacy and Presbytery* (1660), 2 ff, show the continuity of the argument that the Reformation had never been carried through and needed completion.

[5] Cf. William Bates in his funeral sermon for Thomas Manton: "The Preaching of the Word is the principal Part of the Minister's Duty, most essential to his Calling, and most necessary to the Church. For this End chiefly, the several Orders in the ministerial Office were instituted . . ." (*Works* [2nd edn, 1723], 682).

and stricter moral standards and discipline for both clergy and laity. But unanimity on these basic aims was by no means carried over into agreement on the methods or organization to be adopted to achieve them; nearly a century of tension between would-be revolutionaries and more moderate reformers lay behind the different policies and often open quarrels of the Civil War and Interregnum. A common frustration at the slowness with which they seemed to be achieving their aims, and general resentment of the persecution they suffered, still masked the deepest divisions among them; the Calvinism they shared was as yet a powerful cement. The rapidity with which the apparent unity of the left wing was to be shattered was one of the greatest surprises of the Great Rebellion, and, in this context, one of its most significant consequences.

The differences between the right and left wings were obvious and well defined; the lines between the centre and the left and right wings hard to draw. Between men of the centre critical of the establishment and men truly of the left the distinction probably lay primarily in the presence or absence of a certain cast of mind, early labelled "Puritan", which has always more or less eluded definition.[1] An extremely sensitive conscience, an unshakable conviction of personal responsibility to God for decisions both great and small, an overwhelming awareness of sin, and constant dependence on the guidance of the Bible are some of its characteristics. Personal seriousness and personal concernment in the furthering of Christ's kingdom were hallmarks of the Puritan; they left him with small sympathy, or even outright condemnation, for many activities which to men with a different, and not necessarily a less Christian, outlook,

[1] Two of the most illuminating recent analyses of Puritanism are those by William Haller in *The Rise of Puritanism* (New York, 1938) and its sequel *Liberty and Reformation in the Puritan Revolution* (New York, 1955), and by G. F. Nuttall in *The Holy Spirit in Puritan Faith and Experience* (Oxford, 1947) and *Visible Saints: the Congregational Way, 1640–1660* (Oxford, 1957).

seemed harmless or even praiseworthy. Richard Baxter's famous autobiographical passage in which he discusses the way his neighbours branded his father as a Puritan draws attention to the fact that before the Civil War this frame of mind might well characterize a man without his consciously or consistently adopting the complete left-wing position, since, as Baxter wrote, his father "never scrupled Common-Prayer or Ceremonies, nor spake against Bishops, nor ever so much as prayed but by a Book or Form . . ."[1] In the great upheavals between 1640 and 1662 men of a similar stamp would almost certainly find themselves on the parliamentary and Puritan side. Among the true centre men, obviously the hardest group to analyse, there must have been many uncommitted to either extreme because they were genuinely moderate or even somewhat confused in their opinions, or because disputing over institutions or ceremonies seemed irrelevant to their essential faith and duty as Christians. Those in the Great Tew circle who were feeling their way towards a Latitudinarian position belonged primarily here, in spite of the attraction of other members to Laudianism.[2] No doubt there were also natural time-servers, Vicars of Bray for whom self-preservation was the prime consideration.

When the restoration of the King in 1660 made a new settlement of religion necessary, the situation was infinitely more complicated than it had been twenty years earlier. A bare recital of the major ecclesiastical changes in these years explains something of the legacy of frustration and appetite for revenge which were to bedevil the negotiations of 1660–2. In 1640 a series of attacks on the bishops and the principle of episcopacy began a long debate culminating in February 1642 in the exclusion of the episcopate from the House of Lords, while in January of the following year Parliament,

[1] *RB* I.i.§1, cf. §49.

[2] B. H. G. Wormald, *Clarendon: Politics, History and Religion, 1640–1660* (Cambridge, 1951), 247 foll.; H. J. McLachlan, *Socinianism in Seventeenth-Century England* (Oxford, 1951), ch. 5.

though without the King's consent, abolished bishops and deans and chapters, later sequestering their lands.[1] The provision of a substitute system of church government was then referred to the Westminster Assembly, whose deliberations were deeply influenced by the Solemn League and Covenant, by which the English Parliamentary negotiators had agreed with the Scots to reform the English Church "according to the Word of God, and the example of the best reformed Churches", and to root out prelacy and popery.[2] But there was little unanimity on the exact course to be followed, for by now there was no such thing as a united front among Puritans. Strict Presbyterianism was acceptable neither to the growing body of Erastians, who feared presbyters as much as bishops, nor to the Independents, that increasingly influential group whose very existence had barely been discernible in 1640, and whose significance, in this controversy, was that they stood for a decentralized system of church government, diametrically opposed to the closely integrated Genevan system of synods.[3] Presbyterianism of a kind was, nevertheless, theoretically established by ordinances of 1645 and 1646, while the *Directory* was substituted for the Book of Common Prayer.[4] But before a complete and stable organization could be set up throughout the country, the rise

[1] W. K. Jordan, *The Development of Religious Toleration in England* (1932–40), iii.20–30, 39 f, 42; W. A. Shaw, *History of the English Church . . . 1640–1660* (1900), i.118–121; ii.204–13.

[2] Shaw, op. cit., i.142 foll.; Jordan, op. cit., iii.40 foll.; S. R. Gardiner, *Constitutional Documents of the Puritan Revolution* (3rd edn rev., Oxford, 1936), 268.

[3] Jordan, op. cit., iii.34, 45–9, 53 foll.; George Yule, *The Independents in the English Civil War* (Cambridge and Melbourne, 1958), 11 f; on Erastianism, cf. W. M. Lamont, "Episcopacy and a 'Godly Discipline', 1641–6", *JEH* x (1959) 74–89, esp. 87.

[4] C. H. Firth and R. S. Rait (ed.), *Acts and Ordinances of the Interregnum, 1642-1660* (1911), i.582–607, 749–54, 755 ff, 789–97, 833–8, 852–5; Jordan, op. cit., iii.58 f, 80; Shaw, op. cit., i.194–205, 279–90, 353–7; J. H. Hexter, *Reappraisals in History* (1961), 167 f. Bodleian Library Pamphlet c. 70 (1645) contains interesting evidence of the Presbyterian organization in local guise.

of the Independent- and Sectarian-dominated army to political rivalry with, and finally control over, Parliament, undermined what Presbyterian progress had been made and prevented the system's expansion:[1] a curious kind of ecclesiastical anarchy took its place, which allowed wide variety in the doctrine preached and the local organization adopted.[2] Cromwell's government in the main continued this policy of virtual *laissez-faire*, apart from legislation adding to the existing machinery to screen those seeking admission to livings and to remove unfit incumbents, and although attempts were made to prescribe some minimum creed, the Protector died before any statement had been agreed. The revival of Presbyterian political influence after 1658 lasted too short a time to permit any serious reinstatement of Presbyterian church government, and probably achieved little except to resuscitate the fear of strict Genevan discipline.[3]

What actually happened in the parishes during this period is obscure, and, for many of them, likely to remain so, for the evidence available is scrappy and leaves many questions unanswered. It seems undeniable that the majority of Englishmen, clerical and lay, accepted the successive arrangements made by the Long Parliament, the Rump, Cromwell, and the revived Long Parliament without any apparent protest, "as men", it has been said, "had accepted the Church of England in its various manifestations from Henry

[1] For the gradual decay of the system, particularly with regard to lay elders, see Charles E. Surman (ed.), *The Register-Booke of the Fourth Classis in the Province of London, 1646–59* (Harleian Society, lxxxii, lxxxiii, 1953), pp. xvi f; cf. pp. xi f, for a survey of other surviving records of classical presbyteries.

[2] Jordan, op. cit., iii.80, 87 f, 137–40; Shaw, op. cit., ii.21–35, 98–101, 117 foll.; Harold Smith, *The Ecclesiastical History of Essex under the Long Parliament and Commonwealth* (Colchester, 1932) and *VCH Wiltshire*, iii. 101–4 (cf. 40–3) trace some of the ecclesiastical changes in two counties.

[3] Jordan, op. cit., iii.155–60, 164 ff, 246–56; Godfrey Davies, *The Restoration of Charles II* (San Marino, 1955), 297 f; Bosher 102 f, 139 f.

VIII to Elizabeth".[1] The parish structure remained, and tithes were still demanded for the support of the parish minister, in spite of bitter criticism of the system and attempts to abolish it. Presbyterians, Independents, Baptists, and many Anglicans willing to conform fitted for the most part into the loose organization, while many of the radical sects existed, relatively undisturbed, alongside it, unless, like the Quakers, they seemed subversive of the social order.[2] To the Presbyterians, who at one time had seemed so near their goal of bringing the whole country under the Genevan system, the untidy lack of uniformity, almost the anarchy, of these years was a deep disappointment.[3] But though they were frustrated in their general plans, individual Presbyterian ministers had liberty to propagate their views, and, if their parishioners were willing to co-operate, to organize parishes on a Presbyterian basis, with lay elders and strict parochial discipline. Those loyal to the traditional Church of England, the Anglicans (as we may begin to call them), had officially no such latitude. They without doubt suffered most during these years, suspect as they were both ecclesiastically and politically, and often regarded as necessarily reprehensible morally because they spurned the strict Puritan way of life. Yet it would be totally wrong to think that they were persecuted with the determination and efficiency of a modern totalitarian state. The policy of successive governments towards them fluctuated between occasional severity and general mildness, but was at no time really thorough in its repression;[4] even after the tightening up of the laws in

[1] Christopher Hill, *Oliver Cromwell, 1658–1958* (Historical Association Pamphlet 38, 1958), 24.

[2] Margaret James, "The Political Importance of the Tithes Controversy in the English Revolution", *History*, xxvi (1941–2) 1–18; Jordan, op. cit., iii.172–9.

[3] For the changes in Presbyterian thought between 1640 and 1660, see Jordan, op. cit., iii.267–346.

[4] Jordan, op. cit., iii.132, 194 ff, 200 foll.; Bosher 5 f, 8–13, 43 f; P. H. Hardacre, *The Royalists during the Puritan Revolution* (The Hague, 1956), 86 ff, 109 foll.

1655, after Penruddock's Rising, some Anglican clergymen were remarkably active, and John Evelyn, whose *Diary* reflects the changing fortunes of Anglicanism during this period in considerable detail, was never long without their ministrations.[1] Nevertheless the deliberate and at times systematic ejection of Anglican clergy with unpopular religious views, or believed to be hostile to Parliament or the revolutionary governments, had a double importance. First, the proceedings formed a precedent and, albeit in an unworthy sense, gave an excuse for the ejections of Puritans between 1660 and 1662. Secondly, the displaced clergy tended to develop in the wilderness theological and ecclesiastical opinions likely to complicate the future re-establishment of a comprehensive Church.

The widespread and violent attacks on the clergy which characterized the early 1640s were directly provoked by the hatred of Laud and everything to do with his policy; but behind them also lay the deeply-ingrained anti-clericalism and firm Erastianism which had long been manifested in English life. It was with some alacrity, therefore, that early in their sessions both houses of the Long Parliament concerned themselves with the discipline of the clergy, the Grand Committee for Religion of the Commons showing particular zeal. In December 1640 a special body was set up, whose alternative titles—the Committee for Preaching Ministers or the Committee for Scandalous Ministers—well describe its various duties. The compilation of one of its chairmen, John White's *First Century of Scandalous, Malignant Priests* (1643), reports the first hundred cases handled. Popish innovations in ceremonial and doctrine, non-residence, pluralism, failure to preach, hostility to Parliament, and some cases of drunkenness and immorality constituted the main charges; later, active Royalist sentiments became another reason for trial. Those found guilty were normally deprived, and the

[1] John Evelyn, *Diary* (ed. E. S. de Beer, Oxford, 1955), vols. ii and iii, *passim.*

benefice placed under sequestration. During 1643 and 1644 much of the responsibility for purging the Church of those unacceptable to Parliament with its Puritan sympathies was given to a local committee in each county.[1] The Earl of Manchester's instructions to those in the Eastern Association suggest that the element of the witch-hunt was not entirely lacking; one clause, for example, authorized the use, as a near-contemporary gloss put it, of "spirituall blood hounds" since, the document ran, it was "found by sad Experience that Parishioners are not forward to complain of their Ministers", being "loth to come under a powerfull Ministry". Even the fact that secular legislation often made use of informers can scarcely justify such a procedure, and little reliance can be placed on accusations obtained by such means.[2]

To the task of purging the Church of scandalous ministers was joined, as the war progressed, the problem of finding a living for the minister who was acceptable to Parliament, but had lost his benefice at the hands of the Royalists or had never enjoyed due preferment. The House of Commons therefore set up, in December 1642, a new body known as the Committee for Plundered Ministers, which gradually took over the functions previously carried out by the Committee for Scandalous Ministers, adding to them wide additional duties, which were also exercised by their successors, the Trustees for the Maintenance of Ministers. These commissioners dealt, too, with the scrutiny and, if necessary, the ejection of ministers, ordered the payment (where appropriate) of a fifth of the value of the sequestered benefice to the wife of the victim, and exercised a certain amount of

[1] Shaw, op. cit., ii.175–9, 184 f; Jordan, op. cit., iii.62 f; G. B. Tatham, *The Puritans in Power* (Cambridge, 1913), 55 f, 65 foll; Hardacre, op. cit., 40 f. Cf. *RB* I.i. § 117 for Baxter's criticism of ejections for political reasons.

[2] Bodleian, Walker MS. c. 6, foll. 16–18, esp. fol. 17; M. W. Beresford, "The Common Informer, the Penal Statutes and Economic Regulation", *Ec. HR*, 2nd ser., x (1957) 221–37.

patronage.[1] After the vigorous policy of ejection in the 1640s activity declined to some extent, but in 1654 County Committees were set up to conduct a fresh examination of the clergy, as a result of which at least 150 ministers were ejected. This was the last major purge, despite later discussion in favour of renewed activity.[2] The general policy of screening ministers was carried forward in another way by the national Commissioners for the Approbation of Public Preachers, often known as the Triers, who from March 1654 decided on the fitness of presentees to vacant livings. Scrupulous trouble was also taken to see that only men of impeccable moral character and sound Puritan views were accepted for ordination.[3] The work of the Trustees and Commissioners was therefore carefully directed toward the establishment of a zealous Puritan ministry in the Church, and the rooting out of all teaching subversive of Puritan doctrine.

It remains very difficult to form any general conclusions on the justice of the verdicts meted out by these committees. The ejected themselves, who are the source of much of our information, were naturally not always the most impartial reporters,[4] just as those who were refused by the Triers for livings were not inevitably good judges of their own fitness for preferment. Posterity, for instance, has concurred with the Triers' decision that Anthony Sadler was unsuitable to

[1] Shaw, op. cit., ii.189–98; Firth and Rait, op. cit., ii.1000–6.

[2] Firth and Rait, op. cit., ii.968 ff; Shaw, op. cit., ii.246 foll.; *WR* pp. xvii f.

[3] Firth and Rait, op. cit., ii.855–8; i.521–6, 865–74; Shaw, op. cit., i.318–37; ii.142; cf. Surman, loc. cit., p. xv; Nuttall, *Visible Saints*, 87–95.

[4] The most comprehensive account of the fate of the ejected clergy is that of John Walker, *An Attempt towards recovering an Account of the Numbers and Sufferings of the Clergy of the Church of England* (1714), to be read in conjunction with A. G. Matthews's critical commentary, *Walker Revised* (Oxford, 1948), which adds much to Walker's survey. For Wales see Thomas Richards, *History of the Puritan Movement in Wales from . . . 1639 to . . . 1653* (1920), and the same author's *Religious Developments in Wales, 1654–62* (1923).

hold a cure of souls, in spite of his eloquent criticism of their conduct.[1] But the use of informers and reliance upon hostile gossip remain unattractive features of a quasi-inquisitorial procedure, while the fact that so many of the cases were heard by local commissioners gave full opportunity for paying off old scores and precluded any uniform standards of procedure. William Prynne's complaints to the Somerset committee about the injustice suffered by the rector of Swainswick "out of particular malice" because he was thought of as his chaplain indicates that not only Royalists and Anglicans found fault with what was done.[2] John Walker's account of the sufferings of the clergy provides many examples of hardship and injustice, culled from a wide variety of sources of very different reliability. Some have become famous: the ejection of Henry Collier, who with his wife and eleven children was turned out of the rectory of Steeple Langford, Wiltshire, into very deep snow; the constant persecution and plunder of John Manby, rector of Cottenham, Cambridgeshire, whose family was left homeless and hungry; the violence offered first to Thomas Wiborow, rector of Pebmarsh, Essex, and then to his wife and children, who were besieged in the rectory and thrown out by force.[3] But Mr A. G. Matthews's conclusion that "once granted the major injustice of the ejections, in matters comparatively minor [the Committee for Plundered Ministers] did their best to get the injured what justice remained open to them" seems, on the evidence he puts forward, incontestable, for a genuine effort was made to force the intruders to pay fifths to the wives of those they had supplanted, though not always with success.[4] In the context of the settlement at the Restoration, however, the truth (so far as it may be recovered) about

[1] Hardacre, op. cit., 112 f, cf. 113 f; for Sadler's career, *WR* 137 and *DNB*.

[2] Henry Cary, *Memorials of the Great Civil War . . . 1642–52* (1842), i.369–75.

[3] Walker, op. cit., ii.227, 303 f, 396 f.

[4] *WR* p. xxvi; cf. Bosher 241.

the ejections was probably less important than what was widely believed about them. The appearance of pamphlets such as *An Apologetick for the Sequestred Clergie of the Church of England* (1649), with its pathetic references to the griefs of the ejected clergy, created a martyrology more potent than the facts, and did much to breed up Anglican resentment and hatred.[1]

The recent researches of Mr Matthews and Dr R. S. Bosher have revolutionized our knowledge of the fate of Anglicans and the groups among them between 1640 and 1660. Nevertheless the total number of those ejected remains obscure, and is probably irrecoverable. Mr Matthews himself did not publish any overall figure, but preferred to state that, between 1643 and 1660, about 2,425 benefices were at some time under sequestration in England, while about 650 cathedral clergy and 829 men holding university positions were turned out. It is obvious that no total can be constructed from these figures as they stand, largely because pluralists may have lost more than one preferment; for example, of the 1,479 cathedral and university victims, Mr Matthews calculated that only about 780 held no other ecclesiastical office.[2] The same difficulty of pluralism makes untenable any assumption that the number of benefices under sequestration can be equated with the number of men sequestered. Dr Bosher's round figure of 3,600 as representing "the bulk of the Laudian clergy" may or may not be a close estimate, but the figures which he seems to have used to arrive at this

[1] Cf. the Anglican views of the clergy's sufferings in R. Mossom, *An Apology in the behalf of the Sequestered Clergy* (1660), and George Morley, *The Bishop of Winchester's Vindication of Himself from divers False, Scandalous and Injurious Reflexions made upon him by Mr Richard Baxter* . . . (1683), 418 f, 514, with the Presbyterian William Bates's recognition of the part played by Anglican wrath and revenge in what happened after the Restoration (*Works* [1723], 725), and J. Gailhard's comment in *The Controversie between Episcopacy and Presbytery* (1660), 5.

[2] *WR* pp. xiii foll., xx f. Matthews did not include Wales in his revision of Walker's material, although Walker himself dealt with it.

total appear somewhat speculative.[1] Since only about 2,425 out of approximately 8,600 livings (some 30%) were under sequestration, continuity was much greater during these twenty years than used to be thought, although it seems highly likely that time-serving among those who remained in their livings, and the probable Puritanism of most of those who succeeded deceased incumbents, must have played their part in setting the character of the Church as a whole.[2] Mr Matthews was the first to produce evidence of the large number of men who kept their livings throughout or died, still undisturbed, in their benefices, and to point out the influence that, as "collaborators", they must have exerted.[3] Dr Bosher further investigated the careers of these men, and also of the Anglicans out of office who either remained in England or went into exile.[4] Something must be said of each group and its point of view if the situation at the Restoration is to be clear.

The passage already quoted from Matthew Newcomen's sermon sounds a cautionary note so far as any criticism of the "collaborators" is concerned. Some incumbents, as we

[1] Bosher 5 f. This figure of 3,600 seems to be arrived at in the following way:

Matthews's figure of *benefices* under sequestration	2,425
Matthews's figure of cathedral and university *victims* who held no other preferment	780
Clergy who, according to Walker, were harassed but not expelled (cf. *WR* p. xv)	400
	3,605

[2] Cf. Bosher 5.

[3] *WR* pp. xvii f. Examples of incumbents who kept their livings throughout the whole period are (to confine attention to one rural deanery, that of Potterne, in Wiltshire): John Wilton (Chalfield Magna, 1629–78), Henry Colepepper (Enford, 1623–70), Edward Gough (Great Cheverell, 1623–68), William Gunn (Marden, 1636–85), John Northy (Potterne, 1629–68); the incumbents of Steeple Ashton and Upavon, and perhaps one or two other parishes, may also have been unchanged (Salisbury Episcopal Registers).

[4] Bosher 5 f, 27–30, 49 foll.

have seen, were forced for ecclesiastical or political reasons to leave their preferments; others had to resign or were removed because they could not with a good conscience accept the Solemn League and Covenant or, after 1650, the Engagement. But if an incumbent could avoid taking the oaths, or felt that, since they were imposed by force, they were not morally binding, there was little for long periods at a time to prevent him, in spite of Anglican sympathies, from continuing to serve his congregation, and, provided he was not informed against, from using Anglican forms.[1] The ordinances of 1645 substituting the *Directory* and imposing fines and imprisonment for using the Prayer Book were not rigidly enforced, and many may have considered that Charles I's proclamation of 13 November commanding that the Prayer Book be read had better sanction behind it.[2] The breakdown of episcopal authority (probably fairly complete by 1645 or 1646)[3] and the surprisingly feeble lead which the dispossessed bishops gave to the parish clergy left every man free to make the kind of compromise he conceived would work in his circumstances. Many, like the future prelates Robert Sanderson, John Hacket, and Edward Rainbow, must have concluded that they could do more good by a tempered Anglicanism than by refusing entirely to serve under the usurpers, or by deliberately courting ejection. Even "Laudians" like Baxter's opponent Thomas Pierce found it possible to serve a parish under Cromwell, while Sheldon does not seem finally to have severed his connection with his parish of Ickford, Buckinghamshire, till about 1650.[4]

[1] Newcomen, loc. cit., 163; Bosher 4 f, 14 f; *RB* I.i.§99.

[2] Jordan, op. cit., iii.195, 200 f; Robert Steele, *A Bibliography of Royal Proclamations, 1485–1714* (Oxford, 1910), i.319.

[3] At Salisbury, for example, there is a gap in the Bishops' Registers from 1645 to 1660; at Exeter, certain aspects of chapter business went on till the middle of 1646 (D. & C. MSS. 3611[a], 3601).

[4] Bosher 16–23; *WR* 256 f, 49, 38, 76, and references there cited; H. I. Longden, *Northamptonshire and Rutland Clergy from 1500* (Northampton, 1938–43), xi.11.

To some this acquiescence seemed in no sense disloyal to the principles of the Church of England in which they had been reared; to others it was an intolerable betrayal of the very essence of Anglicanism. The difference between the two points of view came to a crisis first over the Engagement, and then over a modified use of the Prayer Book. In both cases Robert Sanderson was an advocate of compromise, opposed by Henry Hammond as the spokesman of those who would make no concession. The second crisis is the more illuminating, for it brought into the open the problem of episcopal authority and the even more important question of the identity of the Church of England. Sanderson argued that a modified use of the Prayer Book would not lead to schism from the true Church of England, since a divergence of practice was the result of necessity and not of intention; he further maintained that, since a rigid adherence to every jot and tittle might deprive faithful Churchmen entirely of the Church's ministrations, the spirit rather than the letter should be observed. Brian Duppa, the most active of the bishops in England, gave Sanderson some support, but the more inflexible Henry Hammond and Herbert Thorndike were irrevocably opposed to his views, which were, understandably, also extremely unpopular with those who, having lost their livings, resented any kind of casuistry which allowed others to continue in any preferment and still call themselves true Church of England men. Gilbert Sheldon, the ejected Warden of All Souls, tried in vain to persuade some or all of the bishops to authorize, with Charles II's approval, a dispensation from strict conformity to the Prayer Book; but the scheme came to nothing when the imprisoned Bishop of Ely, Matthew Wren, refused to further any action. As Dr Bosher has pointed out, the consequences were of the first importance in strengthening the claim of the intransigent Anglicans to represent the true Church of England, for though Sanderson's stand may well have prevented "collaborators" from being openly condemned by their stricter colleagues, their position was inevitably weakened both by the outspoken criticism of their actions and by the lack of any general episcopal support for them.[1]

Intransigence on the part of Anglicans might, of course, be found either among those who had gone into exile or those who remained, deliberately aloof from the present régime in Church and State, in England. There does not seem to have been any contemporary name or nickname in common use to distinguish such men, although at least one writer (albeit as late as 1660) describes as "Canterburians" those who, holding high, apparently "Catholic" views, had "removed the old Land-marks placed by our Protestant Forefathers".[2] Dr Bosher's recourse to the term "Laudian" is, as he himself freely acknowledges, only partly satisfactory;[3] the word has overtones which are not wholly applicable to the Interregnum and Restoration period, and suggests a closer adherence to the archbishop's ideals than some of the leading men among the intransigent Anglicans ever showed.[4] Nevertheless it is difficult to find an alternative term, and indeed it might now prove confusing to use one, since "Laudian" has been

[1] Bosher 13–24; see Jeremy Taylor's *Collection of Offices* (1658: *Works*, viii. 573–701), for a liturgy drawn up by an Anglican during this period.

[2] Henry Hickman, *Laudensium Apostasia: or a Dialogue in which is shewen, That some Divines risen up in our Church since the greatness of the late Archbishop, are in sundry Points of great Moment, quite fallen off from the Doctrine Received in the Church of England* (1660), pref. and *passim*.

[3] Bosher p. xv; cf. the comments of H. R. Trevor-Roper in *JEH* iii (1952) 117.

[4] George Morley, for example, whose dominant position among the "Laudians" is obvious, was certainly thought to retain Calvinist sympathies at least up to the Restoration, and perhaps even later: see *A Supplement to Burnet's History of My Own Time* (ed. H. C. Foxcroft, Oxford, 1902), 67; Anthony Wood, *Athenae Oxonienses* (ed. P. Bliss, Oxford, 1820), iv, col. 154; cf. Morley, *The Bishop of Winchester's Vindication* (1683), 405 f. His attitude to the new organ at New College (of which, as Bishop of Winchester, he was Visitor) suggests that he was not very sympathetic to the spending of money on adjuncts to "the beauty of holiness" (David Ogg, *England in the Reign of Charles II* [Oxford, 1934], i.91).

so generally accepted. In the last resort it is more important to know for what these men stood than how best to describe them, and this Dr Bosher's research has established with a new clarity. Their contention that they alone comprised the true Church of England posed the question of how that body should rightly be defined, particularly since a comprehensive Church under the King as Supreme Governor was nowhere to be found. It was at this juncture that stress on the Catholic elements in the Anglican heritage was specially fruitful, for these served as a clear mark of distinction from all the varieties of Protestantism to be found in the anarchical English Church.[1] Of first importance was the growing conviction that episcopacy was not just the *bene esse*, but the *esse* of a true Church.[2] Of lesser but still great significance was the belief that a written liturgy, generally enforced, was essential, and the Book of Common Prayer gained a new sanctity in this light. The claims of the Eucharist to a central place in worship were maintained, and the Puritan emphasis on preaching scorned; Dean Steward's teaching on a "real but unconceivable presence of Christ in the sacrament" had wide influence among Anglicans.[3] Pamphlets strove to keep alive Anglican practices, and to foster private piety in the Anglican tradition, as Edward Sparke attempted in his *Scintillula Altaris, or, a Pious Reflection on Primitive Devotion: As to the Feasts and Fasts of the Christian Church, Orthodoxally Revived* (1652), or Jeremy Taylor in *The Golden Grove, or, a Manuall of Daily Prayers and Letanies, Fitted to the dayes of the Week . . . Composed for the Use of the Devout, especially of Younger Persons* (1655). Yet there was almost certainly wider agreement on impeccable Royalism as a necessary article of the Anglican creed than

[1] Bosher ch. 1 and 2, *passim*.

[2] *RB* I.ii.§29, and below, pp. 43 foll.

[3] E.g. Herbert Thorndike, *A Discourse of the Right of the Church* (1649), 116 ff; cf. Hickman, *Laudensium Apostasia*, 51, and Gilbert Burnet, *History of My Own Time* (ed. O. Airy, Oxford, 1897), i.296; cf. 244 f. For Steward see *DNB* and N. Pocock, *Life of Richard Steward* (1908).

on Arminian opinions on grace or belief in elaborate ceremonial. The basic faith such men had in common was a conviction that the once-flourishing Church of England, if carefully fostered, would rise again, under the rightful King, from her humiliations. Those who undertook the task of restoring her to strength were, perhaps, not many in number, but they had energy, learning, and unshakable determination.[1]

Among the "Laudians" in England the most influential were Henry Hammond and Gilbert Sheldon, but the correspondence of both shows that they were only at the centre of a large circle.[2] Hammond, who died in 1660 on the eve of the Restoration, was the leading theologian and conscience-keeper of the group; strict and unyielding in many of his views, he was at the same time so obviously a good man that even opponents like Baxter appreciated his worth. His great achievement was to systematize Anglican theology and give it a new standing and self-confidence.[3] Sheldon is *par excellence* a figure of the Restoration, and it is in that context that his character will later be discussed; but even in the Interregnum his administrative ability and power to win the confidence of very different kinds of people are evident, while his energy did something to make up for the supineness of the bishops.[4] Apart from the controversy over the Prayer

[1] Bosher 30 f; cf. David Underdown, *Royalist Conspiracy in England, 1649–60* (New Haven, 1960), 182 f. Cf. also the curious hortatory poems prefacing Edward Sparke's *Scintillula Altaris* (1652), and the preface to Jeremy Taylor's *The Golden Grove* (1655: *Works*, vii.589 ff).

[2] B. M. Harl. MS. 6942 (primarily letters from Hammond to Sheldon) excellently illustrates the membership and interests of this group; the names of those who benefited under Hammond's will are also significant (H. Hammond, *Miscellaneous Theological Works* [Oxford, 1847–50], i, pp. cxvii-cxx).

[3] *DNB*; *RB* I.ii.§66; N. Pocock, "Illustrations of the State of the Church during the Great Rebellion", *Theologian and Ecclesiastic*, xv (1853) 225 foll.

[4] *DNB*; Vernon Staley, *Life and Times of Gilbert Sheldon* (1913); Bosher's assessment of him (p. 29) is illuminating. For a further discussion of him see below, pp. 58, 85 f.

Book, the practical activities of the rigid Anglicans in England were largely concerned with the defence of their position in a series of polemical and expository works (which include among them some of the great classics of the Church of England), the continuation of Anglican ordinations, and the struggle to keep the episcopal succession alive.[1] All were to a greater or lesser degree connected with the emphasis placed on episcopacy. Without the influential arguments of Henry Hammond, Herbert Thorndike, Robert Sanderson, John Bramhall, and Jeremy Taylor, among others, and the less weighty but none the less timely pamphlets of lesser figures, it is doubtful whether episcopal ordination would ever have exercised the attraction it did in view of the difficulty of obtaining it, and the fact that from a short-term standpoint its possession was as likely to be a hindrance as a help to preferment.[2] Evidence from ecclesiastical archives has done much to buttress the statements made by the bishops who survived the Restoration about the many candidates they ordained, and even if the hazards they ran in doing so are hard to assess and easy to exaggerate, they contributed notably in this way to the future of the traditional Church of England.[3] Particularly important was the influence exerted in favour of "Laudianism" by the ejected or dispossessed clergy who found their way into the households of the nobility and gentry, as tutors or unofficial chaplains; how well they imparted their lesson was to be seen in the temper of the young cavaliers in Charles II's Long Parliament.[4] Indeed, the loyalty of so many laymen to the Church of England

[1] Bosher 36 ff, 63–6, 89 foll.

[2] Bosher 38; Norman Sykes, *Old Priest and New Presbyter* (Cambridge, 1956), ch. 3–5 *passim*, esp. 66–9; the Thomason Tracts contain a great number of pamphlets concerned with various aspects of episcopacy. For the Presbyterian attitude to episcopal ordination received after the parliamentary abolition of episcopacy, see Surman, loc. cit., p. xv.

[3] Bosher 38 and n. 1, and authorities there cited.

[4] Ibid., 39 f, 146 f.

during the Interregnum was of incalculable value. Without the courage and resolution of such men as Sir Robert Shirley, whose church-building at Staunton Harold, Leicestershire, still commemorates his firm faith in the Church's recovery, and the kindness of Royalist hosts who sheltered the ejected clergy, as Sir John Pakington did Henry Hammond at Westwood in Worcestershire, Anglicanism would have found it very much harder to survive, and to keep its character intact.[1]

The Anglicans in exile were faced by rather different problems. In the first place they had to win a battle for the survival of the alliance between Royalism and the Church of England: there were many who would have preferred Charles to make his peace either with Presbyterianism or Roman Catholicism, since either arrangement might have attracted money and troops for a successful invasion. Then they were faced with the difficulty of maintaining the Anglican tradition, and emphasizing its distinction; Dr Bosher has shown how much trouble was taken to provide English services with a ceremonial to distinguish them from Calvinist ones, and to prevent apostasy to Rome.[2] The exiles' chief controversialists, John Bramhall and John Cosin, argued in vindication of Anglican orders, and stressed both the Catholic and the Protestant heritage of the Church of England. The securing of Charles II's own allegiance and open support was gradually achieved as he began to depend increasingly on the Anglican Edward Hyde as his chief adviser, while his sincerity seemed proved by his refusal to allow the young Duke of Gloucester's conversion to Roman Catholicism. By the time a restoration of the King became

[1] John Summerson, *Architecture in Britain 1530–1830* (Pelican History of Art, 1953), 108; Bosher 25 f, 32–5, 37; John Fell, *Life of Dr Henry Hammond* (prefixed to Henry Hammond, *Misc. Theol. Works* [1847–50], i, pp. li f).

[2] Underdown, op. cit., 10 ff; Bosher 53 foll.

in any way feasible, the alliance between Royalism and Anglicanism was firmly welded.[1]

It was a development of the utmost consequence that both in England and abroad Anglicans should feel that a defence of episcopal government was essential to the propagation and success of their cause. The late Dr Norman Sykes's work on the development of Anglican ideas on episcopacy from the Reformation to the present day, and the controversy it engendered,[2] has enabled us to see the views of the Interregnum and Restoration in better perspective, and his findings do something to support Baxter's contention that

> there were at that time (*sc.* in the Interregnum), two sorts of Episcopal Men, who differed from each other, more than the more moderate sort differed from the Presbyterians. The one was the old common moderate sort, who were commonly in Doctrine *Calvinists*, and took Episcopacy to be necessary *ad bene esse Ministerii & Ecclesiae*, but not *ad esse*; and took all those of the *Reformed* that had not Bishops, for true Churches and Ministers, wanting only that which they thought would make them more compleat. The other sort followed Dr. *H. Hammond*, and . . . were very new, and very few: Their Judgment was . . . that all the Texts of Scripture which speak of Presbyters, do mean Bishops, and that the Office of Subject-Presbyters was not in the Church in Scripture Times . . . but that the Apostles planted in every Church only a Bishop with Deacons, but with this intent . . . that in time, when the Christians multiplied, these Bishops (that had then but one

[1] Bosher 63–6, 73–7; cf. H[enry] F[erne], *Of the Division between the English and Romish Church upon the Reformation* (1652), 9 ff.

[2] Norman Sykes, *Old Priest and New Presbyter*, and his earlier *The Church of England & Non-Episcopal Churches in the Sixteenth & Seventeenth Centuries* (*Theology* Occasional Papers, N.S., no. 11, 1948); cf. A. L. Peck, *Anglicanism and Episcopacy* (1958), and E. L. Mascall, *The Recovery of Unity* (1958), 163–9. For Sykes's comments on Peck's criticism, see *Theology*, lxi.388 ff. An earlier survey of the same question, still valuable, is that of A. J. Mason, *The Church of England and Episcopacy* (Cambridge, 1914); cf. also J. L. Ainslie, *The Doctrines of Ministerial Order in the Reformed Churches of the Sixteenth and Seventeenth Centuries* (Edinburgh, 1940).

Church a piece) should ordain Subject-Presbyters under them, and be the Pastors of many Churches: And they held that Ordination without Bishops was invalid, and a Ministry so ordained was null, and the *Reformed Churches* that had no Bishops, nor Presbyters ordained by Bishops, were no true Churches, though the Church of *Rome* be a true Church, as having Bishops: These Men in Doctrine were such as are called Arminians: And though the other sort were more numerous and elder . . . yet Dr *H. Hammond* and the few that at first followed him, by their Parts and Interest in the Nobility and Gentry, did carry it at last against the other Party.[1]

But in fact the views of the "New Prelatists" had both a longer and a more complicated ancestry than Baxter recognized, for they went back, in embryo, to Elizabeth's reign. Anglican opinions on episcopacy throughout the century after the Reformation seem, indeed, to have varied in emphasis a good deal according to current stresses. It is understandable that in the middle of the sixteenth century a common faith rather than an identical church order should cement together the Protestant Churches of Europe; while the struggle was a general one with Rome, Calvin's view that "one church should not despise another on account of a variety of external discipline"[2] appeared necessary to many, particularly as Protestants who did not enjoy the benefits of living under a "godly prince" had to make the best arrangements they could in unfavourable circumstances.[3] But even in England, which enjoyed a "godly prince", there was at first little positive support for episcopacy: to some it was a preferable as well as an allowable institution, based on a sound tradition going back to the age of the Apostles; but many Edwardine and Elizabethan reformers disliked it, as corrupted by Rome, or thought of it as a thing indifferent,

[1] *RB* I.ii.§29; cf. I.i.§§109, 140; I.ii.§66 (p. 207).

[2] Quoted by Sykes, *Old Priest and New Presbyter*, 42, from *Institutes*, IV.x.32.

[3] Sykes, op. cit., ch. 1 and 2.

acceptable because the Crown had imposed it rather than because of any scriptural or historical warrant.[1]

It was Presbyterian claims that their system of church government had specific scriptural authority and was the only permissible form which forced Anglicans to reconsider their attitude to episcopacy. A succession of writers in the 1580s and 1590s, in particular Thomas Bilson, argued that episcopacy was of apostolical origin, and thus the episcopal system of church government was not a matter of choice, but the only legitimate form.[2] How the emphasis had changed, for some Anglicans at least, by the first decades of the seventeenth century, is shown by Joseph Hall's opinion that "to depart from the judgment and practice of the universal church of Christ ever since the apostles' times, and to betake ourselves to a new invention, cannot but be, besides the danger, vehemently scandalous", since "that Government whose foundation is laid by Christ, and whose fabric is raised by the Apostles, is of Divine institution". To Laud it was the doctrine of the Church of England that "Bishops might be regulated and limited by human laws, in those things which are but incidents to their calling; but their calling, as far as it is *jure divino*, by divine right, cannot be taken away".[3] Intensified interest in patristic writings, and a more critical attitude towards them, particularly with regard to the authenticity of the Epistles of St Ignatius of

[1] Ibid., ch. 1; cf. J. W. Allen, *A History of Political Thought in the Sixteenth Century* (2nd edn, 1941), 177 f; G. W. Bromiley, *Thomas Cranmer, Theologian* (1956), 50–6; E. T. Davies, *Episcopacy and the Royal Supremacy in the Church of England in the XVI Century* (Oxford, 1950), *passim*; J. W. Allen, *English Political Thought, 1603–1660*, (1938), i. 129 ff, 161 f; Beatrice Hamilton Thompson, in *The Apostolic Ministry* (ed. K. E. Kirk, 1946, repr. 1957), 387–460, for other discussions of these various points of view.

[2] Sykes, op. cit., 58–67.

[3] Quoted by Sykes, op. cit., 66 f., from chapter summaries, presumably by Hall himself, in J. Hall, *Works* (ed. P. Wynter, Oxford, 1863), ix.185, 161, and W. Laud, *Works* (Parker Soc., Oxford, 1847–60), iv.310 f.

Antioch, set in a new perspective the questions of what meaning should be attached to the words *episcopus* and *presbyter*, and whether they should be said to differ *ordine* as well as *gradu*.[1] Henry Hammond's distinctive contribution to the controversy lay in his influential defence of the Seven Ignatian Epistles, whose genuineness had been established by the remarkable scholarship of James Ussher and Isaac Voss, against the attacks of the Huguenot Blondel and English Puritan critics, to whom the Ignatian evidence on the early spread of episcopacy had come as a great shock.[2] Hammond's comprehensive restatement of a view of episcopacy now commonly held by Anglicans at a time when the need was so keenly felt to assert the identity of the episcopal Church of England was of incalculable importance both during the Interregnum and at the Restoration.[3]

But Baxter was on better ground when he maintained that it was new that Anglicans should consider non-episcopal Churches no true Churches.[4] Although it was a conclusion that logically followed from the "New Prelatist" view of episcopacy, it was, as Dr Sykes showed, reluctantly adopted.

[1] Norman Sykes, *From Sheldon to Secker* (Cambridge, 1959), 105 foll.; J. B. Lightfoot, *The Apostolic Fathers* (2nd edn, 1889), II.i, ch. 4 and 5 *passim*, and esp. 239–43, 330–4, 389 foll.

[2] Henry Hammond, *Dissertationes Quatuor, quibus Episcopatus Jura ex S. Scripturis & Primaeva Antiquitate adstruuntur, contra sententiam D. Blondelli, et aliorum* (1651); answered by the London Ministers in *Jus Divinum Ministerii Evangelici* (1654); cf. also John Owen, *The Doctrine of the Saints Perseverance* (1654), preface. Hammond replied in 1654 in *A Vindication of the Dissertations concerning Episcopacie* . . . and *An Answer to the Animadversions on the Dissertations touching Ignatius's Epistles, and the Episcopacie in them asserted*. Cf. also his comments on the word *episcopus* in his *Annotations upon all the Books of the New Testament* (Oxford, 1845), i.350; ii.216 ff, 315, 409; on *presbyter*, i.384–9.

[3] Cf. the tribute made as early as 1653 in Henry Ferne's preface to *Certain Considerations of Present Concernment: touching this Reformed Church of England*.

[4] *RB* I.ii.§29; cf. H. Hickman, *Laudensium Apostasia*, pref., "'Tis notorious that they [i.e. some of the 'Canterburians'] have unchurched all the Transmarine Churches for want of such an Officer as they are not convinced that Christ did ever institute".

As late as the Interregnum the older attitude was still held by distinguished Anglican theologians like John Bramhall and Jeremy Taylor, and even Herbert Thorndike, in spite of his doubts over the validity of ordinations in Calvinist Churches. But theory was one thing and practice another. Faced with the problem of intercommunion with the Reformed Churches of France and Holland, or in England with those who acknowledged the non-episcopal régime, some Anglicans were less sure that charity was the right attitude to be adopted. Bramhall himself, together with George Morley (Calvinist by inclination), Thomas Sydserf, and Richard Steward, were all opposed to intercommunion with the Huguenots, while John Cosin's opinion in its favour was widely criticized.[1] Although there were powerful political arguments for eschewing the Protestant Church in France because of its poor standing with the French monarchy, the springs of this action were partly, if not largely, the result of the growing conviction that episcopacy was an essential ingredient of Anglicanism, and constituted a principle that could no longer be compromised.[2] And if foreign Protestant Churches which had no bishops as the result of political circumstances could not be recognized, no case could be made out for the Presbyterian or Independent Churches of the Commonwealth and Protectorate, since they had deliberately rejected episcopal government.[3] This conclusion was of the utmost importance when the validity

[1] Sykes, *Old Priest and New Presbyter*, 69, 76–81; Bosher 83 f.

[2] Cf. *Certain Letters evidencing the King's Stedfastness in the Protestan Religion* (1660), 14, 33, 40, 43 f; *Correspondence of John Cosin* (ed. G. Ornsby, Surtees Soc., 1869, 1872), i.292. For an indication of the fervour with which the "new" view of episcopacy was held, and the strength of the conviction that the Church of England was distinct from all other Protestant Churches, see the correspondence of Richard Watson in *Calendar of the Clarendon State Papers preserved in the Bodleian Library* (Oxford, 1869–1932), ii.232, 243; iv.18. For Watson, see *DNB*.

[3] Cf. Burnet, *HOT* i.247 f; *Supplement to Burnet's History* (ed. Foxcroft), 70.

of Presbyterian orders was under discussion after the Restoration.

When this growing Anglican preoccupation with episcopacy is remembered, the story of how nearly the episcopal succession in the Church of England died out altogether is all the more surprising.[1] Although concern over the advancing age of the bishops and the number of unfilled vacancies can be traced back to 1651, no constructive measures were attempted till 1655. The full constitutional difficulties then became apparent. There were no chapters to receive the King's *congé d'élire* and letters recommendatory, while the bishops who would have to carry out the consecrations were elderly and timid, living at some distance from each other, and disinclined to come together, or to find any way of surmounting the difficulties. Nothing, therefore, was done. By the year 1659 only eleven English and Welsh bishops were still alive.[2] "I will not mention the age of the Consecrators, though it hath put me into many a fright", wrote Hyde to John Barwick, adding that if he were a Presbyterian, he would keep up endless negotiations and thus "spin out the time till all the Bishops were dead".[3] Yet the second attempt to arrange new consecrations was equally a failure, and again it is difficult to acquit the bishops of making the most of the constitutional difficulties to avoid any action. The devoted efforts of Barwick and Richard Allestree, the exiled

[1] Bosher, 89–100, has traced the story in full.

[2] The ages, according to the *DNB*, of the surviving English and Welsh bishops in 1659 were: William Piers (Bath and Wells), 79; Henry King (Chichester), 67; Matthew Wren (Ely), 74; Accepted Frewen (Lichfield), 71; William Juxon (London), 77; Robert Skinner (Oxford), 68; John Warner (Rochester), 78; Brian Duppa (Salisbury), 71; William Roberts (Bangor), 74. Ralph Brownrigg (Exeter) died in December 1659, at 67, and Thomas Morton (Durham) in September 1659, at the great age of 95. Eight Irish bishops were still living at the Restoration (R. Mant, *History of the Church of Ireland* [1840], i.605); Thomas Sydserf, of Galloway, was the sole surviving Scottish bishop (J. H. S. Burleigh, *A Church History of Scotland* [1960], 238 f).

[3] *State Papers collected by Edward, Earl of Clarendon* (Oxford, 1786), iii.521; cf. 571, 613.

government's agents, and the exasperated pressure of Hyde achieved nothing, and the Restoration came only in the nick of time to preserve the succession. The discreditable story is scarcely a testimonial to episcopal responsibility, and it remains puzzling why the bishops, some of whom (like Juxon, Duppa, and Wren) were trained in the Laudian tradition, were so singularly ineffectual and lacking in public conscience.

It is arguable that with the new emphasis on episcopacy on the one hand, and the rise of Independency and the Sects on the other, any hope that a really comprehensive Protestant Church might be re-established in England was dead long before serious negotiations over the restoration of the King and the terms on which it might be arranged began in 1659. The left and the right were now much farther apart than they had been in 1640, and there could be no going back.[1] Nor were the difficulties only religious; Royalists and Anglicans found it hard to negotiate with men who had approved the execution of Charles I. For the time being, at any rate, there could be no place for the Independents or the Sects in these discussions.[2] But the Presbyterians were in different case, although by some they were hated even more as the original rebels who had begun all the troubles. After their years of political subordination to the Independents, they were now in the ascendant, and clearly the main group to be conciliated if a restoration were to be possible; since the Second Civil War many had been crypto- or even open Royalists.[3] Both politically and ecclesiastically, however, the

[1] For the characteristics of, and main developments in, Independent and Presbyterian thought up to 1660, see Jordan, op. cit., iii.267 foll.

[2] Bosher 116 f; for the story of John Owen's interview with Clarendon, in which he criticized the government's decision not to negotiate with the Independents, see J. Ralph, *History of England* (1744–6), i.52 f.

[3] Cf. *RB* I.ii.§§70, 87, for a catalogue of Presbyterian claims to gratitude from Royalists, and §§4, 23, 284–5, for comments on the characteristics of the Presbyterians. Clarendon's dislike of them was sometimes clearly expressed, e.g. in a letter of 1661 (ed. K. G. Feiling, *EHR* xlii.407 f); for Presbyterian fears of him, see Bosher 111 f.

term "Presbyterian" is easier to use than to define. In the latter context it is habitually applied very loosely: to include, on the one hand, men who stood for a strict Presbyterian church government and discipline, whether on the Scottish or the English model, like Lazarus Seaman, William Jenkyn, or Henry Hickman, and, on the other, men who were first and foremost Puritans, seeking reform in the sense of greater purity in a national Church and among its members. Of men in the first group little need be said here, since with their rigid views they ejected themselves, so to speak, from the established Church, which, given the circumstances, could never have been wide enough to embrace them, and which they would have equally scorned had it had such latitude.[1] Central to this story, however, are the second group, including those sometimes called the "Reconcilers", who were sincerely anxious for a settlement which moderate Anglicans and moderate Puritans could both accept, and were prepared, with the Newport proposals of 1648 and Archbishop Ussher's scheme in mind, and probably, too, Baxter's Association Movement of the Interregnum, to consider a modified episcopacy to that end.[2] Their names are some of the most illustrious in the history of the Church of the Interregnum and of Dissent: the indefatigable but politically inept Richard Baxter, Edmund Calamy (grand-

[1] Nuttall, *The Holy Spirit*, 8–14; Bosher 119 f, 153; *RB* I.ii.§87. For a criticism of Bosher's views on this strict group, cf. James C. Spalding, "The Demise of English Presbyterianism: 1660–1760", *Church History* xxviii (1959) 82, n. 21. John Gailhard's *The Right of the Church Asserted, against the Power usurped over it* (1660) is a detailed statement of the more extreme and at the same time anti-Erastian point of view.

[2] *RB* I.ii.§285; cf. I.i.§§148–9; Ethyn Williams Kirby, "The Reconcilers and the Restoration (1660–1662)", *Essays in Modern English History in honor of Wilbur Cortez Abbott* (Cambridge, Mass., 1941), 49–79; for the Association Movement, see Jordan, op. cit.,iii. 342 f, and G. F. Nuttall, *JEH* i (1950) 197–206. Cf. George R. Abernathy, "Richard Baxter and the Cromwellian Church", *Huntington Library Quarterly*, XXIV (1960–1), 215–31.

father of the martyrologist), Matthew Newcomen, William Spurstowe, Simeon Ashe, Thomas Manton, Anthony Tuckney, Thomas Jacombe, William Bates, and, working very closely with them, Edward Reynolds, whose inclusion in this group or in that of the liberal Anglicans must be a matter of debate.[1] Baxter went out of his way to deny that their aims were Presbyterian, but as with the term "Laudian" for their opponents, common usage to some degree justifies the retention of the word in this context, in spite of its inexactness.[2] It is as difficult to discover the comparative size of these groups among the non-Anglicans as it is to gauge the strength of the Anglican parties, but it is reasonable to suppose that this moderate, reconciling spirit had potentially a large following.

On the political side, Presbyterians played a vital part in the Restoration, and this might have been expected to guarantee a special respect to their ecclesiastical views.[3] In the early stages of the negotiations they were indeed given a great deal of attention. Morley's and Barwick's discussions with the Reconcilers and the general talk of a synod to get to grips with the real difficulties and solve them certainly suggested that a more comprehensive Church was still a feasible objective. But from the beginning frankness was lacking, and there was a risk of serious ambiguity. The Anglicans would not depart from generalities while their political position was weak; the Presbyterians could not win important concessions while their political power was still considerable.[4] The King's Declaration from Breda, published on 4 April 1660, further extended the ambiguity by promising that Parliament, which each side hoped to dominate, should settle the religious problem; equally pregnant

[1] For the careers of these men, see *DNB* and *CR*; for Reynolds, cf. also Spalding, loc. cit., 82, n. 29.

[2] *RB* I.ii.§112; cf.§23. See also below, p. 182.

[3] Godfrey Davies, *The Restoration of Charles II*, 308 f; *CSP Ven. 1659-61* (1931), 141.

[4] Bosher 101 ff; Kirby, loc. cit., 53–8.

of confusion was the King's assurance of a liberty to tender consciences and pledge that no man should be "disquieted or called in question for differences of opinion in matter of religion, which do not disturb the peace of the kingdom", which, by appearing to promise toleration, gave a new hope to those groups which could not expect inclusion in a comprehensive Church.[1] The net result of all the talk and pamphlet controversy and high level negotiation was that so far as the ecclesiastical settlement was concerned, as in other matters, Charles II came back without conditions. Probably no effective conditions could have been laid down; perhaps it was better that none should have been attempted. But with the King's return came a change of incalculable importance. The balance of power within the Church in England altered, almost overnight. For the life of the Church had to go on, and this necessitated a thousand decisions, almost all of them now settled in accordance with the wishes of the Anglican sympathizers who came back as the royal advisers. Had a synod to decide the future of the Church been held before the King returned, the Puritans would have been the party in possession; henceforth, and quickly, it became the Anglicans who held the position of advantage.

At this point it may be useful to recall the main problems confronting all, both clergy and laity, who sought to settle the Church in England, and to examine the characters and opinions of the men most intimately connected with the negotiations. Of the points in dispute, some were old controversies, some the result of recent events. In the first place there was the question of the form of church government to be adopted: was this to be the traditional episcopacy, modified episcopacy, or some kind of Presbyterianism? And

[1] Gardiner, *Constitutional Documents*, 465 ff; George R. Abernathy, Jr, "Clarendon and the Declaration of Indulgence", *JEH* xi (1960) 56, has pointed out that in the draft of the Declaration in B.M. Egerton MS. 2542, foll. 328–9, there is a note in Nicholas's hand by the clause dealing with religion, which reads "This was added by y[e] L[or]d Ch[ancellor]".

what was to be the fate of those who felt unable to conform to it? Secondly, there was the problem of liturgy: should the use of a specified liturgy be legally required, and if so, what form should it take? Thirdly, debate arose about the kind and degree of ceremonial to be enforced. The fourth and fifth problems both arose directly out of what had happened in the Interregnum. It had to be decided how far, on the one hand, non-episcopal ordinations and, on the other, appointments authorized during the last fifteen or twenty years, were valid; the first involved complex theological issues, the second, conflicting claims to the same preferment of men ejected from their livings and men who had since faithfully served the parishes in their stead. Another problem directly arising from recent events was what attitude should be adopted towards those who had taken the Covenant. Lastly, there was the difficulty of determining how the settlement should be made, at what point debate should give place to decisions, and how these decisions should be enforced. For none of these problems was there an easy or universally popular solution, and it is not surprising that the final arrangements left behind them a trail of frustration and disappointment. Yet in one sense the controversies were comparatively simple. The parties were not divided by a direct clash on doctrine: although the seventeenth-century conflict over grace inevitably underlay aspects of the disagreements, it was not a major issue in its own right, as it was in contemporary France or Holland; disputes over the Sacrament were no longer very bitter; the question of authority in the Church was raised more by implication than explicitly.[1] Doctrinal disagreement there undoubtedly was, but it was a disagreement rather embodied in two different traditions than deliberately and systematically formulated.

[1] For the controversies in France and elsewhere, see E. Préclin and E. Jarry, *Les Luttes Politiques et Doctrinales aux XVIIe et XVIIIe Siècles* (vol. xix, 2 pts, of *Histoire de l'Église* [fondée par A. Fliche et V. Martin], 1955).

Perhaps for this reason it was the more difficult to find an accommodation between the two points of view. Yet Dr Nuttall has rightly stressed how close, spiritually, were many Episcopalians in the Church of England to the Presbyterians, Independents, and even some of the Separatists and Sectaries, and that the real gulf lay rather between all these men and the "Laudians".[1]

Among those responsible for making the settlement Charles II and his adviser Edward Hyde (from 1658 Lord Chancellor, Earl of Clarendon from 1661) were inevitably in the forefront of the negotiations. It is not easy to elucidate the policy of either man. Probably the truth about the date of Charles II's conversion to Rome will never be exactly known; but his preferences and prejudices in religion are at least clear. By temperament strongly attracted to Roman Catholicism, he accepted the political necessity of supporting the Church of England; Anglicanism was not, in his eyes, as suitable a religion for kings as Roman Catholicism, but it was not, like Presbyterianism, unfit for gentlemen. Moreover, Anglicans had for long made loyalty to the monarchy almost another article of the Creed, while Presbyterians had needed political defeat to spur them into a proper allegiance, and even then had forced the King to accept the Covenant as a condition of their help.[2] From Charles's point of view the most satisfactory form of settlement was almost certainly a re-estab-

[1] Nuttall, *The Holy Spirit*, 9; cf. however the comments on the decline of Calvinism in G. R. Cragg, *From Puritanism to the Age of Reason* (Cambridge, 1950), ch. 2. The statement made by the Presbyterians from Sion House in July 1660 is noteworthy in this context:

> ". . . wee takeing it for granted that there is a firme agreement betweene our brethren and us in doctrinall truths of ye Reformed Religion, and in the substantiall parts of Divine Worship; and that thes differences are only in some various Conceptions about ye antient forme of Church Gover[n]ment, and some particulars about Liturgy and Ceremonies . . ." (Bodleian Tanner MS. 49, fol. 7).

[2] Burnet, *HOT* i.166 f, 195, 234; ii.472; H. C. Foxcroft, *The Life and Letters of Sir George Savile, Bart., First Marquis of Halifax* (1898), ii.343–7

lished Church of England, accompanied by toleration for both Roman Catholics and Dissenters, for such would ensure the greatest measure of political support for his régime, and perhaps prepare the way for an eventual conversion of the whole country to Roman Catholicism. For such a policy, hinted at in the Declaration of Breda and explicit in the 1672 Indulgence, he strove long and unsuccessfully against opposition that might well have daunted many men; even with his tempered action, no ecclesiastical group really trusted him.

Clarendon's ecclesiastical standpoint has for long been the subject of intermittent debate. But though in his *Life* he stressed the continuity of his policy and its essentially Anglican character, from 1642 to at least 1663 he appears at times to have been prepared to work for some degree of limited comprehension or toleration alongside the established Church; his bitter reflection that "it is an unhappy policy, and always unhappily applied, to imagine that that classis of men can be recovered and reconciled by partial concessions, or granting less than they demand", is probably his epitaph on such attempts to find agreement with the Puritans.[1] Dr B. H. G. Wormald's penetrating study of his religious ideas, so much influenced by the Great Tew circle and in some respects so much the same even in the 1670s, shows how he was exposed to the Latitudinarian opinions which characterized some of the group, and, deriving from them a conviction that the essentials of Christianity were simple and few, was probably by no means averse to compromise over things indifferent. What he feared, Wormald argued, were the political consequences of tampering with the established order in the Church; when political stability was the primary objective, as at the Restoration, ecclesiastical change should not be resisted if it seemed desirable.[2]

[1] Edward, Earl of Clarendon, *Life* (Oxford, 1857), i.546.

[2] Wormald, *Clarendon*, 240 foll., 280 ff, 304–14; for evidence that Clarendon retained, even in his second exile, much the same ideas as earlier, 261 foll.

An examination of Clarendon's letters and papers for the Restoration period convinced Dr K. G. Feiling "that Clarendon's action was less consistently Anglican than his memoirs or his sons claim, and depended, like that of his rivals, rather upon political exigencies and personal factors", while Professor G. R. Abernathy's detailed study of the background of the 1663 Indulgence attempt has persuaded him of the continuity of Clarendon's efforts to achieve comprehension and toleration.[1] Dr Bosher is the principal modern exponent of the view that Clarendon's policy was consistently Anglican, and that the apparent inconsistencies in it were political manoeuvres adopted as the means to an end, although he admitted that "as a responsible statesman, [he] naturally showed himself more sensitive to political considerations than did ecclesiastics".[2] That during his years on the Continent and right up to the eve of the Restoration Clarendon expressed himself strongly, and often, in favour of the re-establishment of the Church of England in its old form, without concessions over episcopacy in particular, seems clear from Bosher's survey of the evidence.[3] But thenceforth the interpretation of his policy depends more on his actions than his words, and it would certainly appear more in accord with his political aims manifested, for example, in the Act of Indemnity and Oblivion, that the Church should be re-established so as to be a bond of unity rather than a cause of renewed strife. For a time, at least, it would seem that his strategy as well as his tactics must have been, to a greater or lesser degree, empirical. Right up to the elections in the spring of 1661 Presbyterian political strength was incalculable; the ease with which the Army was paid off was

[1] K. G. Feiling, *EHR* xliv (1929) 289 ff, esp. 290; xlii (1927) 407 f; Feiling, *History of the Tory Party, 1640–1714* (Oxford, 1924), 104 f; Abernathy, loc. cit., 55–73.

[2] Bosher 275; cf. 55 f, 144 f, 149 f, 216 ff, 242 f, 258, 267–70, and *passim.*

[3] Bosher 55 f, 88 f, 93 foll. 106 foll., 109 f, 113 f, 123 f, 136–40; cf. Abernathy, loc. cit., 55 f.

unexpected; for months no settlement of the revenue was achieved. Popular enthusiasm for King and Church was a surprise, and for long mistrusted, as Government alarm over the Presbyterian success in the City elections showed. These and many other factors had to be taken into account; but perhaps the most remarkable and unpredictable thing was the appearance in 1661 of a fiercely Anglican House of Commons, determined to settle the Church in its own way, despite royal promises and statesmanlike procrastinations.[1]

The most cogent argument against accepting Abernathy's interpretation of Clarendon's policy is the evidence advanced by Bosher of his close partnership with Sheldon and the leading Laudian divines, whose attitude was not, with some possible exceptions, favourable to compromise with either the critics or the enemies of the Church.[2] It seems nevertheless possible that these men may only up to a point have been working for an identical aim; all wanted to restore the Church of England, but whereas by late 1661 or early 1662 many Churchmen were relieved that circumstances had made possible a wholly conservative settlement by which traditional Anglicanism could be established again, the Lord Chancellor, well aware of the King's wishes and genuinely afraid of too narrow a Church, persisted in seeking a more liberal solution either through comprehension or toleration.[3] Unfortunately so little is explicitly known of the real hopes not only of Clarendon but also of both Sheldon and Morley (the latter almost certainly Clarendon's chief friend among the bishops) that it is difficult to tell if such an interpretation

[1] Feiling, *Tory Party*, 98–104; Ogg, op. cit., i.155–8; Bosher 208–12.

[2] Bosher 137 f, cf. 55 f.

[3] Cf. Clarendon, *Life*, i.546 f which it is tempting, although perhaps dangerous, to see as Clarendon's embittered and disillusioned comment on an ecclesiastical policy in which he had once believed. Burnet (*Supplement to Burnet's History* [ed. Foxcroft], p. 56) refers to a change in Clarendon's attitude to church matters after his daughter's marriage to the Duke of York, in gratitude to the bishops who had then supported him, but this seems unlikely.

is likely. Sheldon remains one of the most elusive personalities of the time; no contemporary wrote a full biography, and his own correspondence and published work is singularly unilluminating. Burnet (a younger contemporary who did not know him well) thought him a clever business man, quick-witted and of sound judgement, but insincere in his personal relationships. "He seemed", he wrote, "not to have a deep sense of religion, if any at all: and spoke of it most commonly as of an engine of government, and a matter of policy; and by this means the king came to look on him as a wise and honest clergyman, that had little virtue and less religion."[1] Curiously enough Clarendon, who knew him so well as a fellow-member of the Great Tew circle, and, even if later they disagreed over some things, had apparently liked him so much, never—and perhaps the omission is indicative of later friction—wrote a full character of him; the brief comments on his learning, gravity, and prudence, and the preservation of Sir Francis Wenman's observation that "Dr Sheldon was born and bred to be archbishop of Canterbury", scarcely make up for the loss.[2] It is impossible to concur with Burnet's opinion that Sheldon had no sense of the true concerns of the Church, at any rate as an institution; he was not a man of obvious spirituality or theologically articulate but he numbered among his friends the most eminent Anglicans of his time, some of whom, like Henry Hammond, were "Laudians" in the best sense.[3] That he was a strong character, with a sense of authority and great moral courage, is clear from all the evidence of his dealings.

For the most part, the other Anglicans who played a leading rôle in the Restoration were those who had avoided compromising themselves with the revolutionary régimes of

[1] Burnet, *HOT* i.313 f; cf. *Supplement to Burnet's History* (ed. Foxcroft), 67, for a slightly different version. Cf. also Samuel Parker, *History of His Own Time* (1727), 31–55; Wood, *Athenae Oxonienses* (ed. Bliss), iv, coll. 853–9.

[2] Clarendon, *Life*, i.34 f, 39 f, 45 f, 570; Wormald, op. cit., 244, 262.

[3] Pocock, *Theologian and Ecclesiastic*, vi-xvi (1848–54) *passim*.

the Interregnum: men like George Morley, John Earle, and John Cosin, who had spent much of the time abroad, or who, like Peter Gunning, Humphrey Henchman, or Henry Ferne, had maintained their Anglican integrity though they had stayed in England. Many of them were well known at Court and had sound political contacts: Earle was Charles II's leading chaplain, Morley was closely associated with Clarendon, Cosin had served the Anglicans at Queen Henrietta Maria's court.[1] Almost without exception they were, as their correspondence shows, convinced that the safety of the Church of England and the Stuart dynasty were indissolubly bound together, and animated with a double distrust of the Presbyterians as destroyers of the rightful order both in Church and State. Morley, through his connection with the Lord Chancellor and his Calvinist sympathy with the Puritans, was the most important among them; at times he seems to have played an even more important part than Sheldon in the negotiations. Quick-tempered, outspoken, and sometimes too passionate, he lacked Sheldon's *finesse*, but Clarendon and Burnet emphasize his honesty and personal goodness.[2]

That the out-and-out collaborators had little standing or influence in this period of reaction is intelligible. More surprising is the comparatively small part—though it can be underrated—played in the negotiations by the surviving bishops, who might have been expected at this juncture to resume their authority as the rightful leaders of the Church. But the poor figure they had cut during the Interregnum was not forgotten, nor was their churchmanship, except for that of Wren, Duppa, and possibly Juxon, such as would easily find favour.[3] There was, however, another group of

[1] Bosher, ch. 2 and 3 *passim*, esp. 29 ff, 49 ff.

[2] Burnet, *HOT*, i.314 f; cf. *Supplement to Burnet's History* (ed. Foxcroft), 67–70; Clarendon, *Life*, i. 46 f; cf. Bosher 50.

[3] Bosher 125 f, 150 f, and *passim*; the surviving bishops were, however, consulted in the summer of 1660 on the Puritan proposals about Church government, ibid., 166 f; cf. also below, p. 70.

men whose comparative neglect in making the settlement probably had serious consequences. Those who had conformed, while at the same time keeping up a strong feeling for the traditional episcopal Church of England which had in it nothing of the exclusiveness of the rigid "Laudians", were probably of all people the most likely to be able to understand the outlook of both a Hammond and a Baxter, and to bridge the gap between them. A list of such men is difficult to compile; but some case may be made out, for example, for the inclusion of John Gauden and Thomas Fuller. Gauden's *Eikon Basilike*, although a highly questionable literary deception, was a tribute to King and Church to be set alongside his collaboration; Fuller's outlook was tempered by a scholar's detachment. With men of this mind, "moderate Conformists that were for the old Episcopacy", Baxter thought compromise was possible, and he spoke appreciatively, for example, of Gauden's attitude during the Savoy Conference.[1] But it is noticeable that few or none of the men who fall into this class had the personality, vigour, or political contacts to make their point of view known or to get it adopted. Gauden, in particular, was hated by Clarendon, and no one who reads his querulous letters to the Lord Chancellor after he had received only the poor bishopric of Exeter can fail to understand this sentiment.[2]

Dr Bosher's reconstruction of the course of events between 1660 and 1662 presents government and Anglican policy as at best disingenuous, and at worst double-faced. He argues, in effect, that under cover of prolonged negotiations based on the Breda promises and extended by the Worcester House Declaration of October 1660, the Presbyterians were lulled into a state of inaction until their political strength had been

[1] Bosher 120 ff; *RB* I.i.§140; on Gauden, *RB* I.ii.§236; on Fuller, Jordan, op. cit., iii.199 f; Bosher 27 f.

[2] *Clarendon State Papers*, iii, app., pp. xxvi f, xcv f; cf. his self-satisfied letter to the Earl of Bristol about his behaviour during the Interregnum, p. xcvii.

broken, and their unity shattered, by the promotion of some of them and quarrels among the rest. Meanwhile the Anglicans recaptured the establishment and reinstituted episcopacy on the old model, saw the Anglican-dominated Cavalier Parliament substituted for the uncertain-tempered Convention, and only summoned the Savoy Conference as an earnest of the good faith they so conspicuously lacked, when Presbyterian influence in London seemed to be on the increase, yet the Conference's decisions could safely be overruled by the revived Convocation. The Act of Uniformity and the revised Prayer Book were therefore only the inevitable coping stones on the already reconstructed building, the designs for which had been decided upon some two years earlier, by a small group of "Laudians" working in close co-operation with Clarendon and the King. The ejections of the outmanoeuvred Nonconformists in 1662 were accordingly the consequence of a long-matured political strategy as well as of tactical triumphs since the Restoration.[1] There are grounds, however, as we have seen, for a reconsideration of some aspects of this interpretation.

In the period between the King's return in May 1660 and the apparently generous concessions offered to the Puritans in the Worcester House Declaration of October, almost all the major points of controversy dividing the two sides became clear, as did their different assumptions. To Anglicans, the restoration of the episcopal Church of England, unlawfully dispossessed, to its traditional place in the land, was axiomatic; concessions, if they had to be made, would be of grace and not of right. For Puritans, however, the question at issue was rather one of reorganization; the remodelling of the Church so that it might comprehend at least some of those who could not conscientiously accept her present rules and teaching. From the beginning these two different assumptions seem to have led to a fundamental misunderstanding of what may be called the area for manoeuvre. It soon became

[1] Bosher 138, 144, 149 foll., 208–18; cf. 88 f.

difficult, when more precise problems in making a settlement had to be faced, for either side to understand and sympathize with the other's expectations. But given the assumption that concessions, whatever they might be, would be within the framework of a restored episcopal Church in which the Royal Supremacy was a reality, an assumption the moderate Puritans seem to have accepted, there was nothing necessarily double-faced in the basic policy of the Government and the Anglican leaders in the summer and early autumn of 1660, unless the Declaration of Breda were to be regarded as abrogating all previously established ecclesiastical order.[1] The Presbyterians were certainly not neglected. About ten of their divines were appointed as royal chaplains, and invitations sent to some of them to preach at Court.[2] The King also invited them to talk about the future of the Church, and to prepare proposals for a general discussion with the Anglicans. Their paper, presented on 10 July, is a good illustration of what, at this stage, they were ready to accept. Baxter emphasized that their demands were deliberately kept moderate; they acquiesced, for example, in Ussher's scheme, although at bottom opposed to episcopacy in any form. Other requests were for a new Prayer Book or a substantial revision of the old one and a simplified non-"Laudian" ceremonial as well as a dispensation for Puritans from some of the most criticized of the older requirements, such as the use of the cross in baptism, the wearing of the surplice, and bowing at the name of Jesus. They asked the King to suspend the 1559 Act of Uniformity, and the need for the usual oaths and subscriptions, and to safeguard the position of Puritans in benefices by recognizing Presbyterian orders and preventing fresh appointments to benefices where there was no living counter-claimant to the occupying incumbent.[3]

[1] Cf. the statement of the English Puritans sent to their Scottish friends in August 1660, printed in R. Wodrow, *History of the Sufferings of the Church of Scotland* (Glasgow, 1829–30), i.54.

[2] Kirby, loc. cit., 60; *RB* I.ii.§§88–9.

[3] *RB* I.ii.§§90–6 (text of paper, pp. 232–42); Bosher 153 f.

Charles remarked that he was glad they were "for a Liturgy, and yielded to the *Essence* of Episcopacy", and therefore "doubted not of [their] Agreement with much more"; but Baxter and his colleagues were bitterly disappointed with the temperate yet firm defence of the *status quo* which a few days later the surviving bishops made to their proposals.[1] The gulf so soon revealed between the right-wing Puritans and men who were certainly not among the most intransigent of Anglicans was significant and disquieting.

While such talks were going on, the Church of England was taking on again its traditional form, with widespread public approval. From the middle of June a small group of Anglican advisers, consisting of Sheldon, Morley, and Earle, all "Laudians" in Dr Bosher's sense, had been recommending men of strong Anglican views and generally impeccable Royalist background to fill many vacancies in the Church, and by autumn most cathedral chapters were again at full strength. The Prayer Book was widely used, and ceremonies were revived in some places. In spite of a proclamation that for the time being all incumbents were to remain in their parishes irrespective of other claimants, many were ejected in favour of Anglicans. The universities were purged of all "intruders", and the Royalist survivors returned. As a result of such activities, the party dominating the Church had, by the end of the summer, entirely changed, while theological controversy became more lively.[2]

Since Royalists and Anglicans could at best only hold their own in the Convention Parliament, the Government obviously did not wish to embark as yet on any parliamentary settlement of religion. Prynne's Bill to limit severely the classes of sequestered Anglicans to be allowed to regain their former

[1] *RB* I.ii.§§97–101; the bishops' answer, pp. 242–7, cf. 248–58; cf. Bosher 166 f.

[2] Bosher 156–66; F. J. Varley (ed.), *The Restoration Visitation of the University of Oxford and its Colleges* (Camden Miscellany, xviii, Camden Soc., 1948); J. B. Mullinger, *The University of Cambridge* (Cambridge, 1911), iii, ch. 5 *passim.*

livings, and to confirm the tenure of many existing incumbents, may not, however, have been unacceptable to Clarendon and some of his colleagues, for it conveniently delayed an extensive change in the parishes while the Government was still unsure of its strength and afraid of successful subversive action against it. But its passing through Houses thin in Anglicans in the late summer certainly ran counter to "Laudian" plans.[1] More reassuring to Anglicans was the election, beginning during the recess, of bishops to fill the vacant sees, which, in spite of the alarm felt earlier about the age of the surviving prelates, had not yet been done.[2] Clearly this had to await the reconstruction of the cathedral chapters, if it were to be done in traditional form; another delaying factor may have been the need to recover the bishops' lands from their lay purchasers.[3] The timing of this action, when Presbyterian parliamentary influence had just shown its dangerous strength, may well have been carefully calculated, to offset the fear of such moves as Prynne's Bill. But it does not in itself prove that the Government had no intention of any compromise with the Puritans; even the most liberal terms offered them did no more than suggest a modified episcopacy, not that there should be no bishops at all.

Three only of the surviving bishops were translated to new sees: Duppa to Winchester, Frewen to York, and the old

[1] Bosher 167–79; cf. Abernathy, loc. cit., 57 f. Bosher thinks that Thorndike must have been misinformed when he stated that the Bill had Court support, but it is noteworthy, perhaps, that he was a prebendary of Westminster, and, writing from there, may have been in touch with well-informed political circles (Bosher 176, n. 2, quoting B.M. Harl. MS. 3784, fol. 2).

[2] Bosher 179–82.

[3] Bosher 161 f; B.M. Harl. MS. 3784, fol. 2. Two somewhat obscure letters of Roman Catholic provenance suggest that the King was trying to hold up the appointment of bishops, presumably to further Roman Catholicism, but it is unlikely that this was a major factor in the delay (Bodleian Clarendon MS. 73, foll. 182–5, 196; cf. Bosher 173 f).

and ineffectual Juxon, presumably merely as a courteous gesture, to Canterbury. The real leaders were among those consecrated on 28 October in the first ceremony of its kind to be held for sixteen years: Gilbert Sheldon to London, George Morley to Worcester, and Humphrey Henchman to Salisbury; with them were Robert Sanderson, destined for Lincoln, and George Griffith, for St Asaph. On 2 December seven more bishops were consecrated: Gauden to Exeter, Laney to Peterborough, Lloyd to Llandaff, Lucy to St David's, Sterne to Carlisle, Walton to Chester, and Cosin to Durham. The episcopal bench was finally filled, except for Lichfield and Sodor & Man, on 6 January 1661, when Ironside was consecrated to Bristol, Nicholson to Gloucester, Monk (the General's brother) to Hereford, and Edward Reynolds to Norwich.[1] Not all these men were original choices. In October 1660, attempts had been made to discover if Baxter would accept the see of Hereford, Edmund Calamy that of Lichfield, and perhaps Richard Gilpin that of Carlisle; Manton, Bates, and Bowles, three other Presbyterians or right-wing Puritans, were offered deaneries.[2]

The Puritan dilemma whether to accept these preferments was closely connected with the next series of discussions, which began in early September with the Government's request for comment on the draft of a proposed Declaration on Religion. Dr Bosher, who sees the Government's policy up to this time as one carried out on two levels, one the fundamental re-establishment of the Church and the other the temporary conciliation of the Presbyterians, regards these negotiations and the Declaration to which they led as expedients to keep the Puritans in play and to cover up the fact that the form of the Church settlement was already

[1] Bosher 181–4; *Handbook of British Chronology* (ed. F. M. Powicke and E. B. Fryde, 2nd edn, 1961), 202–80. Cf. B. M. Egerton MS. 2542, foll. 265–71 for memoranda, mostly of July 1658 (amended 1659) on proposed preferments.

[2] *RB* I.ii.§§118–27; Bosher 193 f, and n. 3, p. 193.

decided along rigid, traditional lines. To Professor Abernathy, however, the discussions, Declaration, and offers of preferment reflect Clarendon's sincere wish to set up a more comprehensive Church.[1] Men of the time were equally puzzled how to interpret the concessions. Baxter and his colleagues

> all thought that a Bishoprick might be accepted according to the Description of the Declaration, without any Violation of the Covenant, or owning the ancient Prelacy; but all the Doubt was, whether this Declaration would be made a Law (as was then expected) or whether it were but a temporary means to draw us on till we came up to all the Diocesans desired; and Mr *Calamy* desired that we might all go together, and all refuse, or all accept it.[2]

In the event they did not all act together. Baxter refused preferment for a variety of reasons, according to his retrospective account, perhaps the most significant being that his "Judgment was fully resolved against the Lawfulness of the old Diocesane Frame". Calamy held up his answer till it was obvious that what was offered was unlikely to have parliamentary confirmation. Reynolds, who is described by Baxter as being in the same dilemma, had already accepted as early as 9 September, and did not withdraw when the Declaration was not legally confirmed. But his opinions seem always to have been so nicely poised between right-wing Puritanism and liberal Anglicanism that his decision is not inconsistent with the rest of his career.[3]

Many hours of debate lay behind the Worcester House Declaration of 25 October 1660, the formulation of the final

[1] *RB* I.ii.§105; Bosher 149 f, 184 f; Abernathy, loc. cit., 56 f.

[2] *RB* I.ii.§119; cf. J. Gailhard, *The Controversie between Episcopacy and Presbytery*, 5, for an example of the view that the offers were "to bribe them thereby to the betraying of their trust and Cause, who, I hope will prefer the keeping of a good conscience to all those worldly preferments . . ."

[3] *RB* I.ii.§§121–4, 127, 125; cf. Bosher 119 and n. on the actual date Reynolds accepted the offer. On Reynolds, see Bosher 118 f and *DNB*.

draft of which, so much more accommodating to the Puritans than they had expected, remains somewhat mysterious.[1] So far as episcopacy went, the most important modifications concerned the concurrence of presbyters in ordination and ecclesiastical censure, in both of which they were to give advice and assistance; episcopal jurisdiction, in the exercise of which cathedral chapters and an equal number of elected diocesan presbyters were to participate; and the provision of suffragan bishops in every diocese. Parochial discipline, "pastoral persuasive power", was to be exercised with regard to all who wished to communicate, and confirmation administered with the co-operation of the minister of the parish. Disputed ceremonies and the use of the Prayer Book were not to be enforced for the time being; a national synod would consider the former, and a commission of Anglicans and Puritans be appointed to review the liturgy. Finally, no oath of canonical obedience or subscriptions were to be demanded at ordination or institution, and assent was to be required only to those of the Articles of Religion concerned with doctrine. Most of the concessions had been discussed before, and some even offered in previous negotiations, but as a whole it was the most generous suggestion of accommodation ever made to the Puritans.[2] Apart from

[1] *RB* I.ii.§§105–115 (text as first sent to the Puritans in September, pp. 259–64; the Puritans' Petition, pp. 265 ff; their other comments, pp. 268–76); Bosher 185 ff, and n. 4 p. 187. The text of the Declaration, with the additions and alterations, is conveniently set out by G. Gould (ed.), *Documents relating to the Settlement of the Church of England by the Act of Uniformity of 1662* (1862), 63–78.

[2] Among the most famous schemes for a modified episcopacy are those of Archbishop Ussher, first published without his knowledge in 1641 and suppressed by Parliament, then republished in 1656, 1659, and 1660, etc., with the title *The Reduction of Episcopacie unto the Form of Synodical Government received in the Ancient Church* (cf. *RB* I.ii.§96 [pp. 238 ff]; *DNB* s.v. Ussher, for the literary history); and Bishop Joseph Hall, *Modest Offer of some meet Considerations . . . concerning a form of Church-Government* (1644, repr. 1660); cf. John Gauden's letter to N. Bernard, September 1656 (*Thurloe State Papers* [1742], v. 598–601). The scheme put forward by Charles I's commissioners at

the question of ordination, not touched on in the final version, it went a good way to meet the criticisms of Baxter and his colleagues; in abrogating the oaths and subscriptions it made it as easy as possible for ministers to conform to the Church. That for long moderate Puritans were still hoping that it would be legally confirmed proves that some thought its concessions really valuable.[1] Nevertheless we know from Baxter's evidence that some of the more liberal Presbyterians had serious doubts whether they could, without compromising their opposition to episcopacy, subscribe an address thanking the King for it, while the stricter ones dissociated themselves entirely.[2]

In the story of the restoration of the Church of England and the birth of Dissent, there is no more crucial or confusing chapter than the episode of this Declaration: crucial, because it presents the greatest concessions ever offered to the Puritans, which yet bore no fruit; confusing, because we cannot be certain of the purpose and sincerity with which it was put forward. That the King himself was personally concerned with it, is clear; he set the talks in motion, and was present at the conference on 22 October at Worcester House, when, according to Baxter, not only the concessions to the Presbyterians were discussed, but also the possibility of a general toleration for those who would not disturb the peace, a proposition Baxter opposed since such liberty might extend as well to Catholics.[3] Who drafted the document is uncertain, although Baxter, Bates, and Burnet

---

Uxbridge in 1645, based on the advice of the clergy at Oxford, has several points in common with the Worcester House Declaration (printed in *EHR* ii [1887] 340 ff, with commentary by S. R. Gardiner); cf. also the negotiations at Newport in 1648 (S. R. Gardiner, *History of the Great Civil War* [1911], iv.217–22).

[1] *RB* I.ii.§276.

[2] *RB* I.ii.§128; Bosher 189–95. For addresses of thanks to the King for the Declaration from a group of Presbyterian and a group of Congregational ministers in London see B.M. Thomason Tracts 669 f. 26, p. 28, and Bodleian Clarendon MS. 73, fol. 314.

[3] *RB* I.ii.§§ 108–10; Bosher 186 ff.

all attribute it to Hyde, who was undoubtedly at the heart of the negotiations.[1] Most important of all, we do not know whether the Declaration set out merely to grant a series of temporary concessions, or constituted a blueprint for a final settlement for the Church. There is a good deal of evidence to support the former view, and nothing in the text explicitly to contradict it. The Declaration may, indeed, be seen as nothing more than an indulgence, authorized by the King's prerogative, reinforcing the Declaration of Breda, and designed to damp down dissatisfaction till a final settlement could be arranged through constitutional channels.[2]

Such an interpretation, however, raises certain problems. For instance, the contents of the Declaration go far beyond what was apparently required to re-establish ecclesiastical peace until a synod could be called, since detailed care is given to changes which could only be effective as long-range reforms, such as the institution of suffragan bishops and the establishment of modified episcopacy, needing several months at least to put into operation. It may of course be maintained that the Declaration was intentionally ambiguous, making promises which were perfectly safe because they could not be soon fulfilled, and would never in fact need to be. Yet this was not apparently the view of George Morley, Hyde's trusted friend and, according to Bates, "the principal Manager of the Conference among the Bishops",[3] who wrote to John Lauder, Baillie of Edinburgh, on 23 October, to report that agreement had been reached on everything but reordination, and went on to add that he hoped the Declaration would "give abundant satisfaction to the honest and peaceably minded men of both partys, &

[1] *RB* I.ii.§108; William Bates, *Works* (1723), 724; *Supplement to Burnet's History* (ed. Foxcroft), 56. Cf. Clarendon, *Life*, i.409.

[2] Bosher 149, 188 ff; *RB* I.ii.§§131–43; B.M. Sloane MS. 4107, foll. 260v, 261; Clarendon, *Life*, i. 408–11, 451 f; *CJ* viii.174.

[3] Bates, *Works*, 724 f.

make them cease to bee parties any longer. . . ."[1] It is very hard to read the full text of Morley's letter without feeling convinced that he regarded the concessions as leading to a permanent settlement, and though, again, it may be argued that men at the centre of events had to show such optimism if the Government's policy were successfully to deceive, such a conclusion is not inevitable. The possibility cannot be dismissed that though such concessions could only in the circumstances, and by such an informal body,[2] be granted temporarily, some men in high places were ready for them to be made permanent when the proper machinery could be set up, and if they seemed likely to bring about the desired concord. There may well have been differences of opinion about what the Declaration might achieve, and men may have concurred with it optimistically, pessimistically, or in a mood of pure cynicism. Similar plans had been much canvassed in the last twenty years; the High Churchman Herbert

[1] Partly printed in T. H. Lister, *Life and Administration of Edward, First Earl of Clarendon* (1837), iii. 110 f; I am much indebted to Mr Thomas Rae, of the Manuscript Department of the National Library of Scotland, for tracing for me the complete letter (Wodrow Papers, fol. 32, no. 9), which I hope to publish *in extenso* soon. I have been unable to discover the connection between Morley and John Lauder (for whom, see G.E.C., *Complete Baronetage* [Exeter, 1900–6], iv.360 f), but Morley writes to him as if he were an old friend.

[2] Morley's list of participants in the Worcester House Conference differs in some respects from Baxter's (*RB* I.ii.§108). Both agree that Sheldon, Morley, Henchman, Cosin, Barwick, and Gunning represented the Anglicans, but whereas Baxter names in addition Hacket and Gauden, Morley omits them but adds Frewen of York, Warner of Rochester, and Sterne of Carlisle. For the Presbyterians, both agree that Reynolds, Calamy, Ashe, Wallis, Manton, and Baxter were present; but while Baxter adds Spurstowe and concludes "and who else I remember not", Morley adds the name of Bates. They agree on the laymen present, though Baxter refers to Arthur Annesley as Lord Anglesey, a title he did not assume till 1661, while Morley refers to him as "Mr. Anslow". Since Morley was writing the day after the conference, his list of names is to be preferred to that of Baxter, writing longer after the event. It is noteworthy that the presence of Frewen and Warner suggests that the neglect of the pre-Restoration bishops in the negotiations after 1660 can be exaggerated (see above, p. 59).

Thorndike in August 1660 wrote in support, not necessarily ironically, of some of the concessions to be found in the Declaration.[1] Baxter was not inclined, even in retrospect, and with the failure of the scheme in mind, to think that nothing but "Deceit and Jugling" was intended.[2] Clarendon in the autumn of 1660, still apprehensive of Presbyterian political strength and uncertain of the popularity of Puritanism, may have been more inclined to try out what the Declaration might achieve than in later life he cared to remember.[3]

But what those behind the policy of the Worcester House Declaration do not seem to have foreseen—and, from the standpoint of strict Anglicans, it was a perilous omission—was that the Presbyterians in the Convention Parliament would try to give the Declaration, whose status was doubtful, the force of law. The weeks that followed the reassembly of Parliament till its dissolution on 29 December were therefore particularly critical. During them the Presbyterians lost their last chance to achieve their aims by political means, for they were not again to have substantial representation in the Lower House. Their failure seems to have been partly the result of a divided Puritan front, for Presbyterian refusal to support proposals for a general toleration led some Independent members to vote against the Bill. But the main cause was Government opposition, which appeared to prove the insincerity of the earlier Declaration.[4] Yet it cannot be assumed that this was so. Royal resentment at the proposed legislation may have been rooted in the apparent slight to the prerogative, while some who were earlier in favour of the

[1] H. Thorndike, *The Due Way of Composing the Differences on Foot preserving the Church* (August 1660), esp. 37 foll. For Thorndike's career at the Restoration, see T. A. Lacey, *Herbert Thorndike* (1929), 110 foll.

[2] *RB* I.ii.§143.

[3] His comments on it are remarkably non-committal. Clarendon, *Life*, i.408–11; cf. 546 f.

[4] Bosher 194–9; Bates, *Works* (1723), 725.

concessions may have considered there was no point in making them permanent when it was already clear that they would not be generally acceptable.[1]

For many Puritans, particularly the more moderate in opinion who seriously considered conforming, the most difficult and most personal question of the time was one that the final draft of the Declaration did not touch upon, that of reordination, for it involved theological issues which went to the root of their differences with the Anglicans over episcopacy and grace.[2] Only comparatively few of those admitted to benefices since the breakdown of episcopacy in the early 1640s had been ordained by a bishop; the majority had received ordination at the hands of chosen presbyters or had been received, with solemn prayer, as ministers before an Independent congregation, after careful examination into their knowledge, ability to preach, suitability of character, and, above all, true calling.[3] From the autumn of 1660 Anglican pressure that those holding benefices should receive episcopal ordination grew steadily, and there were many, either conformist by nature or Anglican by preference, who did not scruple to seek it, unconcerned at the

[1] Cf. B.M. Sloane MS. 4107, foll. 260–4v, a draft in Clarendon's hand, which, with reference to this declaration among others, emphasizes the King's prerogative in ecclesiastical affairs, and power of granting indulgences; cf. Abernathy, loc. cit., 62.

[2] Bosher 207; Kirby, loc. cit., 66 f; Bodleian Clarendon MS. 72, fol. 199v (Morley to Hyde, 4 May 1660). The Puritans suggested that the words "That such as have been ordained by Presbyters, be not required to renounce their Ordination, or to be re-ordained, or denied Institution and Induction for want of Ordination by Bishops" should be added to the Worcester House Declaration, but the final draft left them out (*RB* I.ii.§107 [p. 276]); cf. Bosher 185, n. 2, and Gould, op. cit., 77, who say that the clause was in the original draft, but this does not seem to be so (cf. *RB* I.ii. 259–64).

[3] Firth and Rait, op. cit., i.521–6, 579, 865–70, 1199–1204; ii. 1461 f; Surman, loc. cit., pp. xiii f, 33 ff, 75 f, etc.; Nuttall, *Visible Saints*, 88 foll. The letters of orders granted by the First Classical Presbytery of the Province of London on 8 April 1653 to Simon Patrick have survived (Bodleian Tanner MS. 52, fol. 6; cf. Patrick's *Autobiography* [Oxford, 1839], 23 f, and *DNB*).

theological implications of such a course with regard both to the validity of their previous orders, and the status and function of bishops and presbyters.[1] The abnormally large ordinations held by many of the newly consecrated bishops and their senior colleagues on the bench in these months shows how great was the demand, as does the frequency with which both orders were conferred on the same day.[2] But to many of the stricter Presbyterians and Independents the requirement posed extraordinary difficulties, for not only were there, in their view, insuperable theological obstacles, but the oaths and declarations demanded seriously taxed their consciences. To Zachary Crofton, reordination was

> a most ridiculous fancy, notorious fallacy, and false interpretation, never known in the Church under all the Controversies about the Churches Ministry, not rationally . . . to be *required* by any that design not to delude the simple, nor *subjected to* by any who intend not to the keeping of a Living, or gaining some preferment to cheat their consciences, and expose their Ministry, with Gods Church, and true Religion, to scorn, contempt, and ruine. . . .[3]

For the "New Prelatists" among the Anglicans, there was no alternative to reordination; they could never acknowledge that presbyters could do a work in their view specifically and historically reserved to bishops. For the Church of England to admit those not episcopally ordained would be

[1] Bosher 207; a similar problem had arisen during the Interregnum over the validity, from a Presbyterian point of view, of episcopal orders received since the abolition of episcopacy (Surman, loc. cit., p. xv).

[2] Anne Whiteman, "The Re-establishment of the Church of England, 1660–1663", *TRHS*, 5th ser., v (1955) 115 f; see *Correspondence of John Cosin* (ed. G. Ornsby, Surtees Soc., 1869, 1872), ii.32 f, for a list of men he admitted to Holy Orders on 22 September 1661.

[3] [Zachary Crofton,] *A Serious Review of Presbyters Re-ordination by Bishops* (1661), 10; cf. *RB* I.ii.§403; Henry Hickman, *Laudensium Apostasia*, pref. and 59; G[iles] F[irmin], *Presbyterial Ordination Vindicated . . . in Defence of his own Ordination* (1660), and William Prynne, *The Unbishoping of Timothy and Titus* (1636, repr. 1660, 1661), 1–3, 27 f, 33, 35 for other evidence of the importance of this issue.

to separate from the whole Catholic tradition.[1] Nor did precedents by which the ordinations of foreign Churches had been accepted as valid apply, since in such cases episcopal ordination had not been possible; as Thorndike, who held that the Church of England could not acknowledge Presbyterian orders without renouncing unity with the Catholic Church, wrote:

> Let the difficulty of procuring Ordinations, and having Bishops, render them excusable to God. Those that are ordained by Presbyters against Bishops, on purpose to set up Altar against Altar, how can we count them ordained refusing the concurrence of the Church to their Ordinations?[2]

But conditional reordination seemed a tolerable solution to some Anglicans; such a course, according to Morley,

> implys not a Nullity, but only an incertainty, together with an Illegality of their former pretended Ordination, which if it were good, the after Ordination is a Nullity; but if it were not good, then the super-Ordination is necessary, soe that it may doe them good, but it can doe them noe hurt. . . .[3]

Such "an ascertaining or a confirming Act, as publick Marrying again would be, after one is privately married, in case the Law would bastardize or disinherit his Children else", however, did nothing to meet the Presbyterian conviction that presbyters and bishops differed only *gradu*, not *ordine*, or to reconcile men certain that they had long been in orders to a suggestion that their ministry had perhaps been hitherto invalid.[4] Men like Philip Henry and John Howe

[1] *RB* I.ii.§291, cf. §109; H. Thorndike, *The Due Way of Composing the Differences* (1660), 27 f, 61.

[2] Thorndike, op. cit., 61; R. Baxter, *A Petition for Peace* (1661), 10. Cf. Sykes, *Old Priest and New Presbyter*, 69 foll., 87 foll., 118 foll., and Ussher's views, *Whole Works* (ed. C. R. Elrington, Dublin, 1847), i.258 ff.

[3] Nat. Lib. of Scotland, Wodrow Papers, fol. 32, no. 9 (the text in Lister, op. cit., iii.110 is not wholly correct); for the continuity of Morley's views, cf. Bodleian Clarendon MS. 72, fol. 199ᵛ.

[4] *RB* I.ii.§291.

found it impossible to accept reordination in such circumstances, and left the Church.[1] No official compromise was ever accepted in this matter, in spite of frequent discussion, and much was therefore left to the initiative of individual bishops to make entry into Anglican orders easy, as did Sydserf, Bishop of Galloway, who imposed no rigid conditions, and Gauden of Exeter, who specifically told his candidates that they had been ordained "by the hands, prayers and benediction of a Bishop, assisted with the company and Counsel of his venerable Presbyters . . .", or difficult, like George Hall of Chester, who demanded that those he reordained should repudiate their previous orders.[2]

By the close of 1660, it must have seemed likely to all observers that the Church would be re-established in the old form. Not only the consecration of new bishops tended towards this impression; there also seems to have been something of a spontaneous swing in favour of traditionalism in the Church, manifested, for example, by the Grand Jury of Dorset, which in September 1660 presented incumbents for not using the liturgy enjoined by Elizabethan legislation, and complained of dangerous and illegal conventicles of sectaries.[3] In January 1661 Venner's ill-conceived and abortive rising did great harm to the Puritan cause by re-identifying it with revolt, and all over the country justices of the peace and judges were prepared to prove their Anglican zeal by repressive measures which, in view of the Declaration of Breda and perhaps the Worcester House Declaration, were of

[1] M. Henry, *The Life of . . . Philip Henry* (1825), 97; H. Rogers, *The Life and Character of John Howe* (2nd edn, 1863), 117 f.

[2] Bosher 207; *Joannis Episcopi Exoniensis Consilia et voce & scripto tradita XLIIII. Fratribus Filiisque, Sacris Ordinibus per ipsum Episcopum & primores Presbyteros in Ecclesia Cathedrali Exoniensi more patrio, prisco & Catholico initiatis, Januarii 13. 1660* (1661), 16; Henry, op. cit., 97; Kirby, loc. cit., 66 f.

[3] Bosher 199–207; *RB* I.ii.§132; Bodleian Clarendon MS. 73, foll. 218–19.

doubtful legality.[1] In the dioceses the old administrative machinery slowly ground into action; what happened in the parishes is for the most part obscure, but the replacement of some incumbents by their ejected predecessors must have brought Anglican orthodoxy back into many places, as must in others the swing of time-servers.[2] But there was still hope that some at least of the points at issue might be settled by compromise, and to this end invitations were sent out to both Anglicans and Presbyterians on 25 March 1661 to attend further discussions at what was to be known as the Savoy Conference. It has been argued that the unexpected—and, to the Government, highly alarming—election of four Presbyterian members for the City in the new Parliament, and a real though probably unfounded fear of Presbyterian plots, lay behind this move, an attempt to show that the ultimate settlement of the Church was still an open question. It is also maintained that the resounding Royalist and Anglican triumphs at the polls in the rest of the country so renewed the Government's confidence in the soundness of their position that they were emboldened on 10 April to issue writs for a Convocation which, after some months of restored episcopal discipline in the dioceses, might be expected to consist of proctors solidly for the continuation of the *status quo* in the Church. Certainly, as in the case of Parliament as a whole, the elections were completely satisfactory from the Anglican point of view. But the fact that at first Convocation's terms of reference were strictly limited suggests that the Savoy Conference was to be given a real chance to produce something constructive. The Government's action in preventing a premature Bill for uniformity, originating in the fanatically Anglican House of Commons, from proceeding through the Lords, may also have sprung

[1] Bosher 145, 205 f.

[2] Bosher 206 ff; Whiteman, loc. cit., 113 foll.; Sykes, *From Sheldon to Secker*, ch. 1 *passim*. According to Matthews, *CR* pp. xii f, 695 incumbents were ejected in 1660; cf. Wodrow, op. cit., i.51 f.

from this desire to see if a compromise settlement were possible.[1]

But unfortunately hopes that the Savoy Conference would result in an agreement between Anglicans and Puritans were doomed to failure. It is the concern of another chapter to discuss the meeting in detail; here only the main points must be noted. The principal business was the consideration of the liturgy, in fulfilment of the promises made in the Worcester House Declaration.[2] It was for long thought that Anglican tactics were deliberately unfair, in that the Puritans were encouraged to ruin their case by a comprehensive statement of their objections to the Prayer Book, which could only serve to exacerbate strained relations; but Baxter indeed seems to have welcomed this plan, and persuaded his colleagues to agree to it. Dr Bosher's research, by establishing the order of procedure, has also shown that it was not until July that the Anglicans despaired of any concord, when ample time had been spent on a Puritan statement of objections to the liturgy and Anglican answers to the criticisms, and another period allotted for further Puritan deliberation. Finally, and only in the first week of July, did the Puritans bring in Baxter's new liturgy, which had no chance of acceptance. The decision was then made to keep the old Prayer Book, with only a few alterations and additions. Dr Bosher's reconstruction of events upholds his conclusion that "the Anglicans, contrary to the generally accepted version, did entertain some hope of satisfying the more moderate Puritans, and did not embark on the Conference with a pre-determined attitude of *non-possumus*".[3]

It would be difficult to find a sadder example of misapplied zeal than Baxter's determination to strive with the Anglicans almost single-handed in these discussions. Not only were his tactics misconceived; he was also already on such

[1] Bosher 208–15, 224 f, 228 f, 230; cf. Abernathy, loc. cit., 57.
[2] For the terms of the commission, see *RB* I.ii.§170.
[3] Bosher 226–9; *RB* I.ii.§171; B.M. Add. MS. 28,053, fol. 1.

uneasy terms with the Anglican leaders—particularly Morley—that his criticisms and suggestions were unlikely to get a ready welcome.[1] A man with a more flexible political sense must have grasped that whatever wide concessions might have been hoped for at an earlier stage in the negotiations, Anglican fortunes had now risen so decisively that there was no longer any question of attaining the Puritan ideal; it was merely a matter of what could be salvaged from the wreck of their hopes. Baxter records that he moderated the criticisms and requests put forward;[2] but a perusal of the papers the Puritans produced gives the impression that they did not find it possible to distinguish between matters which to those without a Puritan conscience seemed of minor importance, and matters of generally acknowledged significance. Baxter's burning sincerity and indefatigable spirit, merits though they were, were less useful to the Puritans at this juncture than political suavity and *finesse* could have been; but these were qualities utterly despised by the Puritan negotiators of this generation, and it is a measure of their integrity as men that this was so.

The failure of the Savoy Conference, together with renewed episcopal supervision in the dioceses in the autumn of 1661 and the growing strength of anti-Presbyterian feeling in the country, condemned the Puritans henceforth to the fighting of a rearguard action only. The existence of a Royalist and Anglican Parliament, a phenomenon surely unthinkable to men who remembered the Short and Long Parliaments, reconciled Anglicans to the implementation of one of the promises made at Breda: that the settlement of religion should be parliamentary.[3] Some of the problems awaiting solution in 1660 were already decided. Traditional episcopacy was firmly re-established, and so far as the liturgy

[1] *RB* I.ii.§236; for Baxter's comments on Morley, §§81, 109, 199–203, 209, 216 ff, 236, 249 ff, 275, etc.

[2] *RB* I.ii.§174, cf. §99.

[3] Bosher 239.

went, the Prayer Book was unlikely to be substantially modified; not the revival of ceremonial but rather the degree and manner of its enforcement were now in question. The outstanding matters for settlement were, by the winter of 1661–2, reduced to four: the final revision of the Prayer Book, the definitive formulation of the legal conditions of conformity with the Church of England, the fate of those ordained or appointed to livings during the period of Puritan domination, and the liberty to be allowed to those who found themselves outside the Church. The passing of the Corporation Act in December 1661, with its clauses imposing oaths, declarations, and a sacramental test on all who wanted municipal office, had already deprived nonconformist laymen of full civil rights.[1]

The somewhat untimely zeal of the House of Commons in framing a Bill of Uniformity in the summer of 1661 has already been noticed.[2] The Government was equally embarrassed by the ingenious attempt made soon after Parliament's reassembly in November 1661 to amend Prynne's Act of 1660, confirming several classes of Puritan ministers in their livings, in such a way that very few such incumbents would have been safe from ejection; in addition it was planned that the Act should not, either in its amended or unamended form, serve to confirm in his living any minister not episcopally ordained by 25 March 1662, or who had not administered Holy Communion according to the liturgy of the Church of England for a full year past. Puritan alarm at the prospect of such legislation was understandably extreme. Nor, it seems, was it at all to the taste of the Government. The revised Bill was at first held up in the Lords and then the amendments were defeated; the Commons naturally refused consent to the original Bill when it came back to them from the Upper House. Authorities are agreed that the amended Bill's passage was stopped in the Lords by the

[1] *Statutes of the Realm* (1810–28), v. 321 ff.
[2] See above, pp. 76 f.

action of Clarendon, with the help of Sheldon, Morley, Sanderson, Reynolds, Gauden, and two other bishops, together with the Duke of York. But whereas Dr Bosher sees Clarendon's intervention as "his first open attempt to stem the tide of Anglican reaction", Professor Abernathy regards the Lord Chancellor's move as perfectly consistent with his sustained policy of working for comprehension.[1] However his action is to be interpreted, it is obvious that the amended Bill would have created highly undesirable, and even really dangerous, disturbance throughout the Church.

Clearly a better and fairer way of testing uniformity would be provided by the terms of the Act of Uniformity, the promotion of which now required the completion of the work on the revised Prayer Book. The draft text, conservatively and sparingly altered, was submitted to the King on 24 February 1662, and referred to the Lords a day later; by 17 March it had been approved by that House. The Bill of Uniformity, passed by the Commons but neglected by the Lords in the last session, was at last seriously considered by the Lords, who added certain amendments making the provisions more exacting; for example, subscription to all the Thirty-nine Articles, a solemn declaration against the Covenant and affirming non-resistance, and the deprivation of all not in episcopal orders by St Bartholomew's Day.[2] These can scarcely have been offset by a proviso that fifths should be paid to ejected incumbents in certain cases.[3] Particular interest attaches to the other ameliorating proviso, which would have given the King authority to allow any incumbent in possession of a living on 29 May 1660 to refrain from the use of the surplice or the sign of the cross in baptism, as long as he arranged for another to baptize for him when the full

[1] Bosher 239–44, esp. 242; Abernathy, loc. cit., 58.

[2] Bosher 244–50; on the revision of the text of the Prayer Book, see G. J. Cuming, "The Making of the Durham Book", *JEH* vi (1955) 60–72, and the same author's "The Prayer Book in Convocation, November 1661", ibid., viii (1957) 182–92.

[3] Bosher 250.

Anglican rite was wanted, and did not write or speak against the liturgy, rites, or ceremonies of the Church of England. Introduced into the Lords by Clarendon on the King's instructions, this clause would have given Charles power, in Professor Abernathy's words, "to create a nonconformist branch of the Church of England by letters of dispensation to individual ministers", and might well have kept in the establishment many men who on the final terms of the Act of Uniformity could not conform. With the help (it is noteworthy) of Sheldon, Morley, Gauden, and Reynolds, Clarendon carried the proviso against the opposition of his enemy Bristol and other critics, only to see it and the proposal about fifths cast out by the Commons. Nor was he successful in getting rid of the clause condemning the Covenant.[1] The Act of Uniformity finally passed both Houses after a conference on 30 April, and received the royal assent on 19 May, without any provision for mitigating its requirements. If it had been Clarendon's aim, as seems possible, to avoid a rigid, unaccommodating settlement, he had not succeeded.[2]

The revised Prayer Book and the Act of Uniformity together set out the conditions for conformity to the Church of England, and settled the fate of Puritan incumbents who, by 24 August 1662, had to decide whether they could with a good conscience stay in the Church, or must suffer deprivation. The main stumbling-blocks were familiar to them: their Elizabethan forbears would have understood almost all the points at issue even if their form were a little different a hundred years later. The Act of Uniformity required every minister to read Morning and Evening Prayer, celebrate

[1] Abernathy, loc. cit., 59 ff; Bosher 250–4; for drafts of the provisos, Bodleian Clarendon MS. 76, foll. 156–63, and for one concerning ordination, Bodleian Carte MS. 81, foll. 109–11. For the Crown's use of dispensation in modifying the application of the Corporation Act, see J. H. Sacret, "The Restoration Government and the Municipal Corporations", *EHR* xlv (1930) 252.

[2] Bosher 253 f; Clarendon, *Life*, i.568.

Holy Communion and administer Baptism according to the Prayer Book, and to declare his "unfeigned assent and consent to all and everything" contained in that book and in the Ordinal, openly and publicly before the congregation. In addition, he had to take oaths of canonical obedience and non-resistance, and to abjure the Covenant, in terms which included an acknowledgement that it was not binding either on the swearer of the oath, or any other person. Acceptance of the Prayer Book inevitably, too, involved acceptance of the traditional ceremonies and customs associated with it: kneeling at Holy Communion, the use of the cross in baptism, bowing at the name of Jesus, and the wearing of the surplice.[1] Episcopal ordination was also made compulsory, its lack being made *ipso facto* a cause for deprivation.[2] And enforcing the whole traditional system were the bishops, their powers neither restrained nor strengthened by the co-operation of presbyters, as the Worcester House Declaration had suggested. The innovation most longed for by some Puritans, the general introduction of parish discipline, also mentioned in the Declaration, would never now be introduced.[3] It was the bitter fate of the Puritans not only to lose their preferments but to feel that nothing of all they had fought for so single-mindedly would come to fruition within the framework of a national comprehensive Church, in which most of them believed as firmly as their Anglican opponents. Men like Calamy and Baxter, Manton and Bates had no desire to found a sect, and only the witness they felt they must make, and their responsibility to their congregations, led them to carry on their ministry outside the Church. Some, like John Ray and Zachary Crofton, resigned their preferments and became conforming members, but as if they had been laymen, of the Church of England.[4]

[1] *Statutes of the Realm*, v.364–70. [2] Ibid., v.367.

[3] Cf. *RB* I.ii.§106 (pp. 269–72).

[4] For biographical details of these men, and others ejected in 1662, see A. G. Matthews, *Calamy Revised*, *passim*, and C. E. Surman, *A. G. Matth ws' Walker Revised; Supplementary Index of "Intruders" and others*

The conditions demanded by the Act of Uniformity were, then, admittedly not easy; they required more than had ever been asked for before from ministers in the Church of England, and asked for it with a new precision particularly hard on men with minds so scrupulous that the exact wording of every phrase and the exact meaning of every word had to be examined with meticulous and personal care, as the discussions over the demand for "consent" and "assent" to the contents of the Prayer Book showed.[1] The revisers of the liturgy, it is true, had paid some respect to Puritan wishes expressed in the talks of 1661, and the result was a disappointment to some High Churchmen who would have liked something more akin to the 1549 text, but the final version was still full of things in which Puritans could not acquiesce. When it became clear that the non-subscribers would be many, the politicians seem to have been more concerned than the Anglican clergy themselves. Clarendon's speech at the adjournment on 19 May reaffirmed his desire for eventual comprehension; throughout the summer there was talk of a toleration or an indulgence.[2] The Lord Chancellor made two attempts to mitigate the effects of the Act: the first in June, when he tried unsuccessfully to get a general suspension of it; the second in August, when the opposition of Sheldon prevented a scheme by which individual dispensations might have been granted by the King.[3] But the Anglicans who opposed any suspension or indulgence also had a reputable point of view. They had also fought hard for the re-establishment of what they considered to be the essentials of their Church: episcopal government, a

---

(Dr Williams's Library, Occasional Paper, no. 2, 1956); on Ray, C. E. Raven, *John Ray, Naturalist* (2nd edn, Cambridge, 1950), 57–61, and below p. 159, n. 2; on Crofton, J. A. Dodd, *EHR* x (1895) 53.

[1] *RB* I.ii.§285; G. R. Cragg, *Puritanism in the Period of the Great Persecution* (Cambridge, 1957), 8.

[2] Bosher 244–9, 254 foll.; cf. *RB* I.ii.§276; Cuming, *JEH* viii.184 f, 187.

[3] Bosher 259–64; Abernathy, loc. cit., 61–4.

standard liturgy, adherence to a minimum of ceremonial. Some, like Thorndike, felt that it was their prime duty to retain what they had in common with the communion of the Catholic Church, and saw the problem of unity in different terms.[1] Within limits they had been prepared to make concessions to Puritan scruples, certainly once they had won their main position, perhaps even before. But on other points they could compromise no more than the Puritans, so that the area in which agreement was possible was from the first small.

In the skirmishing that accompanied the re-establishment of the Church of England between 1660 and 1662, neither side has an entirely creditable record. Because they were ultimately the losers, and because the results of their defeat were so tragic for themselves and for the unity of the Church, the Puritans command a sympathy which, perhaps, they do not in all respects deserve. It is easy to see them as the helpless victims of a powerful and vengeful Royalist and Anglican machine, which remorselessly drove them to their doom. But in the Convention Parliament their party played their political cards as ruthlessly as did the Anglicans after the next election, and with as little regard for the injustice they might do to individuals who also had a case worth arguing. They were certainly unfortunate in that no clerical leader with first-rate political capacity emerged from their ranks, and they were poorly supported by their lay friends who, bought off with honours and office, left the ministers to fight virtually alone.[2] Yet when all that is said, it is difficult to acquit the Puritans of a certain blindness in their conduct of affairs: an unwillingness to see that Presbyterians and Independents had to stand together; a fundamental inability to distinguish between essentials and superficialities which

[1] Cf. Thorndike, *The Due Way of Composing the Differences*, 3–16, 38, 57 f, and Matthew Poole, *Evangelical Worship is Spiritual Worship* (1660), 19 f.

[2] Feiling, *History of the Tory Party, 1642–1714*, 103; Bosher 147 f; *RB* I.ii.§111.

weakened the respect their opponents were prepared to pay to their scruples, and a political obtuseness as to what, at any time, was a feasible rather than an ideal policy.[1] Good men though their leaders were, and good as was much in their cause, they were often too ready to attribute honest disagreement with their own point of view to mere obstinacy or even deliberate malice; they were dangerously sure that they alone had right on their side. "...We spoke to the Deaf", wrote Baxter of the failure of the Savoy Conference;[2] but deafness was not the infirmity of one side only. Both Anglicans and Puritans, in the prolonged controversies, had difficulty in hearing the voice of charity and the arguments of reason.

The Anglicans from the start had many advantages: the support of the King for at any rate much of their programme, zealous lay co-operation, the legal argument that they were the legitimate heirs kept from their heritage by wicked usurpers. Much in the political situation, after the first few months, was overwhelmingly in their favour, and they knew how to exploit it, deliberately, and, at times, somewhat unscrupulously. They could afford to offer concessions, but how far they were ever ready to compromise with the Puritans except on a superficial level remains uncertain; undeniably, if we knew more of the mind of Charles II, Clarendon, Morley, and Sheldon, the chief architects of the settlement, we could better judge the sincerity with which the negotiations were carried out. None of them, it appears, was wholly averse to some degree of accommodation; even Sheldon voted for the unsuccessful proviso to allow the King to dispense with the requirements of the Act of Uniformity in favour of individual ministers.[3] But of the four men, his aims were perhaps the simplest: to restore the Church of England to its traditional form, with as few changes as possible, and, once this had been achieved, to refuse any

[1] Cf. *RB* I.ii.§263.

[2] *RB* I.ii.§192, cf. p. 156, below.

[3] Above pp. 80 f.

further negotiations. Yet with all his strength, courage, and decision, he could, it seems, be strangely blind to the implications of his actions, or of what he acquiesced in. The prominence of Parliament and comparative inconspicuousness of Convocation in the making of the 1662 settlement further weakened the Church in its relations with the State, while his short-sighted agreement of 1664 with Clarendon over the taxation of the clergy, which led almost immediately to the virtual suspension of Convocation, deprived the Church of its official mouthpiece and stripped it of its last shred of independence.[1] Perhaps some similar defect of vision played a part in his making of the 1662 settlement; perhaps he did not really believe that the intensely individual Puritans, with whom he had to deal, could ever become the founders of the permanent force in English life which Dissent turned out to be. Odd remarks that he is said, on not very good authority, to have made at this time, are often quoted to support the view that he did not regret the removal of the Puritans from the Church, and this may be true.[2] But it seems more likely that he thought that the judicious use of force would soon restore uniformity, and counted the temporary suffering cheap if a really united and disciplined Church could thereby soon be achieved. Such a view now wins no sympathy, but it was still a common attitude in Europe in the middle of the seventeenth century, and sincerely held by Churchmen of more obvious spirituality than Sheldon.[3]

It is exceedingly difficult to sum up the issues at stake between the Anglicans and the Puritans without recourse to a distorting simplicity. Indeed Presbyterians, Independents, Baptists, and Sectaries of all kinds found different difficulties

[1] Bosher 281 f; Sykes, *From Sheldon to Secker*, 41–4.

[2] Bates, *Works* (1723), 725; Bosher 271.

[3] Bosher 265; cf. for example the views of Bossuet (A. Rébelliau, *Bossuet, Historien du Protestantisme* [3rd edn, Paris, 1909], *passim*), and for a valuable general survey, Jean Orcibal, *Louis XIV et les Protestants* (Paris, 1951), 20 foll.

in coming back into a comprehensive Church; by 1660 only right-wing Puritans even wanted to do so. For those who would have liked to conform, albeit very much on their own terms, there were problems over the form of the liturgy and the degree of ceremonial very hard to resolve. But the dispute seems at bottom to have been more over the nature of episcopacy and the power and authority of bishops, projected inevitably into the question of the validity of orders. As we have seen, Anglican views on episcopacy had for the most part considerably hardened in the last few decades, and the gulf between the right and the left in the Church inevitably widened at the same time. In addition, the ferocity of the attack on the bishops at the beginning of the Great Rebellion bred its own reaction; men who had earlier been but lukewarm supporters of the traditional form of church government now felt convinced that ecclesiastical stability and political and social order rested on episcopacy. Of the general trend of Puritan thinking about bishops it is more difficult to speak. That there were Puritans who agreed in principle to some form of modified episcopacy is undeniable, but their fundamental antipathy to, and mistrust of, the institution seems to have made it very hard—perhaps impossible—for them to agree on the amount of modification they would find tolerable and practical, for in the last analysis there was little in episcopacy which seemed to them theologically convincing. The "parish discipline" on which they set so much store fitted uneasily into the diocesan system, while they had long ago lost faith in episcopal discipline exercised through the church courts. Other Puritans, perhaps even the majority, seem to have been irrevocably hostile to episcopacy in any form, and having once escaped from its control found it intolerable to return under it. For them the authority to be followed in church government and Christian discipline was what they found in, or deduced from, Scripture, often interpreted by Geneva; they reserved their right to reach their own conclusions about liturgy and ceremonial, without the guidance of episcopal authority.[1] It is certainly arguable that by 1660 no concessions, save the general abolition of episcopacy which to Anglicans was unthinkable, could have kept all of them, or even a substantial part, within the Church. And even if a compromise settlement could have been reached, it is by no means certain that it could long have survived the stresses and strains seemingly inescapable when men with fundamentally different attitudes try to exist in the same institution. For the Puritan mind, so difficult to define but so clearly to be seen at work in this period, valued its search for perfect faith and order more than compromise and acquiescence for the sake of peace.

The tragedy of the split and the human suffering involved must not be allowed to detract from the importance of the fundamental issues at stake or the sincerity of the men faced with them. Newcomen's reminder that consciences varied in tenderness must be paralleled by a recognition that men genuinely differed, as they still do, about church government and discipline, liturgy and ceremonial. Sometimes disagreements of this kind can be glossed over, or some exterior danger may reduce their immediate importance. But it is a phenomenon of human existence that recurrently religion and the means by which it is expressed and regulated possesses the minds of some of the finest men in a generation; and in such periods, of which the mid-seventeenth century was one, it is scarcely to be expected that they will find compromise satisfactory in matters which touch on questions beyond earthly solution.

[1] Cf. Baxter's Draft of a Declaration of Religion, 4 April 1660, for a good statement of this point of view (Richard Schlatter, *Richard Baxter & Puritan Politics* [Rutgers University Press, New Brunswick, N.J., 1957], 144).

2

THE SAVOY CONFERENCE

and the Revision of the Book of Common Prayer

E. C. RATCLIFF

AFTER some eighty-five years of troubled life, the Book of Common Prayer established by the Elizabethan Act of Uniformity in 1559, and revised under the royal authority of James I in 1604, was abolished by an Ordinance of Parliament bearing date, "DIE VENERIS, 3 *Januarii* 1644" (1645).

The abolition was an outcome of the "solemn league and covenant for Reformation and Defence of Religion" etc., into which the same Parliament, later to be known as "the Long", together with the Scottish Convention of Estates, had entered in the previous year. Reformation of worship in England and Ireland was among the declared aims of the Covenant. To this, therefore, the Ordinance alludes in its preamble:

> The Lords and Commons assembled in Parliament, taking into serious consideration the manifold Inconveniences that have arisen by the Book of Common-Prayer in this Kingdom, and resolving, according to their Covenant, to reform Religion according to the Word of God, and the Example of the best Reformed Churches, have consulted with the Reverend, Pious and Learned Divines,[1] called together to that purpose; And do judge it necessary that the said Book of Common-Prayer be abolished.

The Ordinance then decrees the repeal of the Edwardine and Elizabethan Acts of Uniformity, the Elizabethan Act for providing a Welsh version of the Prayer Book, and those provisions of an Act of 1567 which established the Ordinal of 1552. The Ordinance next enjoins that "the said book of Common-Prayer shall not remain, or be from henceforth used in any Church, Chappell, or place of Publique Worship, within the Kingdom of England, or Dominion of Wales".[2]

[1] I.e. of the Westminster Assembly.

[2] The text of the Ordinance was printed at the beginning of the *Directory*, and can be found in T. Leishman (ed.), *The Westminster Directory* (Church Service Society, Edinburgh, 1901), 5 ff.

As far, then, as they could do so without the King's assent, the Lords and Commons had both "taken away" the Prayer Book and also destroyed its legal foundations. Yet the Ordinance did not meet with as ready and wide an obedience as the Parliament expected and desired. On 23 August 1645, because "there hath been as yet little fruit of the said Ordinance", the Parliament took measures to reinforce it by issuing a second Ordinance attaching penalties to the use of the Prayer Book, not merely in any public place of worship but now also "in any private place or family within the Kingdom of England"; and ordering, under penalty of a fine, churchwardens or parish constables to remove from churches and chapels into the custody of the Parliamentary County Committees all copies of the Prayer Book "to be disposed of as the Parliament shall direct".[1] Henceforward, the forces of the law could be invoked against any use of the Prayer Book for purposes of worship.

A study of the *Directory for the Publique Worship of God*, which the Ordinance of 3 January substituted for the Prayer Book, is outside the scope of this chapter. The Preface of the *Directory*, however, calls for a brief notice, because it specifies the chief of the "Inconveniences" of the Prayer Book mentioned in the Ordinance.[2] When that Book was first set forth, so the Preface allows, it was a matter for rejoicing in that it provided a form of public worship "in our own tongue". On the other hand, long and sad experience has shown that, notwithstanding the good intentions of its compilers, the Prayer Book "hath proved an offence, not only to many of the godly at home, but also to the Reformed Churches abroad". In particular, "the many unprofitable and burdensome ceremonies contained in it have occasioned much mischief" by disquieting the consciences of many good ministers and people who could not "yield unto" the ceremonies, so

[1] For the text of the Ordinance see C. H. Firth and R. S. Rait (ed.), *Acts and Ordinances of the Interregnum 1642–1660* (1911), i.755 ff.

[2] For the text of the Preface see Leishman, op. cit., 9–14.

that "sundry good Christians have been, by means thereof, kept from the Lord's Table; and divers able and faithful ministers debarred from the exercise of their ministry". It was not necessary for the Preface to name the ceremonies,[1] which were the cause of offence. They were well known to every reader, whether Puritan or Prayer Book man. They had been the subject of complaint forty years before in the *Millenary Petition*.[2] The first clause of the *Petition* had requested "that the cross in baptism, interrogatories ministered to infants, confirmation, as superfluous, may be taken away . . . the cap and surplice not urged;[3] that examination may go before the communion; that it may be ministered with a sermon;[4] that divers terms of priests and absolution, and some other used, with the ring in marriage, and other such like in the book [i.e. of Common Prayer], may be corrected . . . no ministers charged to teach their people to bow at the name of Jesus;[5] that the canonical Scriptures only be read in the Church". Puritan objection against the ceremonies was not new in 1603; it had acquired formidable strength by 1645, and to the men of that day the issue of the *Directory* must have seemed an assurance that the question of the ceremonies was settled for ever.

To its condemnation of the ceremonies, the Preface of the

[1] The term "ceremony" is used in this context not only of a ceremonial action, such as making the sign of the cross on an infant at baptism, but also of any liturgical rite or usage, and of anything therewith connected, so that confirmation and wearing a surplice are both "ceremonies".

[2] See Gee and Hardy, *Documents Illustrative of English Church History*, (1921), no. 88.

[3] The use of the surplice was covered by the Ornaments Rubric of the Elizabethan Prayer Book. The wearing of the square cap was enjoined by no. 30 of the Royal Injunctions of 1559, and ordered by Archbishop Parker's "Advertisements" of 1566.

[4] Not all ministers possessed a licence to preach, and a sermon was not an invariable element of the Communion service; but it was a Puritan tenet that (in the words of Cartwright) "the life of the sacraments dependeth of the preaching of the Word of God".

[5] Enjoined by no. 52 of the Royal Injunctions of 1559.

Directory appends two further complaints against the Prayer Book. First, "Papists boasted that the book was a compliance with them in a great part of their service"; and second, "the Liturgy hath been a great means . . . to make and increase an idle and unedifying ministry, which contented itself with set forms made to their hands by others, without putting forth themselves to exercise the gift of prayer, with which our Lord Jesus Christ pleaseth to furnish all His servants whom He calls to that office". The approval of extemporized prayer was a concession to the Independents. The Presbyterians, who followed the Calvinist tradition, had no scruple against a fixed framework of worship and set prayers; they commonly employed them, as Calvin himself had done. The Independents, on the other hand, maintained that both framework and prayers should be free.[1] The *Directory* provides for free prayers, usually upon set themes, within an appointed framework, and thus is a compromise between the two methods of applying the basic principle of Puritan worship. That principle is stated, in temperate terms, in the conclusion of the Preface of the *Directory*, "our care hath been to hold forth such things as are of Divine institution in every Ordinance; and other things we have endeavoured to set forth according to the rules of Christian prudence, agreeable to the general rules of the Word of God". The Puritans were never tired of arguing against their opponents that God, who had revealed himself as a "jealous God", must be worshipped only according to the rules laid down in his Word. Such a conviction was irreconcilable with the persuasion of the conformist who held it legitimate to proceed in accordance with the proposition, contained in the 20th of the Thirty-nine Articles of Religion, that "it is not lawful for the Church to ordain anything that is contrary to God's Word written". In the Puritans' opinion the proposition was inadequate and misleading, if not formally erroneous; it

[1] For a discussion of the points at issue see Horton Davies, *The Worship of the English Puritans* (1948), ch. 8.

could be used to cover "compliance with the Papists" in much of their service, the offending ceremonies, and lack of true discipline, together with prelacy and all the other evils of the established Church. The Puritans affirmed that worship must be "agreeable to the Word of God", that is, that the manner and details of worship must possess the positive warrant of Scripture. Scripture was (to quote Dr Horton Davies) the Puritans' "all-sufficient manual for all liturgical matters".[1]

The Preface of the *Directory* is concerned solely with religious objections to the Prayer Book. The Puritans were wont, however, to allege another objection, one of a totally different character, by means of which they sought rather to embarrass the Government than to set out their own case. Whereas the Prayer Book of 1559 derived its legality, as its Edwardine predecessors had done, from an Act of Parliament having the Sovereign's assent, the alterations made in the Elizabethan Book in 1604 rested on the authority of no more than letters patent of King James I and a royal proclamation.[2] The alterations, which were few and not specially of a kind to exacerbate Puritan susceptibility, left the character of the Prayer Book unchanged;[3] but they were never submitted to Parliament for consideration and consent.[4]

[1] Ibid., 50.

[2] For the text of the proclamation "for the authorizing and uniformity of the Book of Common Prayer to be used throughout the realm", dated 5 March 1603 (/4), see no. 89 in Gee and Hardy, *Documents*, etc. The proclamation was printed after the Elizabethan Act of Uniformity in impressions of the Prayer Book issued in the reigns of James I and Charles I.

[3] The principal alterations were the addition of the Questions and Answers on the Sacraments to the Catechism, of a suffrage and prayer for the Queen, Prince Henry, and the rest of the "Royall progenie" in the Litany, and of six Occasional Thanksgivings appended to the Litany. Also four Apocryphal lessons were replaced by four Canonical, presumably as a concession to the Millenary Petitioners and those who represented them at the Hampton Court Conference.

[4] Neither were they submitted to the Convocations. No. 80 of the Canons of 1603, however, recognized the Jacobean Book as a necessary furnishing of churches.

On this ground, the Puritans declared the Book of 1604 to be wanting in legality and consequently to be not binding.[1] This legal objection could not be mentioned in the Preface of the *Directory*, not merely because it would have been out of place among the religious "Inconveniences" therein cited but also, and more important, because the *Directory* itself, though having the sanction of Parliament, lacked the assent of the Sovereign, and so was exposed to the sort of objection which the Puritans themselves had raised against the Jacobean Prayer Book. No constitutionally-minded conformist and no royalist could regard the *Directory* as legally substituted for the Prayer Book, or the Prayer Book as lawfully abolished.

Such is the contrariness of human nature that a possession, which a man has been accustomed to value lightly or not at all, becomes to him an object of worth and affection, once it is taken away. The Prayer Book was no exception to this rule; abolition of the Book led to a new esteem for it. Its quality was made apparent by contrast with the system of worship which had superseded it. When, under the Protectorate of Oliver Cromwell, the Independents acquired full liberty of worship, their free proceedings were calculated further to enhance traditional Anglican liturgical order in Anglican eyes, and, not improbably, in other eyes as well.[2] It was reported in 1653 that "conventicles for Common Prayer are frequent and much desired in London".[3] Cromwell's own mind was in favour of toleration; and so far was the law from being strictly enforced in the capital that the Prayer Book was openly used in several city churches. There is ground for supposing that in the country, no less

[1] They refused to allow that the power to ordain further rites and ceremonies, which the Act of Uniformity of 1559 vested in Queen Elizabeth I, extended to her successor.

[2] For an account of Independent procedure see John Evelyn, *A Character of England*, in *Miscellaneous Writings* (1825), 152 f (the passage is quoted in *The Diary of John Evelyn*, ed. Austin Dobson [1906], ii.53, n. 1).

[3] *Calendar of the Clarendon State Papers* (ed. O. Ogle *et al.*) ii.234; Bosher 11.

than in London, the services of the Prayer Book were being read in the churches. Moreover in many private houses, alike in town and country, the services were read by clergymen who, ejected from their parishes for nonconformity, were maintained as chaplains and tutors, or by visiting clergymen, such as Evelyn's Mr Owen who, on 25 October 1653, "preached in my Library at Says Court" and afterwards "administred to us all the Holy Sacrament".[1] Up to the end of 1655 Anglicans determined to worship and to receive the Sacraments according to the use of the Prayer Book found it not impossible or even too difficult to do so.[2] Attempted Royalist risings in the course of 1655 prompted a sterner policy. An Order of the Lord Protector, dated 4 October, prohibited Royalists from keeping ejected clergymen in their houses as chaplains or tutors, and forbade all such clergymen to keep any school, to preach in public or private (except to their own families), to administer the Sacraments, to solemnize marriages, "or use the Book of Common-Prayer or the forms of prayer therein contained", under penalties.[3] The first of January 1655/6 was appointed to be the day on which the Order should take effect; and the penalties were three and six months' imprisonment respectively for the first two offences, and banishment for the third. A proclamation issued on 24 November confirmed the Order.[4] Before 1 January, however, some "tenderness" was promised to those offenders who should show themselves tractable to the Government. Once again, in the event, the rigour of the law was not enforced. At the same time, the conditions of life were made markedly harder and more hazardous for the majority of those Anglicans who valued

[1] *Diary*, ed. E. S. de Beer, iii.89. For Richard Owen, see *Walker Revised*, ed. A. G. Matthews (Oxford, 1948).

[2] See W. K. Jordan, *The Development of Religious Toleration in England*, iii (1938) 194 ff.

[3] See *Harleian Miscellany*, vi (1810) 420 f.

[4] The relevant passages of the proclamation are printed in Gee and Hardy, *Documents* etc., no. 112.

the corporate worship and observances of their religion. Yet, in spite of the threat of penalties, the Prayer Book was not effectively suppressed. Evelyn records that, on 3 August 1656, he went "to Lond⟨on⟩, to receive the B⟨lessed⟩ Sacrament, & was the first time that ever the Church of England was reduced to a Chamber & Conventicle, so sharp was the Persecution . . . In a private House in Fleetestreete Dr Wild preachd . . . we had a greate meeting of zealous Christians who were generaly much more devout & religious, than in our greatest prosperity". On Christmas Day, Evelyn was again at Dr Wild's lodgings to receive "the blessed Sacrament".[1] A year later, the Council advised the Lord Protector "to send for Mr Guning and Dr Taylor,[2] and require an account of the frequent meetings of multitudes of people held with them, and cause the ordinance for taking away the Book of Common Prayer to be enforced".[3] At Luton, in May 1658, Thomas Jessop, a minister, reported that he was "struggling against a malignant and prelatical party, because I was not episcopally ordained, and they now withdraw the people from my communion and worship in prelatical form".[4] Almost on the eve of the restoration of the monarchy, Parliament was still considering how "to peruse the several Ordinances, and Acts for abolishing of the Book of Common Prayer . . . and to provide against the useing of other superstitious Ceremonies, and practizes in divine worship".[5] It was harder to abolish the Prayer Book than it had been to impose it.

When King Charles II returned to England in May 1660, he came not to begin a reign but in the twelfth year of a

[1] *Diary*, ed. E. S. de Beer, iii.181, 185.

[2] Peter Gunning, formerly Fellow of Clare College, Cambridge, officiated at the chapel of Exeter House in the Strand during the Interregnum. Jeremy Taylor, formerly chaplain to Charles I, and author of *Holy Living* and *Holy Dying*, also officiated there.

[3] *CSPD 1657–8*, 159.

[4] *CSPD 1658*–9, 37. For Thomas Jessop, see *CR*.

[5] *Mercurius Politicus*, no. 556 (24 Feb. to 3 March 1659), 261.

reign begun on 30 January 1649. So the Convention Parliament, which had invited the King to return, had unequivocally declared. Moreover, the King's return was unconditional. It was to be expected, therefore, that the Elizabethan Church Settlement would be restored with the monarchy. Some move in this direction was, indeed, made. Parliament, by its Act "for Confirming and Restoring Ministers" to their livings, made cautious arrangements for the removal of intruders. Deans and canons returned to their cathedral and collegiate churches, and resumed their corporate existence. But no official action was taken in regard to the position of the bishops, or about a general restoration of the Prayer Book. The Prayer Book had duly been restored in the Chapel Royal, and in most, if not all, the cathedrals. In some places, also, strict legalists had restored the Book as being the only form of worship lawfully authorized. According to John Evelyn, however, it was not until July that "from hence forth was the Liturgie publiquely used in our Churches, whence it had ben for so many Yeares banish'd".[1] Even so, the use of the Book depended upon the *motu proprio* of the minister. Nothing had yet been done to put in force the Elizabethan Act of Uniformity. For hesitancy in restoring the general use of the Prayer Book the King himself was in part responsible.

By the Declaration of Breda, of 4/14 April 1660, Charles had promised "a liberty to tender consciences, and that no man shall be disquieted or called in question for differences of opinion in matter of religion, which do not disturb the peace of the Kingdom".[2] *Prima facie*, Charles's vague "indulgence" could extend to forms of worship, if not to ecclesiastical government. But the exact scope of the indulgence, and the method of implementing it, Charles

[1] *Diary*, 8 July 1660, ed. E. S. de Beer, iii.251 f. On the same day another famous diarist went to the Chapel Royal, Whitehall, where "I heard very good music, the first time ever I remember to have heard organs and singing men in surplices in my life" (*The Diary of Samuel Pepys*, ed. Henry B. Wheatley [1902], i.195).

[2] For the text see Gee and Hardy, *Documents* etc., no. 114.

diplomatically referred to the Convention Parliament. That Parliament, with equal diplomacy, abstained from acting in the matter. The next important step was taken in June. The King received from the Presbyterian ministers an Address containing certain proposals. The Address had been drawn up at Charles's own instance, and was, in fact, a memorandum dealing with the twin problems of government and worship, and indicating the terms on which the Presbyterians could come to an agreement with the Anglicans.[1] The King had expressed the purpose of bringing the two parties to an "accommodation".

In their preamble, the Presbyterians spoke of themselves as "taking it for granted that there is a firm agreement between our brethren and us in the doctrinal truths of the reformed religion, and in the substantial parts of divine worship, and that the differences are only in some various conceptions about the ancient form of church-government, and some particulars about liturgy and ceremonies". In regard to government, the Presbyterians, while dissenting "from that ecclesiastical hierarchy or prelacy disclaimed in the covenant",[2] declared that they had not renounced "the true ancient primitive episcopacy or presidency as it was ballanced and managed by a due commixtion of presbyters therewith", and that they would submit to such episcopacy, if it were constituted. As "a ground-work towards accommodation" they offered to the King for consideration Archbishop Ussher's *Reduction of Episcopacy unto the form of Synodical Government received in the Ancient Church.*[3] In regard to

[1] For the text of the Address see E. Cardwell, *A History of Conferences* (1841), 277–86.

[2] I.e. the Solemn League and Covenant of 1643 which defined prelacy as "Church government by archbishops, bishops, their chancellors and commissaries, deans, deans and chapters, archdeacons, and all other ecclesiastical officers depending on that hierarchy": see Gee and Hardy, *Documents* etc., 571.

[3] Edited after Ussher's death by his chaplain, N. Bernard, and published in 1656. It has been doubted whether the *Reduction* represented the deliberate mind of Ussher: see A. J. Mason, *The Church of England and Episcopacy* (1914), 120 f.

worship the Presbyterians had a definite proposal to present. They affirmed that they accepted "the lawfulness of a liturgy, or form of publick worship", on the condition, however, that it conformed with certain requisites: it must be "agreeable unto the word of God"; it must not be "too tedious in the whole, nor composed of too short prayers, unmeet repetitions or responsals";[1] it ought "not to be dissonant from the liturgies of other reformed churches; nor too rigorously imposed": and finally it must allow for the minister "to make use of those gifts for prayer and exhortation which Christ hath given him for the service and edification of the Church". At this point, the Prayer Book received an unfavourable notice. The Presbyterians observed that the Book "hath in it many things that are justly offensive and need amendment", and further that as it had long been discontinued and was a cause of dissatisfaction to many pious and loyal persons, both ministers and people, its reimposition would inevitably create "sad divisions and widening of the breaches which it was the King's endeavour to heal". Accordingly, the Presbyterians submitted the proposal that "some learned, godly and moderate divines of both persuasions", chosen without bias to one side or the other, should be commissioned either to compile a liturgy in conformity with the requisites stated and "as much as may be in Scripture words", or, at the least, to "revise and effectually reform" the Prayer Book, adding or inserting "some other varying forms in Scripture phrase, to be used at the minister's choice". The Presbyterians then turned to deal with the old and vexed question of the "divers ceremonies formerly retained in the Church of England". They repeated the customary Puritan objections against the ceremonies, as being contrary to the will of the "jealous God" of Scripture, and rejected by many of the Reformed Churches abroad; and they proposed that the

[1] I.e. the responses in the Litany and the people's *Answers* in other services. Puritan objection to these was of long standing, and had been expressed in *A Second Admonition to the Parliament* issued in 1572.

use of the surplice, the sign of the cross at baptism, and bowing at the name of Jesus should be abolished. They requested, also, that kneeling at communion and the observance of "such holydays as are but of humane institution"[1] should not be imposed upon those who disapproved of them on grounds of conscience. In conclusion, the Presbyterians referred to certain other ceremonies which they conceived to have no foundation in the law of the land, "as erecting altars, bowing towards them,[2] and such like"; they proposed that the King should take measures "to prevent the imposing and using of such innovations for the future".

It will be perceived that the Presbyterians' Address exhibits the traditional Puritan ideas which had found expression in the *Directory* and in the liturgical clause of the *Millenary Petition*. It must have been obvious to the King and to his advisers, as to the authors themselves, that the Address proffered small, if any, real concession to the Anglicans. The matter of church government apart, it was clear that if the Presbyterian proposals were accepted, and either a new liturgy drawn up or the Prayer Book reformed, the result would be little to the taste of Anglicans who stood by their inherited forms of worship. A new liturgy, although containing set prayers, would be remarkably like the *Directory*; and a Prayer Book shorn of the ceremonies and other features repugnant to the Presbyterians would be remarkably unlike the historic Book of Common Prayer. Nevertheless, having played a dominant part in his restoration, the Presbyterians counted upon the sympathetic support of the King. Possibly, also, they expected the Anglicans to be too apprehensive of Independent republicanism and insurgency to be other than amenable to Presbyterian proposals, once the principle of a

[1] These had been settled by the Act of Parliament, "for the Keeping Holy-Days and Fasting-Days", of 1551. The Puritans objected to the observance of all holy days but Sunday.

[2] An allusion to no. 7, "A declaration concerning some rites and ceremonies", of the Canons of 1640, which were confirmed by the King, but were condemned by the Long Parliament.

liturgy had been granted. By mid-June, however, the Anglican reaction had begun to set in. On 26 June, James Sharp, representative of the Scottish Kirk at the Court in London, wrote to the ministers in Edinburgh: "Petitions come up from counties for episcopacy and Liturgy. The Lord's anger is not turned away. The generality of the people are doting after prelacy and the Service-book."[1] By the autumn, the vacant bishoprics had been filled, and new bishops consecrated or about to be so; and the magistrates were enforcing use of the Prayer Book by resort to the Elizabethan Act of Uniformity. When the King gave his answer to the Presbyterians' Address, the old Church Settlement was coming alive again.

Charles's answer, dated 25 October 1660, was cast in the form of a *Declaration to all his loving subjects of his kingdom of England and dominion of Wales, concerning ecclesiastical affairs*.[2] He spoke of episcopal authority as "the best support of religion"; but displayed no interest in synodical episcopacy. He consented to appoint "an equal number of learned divines of both persuasions" to review the Prayer Book in accordance with the terms of the Presbyterian proposals, inclusive of making "some additional forms (in the scripture phrase as near as may be)"; and was agreeable that "it be left to the minister's choice to use one or other at his discretion". Until the revision had been accomplished, the King undertook that "none be troubled or punished" for not fully using the Book. Of "the Liturgy of the Church of England contained in the Book of Common Prayer, and by law established" the King stated that it was "the best we have

[1] See R. Wodrow, *The History of the Sufferings of the Church of Scotland* (1827), i.44. For Sharp's comments on the Address see ibid., 46: Sharp expressed disapproval of the acceptance of "moderate episcopacy and reformed Liturgy". Nevertheless, in 1661, he was ordained deacon and priest, and consecrated Archbishop of St Andrews, in one day at Westminster Abbey, and became an opponent of Presbyterianism (ibid., 239). He was murdered in 1679.

[2] For the text see E. Cardwell, op. cit., 286–98.

seen, and we believe that we have seen all that are extant and used in this part of the world". Moreover, he noted, it was rightly reverenced by the most learned men in the Reformed Churches. About compiling a new liturgy, on the other hand, nothing at all was said. Concerning the ceremonies, Charles referred to them as "introduced by the wisdom and authority of the Church", and proceeded: "We shall say no more, but that we have the more esteem of all, and reverence for many of them, by having been present in many of those Churches, where they are most abolished, or discountenanced". This reminiscence of attending the services of the Reformed Churches of France and Holland was followed by the affirmation that every national Church, "with the approbation and consent of the sovereign power", may introduce such ceremonies as tend to edification,[1] "though the necessary practice thereof cannot be deduced from Scripture". The King therefore refused to abolish the ceremonies: but to those who were aggrieved by them he granted, out of his compassion, an indulgence for omitting them. Yet there was an exception in regard to the surplice; it was to be retained in the Chapel Royal, in cathedral and collegiate churches, and in the college chapels at the two universities. In all matters of that kind it was his intention, so the King declared, after some lapse of time and after the conference of the divines, to take the advice of a national synod, and thereafter to "use our best endeavour, that such laws may be established, as may best provide for the peace of the Church and State". For all its concessive tone, the Declaration could not have been other than ominous to the Presbyterians and other dissenters from the Anglican Church. The passages dealing with the Prayer Book and the ceremonies could be taken to intimate that the King and his revisers were contemplating a conservative revision of the Book. Again, the reference to a national synod, that is, to the Convocations (which had not yet been

[1] Cf. Article 34, "Of the Traditions of the Church".

recalled into existence), and to legislation, that is, to Parliament, strongly suggested that the royal indulgence might not be permanent. The Convention Parliament was dissolved on 29 December; much, if not everything, would depend upon the Parliament succeeding it.

On 25 March 1661, the King issued his commission to twelve bishops and twelve Presbyterian divines, requiring them to meet within the ensuing four months in the Master's lodgings in the Savoy "to advise upon and review" the Book of Common Prayer, "comparing the same with the most ancient Liturgies which have been used in the Church, in the primitive and purest times". The nominal leader of the bishops was the aged Accepted Frewen, Archbishop of York. The actual leader was Gilbert Sheldon, Bishop of London, who during the Interregnum had favoured the use of an amendment of the Prayer Book which could be considered as falling within the limit of the law. Another "amendment" commissioner was Robert Sanderson, Bishop of Lincoln, a former Regius Professor of Divinity at Oxford.[1] John Gauden, Bishop of Exeter, was a convert from Puritan religious and political principles, and had become an apologist of episcopacy and the Prayer Book. The liturgist among the bishops was, of course, John Cosin, Bishop of Durham. Both he and George Morley, Bishop of Worcester, had been Anglican chaplains on the Continent during the Interregnum. The leader of the Presbyterians was Edward Reynolds, a former member of the Westminster Assembly. As Dean of Christ Church, Oxford, he was the first Puritan Vice-Chancellor of the University, but was ejected from office on account of his dislike of the Engagement of 1649.[2] In

[1] Sanderson's form of amendment is printed in W. Jacobson, *Fragmentary Illustrations of the History of the Book of Common Prayer* (1874), 3–40.

[2] An undertaking to "adhere to this present Parliament . . . in the maintenance and defence of their resolutions concerning the settling of the government of this nation for the future in way of a Republic, without King or House of Lords".

1660, on the King's return, Reynolds became a conformist, and was one of those Presbyterians ready for reconciliation with the Anglicans. Shortly before the setting up of the Savoy commission, he was appointed to the bishopric of Norwich, still professing his attachment to the principles of synodical episcopacy. To Reynolds and Edmund Calamy was entrusted the nomination of the Presbyterian members of the commission. Of the company which they assembled, Calamy himself was neither the least distinguished nor the least able. In his younger days, at Cambridge, he had been known as a strict Calvinist and as an assailant of Arminianism. He had also been a constant adversary of episcopacy, both synodical and prelatical. Whereas Reynolds was by nature a moderate man, Calamy, of Huguenot origin, was by mental inheritance perhaps too French willingly to accept compromise. Nevertheless, as a monarchist, he shared the Presbyterians' fear of the Independents and other "sectaries" and was prepared, in 1661, to come to a settlement with the Anglicans. He felt unable, however, to follow Reynolds in accepting the offer of a bishopric. Also prominent among the Presbyterian commissioners were John Wallis, Savilian Professor of Geometry at Oxford, and Matthew Newcomen, who, like Calamy, was a London minister. The most conspicuous member of the Presbyterian side, indeed, of the commission as a whole, was Richard Baxter.

Baxter, for his importance both inside and outside the commission, demands a closer notice. He was the son of a Shropshire freeholder who, by teaching the boy to read the Bible at an early age, developed in him a natural bent towards religion. For education the young Richard was sent first to Wroxeter Free School, and next to read under Richard Wickstead, chaplain at Ludlow Castle. Then, instead of going to one of the universities, he was placed, through Wickstead's interest, under Sir Henry Herbert, Master of the Revels, who, Baxter records in his *Life*, "would quickly set me in a rising way". But the serious Baxter soon had enough of the Court. "When I saw a Stage-Play instead of a Sermon on the Lord's-days in the Afternoon, and saw what Course was there in fashion, and heard little Preaching, but what was as to one part against the Puritans, I was glad to be gone".[1] After about a month, his mother fell ill, and he returned home at Christmas 1634, having renounced his "Expectations" from Whitehall. Baxter was then eighteen years old. At home, he proceeded to educate himself in practical divinity and in the points at issue between conformists and nonconformists. He had already begun to study the schoolmen, whose logic and metaphysic he found to be specially suited to his mental "Disposition". Aquinas, Duns Scotus, Durandus of St Pourçain, and William of Ockham gave him great intellectual satisfaction;[2] their logical method, their distinctions and analyses, formed his studies in theology, and left a permanent imprint on his mind. Extraordinary escape from being trampled to death by horses on two occasions gave him a sense of divine protection and choice; the sense seems to have been deepened by recovery from an illness which lasted for nearly two years, and from which he recovered in his twenty-third year. The thought of ordination had come to Baxter in boyhood; in 1638 he was ordained to the mastership of Dudley School, but after only nine months went to Bridgnorth as assistant to the rector. He found the people ignorant and dead-hearted; though he preached fervently, he says, the conversions which followed were too few. But his reputation as a preacher had gone abroad. He was invited to be "Lecturer", or stipendiary preacher, at Kidderminster. There in 1641–2 and from 1647 to 1660 Baxter exercised a ministry remarkable as much for pastoral work as for preaching. By this time, he had reached a moderate Presbyterian position; if now anti-prelatist, he was yet prepared to accept a synodical episcopacy; if he found fault with the Prayer Book, he nevertheless allowed the lawfulness and propriety of a liturgy. As to the ceremonies, he

[1] *RB* I.i.§10. [2] *RB* I.i.§5.

was content to ask the liberty not to use them. During the Civil War, Baxter was from 1645 to 1647 a chaplain to the Parliamentary Army, an experience which proved disagreeable, because "when I came to the Army among Cromwell's Soldiers, I found a new face of things which I never dreamt of: I heard the plotting Heads very hot upon that which intimated their Intention to subvert both Church and State".[1] Baxter's experiences with the Army, and what he observed under the Protectorate, persuaded him that political stability and an ordered church settlement were the first necessities of the nation; and he was ready actively to support any compromise, which he could deem permissible, in order to attain them. A consistent royalist in holding Charles II to be the rightful sovereign, Baxter took a part in promoting Charles's return. In recognition of his services, he was made a royal chaplain, and a bishopric was offered to him.[2] The latter he declined, because his judgement was "fully resolved" against prelacy.[3] It might seem that a leader of such strong character, single-mindedness, learning, and varied experience of men would have been an immeasurable strength to the Presbyterian cause in the events of 1661, and not least at the Savoy Conference. But as he himself reveals in his *Life*, Baxter suffered from defects which made him as awkward an ally as he was a difficult opponent. Unable patiently to tolerate dissent from his opinion, he was apt to discern a lack of wisdom, or an evil will, in those who opposed him. He was impatient, also, with whatever he regarded as illogical and "disordered". His impatience led him into tactless behaviour. Not having learned, at a university, the art of "disputation", and being always

[1] *RB* I.i.§73.

[2] The bishopric was Hereford; the offer was made privately for fear that it might be publicly refused (*RB* I.ii.§118).

[3] I.ii.§121. Baxter suggested to Hyde that he might be able to accept a bishopric, if the *Declaration* of 25 October 1660 became law, but he held himself free to refuse. *RB* leaves no doubt that Baxter had no intention of becoming a bishop on the "Diocesan Frame".

zealous for the triumph of the truth, as he saw it, he would take upon himself, at conferences, the office of chief speaker, often with "vehemence", so that he irritated colleague and opponent together. The failing was intimated to him. He was aware that he was "unacceptable" and "distasted"; he accepted the fact, apparently without even suspecting the cause. While, therefore, he sincerely desired accommodation with the bishops, he was not the most likely figure to bring it about, or to promote it. Though he might intend *suaviter in re*, he was certain to show himself *fortiter in modo*. When Reynolds and Calamy first invited him to become a member of the Savoy commission, Baxter professed unwillingness to accept, because he had found that his part in recent discussions had made him "unacceptable with my Superiours", and other men, less disliked, "might be fitter".[1] This plainly half-hearted refusal was overruled. Whatever disadvantage Reynolds and Calamy may have apprehended from Baxter's presence, they could have apprehended only greater from his absence. We may be glad that Baxter complied, if only because he wrote an account of the proceedings of the conference.[2] It is inevitably a biased account; but the bias is so patent that often we may reasonably conjecture the truth.

In addition to the twenty-four principals, eighteen assistants were appointed, nine to each side. It was their function to supply the place of absent principals, and so to maintain the activities of the commission. According to Baxter, the most distinguished of the Presbyterian assistants, John Lightfoot, author of *Horae Hebraicae et Talmudicae*, attended only once or twice. One or two came not at all. Thomas Jacombe and William Bates, on the other hand, appear to have taken a full share of the work. They were London ministers, and had to bear neither the inconveniences of travel nor its expense. Several Anglican assistants, among them Peter Heylyn, Laud's apologist, also failed to attend. The most assiduous, as well as talkative, of the Anglican

[1] *RB* I.ii.§170.

[2] *RB* I.ii.§§170–240 (pp. 303–69).

assistants were John Pearson, author of *The Exposition of the Creed*, and Peter Gunning, at that time Lady Margaret Professor of Divinity at Cambridge, and Master of Corpus Christi College.

The first meeting of the Savoy Conference was held on 15 April, Monday in Easter week. The proceedings opened with the reading of the King's commission. To the general instruction, directing the commissioners to advise upon and revise the Prayer Book, comparing it with the most ancient liturgies, were added two particular terms of reference:

(i) to consider the several directions, rules, and forms of prayer, and things contained in the Prayer Book, and to advise upon and consult about them, and about the objections and exceptions raised against them; and

(ii) if occasion be, to make such reasonable alterations, corrections, and amendments in the Book, as the commission shall agree to be necessary and expedient for satisfying tender consciences and restoring religious peace, "but avoiding, as much as may be, all unnecessary alterations of the forms and Liturgy wherewith the people are already acquainted, and have so long received in the Church of England".

In conclusion, the commissioners were directed to present a written and signed report to the King, when they had reached agreement concerning what was necessary and expedient "for the altering, diminishing or enlarging the said Book of Common Prayer or any part thereof".

The Savoy terms of reference call for a passing comment. They are considerably more restricted than the terms promised in the *Declaration* of 25 October. They do not include, for instance, the drawing up of additional and alternative forms of service. In fact, they appear to contemplate little more than a revision of the Jacobean Prayer Book; and the limiting clause in (ii), "but avoiding . . . all unnecessary alterations" etc., points to a strictly conservative revision. Yet the mention of "enlarging" in the concluding direction is patient of interpretation in harmony with the *Declaration*, although, of course, it can equally be taken to mean no more than the provision of supplements, where supplements seemed to be desirable.[1] We may suppose the ambiguity to have been deliberate. It could have been no easy matter, in drafting the terms of reference, to devise phrases which would not displease one side or the other. The Presbyterians were sincere in their wish for a revised Prayer Book; but the kind of revision which they contemplated was radical. The bishops, on the other hand, had no wish for revision (and here they were undoubtedly representative of Anglican feeling generally). When they had been asked for their opinion of the Presbyterian proposals for revision, they gave a lengthy answer which may be summarized in Jeremy Collier's sentence: "they pronounce the offices in the Common Prayer altogether unexceptionable".[2] They expressed themselves not unwilling, however, to change anything, if it were proved to be "justly offensive to sober persons".

These contrasted attitudes of mind to the purpose of the conference made themselves manifest at the first meeting, as soon as the question of procedure was broached. When the royal commission had been read, Archbishop Frewen made a short speech committing the conduct of the business to Sheldon, Bishop of London, who, said the archbishop, knew more of the King's mind in the matter. Sheldon then addressed the Presbyterians, and said that as it was they who had proposed the conference and desired alterations in the Liturgy, there was nothing to be said or done until the Presbyterians had submitted to the bishops, in writing, all their objections to the Prayer Book and all the additional forms and alterations which they desired.[3] It will be noticed

[1] E.g. the provision of a rite for the baptism of adults.

[2] *Ecclesiastical History*, ed. T. Lathbury (1852), viii.390. For the text of the bishop's answer see *RB* I.ii.§101 (pp. 242–7).

[3] *RB* I.ii.§171.

that, in referring to "all the additional Forms" desired by the Presbyterians, Sheldon was allowing the widest interpretation of the terms of reference. With one exception, the Presbyterians demurred to Sheldon's proposition; they would have preferred discussion, since "by Conference we might perceive as we went what each would yield to, and might more speedily dispatch, and probably attain our End; whereas Writing would be a tedious, endless Business".[1] The exception was Baxter. Although imputing unfriendly motives to Sheldon, Baxter pressed upon his colleagues arguments in favour of Sheldon's plan, among them the consideration "that we were engaged to offer them new Forms (which was the Expedient which from the Beginning I had aimed at and brought in, as the only way of Accommodation, considering that they should be in Scripture Words, and that Ministers should choose which Forms they would)".[2] Baxter omits to record how his colleagues received his arguments. He merely states that "upon these Reasons I told the Bishops that we accepted of the Task which they imposed upon us".[3] It was agreed, however, that objections to the Prayer Book might be submitted at one time, and additions at another. The two parties then withdrew.

What next occurred on the Presbyterian side must be recounted in Baxter's own words. "When we were withdrawn, it pleased our Brethren presently to divide the undertaken Work: The drawing up of *Exceptions against the Common-Prayer*, they undertook themselves, and were to meet from day to day for that end: The drawing up of the *Additions or new Forms* they imposed upon *me alone*, because I had been guilty of that Design from the beginning, and of engaging them in that piece of Service (and some of them thought it would prove odious to the Independents, and others who are against a Liturgy as such)".[4] We have here an interesting revelation. It had been plainly no part of the original

[1] *RB* I.ii.§171. [2] Ibid. [3] Ibid.
[4] *RB* I.ii.§172.

Presbyterian intention to put forward any "new forms", and certainly not the alternative Reformed Liturgy upon which Baxter's mind was set. Procedure by discussion, which the other Presbyterian commissioners would have preferred and which was suggested by the commission's terms of reference, would, at the least, have jeopardized Baxter's project, and possibly would have prevented its execution. How he contrived to "engage", or commit his colleagues to his project, or how far they conceived themselves to be committed to it before the first meeting, Baxter neglects to inform us. However, Sheldon's unexpected proposition, upon which he "resolutely insisted", provided the opening which Baxter required. The demand for a catalogue of *Exceptions* could be conceded in return for the admission of his own "Work" as he termed his projected liturgy. His colleagues had no course but to acquiesce; but an uneasiness on their part can be discerned in Baxter's narrative. We are led to wonder whether Sheldon had acquired some knowledge of the Presbyterian deliberations, and whether Sheldon's proposition was totally unexpected by Baxter. Be that as it may, Sheldon's ruling on procedure suited both Baxter's immediate project and also, as he believed, his design for the future. On the assumption that the King's *Declaration* of 25 October 1660 would continue in force, Baxter planned to employ the conference as a means of ensuring a liturgy which "Brethren that scrupled the use of the Common Prayer" would receive without objection.[1]

The division of labours settled, Baxter retired to draw up his liturgy. It was entirely his own composition: "I could not have time", he says, "to make use of any Book, save the Bible and my Concordance".[2] The work occupied him for a fortnight. At the end of that period he rejoined his colleagues, to find them still employed on their catalogue of exceptions. Since absorption in their task precluded them from giving immediate attention to his liturgy, Baxter was drawn in to

[1] *RB* I.ii.§173. [2] *RB* I.ii.§172.

assist with the catalogue. His principal function was to bar such objections against the Prayer Book as would not bear weight. At the same time, he took upon himself to compile a list of the faults "which were they which I most disliked in the Forms".[1] He insisted to his colleagues that he had never agreed with those who charged the Prayer Book "with false Doctrine, or Idolatry, or false Worship in the Matter or Substance";[2] he regarded the Book as defective and disordered indeed, yet permissible when no better was to be had. When he submitted his list to them, "the Brethren reduced it to a few brief Exceptions in general, and would not by so particular an Enumeration of Faults provoke those that we had to do with (which I misliked not)".[3] The tone of Baxter's document was certainly hypercritical, and sometimes carping; whereas the "Brethren", as Baxter testifies, were solicitous not to offend. Their own document, though necessarily critical of the Prayer Book, was reasoned, dignified, and courteous in expression.

The Exceptions against the Book of Common Prayer and *The Answer of the Bishops to the Exceptions of the Ministers* are both well known.[4] It will therefore be enough to recall their broad outline and character. The *Exceptions* falls into two parts, a general and a particular. The first or general part is a tabulation of the historic Puritan objections to the Prayer Book and the ceremonies, with some new matters added, among which are several of Baxter's points. The old complaint that the Prayer Book is a "compliance" with the Papists is tactfully handled, and skilfully used to support the case for revision of a Presbyterian type. "Our first reformers" varied as little as they well could from the Romish forms in order to draw the Papists into communion with the Church of England; accordingly, in the changed state of things now

[1] *RB* I.ii.§174. [2] Ibid. [3] Ibid.

[4] The text of the two documents is printed in E. Cardwell, op. cit., 303–63. The text of the *Exceptions* (but not of the *Answer*) is printed in *RB* I.i.§174 (pp. 316–33).

prevailing, it is asked that the Prayer Book should be so "composed" as to render it acceptable to "all those who in the substantials of the protestant religion are of the same persuasion as ourselves". The requisites for such a "composure", or rearrangement, of the Prayer Book services is indicated in the ensuing paragraphs. Because, according to Scripture, the minister is "the mouth of the people to God in prayer" and the people's proper part is to attend reverently and in silence, all responses should be omitted and the people's vocal participation in the liturgy limited to saying *Amen.* For the same reason the Litany should be "composed into one solemn prayer to be offered by the minister". Because the phraseology of the services implies wrongly that all persons in the communion of the Church are "regenerated, converted and in an actual state of grace", such phraseology should be "reformed". The Collects being generally short and being "neither agreeable to scriptural examples, nor suited to the gravity and seriousness" of corporate prayer, the petitions of some of them should be composed into "one methodical and intire form of prayer". Further, the observance of saints' days and their vigils, being "without any foundation (as we conceive) in Scripture", should be omitted. Also, because the Apocryphal books are not Scripture, no lessons should be read from them. Furthermore, it was asked that all epistles and gospels should be taken from the version of 1611. Turning, then, to that old subject of discord, the ceremonies, the Presbyterian commissioners recapitulate the traditional complaints and objections; and request either that the ceremonies be totally abolished, or that the bishops will join in petitioning the King to confirm and continue "to us and our posterities" the indulgence granted in the *Declaration* of 25 October, and also to extend the same indulgence "to such as do not yet enjoy the benefit thereof".[1] The general part of the *Exceptions* concludes with the observation, respectfully expressed, that it has not been

[1] I.e. the Independents and other groups.

possible, after inquiry, to find any complete and authentic primitive liturgies with which to compare the Prayer Book. The second part of the document is a catena of critical comments upon and suggested amendments of particular features of the Book. Some of the suggestions are trivial, such as that to alter the description attached to "sin", in the Litany, from "deadly" to "heinous" or "grievous"; or the suggestion to remove the initial word from the phrase, "all that travel by land or by water" (also occurring in the Litany), on the ground that "all" seems "liable to just exceptions". Of importance, on the other hand, is the request that the Black Rubric, or Declaration on Kneeling of 1552, should be restored at the end of the Communion Service "for the vindicating of our Church in the matter of kneeling at the sacrament (although the gesture be left indifferent)".[1] Still more important is the comment on a central feature of the Communion Service:

Prayer at the Consecration

Hear us O merciful Father, etc., who in the same night that he was betrayed, took bread, and when he had given thanks, he brake it, and gave to his Disciples, saying, Take, eat, etc.

We conceive that the manner of the consecrating of the Elements is not here explicite and distinct enough, and the Ministers *breaking of the Bread* is not so much as mentioned.

It often passes unrecognized that objection is made in this comment to something more than the lack of a direction to break the bread. The petition preceding the Institution-narrative is criticized for being indeterminate. Its phrases do not refer expressly to consecration; and by contemporary English Presbyterian usage the minister celebrating a Sacramental Ordinance prayed that God would sanctify the element used, whether the bread and wine at the Lord's Supper or the water at Baptism.[2] The *Exceptions* has the

[1] See below, p. 139 f.

[2] The *Directory* orders the minister to pray God "so to sanctify these Elements both of Bread and Wine, and to bless His own Ordinance, that we may receive by faith the Body and Blood of Jesus Christ, crucified for us" (T. Leishman, *Westminster Directory*, 51). The Prayer Book petition reflects a sacramental doctrine less "high" than the

latter in view when it comments on a prayer in the Order of Public Baptism in these terms:

In the first Prayer	
By the Baptism of thy welbeloved Son, etc., didst sanctifie the Flood Jordan, and all other waters to the Mystical washing away of Sin, etc.	It being doubtful whether either the Flood Jordan, or any other waters were sanctified to a Sacramental use, by Christ's being baptized, and not necessary to be asserted, we desire this may be otherwise expressed.

The particular exceptions are to be understood, of course, in the light of what precedes them; yet on balance they are rather more moderate than the general exceptions would prepare us to expect. *Exceptions* concludes with a notification that its authors will shortly offer some "new Forms" in which they have made "a considerable progress". The reference is to Baxter's liturgy.

The bishops' *Answer* to the *Exceptions* naturally follows the twofold division of the latter. In each of its parts the *Answer* meets the Presbyterian objections point by point, and vigorously upholds the usages of the Prayer Book. On the ceremonies the bishops assert the Church's power to impose the use of them, and, as doubtless was foreseen, oppose the abolition of them; "Were the ceremonies to be laid aside", the bishops observe, "there would be the same divisions". Nevertheless, the bishops were not altogether unyielding. They made seventeen concessions to the Presbyterians, none of which, however, touched matters of principle. Two of the concessions deserve notice: "We are willing that all the epistles and gospels be used according to the last translation"; and "That the manner of consecrating the elements

---

Presbyterian. The Prayer Book of 1552, unlike the Book of 1549, contained no petition for the consecration of any material object.

The *Directory* petition recalls the clause in the Communion Service of 1549, ". . . vouchsafe to bless and sanctify these thy gifts and creatures of bread and wine, that they may be unto us the body and blood" etc.

In its directions for the administration of Baptism the *Directory* orders that "Prayer is also to be joined with the Word of Institution for sanctifying the water to this spiritual use" (Leishman, op. cit., 44). "The Word of Institution" refers to Matthew 28.19.

be made more explicit and express, and to that purpose those words be put into the rubr[ic], *Then shall he put his hand upon the bread and break it, then shall he put his hand unto the cup*".[1] The petition "Hear us, O merciful Father" etc. was left unchanged.[2]

It took the bishops time, first to digest the *Exceptions*, and then to formulate their *Answer* to them. Meanwhile the Presbyterian commissioners were occupied with Baxter's Liturgy. "I made it an *intire Liturgy*", Baxter informs us, "but might not *call it so*, because our Commission required us to call it *Additions to, or Alterations of the Book of Common Prayer*."[3] To make the Liturgy complete, Baxter put in "the *Directive Part* called Rubricks", and also added "*Forms of Order and Discipline* partly . . . to shew the difference between their kind of Discipline in Chancellors Courts, and ours by Pastors in Christian Congregations".[4] Baxter's colleagues studied his liturgy often and carefully. They had certain misgivings about it. "At first", Baxter says, "they would have had no Rubrick or Directory, but bare Prayers, because they thought our Commission allowed it not".[5] Eventually they gave way before Baxter's arguments, and resolved to include the rubrics. The final revision of the "reformed Liturgy" is best described by Baxter himself: "they past it at last in the same Words that I had written it, save only that they put out a few Lines in the Administration of the Lord's Supper, where the Word *Offering* was used; and they put out a Page of Reasons for Infant Baptism, which I had annexed to that Office, thinking it unnecessary; and they put the larger Litany into

[1] The usages here sanctioned had, in fact, been practised among Anglicans widely, if not universally, since Jewel's time.

[2] The bishops did not count the petition as part of the consecration of the elements. It had become Anglican tradition to reckon consecration as effected by the "joining" of the Words of Institution to the elements (see E. C. Ratcliff, "The English Usage of Eucharistic Consecration, 1548–1662", Part 2, in *Theology*, vol. ix. no. 445 [July 1957] 273–80).

[3] *RB* I.ii.§173. [4] Ibid. [5] *RB* I.ii.§175.

an Appendix as thinking it too long: and Dr *Wallis* was desired to draw up the Prayer for the King, which is his Work (being after somewhat altered by us). And we agreed to put before it a short Address to the Bishops, professing our readiness in Debates to yield to the shortning of any thing which should be too long, and the altering of any thing that should be found amiss."[1] The short prefatory Address includes two further matters, both important, though neither is mentioned by Baxter. First, in explaining their submission to the bishops of a complete liturgy, the Presbyterian commissioners appealed to that clause in the terms of reference, in which mention is made of "enlarging" the Prayer Book. Second, they indicated what was to be done with their "alterations and additions": the "several particulars thereof" were to be inserted into the Prayer Book at the appropriate places, and it was to be left to the minister's choice to use one or other. As authority for this arrangement, the Presbyterian commissioners appealed, behind their terms of reference, to the *Declaration* of 25 October 1660.

The *Reformed* or *Savoy Liturgy*[2] is so little known, and nowadays is so little accessible, that a brief description of it and of its principal features may not be amiss. The contents of the Liturgy are as follows:

(i) The Ordinary Public Worship on the Lord's Day.
(ii) The Order of celebrating the Sacrament of the Body and Blood of Christ.
(iii) The Celebration of the Sacrament of Baptism.
(iv) Of Catechizing, and the Approbation of those that are to be admitted to the Lord's Supper.
(v) Of the Celebration of Matrimony.
(vi) The Visitation of the Sick, and their Communion.
(vii) The Order for solemnizing the Burial of the Dead.

[1] *RB* I.ii.§182.

[2] A reprint, under the title *The Savoy Liturgy*, was published in 1847 as no. iv of the series *Reliquiae Liturgicae* edited by Peter Hall. The text without the prefatory Address to the Bishops will be found also in *The Practical Works of the Rev. Richard Baxter*, ed. W. Orme (1830), xv. 450–527.

(viii) Of Extraordinary Days of Humiliation, and Thanksgiving; and Anniversary Festivals.

(ix) Of Prayer and Thanksgiving for particular Members of the Church.

(x) Of Pastoral Discipline, Public Confession, Absolution, and Exclusion from the Holy Communion of the Church.

APPENDIX:

(xi) A Larger Litany, or General Prayer, "to be used at discretion".

(xii) The Church's Praise for our Redemption, "to be used at discretion".

Of this list, (i), (ii), (iii), (v), (ix), and (xi) could have been considered as alternative to provision made in the Prayer Book, (vi) and (vii) consist only of general directions, with suggested Scripture lessons for (vii). (iv) and (x) provide for the maintenance of traditional Puritan discipline; (viii) consists of directions for amending or replacing observance of the fasting and festival days enjoined by the Prayer Book; (xii) is a novel feature without parallel in the Prayer Book.

The characteristics of the Savoy Liturgy are fully exhibited in the service entitled, "The Ordinary Public Worship of the Lord's Day", which can be properly understood and estimated only if it be set out schematically:

(a) A preparatory prayer for God's assistance (a shorter alternative is provided for use "when Brevity is necessary").

(b) The Apostles' or Nicene Creed by the minister, "And sometimes Athanasius' Creed".

(c) The Ten Commandments.

(d) Sentences of Scripture moving the people to penitence and confession.

(e) Confession of sin and prayer for pardon and sanctification, ending with the Lord's Prayer (a shorter alternative is provided).

(f) Sentences of Scripture strengthening the faith of the penitent.

(g) Sentences of Scripture informing the people "what you must be, and do, for the time to come, if you would be saved".

(h) Psalm 95, or 100, or 84, followed by "the Psalms in order for the day".
(i) A chapter of the Old Testament.
(j) A Psalm, or Te Deum.
(k) A chapter of the New Testament.
(l) The Prayer for the King and Magistrates.
(m) Psalm 67, or 98, or some other Psalm; or Benedictus, or Magnificat.
(n) Prayer for the Church extemporized by the minister in the pulpit.
(o) Sermon "upon some text of Holy Scripture".
(p) Prayer "for a blessing on the word of instruction" and for any matters not mentioned in (n).[1]
(q) Dimissory Benediction.

Such, in outline, is Baxter's service for Sunday morning. It is composed of elements of Morning Prayer, Litany, and Ante-Communion, without the repetitions, redundancies, and other "unmeet" medieval liturgicalia of the Prayer Book; and it exhibits the logic and order which Baxter desired in worship as in other procedures. The service is not as rigid as the outline might suggest: at his discretion, for instance, the minister could omit (d) and (f); and if he should think it needful "to be longer" on one part of the service, a rubric allowed him to abbreviate others. Also, a hymn of "Thanksgiving for Christ" and another hymn are attached to the service for use after the sermon at the minister's discretion. The two hymns, and indeed the other forms of the Liturgy, are constructed of phrases of Scripture, the references being inserted in the margin in order to authenticate, to the scrupulous, the divine source of the material employed. Although this genre of liturgical composition would appeal to few, if any, nowadays, the deftness and dignified effect of Baxter's constructions must be admired.

When "the Sacrament of the Body and Blood of Christ" was to be administered, the celebration was to follow (p). In

[1] A set form of "General Prayer" is provided. When the Larger Litany was said, it occurred at this point.

substance, the service corresponds with that part of the Prayer Book Communion which begins with the Prayer of Humble Access. First, however, the minister, at his discretion, could recite, in his own words or in a form provided, an "explication of the nature, use, and benefits of this Sacrament", together with an exhortation to "see here Christ dying in this holy representation".[1] After the first prayer, the minister proceeds to the consecration. If the elements are not already on the table, he receives and places them there, and recites a short prayer which ends with this petition:

> Sanctify these thy creatures of bread and wine which, according to thy institution and command, we set apart to this holy use, that they may be sacramentally the body and blood of thy Son Jesus Christ. *Amen.*[2]

The Institution narrative of 1 Corinthians 11 is then recited (but it may be recited before the preceding prayer). There follows a prayer addressed to Christ, in which the minister asks:

> We beseech thee, by thine intercession with the Father, through the sacrifice of thy body and blood, give us the pardon of our sins, and thy quickening Spirit, without which the flesh will profit us nothing. Reconcile us to the Father: nourish us as thy members to everlasting life. *Amen.*

Then the minister breaks the Bread and pours the Wine from the flagon into the communion-cup, "in the sight of the people". The formula which may be said at the breaking of the Bread is noteworthy.

> The body of Christ was broken for us, and offered once for all to sanctify us: behold the Lamb of God, that taketh away the sins of the world.[3]

[1] *Savoy Liturgy*, ed. P. Hall, 61.

[2] Ibid., 68. Although Baxter provides a consecratory petition in the Lord's Supper, he follows the Prayer Book in omitting a consecration of the water from his baptismal service.

[3] Ibid., 70.

Discretionary latitude is allowed to the minister at the consecration. If he will, he may consecrate and administer the Bread first, and then proceed to the Wine; he may also use a combination of the several prayers into one form. Similarly the communicant may sit, stand, or kneel at the administration, as he pleases. The service concludes with a post-communion prayer; a short exhortation, "if there be time"; a hymn in metre, or a Psalm of praise; and a blessing.

It would be interesting to recover the "few lines . . . where the word *Offering* was used", and excised from the service by Baxter's colleagues. Possibly Baxter's doctrine of Offering was too "high". It will have been apparent from the passages quoted above that the doctrine of Baxter's service is markedly higher than the doctrine expressed or implied in the Communion Office of the Prayer Book of 1552 or 1559. The conception expressed in Baxter's service is thus summed up in the preliminary exhortation:

> The Lord's Supper, then, is an holy Sacrament, instituted by Christ: wherein bread and wine, being first by consecration made sacramentally, or representatively, the body and blood of Christ, are used by breaking and pouring out to represent and commemorate the sacrifice of Christ's body and blood upon the cross once offered up to God for sin; and are given in the name of Christ unto the Church, to signify and solemnize the renewal of his holy covenant with them, and the giving of himself unto them, to expiate their sins by his sacrifice.[1]

It is curious that Baxter finds no place in his service for an equivalent of the theme of the Preface, "It is very meet, right . . . that we should . . . give thanks unto thee". Perhaps his private sense of logic led him to connect thanksgiving with the Ordinary Worship of Sunday. This failure apart, Baxter's conception of the liturgical action of the Lord's Supper is nearer to the historic western tradition than the conception which Cranmer embodied in the Communion Service of the Prayer Book of 1552.

[1] Ibid., 57. It will be observed that Baxter's doctrine is more advanced than Laud's.

How did the bishops receive the Savoy Liturgy? Baxter complains, in his account of the conference, that "the generality of the Bishops and Doctors present never knew what we offered them in the reformed Liturgy . . . nor in any of our Papers, save those few which we read openly to them . . . it seems before they knew what was in them, they resolved to reject our Papers, right or wrong".[1] The bishops have often been censured for the hostile attitude of which they are here accused. But, as far as the Savoy Liturgy is concerned, Baxter is misleading. From a reading of his narrative, we might suppose that the liturgy had been delivered to the bishops at the end of May.[2] Dr R. S. Bosher, however, has brought to light a document which puts a different complexion on the matter. The document is an account of the conference written four days after its close by the Prolocutor of the Lower House of Canterbury Convocation, Dr Henry Ferne, Dean of Ely. Ferne states, "In the first week of July, they brought in their form of Liturgy".[3] Ferne could not know, and Baxter does not reveal, why the Presbyterians took so long to submit the Liturgy. Was his colleagues' resistance to Baxter's arguments longer and stronger than Baxter implies? 24 July, the date appointed for the close of the conference, was in sight, when the Liturgy was brought to the bishops. They had but little time to examine it. From another document, also brought to light by Dr Bosher, we learn what impression the Liturgy made upon the Anglican commissioners. One of the assistants, John Hacket, writing to a friend on 8 July, informed him:

> Since we parted at London, a composure of a Liturgy (some say it was Mr Baxter's pen) was brought to the bishops. It was sent to me immediately to look it over, and in three nights'

[1] *RB* I.ii.§190.

[2] The last date which Baxter has mentioned before the reference to the passing of his liturgy is 22 May, see *RB* I.ii.§181. Baxter is vague in his dating of the events of the conference.

[3] Add. MSS, 28,053, 1; Bosher 227.

warning for my answer. I was sorry to see that it was so unconsonant, so quite different in the frame from our Liturgy. Which produceth this result, that since the disagreeing party keep such a distance from the old Reformed way, the ancient Prayer Book shall be held up with some few alterations and additions. This I communicate to yourself privately, till you see it really done, as I sub-intimate to you.[1]

Apparently, then, there was on the Anglican side a readiness to receive and consider the Presbyterians' promised "new forms", and an expectation that the forms would not be too unlike, in shape, the services and prayers of the Prayer Book. The expectation was disappointed. The Savoy Liturgy offered the bishops nothing which they were able to use. The only alternative open to them was (as Hacket "sub-intimated") a conservative revision of the Prayer Book. But for the execution of such an undertaking the Convocations, which had been restored to life in May and were now in session, might claim to be recognized as the proper body. In fact, voices had already been raised in assertion of the Convocations' right in the matter against the Commission.[2]

Doubtless with this situation in mind, the Anglicans put to the Presbyterians a final question in traditional Anglican form; they asked "Whether there be anything in the Doctrine or Discipline, or the Common Prayer, or Ceremonies, contrary to the Word of God". The Presbyterians were to have satisfaction, if they could make a case; if they could not, they were invited to put forward what they would ask on grounds of expediency, "and acknowledge it to be no more". Their request was then to be submitted to "the consideration and judgement of the Convocation, who are the proper and authentick Representatives of the Ministry".[3] If the Anglicans had hoped to effect, at the eleventh hour, a

[1] Ibid., 228. Hacket was soon to be appointed Bishop of Lichfield.

[2] See Peter Heylyn's letter to a minister of State quoted in Jeremy Collier, *Ecclesiastical History of Great Britain*, ed. F. Barham (1841), viii.444.

[3] *RB* I.ii.§207.

compromise of a practical kind with the Presbyterians, they had reckoned without Baxter. When he had studied the Anglican paper, "I perceived", said Baxter, "that it was a cunning snare for us".[1] He took it to be an attempt to divide the Presbyterian side; "they thought that one would take for *inexpedient* only, which others took to be *sin*".[2] Baxter composed an answer to the bishops' paper. Then followed a formal disputation, in which three of each side, partly in speech and partly in writing, debated the Anglican question and proposals. Baxter focused the dispute upon one point, that of kneeling at reception in the Lord's Supper. While he admitted kneeling to be neither sinful in itself nor unlawful, he contended that the imposition of it as a condition of communion was contrary to the Word of God, and therefore sinful. In proof of his case, he cited Romans 14.1–3 and 15.1.[3] The Anglicans denied the pertinence of the Pauline passages, and maintained that Baxter had proved nothing. The disputation, not the least heated and barren of the interchanges of the conference, was still proceeding on the last day. Baxter was desirous of continuing it, "as Private Men Voluntarily among ourselves". Gunning also was ready to continue. Bishop Morley, a moderator in the disputation, ruled, however, that it was unfitting to continue after the King's commission had expired. Instead, it was agreed to report to the King that the conference had ended in disagreement.

The failure of the conference, according to Baxter, was the fault of the bishops; they had "resolutely insisted on it, that they had nothing to do till we had proved that there was any necessity of Alteration [in the Prayer Book], which we had not yet done".[4] The Anglicans, on the other hand, ascribed the failure to Baxter himself. Baxter's own account of his behaviour at the conference gives colour to the charge. He took control of the Presbyterian side, doing so, we are led to

[1] Ibid.
[2] *RB* I.ii.§208.
[3] *RB* I.ii.§§222–4 (pp. 348–56).
[4] *RB* I.ii.§192.

surmise, because he could not count upon the whole-hearted and constant support of his colleagues in the furtherance of his aim. He had hoped and believed that the bishops would eagerly accept his Reformed Liturgy as an alternative to an unchanged or almost unchanged Prayer Book. The Established Church would then have two uses until such time as, the superiority of the Reformed Liturgy having been proved in practice, the Prayer Book fell into desuetude, leaving Baxter's Liturgy, with its pastoral discipline and a moderate episcopacy, unchallenged in the field. If Baxter's aim were realized, the Presbyterians would gain, in course of time, all that they had been asking since 1603. Ecclesiastical politics, like secular, is the art of the possible. Baxter, a visionary, had little conception of the art.[1] Having irritated his opponents, he was surprised and mortified by their indifference (as it seemed) to his "Work". It does not appear to have occurred to him that the bishops would see in his project the promise, not of peace, but of a continuance of strife.

Could the conference have succeeded, had Baxter not been a member of it? In their readiness to admit and consider Baxter's Liturgy, the bishops showed themselves to be not opposed to all idea of an accommodation with the Presbyterians, as Baxter afterwards alleged that they were. The bishops were also convinced that, had his colleagues been left to themselves, they would have been more conciliatory than Baxter permitted them to be. It is not impossible that the two sides would have reached a compromise. It is hardly possible, however, that the compromise would have long survived the conference which produced it. On one hand, the extreme Presbyterians and (we may suppose) Baxter would

[1] Gilbert Burnet, no enemy of the Presbyterians, says that Baxter persuaded his colleagues that they were bound "to offer everything that they thought might conduce to the good or peace of the Church, without considering what was like to be obtained, or what effect their demanding so much might have, in irritating the minds of those who were then the superior body in strength and number" (Burnet, *HOT* i.320).

have denounced the kind of compromise which the bishops could have accepted; and, on the other hand, the new Parliament would have quashed any compromise whatsoever.

In the new House of Commons, which had been elected as the Savoy commission was entering upon its labours, the predominant majority consisted of Royalist and Anglican gentry, "Cavaliers", many of whom had been tutored in youth by ejected Anglican clergymen. They represented the class which, by fines and loss of their land, had suffered most during the Interregnum. For these men, the Prayer Book was the symbol of their cause in its religious and ecclesiastical aspects. They remembered with anger the proscription of their Church and its usages; they cherished a bitter resentment against the authors of its overthrow, whether Presbyterian or Independent. The Cavalier Parliament met on 8 May. On 17 May, the Commons resolved on the public burning of the Solemn League and Covenant. On 26 May, with the exception of three or four members who were suspended from sitting because of refusal, the Commons received the Sacrament according to the use of the Prayer Book. On 18 June, by repealing an Act of the Long Parliament, the Cavalier Parliament restored the bishops to the House of Lords. A week later, on 25 June, the Commons, disregarding the conference proceeding at the Savoy, initiated measures "for confirming the Liturgy of the Church of England". It was the intention of the Commons to procure the passing of a new Act of Uniformity, so drafted as to supply the defects of earlier legislation and to ensure conformity with the Prayer Book "for the time to come". A Bill for Uniformity was read three times; a search for the "Original" Liturgy of 1552 having been unsuccessful, a copy of the Jacobean Book, printed in 1604, was annexed to the Bill at its third reading on 9 July. Both the terms of the Bill and the adoption of the Book of 1604 left no uncertainty about the mind of the Commons concerning Prayer Book revision and the legality of the Jacobean Prayer Book. On 10 July the Bill was sent to the Lords, but had not been read once before their adjournment on 30 July.

The Commons' Bill for Uniformity together with the failure of the Savoy Conference could have provided an excuse for proceeding no further with the revision of the Prayer Book. The King and the Government had gone too far, however, to let the matter drop. In the new Convocations, also, there was known to be some feeling in favour of tidying up the Book and of modernizing its more archaic features, while leaving its essential character unchanged. During May, indeed, Canterbury Convocation had already accomplished an important piece of modernizing revision. It had drawn up the "Form of Baptizing the Adults" which is still in use; and it had composed Forms of Prayer for 30 January ("the Day of the Martyrdom of the blessed King Charles the First") and 29 May (the Birthday and Restoration of King Charles II) and a prayer for Parliament. The Government may well have hoped that the Convocations could make enough alterations in the Prayer Book as to give a semblance of fulfilling the promises made in the *Declaration concerning ecclesiastical affairs*, and at the same time to reconcile the more moderate Presbyterians to the use of the Book. By 26 July it was too late to proceed immediately; and the King's letters authorizing revision were not issued to the Convocations until October. On 21 November, the first day of its reassembly, Canterbury Convocation took the initial steps towards the work. The Upper House appointed a committee of eight bishops, inclusive of one from the York Upper House, Cosin of Durham, to proceed in the business. Two days later, the committee presented the first part of the revision; and the Upper House, having approved the work, sent it for amendment to the Lower House, with which were sitting proxies of the Lower House of York. Four days afterwards the Prolocutor returned the revision with a schedule of amendments. The second part was accomplished with equal dispatch. By 20 December the whole revision was concluded, approved, and subscribed by the members (or their proxies) of both Houses of both Convocations. The Restoration Prayer Book, unlike its predecessors, possessed the authority of a National Synod of the Church of England.

From the speed with which the revision of 1661 was carried through, it is clear that the greater part of the work had been done by 21 November. Sheldon is reported to have admitted as much to the Clerk in the Convocation;[1] he had doubtless been forewarned by Clarendon of the Government's intention to authorize revision. According to Clarendon, "the bishops had spent the vacation [i.e. from August to mid-November] in making such alterations in the Book of Common Prayer, as they thought would make it more grateful to the dissenting brethren, for so the schismatical party called themselves; and such additions, as in their judgments the temper of the present time and the past miscarriages required".[2] In the following paragraph, however, Clarendon states that "the bishops were not all of one mind". Some of them, like the Commons, thought it best "to restore and confirm the old Book", which had been the subject of "so many scandals and reproaches", and changes in which would be taken as proof of the justice of Puritan complaint. Other bishops thought it would be "great pity" not to gratify the dissenters "in those small particulars, which did not make any important difference from what was before".[3] Unfortunately Clarendon gives no names. Who, then, were "the bishops" said to be occupied with revision during the vacation of 1661? There is no trace of an episcopal committee; and it is known that the bishops were employed in visiting their several dioceses during the vacation. It seems probable that Clarendon was recalling information according to which proposals for revision, made by two bishops,

[1] [E. Pearse,] *The Conformists Plea for the Nonconformists* (1682), 28.
[2] *Life . . . written by himself* (Oxford, 1857), i.544.
[3] Ibid., 545.

were being co-ordinated for consideration by the rest of the bishops in the November Convocations.

The two bishops were Wren and Cosin, neither of whom was regarded as a friend of the dissenters. Matthew Wren, Bishop of Ely, had been concerned with the issue of the Scottish Prayer Book in 1637. On this account, and because he was also learned in liturgy, he is generally assumed to have wished for a revision of the English Prayer Book along Scottish lines. His rôle in the affair of the Scottish Book, however, was subordinate, and there is no reason to suppose that he differed from Laud who preferred the English Book. There is, rather, reason to suppose that Wren had no special liking for the Scottish Book. Early in 1660 he drew up his *Advices*,[1] a series of alterations which he wished to see introduced into the English Book. It is remarkable that he recommended the adoption of none of the more striking and distinctive Scottish features. On the other hand, he desired some changes of a kind likely to please the Presbyterians. He proposed, for instance, that archaic or obscure words or modes of expression should be changed; "One general rule would be, that every word throughout (as much as can be) should be commonly understood". He proposed also to expand several of the prayers and collects so as to soften the effect of Cranmer's terseness.[2] He suggested that the canticles should be introduced by short invitations, such as "Let us give Praise unto God, as old Simeon did"[3] for Nunc Dimittis. Another of Wren's rules was "that whatsoever is not very perfect and right, be it never so small, should now be set

[1] For a reprint of the *Advices* see W. Jacobson, *Fragmentary Illustrations*, 43–109.

[2] The present collect of Trinity Sunday, no improvement upon Cranmer's rendering of the Latin, is an example of Wren's method. Another example, fortunately not adopted, occurs in the collect of the Fourth Sunday after the Epiphany; for the phrase "stand upright" Wren proposed "stand in that integrity we ought to do" (W. Jacobson, op. cit., 67, 69).

[3] Ibid., 60.

right, to prevent all after quarrels; yet all care now to be had, that, in setting it right, it be done with as little alteration as may be".[1] If Wren was ready to concede that the Prayer Book was capable of improvement in some of the respects in which it offended dissenters, it is nevertheless evident that he was content with the broad pattern of its services. He was prepared to make the Book more intelligible, and in some ways more congenial to the sentiment of his day, but he was not prepared to modify any rite or ceremony. His proposals could satisfy only the most moderate of objectors.

Cosin's proposals for revision are preserved in a Prayer Book printed in 1619, now in the Cosin Library at Durham, and hence designated the *Durham Book*.[2] The proposals, which are entered in the margins of the services to which they refer, reveal the influence of several sources, chief among which were the Scottish Prayer Book of 1637 and Wren's *Advices*. It is clear that Cosin had Wren's document before him. Mr G. J. Cuming has accordingly suggested that Cosin was prompted to formulate amendments of his own by studying the proposals of his former associate. The Durham Book was, in fact, a note-book for revision of the Liturgy, and was used as such. Some of the entries are in the hand of William Sancroft, Cosin's chaplain; among these, Mr Cuming notes, are the concessions granted by the bishops at the Savoy Conference. If the concessions were entered soon after the conference ended, the Durham Book brings us to the eve of the summer vacation of 1661. The condition of the entries, however, was not such as to allow of the Book being laid before the bishops. During the vacation, therefore, when Cosin was visiting his diocese, the entries, or

[1] Ibid., 46.

[2] See *The Durham Book*, ed. G. J. Cuming (1961). See also Mr Cuming's "The Making of the Durham Book", in *JEH* vi (1955) 60–72. Mr Cuming's examination of the entries is the most informed, and his handling of the subject the most satisfactory, of those hitherto offered.

most of them, were neatly copied out by Sancroft in a Prayer Book dated 1634 and generally cited as Sancroft's *Fair Copy*. Mr Cuming suggests, with high probability, that Wren supervised this stage of the work, and that the *Fair Copy* represents proposals which Wren and Cosin had agreed to submit jointly to the bishops at the November Convocation.

Is there any one of Cosin's own proposals which may have been intended to "gratify the dissenting brethren"? It is possible that there is; and it is one which is commonly assumed to have been more likely to offend them. The Communion Service in the Durham Book contains an alternative Consecration Prayer almost identical with that in the Scottish Prayer Book.[1] It was copied out on a separate sheet and inserted into the *Fair Copy* by Sancroft, who added the note "both left to censure". The bishops were to decide whether to retain the current form, which on the basis of the *Advices* we may take to have been Wren's preference, or to adopt the alternative which may be accepted as Cosin's. The alternative would have met the Presbyterians' exception that the manner of consecrating the elements was not "explicite and distinct enough".[2] In the alternative, the Scottish petition, "vouchsafe so to bless and sanctify . . . these thy gifts and creatures of bread and wine", expresses the intention of consecration with a definiteness wanting from the English petition. The alternative Consecration Prayer would also have gone some way towards meeting Baxter's objections noted in his "list of faults". Of the Prayer Book, he objected that "It is a disorder . . . to begin in a Prayer and end in a Narrative", and that "The Consecration, Commemoration . . . are not distinctly enough performed".[3] In Cosin's alternative Prayer, the Institution Narrative is followed by the "Memoriall, or Prayer of Oblation", which contains a commemoration of Christ's

[1] For the text of the alternative Consecration Prayer, see Appended Note below, pp. 147 f.

[2] See above, p. 116.

[3] *RB* I.ii.§174 (p. 312).

Passion, Resurrection, and Ascension. Cosin's concessions to Baxter do not end here. Into the Prayer of Oblation he introduced two sentences which appear to have been inspired by the Savoy Liturgy. In that Liturgy, the liturgical action of the Communion Service is declared to be a representation of Christ's Death, and mention is made of his Heavenly Intercession. The English and Scottish Consecration Prayers ignore both these matters. Cosin rephrased a passage in the Prayer of Oblation thus: "... by the Merits & Death of thy Sonne Jesus Christ, now represented unto thee, & through faith in his Bloud, who maketh Intercession for us at thy right Hand ..." It is difficult to resist the impression that Cosin drew from the Savoy Liturgy two elements which he recognized as integral to a rightly formulated Consecration Prayer. That Baxter would have regarded Cosin's phrases as adequately expressing the two ideas is improbable; but there is little doubt that he and his Presbyterian colleagues would have approved the greater length of Cosin's Prayer, if nothing else.

Cosin's Consecration Prayer was never submitted to the Convocations. A note written by Sancroft against the original entry in the *Durham Book* runs: "My LL.ye BB. at Elie house Orderd all in ye old Method".[1] The Bishop of Ely's house, in Holborn, was the appointed meeting-place of the bishops' revision committee. When, then, the matter came up for "censure", the bishops discarded Cosin's Prayer, and retained the current usage. It is possible that Cosin himself was the sole member of the committee who desired his Prayer; but whatever the personal preferences of the other members of the committee, it would have been surprising had they done other than they did. Although Cosin's alternative was undeniably covered by the Convocations' terms of reference, nevertheless, had so notable a change in so familiar a service as the Communion been presented to Parliament, it would have been certain of rejection, and

[1] See G. J. Cuming, *The Durham Book*, 180, no. 268.

could easily have provoked refusal to sanction revision of any sort.

The terms of reference set out in the King's Letters of Business were unrestricted, and included the Ordinal as well as the Prayer Book.[1] The Convocations were instructed merely to "review" the two Books, and to "make such additions or alterations in the said Books, respectively, as to you shall seem meet and convenient". How was the instruction carried out? A general answer to the question is given in the neat summary composed by that bishop who, according to Izaak Walton, played a dominant part in the Synod both in guiding its deliberations and in expressing its mind and will.[2] Sanderson, in his Preface to the revised Prayer Book, wrote:

> That most of the Alterations were made, either first, for the better direction of them that are to officiate in any part of Divine Service, which is chiefly done in the Kalendars and Rubricks: Or secondly, for the more proper expressing of some words or phrases of ancient usage in terms more suitable to the language of the present times. . . : Or thirdly, for a more perfect rendering of such portions of holy Scripture, as are inserted into the Liturgy; which, in the Epistles and Gospels especially, and in sundry other places are now ordered to be read according to the last Translation.

An example of "better direction" is offered by the rubrics relating to an additional consecration and to the disposal of the unconsumed elements, consecrated and unconsecrated, at the Communion. Of additions Sanderson wrote:

> it was thought convenient that some Prayers and Thanksgivings, fitted to special occasions, should be added in their

[1] Until 1661 the Ordinal was reckoned as distinct from the Prayer Book, the title of which contained no mention of the Ordinal, although the two were commonly bound up together. The authority of the Ordinal derived from an Act of Parliament of 1565.

[2] *The Life of Dr Robert Sanderson, late Lord Bishop of Lincoln* (see Walton's *Lives of Donne*, etc., ed. V. Blackburn [1895], 220).

> due places;[1] particularly for those at sea, together with an Office for the Baptism of such as are of riper years; which . . . by the growth of Anabaptism, through the licentiousness of the late times crept in amongst us, is now become necessary, and may be always useful for the Baptizing of Natives in our Plantations, and others converted to the Faith.

Sanderson propounded finally that the reason for changes would readily appear, if the passages exhibiting them were compared with the parallel passages in the former Book. The impression which Sanderson's statements convey is one of a revision strictly practical and therefore moderate. The impression is not false. The liturgical interest associated with the Laudians was not in evidence. The principles animating the revision were rather those of Wren's *Advices* than of any ideal ancient liturgy, eastern or western. It is significant that the allusion to "the most ancient liturgies" introduced into the terms of reference of the Savoy commission was not repeated in the instruction to the Convocations; we may infer that the ancient liturgies were only cited to counterbalance the Presbyterians' appeal, implicit in the Directory and explicit in their Address to the King, to the liturgies of the continental Reformed Churches. By October 1661, the bishops were no longer in fear of a Genevan revision of the Prayer Book. The ancient liturgies had become irrelevant. If the Convocations sought the old paths, the paths were English, and antiquity was not seen to extend beyond the reign of Edward VI. In the issue the Anglican churchman, jealous at last for the Prayer Book, which had been sanctified for him by the halo of proscription and by its connection with the cause of the Martyr King, saw no essential difference between the old Book and the new.[2] The shape of the services remained as it was. If Psalms had been added to the Burial Service, and its internal components transposed, the change

[1] A reference to the *Prayers and Thanksgivings upon several occasions* to be used at the end of the Litany or of Morning and Evening Prayer.

[2] For a detailed account of the corrections and changes see F. E. Brightman, *The English Rite* (1915), vol. i, pp. cciv-ccxxv.

was slight and not without practical advantage; moreover, the revised pattern was hallowed by the usage of Dr Sanderson in the penal days, when the old service might not be read.[1] As for the ceremonies, the surplice, the sign of the cross at baptism, confirmation, and the ring in marriage, all these retained their traditional use and place in the revised Book. The Synod might not unreasonably claim that the small changes which it had introduced, although not a few, had made the Prayer Book even more the same thing than it was before.

The most noteworthy of the alterations occur, not in the Prayer Book proper, but in the Ordinal. They call for a short notice to themselves. The formulae of ordination to the priesthood and the episcopate were amplified, as may be seen from the synoptic presentation of the texts:

The priesthood

1552 (1559)	1661
Receiue the holy ghost: whose sinnes thou doest forgiue, etc.	Receive the Holy Ghost, *for the Office, and work of a Priest, in the Church of God, now committed vnto thee by the imposition of our hands.* Whose sins thou dost forgive, etc.

The episcopate

Take the holy ghost, and remember that thou stirre vp the grace of God, which is in thee by the imposition of hands: for God, etc.	Receive the holy Ghost, *for the office and work of a Bishop in the Church of God, now committed vnto thee by the Imposition of our hands, in the Name of the Father, and of the Son, and of the holy Ghost. Amen.* And remember that thou stir vp the grace of God, which is *given* thee by *this* Imposition of *our* hands. For God, etc.

What was the reason for these amplifications? A few years previously, a Roman Catholic controversialist had impugned the validity of Anglican ordinations on several counts, among them an alleged defect in the ordination formulae:

> The intention of the Ordainer expressed by generall words, indifferent and appliable to all, or divers degrees of holy

[1] See W. Jacobson, *Fragmentary Illustrations*, 36 f. Sanderson's usage was probably followed by others.

> Orders, is not sufficient to make one a Priest, or a Bishop. As for example, *Receive the holy Ghost*, these words being indifferent to Priesthood, and Episcopacy, and used in both Ordinations, are not sufficiently expressive of either in particular; unlesse Protestants will now at length professe themselves Presbyterians making no distinction betweene Priests and Bishops; but they are as farre from that, as we Catholicks. In the words, or forme whereby Protestants ordaine Bishops, there is not one word expressing Episcopall power, and authority.[1]

The Roman Catholic writer here makes an indirect reference to the Presbyterian assertion, mentioned also by Burnet, that the use of the words, *Receive the holy Ghost*, for bishop and priest alike was enough to prove "both functions the same".[2] Bishop Bramhall replied to the Roman Catholic argument by maintaining that "the rest of the Office" in each case determined the sense in which the words were used, and was itself enough to prove a distinction of order between episcopate and priesthood.[3] Bramhall may be said to have expressed the mind of the Church of England upon the subject; but the amplifications of 1661 indicate that the Anglicans had learnt from the Roman Catholic controversialist the necessity, and the method, of answering the Presbyterian assertion.[4]

The Convocations had been commanded to present the result of their labours to the King. They duly obeyed; but no action is recorded in regard to the revision for two months. In the meantime the Commons, ignoring but hardly ignorant of the liturgical activity of the Convocations, had pressed the Lords to proceed with the Uniformity Bill sent to the Upper House in July. On 28 January 1661/2

[1] *A Treatise of the Nature of Catholick Faith and Heresie*, by N. N. (Rouen, 1657), 22. The writer was the Irish Jesuit, Peter Talbot, who in 1669 became titular Archbishop of Dublin.

[2] G. Burnet, *History of the Reformation*, ed. N. Pocock (1865), ii.252.

[3] *The Consecration and Succession of Protestant Bishops justified* (The Hague, 1658: reprinted in Bramhall's *Works* [Library of Anglo-Catholic Theology], ii [1844] 162 ff).

[4] According to Humphrey Prideaux, Gunning and Pearson were "the prime advisers" of the amplifications: see his *Validity of the Orders of the Church of England made out against the Objections of the Papists* (1688), 43.

the Commons addressed a second message to the Lords, desiring them "to give dispatch to the Bill of Uniformity". The Commons were obviously anxious about the length of time being taken to reimpose the use of the Prayer Book, and were determined to reimpose it as quickly as possible. The Lords would not be hurried. They had given two readings to the Bill, and had appointed a committee to consider it. On 13 February, the committee reported that it "expected a book of Uniformity to be brought in", and the Bishop of London said that the Book would be brought in "very shortly".[1] The Lords decided to wait for it, and gave no third reading to the Commons' Bill. Before the new Book was brought in, however, an interval of twelve days was still to elapse.

As yet the revision had not been considered by the Privy Council. The King ordered the revised Book to be brought to the Council on 21 February. That day and the following Monday, the 24th, were devoted to debate on the revision. On the 24th, by order of the Council, Sheldon with four bishops chosen by the others and including Cosin attended the discussion.[2] There is some reason for thinking that an important addition was made to the revision at the Council Board, and that the attendance of the bishops is to be explained accordingly. At some time between 20 December and 25 February the *Declaration on Kneeling*, or Black Rubric, in a slightly revised form was restored to its old position at the end of the Communion Service. The Declaration was not part of the Prayer Book annexed to the Act of Uniformity of 1552; it was added as an afterthought by order of the Council. Consequently the Declaration was not included in 1559 when Parliament re-established the Book which had been enacted in 1552. At the Savoy Conference, as we have

[1] See *Documents relating to the . . . Act of Uniformity of 1662*, ed. G. Gould (1862), Extracts from Journals of Parliament relating to the passing of the Act, 413 f.

[2] White Kennet, *Register and Chronicle Ecclesiastical and Civil* (1728), 631 f.

noticed, the Presbyterians requested that the Declaration be restored. The bishops refused, on the ground that there was not "any great need of restoring it, the world being now in more danger of profanation than of idolatry".[1] Two bishops, however, Morley and Gauden, were known to desire the reinstatement of the Declaration; and two members of the Council, the Earls of Southampton and Northumberland, were in favour of making concessions to the Presbyterians. What had not been done by the Convocations could be done by the King in Council; but it would have been impolitic, as well as contrary to the Government's method of procedure, to do it without the concurrence of the bishops. We may suppose, therefore, that the five representative bishops attended the Council partly to express concurrence in restoring the Declaration, and partly to present an amendment of its text. According to the original text, kneeling at reception of the Holy Communion was not to be taken as meaning "that any adoracion is doone, or oughte to be doone, eyther vnto the Sacramentall bread or wyne there bodely receyued, or vnto anye reall and essenciall presence there beeyng of Christes naturall fleshe and bloude", which are said to be "in heaven and not here". The statement was intended as a denial of the doctrine of Transubstantiation, and of any doctrine connecting the presence of Christ's Body and Blood with the consecrated elements. In its amended form the statement reads, "no Adoration is intended, or ought to be done . . . unto any Corporal Presence of Christ's naturall Flesh and Blood". The new phrase is less exclusive than the old. For an elucidation of it we may turn to Cosin. Commenting on the words of institution, Cosin wrote in his *History of Popish Transubstantiation*:

> This also seems very plain, that our blessed Saviour's design was not so much to teach what the elements of bread and wine are by nature and substance, as what is their use and office and signification in this mystery. For the Body and Blood of our

[1] E. Cardwell, *Conferences*, 354; see above, p. 116.

> Saviour are not only fitly represented by the elements, but also by virtue of His institution Christ Himself is really offered to all by them [*iis mediantibus . . . verissime omnibus exhibeatur*], and so eaten mystically and sacramentally . . . This is the spiritual (and yet no less true and undoubted than if it were corporal [*non minus tamen vera, et indubia, quam si corporalis esset*]) eating of Christ's Flesh, not indeed simply as it is flesh, without any other respect, (for so it is not given, neither would it profit us), but as it is crucified, and given for the redemption of the world. . . . So then none of the Protestant Churches doubt of the real [*reali*] (that is, true and not imaginary [*id est, vera et non imaginaria*]) presence of Christ's Body and Blood in the sacrament.[1]

The new phrase is consonant with this Protestant conception of the presence, and was understood to exclude Roman Catholic doctrine. Cosin himself is a likely author of the phrase.

On 25 February the manuscript fair copy of the revised Prayer Book, now including the amended Black Rubric, and approved by the King with the advice of his Council, was transmitted by the hand of Clarendon to the House of Lords, together with a royal message recommending that the intended Act of Uniformity be related to the revised Book. Clarendon records that "the book itself took up no debate, only the Earl of Northumberland proposed that the old Book of Common Prayer might be confirmed without any alteration or addition, and then the second Act of Uniformity that had been in the time of Queen Elizabeth[2]

[1] Cosin, *Works* (Library of Anglo-Catholic Theology), iv (1851) 17 f (Latin) and 156 f (English). Cosin's *Historia Transubstantiationis Papalis* was written in Latin in Paris in 1656, and was first circulated in MS. It was published in London in 1675; an English version followed in 1676. Both Latin and English are printed in *Works*, iv. It should be added that Cosin held, in common with Calvinists, that the Body and Blood of Christ are present only to the worthy communicant and then only at the moment of receiving the sacramental elements; op. cit., ch. 2,§3 (pp. 19, 157) and ch.4,§5 (pp. 49, 174). For Cosin's emphasis upon the Body or Flesh "as it is crucified", cf. the consecratory petition in the *Directory*, see above, p. 116, n. 2.

[2] The Elizabethan was the third Act of Uniformity.

would be likewise applied to it, whereas a new Act of Uniformity might take up much time and raise up much debate, all which would be avoided by adhering to the old"[1]. If Northumberland were speaking (as he was understood to be doing) for the Presbyterian leaders, the latter were offering, at the eleventh hour, to accept the Book of 1604 with the Elizabethan Act of Uniformity as its sanction. Northumberland's proposal has been described as "a last appeal for compromise".[2] It has, rather, the appearance of being an attempt at adroit manoeuvre. The Elizabethan Act of Uniformity contemplated the possibility of the Elizabethan Prayer Book not being final. According to the penultimate proviso of the Act, "if there shall happen any contempt or irreverence to be used in the ceremonies or rites of the Church, by the misusing of the orders appointed" in the Elizabethan Prayer Book, the Sovereign had power "to ordain and publish such further ceremonies or rites, as may be most for the advancement of God's glory, the edifying of His Church, and the due reverence of Christ's holy mysteries and sacraments".[3] To confirm a Prayer Book which, by revising it, the Convocations had admitted to be imperfect, and to apply to it an Act containing the proviso quoted, would have provided ground for a revival of old controversy and, when the opportunity appeared favourable, for a further trial of strength. The Lords rejected Northumberland's proposal. According to Clarendon, it was said in the House that, had the proposal been made when the King returned to England, "it would have met with a general approbation, and prevented much sharpness and animosity, which had since risen by those who opposed that excellent form" (i.e. the Elizabethan Book).[4] At this juncture, however, to reject the revision which the Convocations had prepared "with

[1] Clarendon, *Life*, i.553.

[2] D. Ogg, *England in the Reign of Charles II* (2nd edn 1956), 45.

[3] Gee and Hardy, *Documents*, 466.

[4] Clarendon, *Life*, i.553.

great deliberation", and which the King had both authorized and approved, would put a high affront upon the Convocations and upon the King himself. The Lords therefore accepted the revision, and having thanked the Convocations for their care in the matter, turned to consider the Uniformity Bill.

The Commons were less gracious but rather more alert than the Lords in their treatment of the revision. It was delivered to them, with the Lords' amendments to the Uniformity Bill, on 14 April. On the 15th, the Commons appointed a Committee of the House to compare the revised Book with the Jacobean and to check the text of the revision with the Convocation's official list of alterations.[1] The committee worked for six hours on the 15th, and completed its labours the next morning. The report of the committee has not survived; had it been other than reassuring, the *Journals* of the House would have recorded the fact. Probably it was the committee which first detected an erratum in the penultimate rubric of The Ministration of the Public Baptism of Infants. In any case, the House desired the correction of the erratum, and the bishops agreed.[2] Later in the same day, 16 April, the question was put "whether debate shall be admitted to the amendments made by the Convocation in

[1] The alterations, as finally determined by the Convocations, were written out by Sancroft in a folio Prayer Book, dated 1636 and known as "the Convocation Book". Both this book and the manuscript fair copy were submitted to Parliament, and both of them were used by the Committee of the House of Commons in the course of its work. For the Convocation Book see *Fac-simile of the Black-letter Prayer-book containing manuscript alterations and additions made in the year 1661* (1871); and for the fair copy see *Facsimile of the original manuscript of the Book of Common Prayer signed by Convocation December 20th, 1661, and attached to the Act of Uniformity, 1662* (1891).

[2] The rubric originally read: "It is certain by God's Word, that persons which are baptized", etc. The bishops agreed with the Commons that "persons" was a scribal error for "children". The correction was written into the manuscript fair copy by Cosin, attended by two other bishops, in the Upper House on 8 May (see *Facsimile*, 258).

the Book of Common Prayer, and sent down by the Lords to this House?" On the division, there were 96 Noes to 90 Yeas. The House thereupon resolved, "That the amendments made by the Convocation, and sent down by the Lords to this House, might, by order of this House, have been debated". In this fashion, by a majority of six votes, the Commons accepted the revised Prayer Book, and saved the dignity of their House for neither amending nor debating the Book. Thereafter the Commons gave their attention to the Lords' amendments to the Bill of Uniformity, spending, as the Lords had done, much more time on the Bill than on the Book. It had been the wish of the King, in order to keep his promise of "liberty to tender consciences" made in the Declaration of Breda, that the Act of Uniformity should contain a proviso empowering him, under certain conditions, to dispense from the use of the surplice and from the sign of the cross at baptism. The Lords had included a proviso to this effect.[1] The Commons, however, rejected it. At the final consultation with the Lords, the Commons' spokesman declared that the proviso would establish schism, and would fail to gratify those for whom it was intended. The Lords were persuaded, and withdrew the proviso. They accepted the other amendments made to the Bill by the Commons, and passed it on 8 May. Eleven days later, in the presence of the King himself, the *Act for the Uniformity of Public Prayers, and Administration of Sacraments, and other Rites and Ceremonies; and for establishing the form of making, ordaining and consecrating Bishops, Priests and Deacons in the Church of England*, having the revised Prayer Book annexed and joined to it, received the Royal Assent. By the fourth Act of Uniformity, of 19 May 1662, the Cavalier Parliament not only reversed the Ordinance of the Long Parliament abolishing the Prayer Book, and restored the Elizabethan settlement of worship in the Church of England; but also sought, by the most stringent

[1] See C. A. Swainson, *The Parliamentary History of the Act of Uniformity* (1875), p. 44, l.518—p. 45, l.555.

provisions which it could devise, to secure the Book, in its revised form, and the whole settlement of which it formed part, from a renewal of attack from within the Church itself, and from a second overthrow.

It was not to be expected that the "Congregationals" and "sectaries", as Baxter termed them, would accept the revised Prayer Book. Revised or unrevised, the Book was wholly objectionable to them; and no settlement retaining even a modified episcopacy and the Prayer Book could have comprehended them within the Church of England. It was not to be expected, either, that Baxter and those who thought with him would regard the revised Book as any substantial improvement upon the unrevised. Archaisms might have been replaced by current forms, a blessing of the water provided at baptism, a renewal of baptismal vows added to confirmation, the term "Consecration" and the manual acts restored to the Communion Service, and new prayers introduced: all these features, welcome in themselves to the Presbyterians, were insignificant in comparison with the fact that the form of the old Book was retained, that the use of the surplice and the sign of the cross was obligatory, and that provision was nowhere made for extemporaneous prayer. The summary judgement which Baxter passed upon the revised Book was that "the Convocation had made the Common Prayer Book more grievous than before".[1] In particular, he objected, with other Dissenters, to the baptismal rubric affirming it as "certain by God's Word" that baptized infants dying before the commission of actual sin "are undoubtedly saved", and he was later reported as, in a heated moment, saying on behalf of the Dissenters "That of the Forty sinful Terms for a Communion with us [the Church party] if Thirty-nine were taken away, and only that Rubrick . . . were continued, yet they could not conform".[2] In such an atmosphere of thought and feeling something more than mere adjustment of the Prayer Book was

[1] *RB* I.ii.§276. [2] [Thomas Long,] *Vox Cleri* (1690), 18.

necessary, if a communion which could be expressed in even a broad uniformity of worship were to be achieved.

Three centuries of that time "which antiquates antiquities" have antiquated not a few of the matters most bitterly debated between Anglicans and their opponents in the seventeenth century. Nowadays Anglicans and Free Churchmen alike can see the past in a truer perspective than was open to their forefathers on either side. Anglicans have learned to see the defects in the Prayer Book. Free Churchmen have learned to use the Prayer Book, and sometimes to improve upon it, in their worship. In 1962 the Book of Common Prayer is not a wall of division, as it was in 1662.

APPENDED NOTE

The text of Cosin's alternative Consecration Prayer as written out by Sancroft on the leaf inserted into his Fair Copy (reprinted from *The Durham Book* (1961), Appendix B, 290 f, edited by G. J. Cuming and published for the University of Durham by the Oxford University Press).

Almighty God, our Heavenly Father, who of thy tender mercie didst give thine only sonne Jesus Christ, to suffer death upon the Crosse for our Redemption; who made there (by his one oblation of himselfe once offered) a full, perfect, & sufficient Sacrifice, oblation, & satisfaction, for the Sinns of the whole world; & did institute, & in his holy Gospel co̅mand us to continue a perpetuall Memory of that his precious Death, & Sacrifice, untill his coming againe: Heare us, ô Mercifull Father, wee most humbly beseech thee; and by the power of thy holy word, & spirit vouchsafe soe to blesse, and sanctifie these thy gifts, & creatures of Bread & Wine, that wee receiving them according to thy Sonne our Saviour Jesus Christ's holy Institution, in remembrance of Him, and to shew forth his Death, & Passion, may be partakers of his most blessed Body, & Bloud

Who in the same night that he was betraied, * tooke Bread, & when he had blessed, & given thanks, he * brake it, & gave it to his disciples, saying, Take, Eat, * This is my Body, wch is given for you; Doe this in remembrance of me.

Likewise after Supper he * tooke the Cup, and when he had given thanks, he gave it to them, saying, Drink ye all of this; for * This is my Bloud of the New Testament wch is shed for you, & for many for the Remission of Sinnes: Doe this, as oft, as ye shall drink it, in remembrance of me. Amen.

Im̅ediately after shall follow this Memoriall, or Prayer of Oblation.

Wherfore, o Lord & Heavenly Father, according to the Institution of thy dearely beloved Sonne, our Saviour Jesus Christ, wee thy humble servants, doe celebrate, & make heere

* The asterisks indicate the points at which directions for the manual acts would be inserted in the margin.

before thy divine Majesty, with these holy gifts the Memoriall, wch thy sonne hath willed, & com̄anded us to make; having in remembrance his most blessed Passion, & Sacrifice, his mighty Resurrection, & his glorious Ascension into heaven; rendring unto thee most heartie thanks for the iñumerable benefits, procured unto us by the same. And wee entirely desire thy Fatherly goodnes, mercifully to accept this our Sacrifice of Praise, & Thanksgiving: most humbly beseeching thee to grant, that by the Merits, & Death of thy Sonne Jesus Christ, now represented unto thee, & through faith in his Bloud, who maketh Intercession for us at thy right Hand, wee, and all thy whole Church may obtaine Remission of our Sinns, & be made partakers of all other Benefits of his Passion. And heere wee offer, & present unto thee, ô Lord, ourselves, our soules, & bodies, to be a reasonable holy, & lively Sacrifice unto thee; humbly beseeching thee, that, whosoever shall be partakers of this holy Com̄union, may worthily receive the most precious Body, and Bloud of thy Sonne Jesus Christ, & be fulfilled with thy Grace, & Heavenly Benediction. And although wee be unworthy, through our manifold sinnes, to offer unto thee any Sacrifice; Yet wee beseech thee, to accept this our bounden duty, & service, not weighing our Merits, but pardoning our offences, through Jesus Christ our Lord, By whom, & wth whom in the Unity of the Holy Ghost all honour, & glory be unto thee, O Father Almighty, world without end. Amen.

3

THE FIRST NONCONFORMISTS

GEOFFREY F. NUTTALL

"WE cannot forget the late disputing Age, wherein most Persons took a Liberty, and some Men made it their Delight, to trample upon the Discipline and Government of the Church. The Hedge being trod down, the Foxes and the Wolves did enter; the Swine and other unclean Beasts defiled the Temple. At length it was discerned, the Smectymnian plot did not only bend itself to reform Ceremonies, but sought to erect a Popular Authority of Elders, and to root out Episcopal Jurisdiction. In order to this Work, Church Ornaments were first taken away; then the Means whereby Distinction or Inequality might be upheld amongst Ecclesiastical Governors; then the Forms of Common Prayer, which as Members of the public Body of Christ's Church were enjoined us, were decried as superstitious, and in Lieu thereof nothing, or worse than nothing, introduced".[1] With these words the Speaker of the House of Commons, Sir Robert Turner, begged leave to introduce to His Majesty the Bill "for the reformation of all abuses in the public worship of God" entitled the Bill for the Uniformity of Public Prayers and Administration of Sacraments. The conflation of biblical references in the second sentence introduces an interpretative element which is disputable. Otherwise one can hardly withhold admiration for so brief and clearly ordered a summary of the ecclesiastical revolution begun twenty-one years earlier. In particular, the reference to "the Smectymnian plot" is shrewd; for, though its position "was really one of conciliation",[2] the *Answer* (1641) of "Smectymnuus" to Bishop Hall's anonymous *Humble Remonstrance* in defence of liturgies and episcopacy had in fact done "much to accelerate the growing movement for the abolition of episcopacy",[3] and extracts from it had been seasonably reprinted.

[1] *LJ* xi.470.

[2] Alexander Gordon, in *DNB*, s.v. Edmund Calamy (1600–66).

[3] Alexander Gordon, in *DNB*, s.v. Stephen Marshall.

Le Roy le veult. The Bill was presented, and the royal assent pronounced, on Monday 19 May 1662. On the following Sunday, 25[1] May, Richard Baxter delivered "the last Sermon that ever I preached in Publick"[2] "unless God cause an undeserved Resurrection".[3] This was in London. At Kidderminster, under the Act of 13 September 1660 for Confirming and Restoring of Ministers, the living had been restored, after thirteen years of sequestration, to Baxter's predecessor, George Dance.[4] In the autumn of 1661 Baxter asked leave of Dance "but once to Administer the Sacrament to the People, and preach my Farewell Sermon to them; but he would not consent".[5] Baxter then visited George Morley, who with the Restoration had become Bishop of Worcester, and sought "liberty to preach in his Diocess"; but, "though I offered him to preach only on the Creed, and the Lord's Prayer and Ten Commandments, Catechistical Principles, and only to such as had no preaching",[6] Morley refused permission.

Henceforth Baxter refrained even from writing to his former flock "past once in a year, lest it should bring Suffering upon them";[7] but "because I could never after tell them publickly (being Silenced)", he at once added to his book then "coming out of the Press", *The Mischiefs of Self-Ignorance* (1662), a short epistle "To my dearly beloved . . . of Kidderminster", explaining "the occasion of my removal

[1] Not 22 May, as Powicke i.215.

[2] *RB* I.ii.§278.

[3] *RB* I.ii.§164; his "resurrection" came on 19 November 1672, "the first Day after ten Years Silence, that I preached in a tolerated Publick Assembly" (*RB* III.i.§227).

[4] For Dance, see *WR* 383.

[5] *RB* I.ii.§247. The sermon from John 15. 22, "prepared to have been preached", which later, with "the last sheet . . . added . . . after I came from you", he intended to send "as my farewell", but refrained "lest it should raise more enmity against you", Baxter eventually printed in 1683 as *Richard Baxter's Farewel Sermon.*

[6] *RB* I.ii.§249.

[7] *RB* I.ii.§254.

from them, and my silencing".[1] This epistle, which is dated 11 November 1661, he still signed "your faithful, though unworthy pastor".[2]

In Worcestershire Baxter was "silenced";[3] but not in London. In February 1661 he had visited Gilbert Sheldon, who had been raised to the bench on the same day as Morley, "to ask him for His License to preach in his Diocess". "I subscribed my promise not to preach against the Doctrine of the Church, or the Ceremonies established by Law, in his Diocess, while I used his License";[4] and the licence was granted.[5] Thus authorized, Baxter had been preaching "once a week"[6] at St Dunstan's-in-the-West,[7] and then at St Bride's,[8] both in Fleet Street, and thereafter "twice a Week",[9] "once every Lord's Day" at St Anne's, Blackfriars, and "on the Week days"[10] at St Mary Magdalen's, Milk Street: the incumbents of these churches, William Bates,

[1] *RB* I.ii.§257. For the controversy between Baxter and Morley which ensued, see William Orme, *Life and Times of R. Baxter* (1830), ii.115, note e. *Richard Baxter, his Account* (1662), published by D.E. (i.e. Edward Bagshaw), was issued, Baxter says, "without my knowledge . . . I desire no such champion" (*RB* I.ii.§260).

[2] Baxter's next piece, *A Saint or a Brute* (1662), also contains an epistle "To my dearly beloved . . . of Kidderminster", dated 7 June 1662, i.e. after his "last sermon"; this is signed "The servant of Christ, and Helper of your joy".

[3] Though used by him also of the ministers ejected in 1662 (e.g. *RB* I.ii.§164–8), it is Baxter's word for this occasion; whence perhaps, as Mr Matthews indicates (*CR* p. xl), its adoption ("Ejected or Silenced") by Calamy in his *Account* (vol. II of *Abridgement*).

[4] *RB* I.ii.§166.

[5] The licence is preserved at Dr Williams's Library: see *Baxter Treatises* (1959), ed. Roger Thomas, 10 b, where its date should be corrected (from 28) to 25 February 1660 (/1), as Powicke i.215, n. 2.

[6] *RB* I.ii.§160.

[7] *The Mischiefs of Self-Ignorance* contains sermons preached at St Dunstan's.

[8] *RB* I.ii.§163.

[9] *RB* I.ii.§278; Powicke, i.215, errs in the phrase "twice a week at Milk Street".

[10] *RB* I.ii.§164.

John Herring, John Gibbon, and Thomas Vincent[1] respectively, though all soon to be "cast out", being at present still in possession.

Thus it was that the sermon from Colossians 2. 6–7 which he expected to be his last Baxter preached not at Kidderminster but at St Anne's, Blackfriars. What purported to be this sermon appeared in the collection issued by "some covetous Booksellers" as *Farewell Sermons* (1663); but they "mangled so both Matter and Style, that I could not own it":[2] "much of it was nonsense".[3] In 1664 Baxter found "among the relics of my scattered pieces" a sermon from the same text, which he had preached at Kidderminster in 1658; and this he desired to publish, "so as to right myself and to cashier that farewell sermon".[3] "I offered it Mr Grig,[4] the Bishop of London's Chaplain, who had been a Non-conformist. . . . But he durst not Licence it."[5] "He utterly refused it; pretending that it savoured of Discontent, and would be interpreted as against the Bishops and the Times".[6] Eventually, with yet another epistle "To my dearly beloved . . . at Kidderminster", dated 31 October 1668, it did appear, under the title *Directions for Weak Distempered Christians*.[7] This was in 1669, at a time "when I was in Prison".[8] But we are running ahead.

[1] For all four, see *CR*.

[2] *RB* I.ii.§168.

[3] *Directions for Weak Distempered Christians*, pref.

[4] For Thomas Grigg, Fellow of Trinity College, Oxford, who was ordained by the Bishop of Norwich in November 1661, see *Al. Ox.* and *Al. Cant.*

[5] *RB* I.ii.§439.

[6] *RB* I.i.§211.2.

[7] Baxter's account in *RB* I.ii.§167, which perhaps betrays some confusion, misled Powicke, ii.1, into identifying the sermon with Pt III of Baxter's *The Divine Life* (1664); but this, though "preached a little before the ending of my public ministry" (ep. to reader), was preached before 13 February 1662, since "the old Queen of Bohemia", whose comment Baxter records, died on that date.

[8] *RB* III.i.§137; the ep. to Sir Henry Ashurst which precedes its second part is dated 14 June 1669, "from my Lodging in New-Prison".

Our examination of the reasons for the place of Baxter's "last sermon" has served to remind us that "silencing" (or ejection) was in progress for some time before 24 August 1662;[1] and also that those "silenced" had difficulty in printing anything in self-defence, or even a farewell sermon. We have still to ask why Baxter refrained from preaching as soon as the Act was passed, instead of continuing until the three months legally permitted had expired.

The reasons he gives himself are these. "A doubtful clause in the Act"[2] led to the interpretation that all "lecturers" (such as himself), as distinct from incumbents, lost their legal right forthwith; and "I would let Authority soon know, that I intended to obey them in all that was lawful."[3] This was in line with his earlier acceptance of his "silencing" by Morley: "since then I never preached in his Diocess".[4] For law, and for duly constituted authority, Baxter's reverence was deep. He adds this further reason: "Because I would let all Ministers in England understand in time, whether I intended to Conform or not: For had I stayed to the last day, some would have Conformed the sooner, upon a Supposition that I intended it."[5] In its regard for facts rather than conventional modesty the unhesitating claim behind these words is characteristic. To Baxter's "power with the religious people of England" Alexander Gordon attributes it that "the Parliamentary establishment" of Presbyterianism "was never carried out in its integrity as a national institution".[6] In 1660 he had accepted a chaplaincy to the King and a few months afterwards had been offered, but had declined, the see of Hereford. Still more recently he had been among, and prominent among, those engaged in the Savoy Conference for the removal of ecclesiastical exceptions and

[1] Mr Matthews reckons (*CR* p. xiii) that as many as 695 ministers were ejected under the Act of 1660, as against 936 ejected under the Act of 1662.

[2] Clause xix.

[3] *RB* I.ii.§278.

[4] *RB* I.ii.§249.

[5] *RB* I.ii.§278.

[6] Alexander Gordon, *Heads of English Unitarian History* (1895), 64.

difficulties. The most cursory examination of his manuscript letters,[1] moreover, reveals the remarkable extent to which, week by week, his advice was sought by correspondents high and low. On 14 June 1661, for instance, James Greenwood, the curate of Old Hutton in the parish of Kendal, Westmorland, wrote, though "a stranger to you by face", to ask "whether I may reade the present Imposed Liturgy or practise & use any of the soe much adored & Cry'd up Ceremonyes without Sin, as also whether it were not better and more safe to lay downe my preachinge ye gospel then practise these if I may not be allowed to preach without Conformity to these?"[2] Baxter had no cause to doubt his responsibility for leadership.

What he does not say, because he took it for granted, is that he knew his own mind. To him the Act was no surprise. It was, rather, the lamentable but natural conclusion of a policy which he had watched shaping itself inexorably, and which he had endeavoured, but failed, to halt. Towards the end of the Savoy Conference "I foreknew and foretold them what they were about to do".[3] "I beg'd their Compassion on the Souls of their Brethren, and that they would not unnecessarily cast so many out of the Ministry and their Communion";[4] "I moved them to some Christian Charity to all those Consciencious Christians, that were to be put away from the Communion of the Church".[5] "But we spoke to the Deaf; they had other Ends, and were other Men, and had the Art to suit the means unto their Ends";[6] "and I perceived that they intended no Abatements, and consequently that they intend the silencing of me, and all that are of my Mind".[7]

Baxter's perspicacity has been confirmed all too clearly by

[1] Cf. G. F. Nuttall, "Richard Baxter's Correspondence: a preliminary survey", in *JEH* i (1950) 85–95.

[2] D.W.L. MSS. 59.5.174. For Greenwood, see *CR*.

[3] *RB* I.ii.§212.

[4] *RB* I.ii.§196.

[5] *RB* I.ii.§211.

[6] *RB* I.ii.§192; cf. p. 85, above.

[7] *RB* I.ii.§212.

Dr Bosher's researches.[1] Even before the Savoy Conference, indeed, he had seen what was coming. "Shall we be Silenced, Imprisoned, Confiscated, Banished, for refusing your Oaths and Subscriptions?"[2] he had asked, in the course of the written discussions which preceded the Conference; "a little Reprival from intended Ejection" he judged to be, in effect, "all the Fruit of this our Treaty"[3] even then. As early as June 1660, in audience with the King, he had begged Charles "to interpose, that so the People might not be deprived of their faithful Pastors".[4] He even asserts that, when in April 1660 he received a letter[5] from Raymond Gaches,[6] the minister of the Reformed Church at Charenton, pressing him to assist in the restoration of the King, "I thought with myself" that this would involve "setting up those Prelates who will Silence me and many a hundred more! . . . but I am for restoring of the King, that when we are Silenced, and our Ministry at an end, and some of us lye in Prisons, we may there, and in that Condition, have Peace of Conscience."[7] This may be regarded as what is nowadays called hindsight; but Baxter's predictions were often as shrewd as his memory was acute.

In his autobiography Baxter spends many pages in the endeavour "to open the true state of the Conformists and Nonconformists" and to give "the Sum of their several Causes, and the Reasons of their several Ways".[8] As he sets these out, there were, in addition to "divers general reasons" for nonconformity, seven matters of controversy between the

[1] See R. S. Bosher, *The Making of the Restoration Settlement* (1951).

[2] *RB* I.ii.§101: "Defence of our Proposals", 16 (p. 254).

[3] *RB* I.ii.§106.

[4] *RB* I.ii.§90.

[5] D.W.L. MSS. 59. 4.32; pr. in A. de la Tour d'Auvergne, *Collection of Letters* (1660).

[6] In his anon. *Patronus bonae fidei* (1672), "Patronus", 42, Lewis Du Moulin, who refers to Gaches as "nunc ὁ μακαρίτης", writes that "amore Baxteri eam linguam addidicit & exantlavit".

[7] *RB* I.ii.§71.

[8] *RB* I.ii.§§284, 286.

two parties: namely, first, acceptance of "the English Diocesan Frame of Government"; secondly, repudiation of the Solemn League and Covenant "as an unlawful oath"; thirdly, the oath that it was illegal "upon any pretence whatsoever" to take up arms against the King; fourthly, "the Oath of Canonical Obedience"; fifthly, the "Reordination" of those not episcopally ordained; sixthly, the declaration of unfeigned assent and consent to everything contained in the Book of Common Prayer, including ceremonies; and seventhly, matters of discipline involved in "Actual Administration according to the Common Prayer and Canons".[1] It is not easy to find elsewhere so full and careful an exposition of the issues, in which attention is given to the arguments on both sides; and Baxter's warning that "my bare Recital" of "the Reasons against our full Obedience to the Imposition of this Conformity" "is no sign of my Approbation of all that I recite, though I be one of those that dare not Conform",[2] makes it possible to feel some confidence in his objectivity.

It will be seen that the seven conditions of conformity, though distinguishable, are inter-related in a number of ways. The second, third, and fourth have to do with oaths and the repudiation of oaths—in itself a tender point which in the seventeenth century raised scruples among groups as different from each other as the Quakers and the Nonjurors. The first, fourth, and fifth turn on episcopacy, and a certain form of it. The sixth issue is the liturgical: it includes both the form of words and the ceremonies to be used in public worship. The seventh issue is one of discipline; though this, again, is linked not only with the sixth but with the first; for, as Baxter puts it, "the seventh Charge against the Diocesan Form (and that which sticketh more than all the rest) is, That it maketh the Church Government or

[1] *RB* I.ii.§§311–416; this section is omitted almost entirely from the abridgement of *RB* edited by J. M. Lloyd Thomas as *The Autobiography of Richard Baxter* (1925).

[2] *RB* I.ii.§303.

Discipline which Christ hath commanded, and all the ancient Churches practised, to be a thing impossible to be done, and so excludeth it", and "the eighth . . . That . . . it setteth up, instead of it, an unlawful kind of Church-Discipline".[1] Although Baxter spends several paragraphs over the repudiation of the Solemn League and Covenant, neither this nor the oaths required were in fact the major issues.[2] In a sense, they were peripheral. In the "Paper of Proposals" to the King which he drew up earlier Baxter reduces the seven issues to the three "Matters in Difference, *viz.* Church-Government, Liturgy and Ceremonies".[3]

In effect these are the same three issues as those Sir Robert Turner mentioned when he presented the Act. We may proceed to examine each of them more closely. To Baxter none of the requirements, in and by itself, was an insuperable obstacle, however objectionable. His own grounds for nonconformity went much wider and deeper. To these we will return. But first let us see how one or other of the requirements in these three main spheres made it impossible for many other ministers to conform.

> Apostatizing from the pure worship of God, to the superstitious Rites and Ceremonies of man, provokes bitterly. . . .

[1] *RB* I.ii.§§321, 332.

[2] Stubborn opposition to repudiation of the Covenant was expressed by Zachary Crofton, ejected from St Botolph, Aldgate, London, in prolonged controversy with John Gauden, who, though retaining his preferments during the Interregnum, conformed at the Restoration and became Bishop of Exeter. John Ray, the eminent naturalist, who preferred "deprivation of my fellowship" at Trinity College, Cambridge, rather than "if I should swallow the declaration" (cf. *CR*), "considered the covenant an unlawful oath" but "declined to declare that it was not binding on those who had taken it" (*DNB*). Laurence Fogg, the rector of Hawarden, Flintshire, who later conformed and became dean of Chester, had obtained episcopal orders and was "Conformable in Worship, Ceremonies and other Matters Ecclesiastical" (Calamy, *Continuation* [1727], 708), but could not subscribe to the declaration against resistance to the King. Cf. also Congreg. Hist. Soc. *Trans.*ix.266 (September 1926).

[3] *RB* I.ii.§96 (p. 233); also pr. as *Two papers of proposals* (1661).

> Symbolizing with Idolatrous worship, persons or things, God allows not . . . . Reader, it is dangerous to Symbolize with the Superstitious Rites, and inventions of men. Do not Judaize, do not Gentilize, do not Romanize but see you Christianize.

We catch here a shorter, sharper note than Baxter would allow himself, at least in print. It expresses indignation and fear: the godly fear of one who accepts implicitly the divine prohibitions in Scripture and the penalties attached to their transgression; and the righteous indignation of one who has argued all this before and may now claim the abbreviations of authority.

The writer, William Greenhill, was an older man than Baxter, born as long ago as 1597–8.[1] In 1628 he was ordained by the Bishop of Lincoln and soon afterwards became rector of Oakley, Suffolk. Here he had not Baxter's good fortune in beginning his ministry in a place "priviledged from all Episcopal Jurisdiction, except the Archbishop's Triennial Visitation".[2] Oakley was in the diocese of Norwich; and in the brief period (1635–8) during which Matthew Wren was bishop, Greenhill was one of a number who, for such offences as "using conceived Prayers before and after Sermons" and "not reading the second Service at the Communion Table set Altarwise", had been "excommunicated, Suspended or deprived, and otherwise censured and silenced".[3] Five years later the wheel had turned and, together with three others[4] suspended by Wren, he is to be found in the Westminster Assembly among the "Dissenting Brethren". He had also been appointed by Parliament chaplain to three of the children of Charles I. From 1641 he was evening lecturer of Stepney, and from 1652 vicar of Stepney also. All through these years he had

[1] Cf. *CR* which identifies Greenhill with a Cambridge graduate from Gonville and Caius; thus correcting *DNB*, which identifies him with an Oxford graduate from Magdalen born in 1591.

[2] *RB* I.i.§21 of Bridgnorth.

[3] *Historical Collections* (ed. John Rushworth, 1692), III. i.353.

[4] William Bridge, Jeremiah Burroughes (rector of the neighbouring parish of Tivetshall), and John Phillip.

been labouring at his *Exposition . . . of the prophet Ezekiel.* The first volume of this work was published in 1645. The phrases quoted above and below are from the preface to the fifth and last volume,[1] which did not appear till 1662.

> Happy be the souls are so resolved, they will buy the Truth whatever it cost them. . . .[2]
>
> Touch not the unclean thing . . . & if non-touching do cause Suffering, casting out, or off, God will receive, be a Father & recompense suffering. . . .
>
> Some say *Imperium sequitur Ecclesia;* the false Church may, but the True Church *sequitur Christum,* It follows Christ. . . .
>
> As Christ will own nothing but what is appointed of the Lord; so those are with him will not own the superstitious appointments of men, but cleave to the Institutions of God, though out of place and despised.

The date of this preface is May ("Third Month") 1662. Under the Act of 1660 Greenhill was already "out of place and despised". He had suffered before and was ready to suffer again. He also evidently expected others to suffer with him; and of earlier opponents of the ceremonies, who, for "refusing the new Conformitie, as they call yt",[3] had shared Greenhill's suspension by Wren, and who were still alive, at least five[4] now again did not conform. Not all bishops were so active in prosecution as Wren; but in the diocese of York Dr Marchant's recent researches reveal a number of

[1] The rarity of this volume, no copy of which is located in Great Britain by D. Wing, *Short-Title Catalogue,* ii (New York, 1948), is remarked in *DNB* ("it is supposed that many copies were destroyed in the fire of London"); a copy is preserved in the library of New College, London.

[2] "Prov. 23.26. Buy the truth and sell it not" stands on the title-page of the volume.

[3] Robert Stansby, vicar of Little Waldingfield, Suffolk, in letter to John Winthrop dated 17 March 1636(/7), printed in Massachusetts Hist. Soc. *Collections,* 4th ser., vii.9; Stansby adds that he had himself been deprived "for refusing the old Conformity", i.e. to the Canons of 1604 or to the reading of the *Book of Sports.*

[4] Thomas Allen, Paul Amyraut, William Bridge, Thomas Mott, and William Powel. Allen and Powel were like Greenhill in being Caius men, Allen and Bridge in being Congregational.

ministers[1] prosecuted during Richard Neile's archiepiscopate (1632–40) for such offences as disuse of the surplice and omitting parts of the Book of Common Prayer, who are also among the ejected of 1660–2. Similar cases can be found in other dioceses. In Essex John Knowles, in London George Hughes had been among those suspended by Laud for "Nonconformity to the Ceremonies".[2] For not bowing to the altar or at the Holy Name, Francis Cheynell, when Fellow of Merton College, Oxford, and Miles Burkitt, when vicar of Pattishall (Nether moiety), Northamptonshire, had been suspended by Sir John Lambe, dean of the Court of Arches and "one of Laud's most active supporters".[3] George Moxon had "met with much Trouble from Dr Bridgeman, Bp. of Chester, for his Nonconformity to the Ceremonies".[4] Thomas Case, also, had been charged in Bridgeman's court with giving the sacrament to those who did not kneel.[5] John Gilpin, the ejected rector of Brinklow, Warwickshire, was another who "had born the Brunt of Persecution former times, for his Nonconformity".[6]

By 1662 none of these men was young. Thomas Case and Elkanah Wales, one of the Yorkshire ministers, were like Greenhill in being born in the sixteenth century, Wales as far back as 1588.[7] So, presumably, was Gilpin, whom

[1] Robert Armitage, Richard Dreaton (Drayton), Nathaniel Rathband, Thomas Robinson, Lemuel Tuke, Elkanah Wales, and Samuel Winter: see R. A. Marchant, *The Puritans and the Church Courts, 1560–1642* (1960). Rathband's "resignation" in 1660 was perhaps not technically an "ejection": "'resignation' at this period may or may not be an 'ejection'" (*CR* p. xxxviii); but what is known of the man, his brother William (ejected in 1662), and his father (suspended earlier) shows where his sympathies were likely to be.

[2] Edmund Calamy, *Account*, 222, of Hughes.

[3] *DNB* s.v. Lambe.

[4] Calamy, *Account*, 129.

[5] *DNB* s.v. Case.

[6] Calamy, *Account*, 750.

[7] The doyen of all the ejected ministers was perhaps Thomas Micklethwaite, who graduated from King's College, Cambridge, in 1596 and was rector of Cherry Burton, Yorkshire, from 1613 to 1662 (rather than Thomas Nuttall, rector of Saxmundham, Suffolk, as *CR* p. lxi).

Calamy calls "the Picture of an old Puritan", who "to the very last preach'd in his Ruff. . . . People us'd to compare him to Father Latimer."[1] The opposition to the ceremonies issued in fact from an old root in English Protestantism. Let us listen to Greenhill once more:

> This should caution us to keep distance from inward approbation of, and outward compliance with, either Jewish ceremonies, or Romish Rites; The first are abrogated by the Lord. . . . The other are the Mark of the Beast, and it is not safe to bear that Mark, Rev. 14.9, 16.2. . . .
>
> Whatsoever is from man in the worship of God hath *aliquid faecis & terrae*, like the man whence it comes and is an unclean thing. . . .
>
> You are to feed on nothing but the sincere milk of the Word, and to Worship God only with Word service, Rom. 12.1, Such as is appointed and ordered by the Word, not contrarie to, or besides it.[2]

In all this we are carried back to the beginnings of the century and beyond: to the deprivation of three or four hundred clergy in 1604–5;[3] to the controversy between Cartwright and Whitgift, in which the drift of the Puritan position (as defined by Hooker) was "that nothing ought to be done in the Church according to any law of man's devising, but all according to that which God in his word hath commanded";[4] to the deprivation of the Dean of Christ Church and the suspension of thirty-seven London clergy in 1565–6 for refusing to wear the surplice;[5] and to the imprisonment

[1] Calamy, *Account*, 750; *Continuation*, 863.

[2] Greenhill adds in the margin: "if λογικὸν γάλα be the milke of the word, λογικὴ λατρεία is the service of the word".

[3] *An Abridgement of . . . the Ministers of Lincolne Diocesse . . . Apology for themselves and their brethren that refuse the subscription and conformity which is required* (1605) was, in fact, reissued in 1660, further abridged, and preceded by extracts from "Smectymnuus", as *The Old Non-conformist, Touching the Book of Common-Prayer, and Ceremonies.*

[4] R. Hooker, *The Laws of Ecclesiastical Polity*, bk III, sect. vii, para. 4 (ed. Keble [Oxford, 1845], i.363).

[5] For a recent study of their case, and of the arguments they advanced, see J. H. Primus, *The Vestments Controversy* (Kampen, 1960).

of John Hooper in 1551, when he was bishop-elect of Gloucester, for similar scruples.[1] Hooper has been called, not without justification, "the father of English Nonconformity". In his own day he was spoken of as the "future Zwingli of England";[2] and in Greenhill's scornful equation of "Romish Rites" with "Jewish ceremonies" we have an echo of Zwingli's fierce teaching concerning the sacraments, that to suppose anything externally applied can cleanse within is to revert to Judaism.[3]

Besides these men who had been suspended earlier for refusing the ceremonies, there were other ejected ministers who had been suspended[4] for other offences, such as refusing to read the *Book of Sports*, or who had at least been presented for some form of nonconformity. When these names are added to those already noted, it may be observed that a number of them had gone into exile in the Netherlands,[5] or in New England,[6] and had since returned. Others[7] were ministers whose fathers had been suspended and had then emigrated. Some, again, had forestalled suspension by emigrating,[8] or simply by moving from one diocese to another.[9]

Among these ministers we may perhaps infer some awareness of one another and of a common stand. We may at least pause a moment over Richard Proud, an older contemporary of Greenhill's at Caius and for some years his neigh-

[1] For Hooper's statement *contra vsum vestium*, see *Journal of Theological Studies*, xliv (1943) 194–9.

[2] See Primus, p. 5.

[3] Zwingli, *Opera* (Turici, 1814), iv.11.

[4] E.g. by Wren: Mathias Candler, Thomas Holborough, and Richard Proud; by Laud: John Beadle, Isaac Knight, and Thomas Weld; and by Juxon: John Goodwin.

[5] E.g. Thomas Allen, Amyraut, Bridge.

[6] E.g. Knowles, Thomas Larkham, Moxon, Weld.

[7] E.g. John Allin, John Bulkley, Isaac Chauncy, Nathaniel and Samuel Mather.

[8] E.g. Robert Parke.

[9] E.g. Thomas Mocket.

bour in Suffolk at Thrandeston. He became rector of this parish in 1623. In 1636 Wren suspended him for not reading the *Book of Sports*. In 1640 he petitioned the House of Commons for restoration to his living; and in 1645, when he was nominated among the ministers to serve in the ninth classical presbytery for Suffolk, he was again "of Thrandeston".[1] Here he remained; but in 1662, at the age of sixty-six or sixty-seven, he was again ejected. In his will he mentions the "sylver knopt spoone marked at the back R.N.P.", explaining that the N. stood for his grandmother's name "when she was a maid as is to be seen in the booke of martyrs".[2] The old man's pride in being (like George Fox) "of the stock of the martyrs"[3] may serve to underline the fact that among those whom we call the first Nonconformists some at least were the conscious inheritors of a tradition, a tradition which ran back into the Reformation itself and which had often involved suffering.

Lemuel Tuke, who was ejected from the perpetual curacy of Sutton-in-Ashfield, Nottinghamshire, is another minister with notable earlier associations. Between 1635 and 1639 he had been charged in the court of the Archdeacon of Nottingham with failure to read the *Book of Sports*, with disuse of the surplice and of the sign of the cross in baptism, with omitting parts of the Book of Common Prayer, and with administering the sacrament to non-kneelants. What is more remarkable is that, prior to his ordination (1623, 1628) by the Bishop of Peterborough,[4] he had been a member of a

[1] Cf. W. A. Shaw, *History of the English Church . . . 1640–1660* (1900), ii.427.

[2] *CR*, with ref. to Foxe's *Acts and Monuments* (ed. Townsend, 1841), vii.373, viii.598.

[3] George Fox, *Journal* (ed. Nickalls, Cambridge, 1952), 1. Matthew Woodman, the ejected vicar of Slinfold, Sussex, was a grandson of the Marian martyr, Richard Woodman, "traditions" of whom "linger in Sussex" (*DNB*); "his ancient Mother" was "warm against Conformity" (Calamy, *Continuation*, 830).

[4] Thomas Dove, who "was charged with remission in allowing silenced ministers to preach" (*DNB*).

Separatist church in London, and earlier still of one in Colchester.[1]

Possibly he was the only ejected minister who had himself been a Separatist. Certainly no other case is known. At the same time, the fierce abhorrence present in Greenhill's manifesto, in such phrases as "Touch not the unclean thing", "the false Church may", and "*aliquid faecis*", will remind anyone acquainted with them of the writings of the Elizabethan Separatists: of the congregation in London in 1571, for instance, who were determined not to have "the fylthy Canon lawe", and whom "god hath seperated from the churches of englande and from the mingled and faulse worshipping therein used . . . saying cume out from among them, and seperate yourselves from them & touche no unclean thing".[2] The necessity to separate from "the false Church" and its "pollutions", with reference to the text just quoted (2 Cor.6.17), was a continuing prime element in the apologia of the Congregational men.[3] Calamy's brief delineation of Lemuel Tuke as "an ancient blind Man: Congregational in his Judgment"[4] is thus likely to be correct.

Another continuing element in Congregational apologia was the limitation of prayer in public worship to the "gift" of utterance, in dependence on the assistance of the Holy Spirit granted during worship.[5] The Independents, as Baxter

[1] See Marchant, 313 f. This reference to the Separatist church in Colchester appears to have escaped the historians of Nonconformity in Colchester.

[2] Cf. A. Peel, *The First Congregational Churches* (Cambridge, 1928), 32 f.

[3] See my *Visible Saints: the Congregational Way, 1640–1660* (Oxford, 1957), ch. 1.

[4] Calamy, *Account*, 530. The conventicles "believed to be held at old Mr Tuke's at Sutton" (*CR*), for going to which a Selston parishioner was presented in 1663, were presumably meetings of the Congregational church formed at Selston by Charles Jackson, the ejected vicar of Selston.

[5] See my *Holy Spirit in Puritan Faith and Experience* (Oxford, 1946), ch. 4; Horton Davies, *The Worship of the English Puritans* (1948), ch. 8.

remarks, were "against a Liturgy as such".[1] This position also can be traced back to the Elizabethan Separatists. "May such old written rotten stuffe be called praier . . . ?" asked Henry Barrow, one of their leaders, in his *Briefe Discouerie of the False Church* (1590).[2] "Their prayer is extemporall", an informer reported of the church in London in 1588: "they teach that all stinted prayers & red service is but babling in the Lords sight & . . . are but cushyns for such idell Priests and Atheists as have not the Spirit of God; and therefore to offer up prayers by reading or writing unto God is plain Idolatry".[3] It is thus, again, not surprising that the most vehement repudiation of the restored liturgy, as of the restored ceremonies, came from ejected ministers who were Independents: men such as John Goodwin,[4] Jeremiah Marsden, or Benjamin Stoneham,[5] each of whom "went so far as to run down Parish Worship as idolatrical".[6]

An example of argument to this purpose is to be found in an anonymous tract issued in 1664 by the minister ejected from Whiteladies Aston, Worcestershire, Robert Brown.[7] The familiar[8] reference to Rev.14.9 is scarcely veiled in its title *Μαρτύριον Χριστιανὸν Κατὰ Θηρ-εικο-δουλευόντων. Or, A*

[1] *RB* I.ii.§172. Philip Henry also notes "several of the Congregational way wholly unsatisfy'd about coming to hear ye service book or any that read it": *Diaries and Letters*, ed. M. H. Lee (1885), 135.

[2] 65.

[3] Cf. H. M. Dexter, *The Congregationalism of the Last Three Hundred Years* (1879), 257.

[4] Cf. his anon. tract, *Prelatique Preachers None of Christ's Teachers* (1663); the attribution of this piece to Goodwin, though queried in *DNB*, has Baxter's support (*RB* III.i.§41) and is accepted by Wing.

[5] Cf. *RB* III.i.§41. From 1644 to 1650 Stoneham was a successor of Greenhill as vicar of Oakley, Suffolk.

[6] Calamy, *Continuation*, 942, of Marsden.

[7] The writer assumed the *nom de plume* Christophilus Antichristomachus; but the attribution of the tract to Brown by Baxter (*RB* III.i.§41), who had known him as a member of the Worcestershire Association, is supported by the appearance of Brown's name on the title-page of a defence of the piece (cf. p. 170, n. 1, below).

[8] Cf. *Visible Saints*, ch. 1.

Christian and Sober Testimony against Sinfull Complyance . . . The Unlawfulness of Hearing the present Ministers of England. "To pray in a form . . .", the writer urges, "is altogether unlawful, being 1. A quenching of the Spirit of Prayer. 2dly, A rendring useless the donation of the Spirit, as a Spirit of Prayer, unto the Children of God." "The present Ministers act in Divine things by vertue of a power received from Idolaters, offer up a Worship abused to Idolatry, with the Rites and Ceremonies of Idolaters". Hence, he concludes, "we assert the present Ministers of England to be Idolaters".[1]

In his attack on "Common-Prayer-Book-Worship" as "not of the appointment of the Lord", Brown refers the reader to "Tracts written by Smectymnuus" and others, including one "by a Learned (but nameless) Author, entituled *A Discourse concerning Lyturgyes and their Imposition*".[2] The writer of this piece holds that "the Book of Common Prayer . . . became from its very Cradle and Infancy a bone of contention to the Church of God in this Nation". "Neither did the Apostles of our Lord Jesus Christ use any Liturgies in the sence spoken of . . .", he argues, "nor did they Prescribe or Command any such to the Churches." For "the first 300 Years after Christ", which was "the time of the Churches greatest purity", "the use of these Liturgies was utterly unknown; which makes the case most deplorable, that it should now be made the Hinge whereon the whole exercise of the Ministry must turn". "The invention of Liturgies" was men's "way to justifie themselves in their spiritual negligence and sloth, and to render a dependance on the Lord Jesus Christ for supplies of his Spirit to enable them unto Gospel Administrations altogether needless".[3]

Some weight attaches to this tract, since it was written by the former Vice-Chancellor of the University of Oxford,

[1] 61 f, 54, 55.

[2] 60. Extracts from "Smectymnuus" were also printed by Vavasor Powell, *Common-Prayer-Book No Divine Service* (2nd edn, 1661); cf. p. 163, n. 3, above.

[3] 37, 20, 28 f, 33.

John Owen, the impress of whose dryly objective manner it bears. Since in 1660 Owen was not in possession of a living from which to be ejected, he does not, strictly, come among those ministers whose nonconformity we are considering; but his influence upon "the first Nonconformists" was so great that it would be artificial altogether to exclude him.[1] What, on reflection, may be thought anomalous is less Owen's presence in this essay than the possession of benefices, from which to be ejected, by Brown or Greenhill or any other Independent[2] who shared their (and Owen's) abhorrence of ceremonies and liturgy. The situation was, in fact, complex. During the Commonwealth and Protectorate the politico-ecclesiastical situation permitted Independency to consist in two parts, distinct but (in modern parlance) "in full communion".[3] While some ministers had adopted, or had remained in, a position of separation even from the Cromwellian Establishment, others (such as Brown and Greenhill) had accepted, or had continued to hold, benefices; although some[4] even of these had resigned their livings before 1660. Owen himself had continued as Dean of Christ Church, Oxford, until two months before the King's return in May of that year.

[1] Cf. Mr Matthews's remark on Owen's inclusion by Calamy that he "could hardly be omitted" (*CR* p. xli). Using the word in its older connotation, Owen describes his father, Henry Owen, vicar of Stadhampton, Oxfordshire, as "a non-conformist all his daies" (*Review of the true nature of Schisme* [Oxford, 1657] 38).

[2] In proportion to the total number of ministers ejected from livings, their number was not great: out of 1,761 (Mr Matthews's total in *CR* p. xiii, which does not include those ejected from livings in the four Welsh dioceses) something like 140, which includes among Independents both those ministers (of whom Brown was one) who favoured, but did not insist on, believers' baptism and those (very few) who did insist on it. See further G. F. Nuttall, "Congregational Commonwealth Incumbents", in Congreg. Hist. Soc. *Trans.*, xiv.3 (April 1943); and *Visible Saints*, 23, n. 1.

[3] For their interrelation and mutual recognition, see *Visible Saints*, *passim*.

[4] E.g. William Ames *fils*, Samuel Lee, Philip Nye.

What is significant for our present purpose is that variation among the Independents in reference to the Cromwellian Establishment did not affect their unity in antipathy to the restoration of the Prayer Book. Exceptions, of course, there were. At least the tone of Brown's book (including its title) was found offensive even by another Independent who was at one with Brown over believers' baptism.[1] But in general Owen's *Discourse*, which, if more moderate in manner, was no less forceful than Brown's *Testimony*, may be taken as presenting effectively grounds for nonconformity felt keenly by the Independents. Other ejected ministers besides Independents felt them too. Thomas Watson, rector of St Stephen Walbrook, London, and Samuel Ogden and William Bagshaw, vicars respectively of Mackworth and Glossop, both in Derbyshire, were Presbyterians. Yet, when Watson was asked for a copy of one of his public prayers he replied, "I do not use to Pen my Prayers; it was no Study'd thing, but utter'd as God enabled me"; while Ogden "thought the Idolizing the Common-Prayer, and placing all Religion in it, was a provocation to the good Spirit of God", and Bagshaw, blessing God "that had help'd . . . to such apt Expressions" a young minister who had prayed with him on his death-bed, added, "There is not a Prayer in all their Book, would have suited my Present Circumstances so well as this has done".[2]

Opposition to the ceremonies and to the liturgy was thus strong among the Independents, as also among the older men, some of whom had already been suspended on these grounds in earlier years. Most of these older men, whether Independents or not, naturally fulfilled the requirement of episcopal ordination.[3] This requirement affected, rather, the younger men, who had been ordained since the abolition of

[1] I.e. John Tombes, who replied to Brown in *Theodulia* (1667; the copy preserved in the library of New College, London, is inscribed *ex dono Authoris* in Tombes' autograph); Brown retorted in *Jerubbaal* (1668).

[2] Calamy, *Account*, 37, 196, 201.

[3] "At least 420 of the ministers [later ejected] were in full episcopal orders before the Civil War": *CR*, p. lxi.

episcopacy in 1643 and had consequently received some form of presbyteral ordination. During the years 1646–60 a variety of modes of ordination had obtained, and it is necessary first to consider these and what was intended by them.

First of all, while no new bishops were consecrated in this period, some,[1] though not all, of those who had been deprived but were at liberty continued to ordain, in secret. No exhaustive study of these ordinations has yet appeared;[2] but we should not expect to find among them the ordination of any minister ejected in 1660–2. Secondly, there was Presbyterian or classical ordination, as laid down in Parliament's *Ordinance* of 1646 *for the Ordination of Ministers by Classical Presbyteries*. This mode of ordination was that which was clearly legal and officially approved. Despite the publication of a number of lists showing the ministers and elders nominated, the "attempt to set up Classes throughout the Kingdom . . . proved abortive":[3] "our Churches yet stand, for the most part, unpresbytered",[4] a Northamptonshire Presbyterian minister lamented in 1652; but in London, Lancashire, and Derbyshire classical ordination was frequent, and there is evidence of its more occasional occurrence in Northumberland,[5] Cheshire,[6] three midland counties,[7] and

[1] E.g. Bridgeman of Chester, Brownrigg of Exeter, Duppa of Salisbury, King of Chichester, Hall of Norwich, Skinner of Oxford, and a number of Irish bishops.

[2] Cf. my *Holy Spirit*, 130 f; S. L. Ollard and K. Major, in *Theology*, xlv (1942) 38, 210 f.

[3] Alexander Gordon, *Freedom after Ejection* (Manchester, 1917), 152.

[4] Daniel Cawdrey, *A Sober Answer to a Serious Question* (1652), 30.

[5] See Calamy, *Account*, 505, for the certificate of ordination of Ralph Ward by the Classical Presbytery of Newcastle-upon-Tyne.

[6] The Cheshire Voluntary Association of ministers, also called the Cheshire Classis, "acquired some little appearance of Presbyterian usage by the admission, in July 1655, of ruling elders among its members" and "was recognised by the Manchester Presbyterian Classis, on 15 April 1656, as a body that could confer ordination": A. Gordon, ed., *Cheshire Classis Minutes 1691–1745* (1919), 106.

[7] Nottinghamshire, Shropshire, and Warwickshire. By a rare oversight, in *CR* the Nottingham Classis is often, though not always, termed the Nottingham Association.

Wiltshire.[1] Thirdly, and outside London and Lancashire perhaps most frequently, there was what may rather be termed presbyteral ordination: that is, ordination by ministers without relation to any classis or presbytery (as a body which included lay elders). This mode of ordination was made legal *pro tempore* by parliamentary Ordinances of 1644 authorizing ordination at large by any seven of twenty-three named ministers, and within Lancashire of twenty-one others.[2] Later, when the endeavour to establish a Presbyterian system had failed, the Instrument of Government of December 1653 could be adduced as a more general authorization for such presbyteral ordination.[3] From 1653 onwards Voluntary Associations of ministers came into being in many parts of the country on the model of Baxter's Worcestershire Association;[4] and some,[5] though not all,[6] of these Associations ordained. Information respecting the extent and character of the Associations still needs to be assembled;[7] but in some counties it appears that ministers not otherwise

[1] Cf. Calamy, *Continuation*, 290, of Nathan Jacob.

[2] See Calamy, *Continuation*, 65, for the certificate of ordination of Samuel Annesley on board the *Globe* by six of the ministers named and one other.

[3] See Calamy, *Continuation*, 227, for the certificate of ordination of James Cave, adducing this authorization, by seven ministers of the Cumberland and Westmorland Association.

[4] For an analysis of its membership, see G. F. Nuttall, in *JEH* i.2 (July-October 1950), 197–206; 37 out of 72 are known to have been ejected in 1660–2.

[5] E.g. Cambridgeshire, Cornwall, Cumberland and Westmorland (cf. n. 3, above), and Devon: see Calamy, *Continuation*, 346, for the certificate of ordination by William Pearse by four ministers of the Devon Association.

[6] E.g. Worcestershire did not; Baxter "never joined in an ordination" (A. Gordon, *Freedom after Ejection*, 153).

[7] Baxter's MS. correspondence at Dr Williams's Library contains references to Associations established or proposed in Cumberland, Dorset, Devon, Essex, Hampshire, Herefordshire, Ireland, Kent, Staffordshire, Somerset, Sussex, and Wiltshire. For the Cheshire Association, see p. 171, n. 6, above. W. A. Shaw, op. cit., app. 3, is confused and untrustworthy.

associated acted together *ad hoc* for ordinations.[1] Whether by Associations or not, such ordination was presbyteral rather than Presbyterian for the further reason that those ordaining frequently included Congregational (and sometimes Episcopal) ministers as well as Presbyterian. Fourthly and lastly, there was Congregational ordination. This differed from Presbyterian in two ways. Though the congregation which had called the minister to be ordained might request those ministers present as representatives of the wider fellowship to act on its behalf, ordination was conceived as performed, essentially, by the congregation itself; and imposition of hands, though commonly practised, was not regarded as of necessity and was sometimes omitted on principle.[2]

In an ecumenical age such variation may seem untidy; but the differences rested on convictions held with exceeding firmness. Giles Firmin, for instance, vicar of Shalford, Essex, had preferred to remain unordained for two years rather than be ordained without imposition of hands by "Congregational Brethren in Essex" who had "cast it away".[3] Earlier George Crosse, who was ejected from Clifton Campville, Staffordshire, remained unordained for as long as nine years, "because he could not find a Bishop in England, nor Ireland, so moderate as to ordain him without imposing Oaths and Subscriptions"; though "when the Presbyteries were set up in London by the Long Parliament, he was one of the first that was Ordain'd there".[4]

In the minds of contemporaries other than Separatists

[1] See e.g. Calamy, *Account*, 831, for the certificate of ordination of Matthew Hill by three ministers; and John Brinsley, *The Sacred Ordinance of Ordination By Imposition of the Hands of the Presbytery . . . at the solemn Ordination of Ministers in the City of Norwich June 11. 1656* (1656).

[2] Cf. *Visible Saints*, 91 ff.

[3] Giles Firmin, *Of Schism* (1658), 119 f; his ordination was presbyteral, but not Presbyterian or classical, for in his *Sober Reply to the Sober Answer* (1653), 8, he makes it clear that no classis had been formed.

[4] Calamy, *Account*, 631.

Parliament had as much right, ecclesiastically, to regulate ordinations in 1662 as in 1646. At one point, however, the Act of Uniformity differed drastically from the *Ordinance for . . . Ordination . . . by Classical Presbyteries:* its regulations were made retrospective. On the earlier occasion episcopacy had been legally abolished, but episcopal ordination had not been invalidated. Nor in the event had episcopal ordination been treated as invalid. In 1652 William Wickins, who had been ordained by Laud, presented the Fourth London Classis with a certificate signed by nineteen ministers[1] that he had been "lawfully ordained". The Classis expressed itself satisfied that he had been "ordained a Presbyter according to the forme of Ordination, wch hath bin held in ye Church of England";[2] and no question of reordaining him arose. If in its *Minutes* a minister who had received deacon's orders only (and whom the Classis proceeded to ordain) is described as "not fully in orders",[3] no episcopalian could quarrel with the description. When John Conant, rector of Exeter College, Oxford, who similarly had earlier received deacon's orders, was ordained in 1652 by presbyters at Salisbury, the late William Hunt, himself a clergyman, does in fact say that this "answered to priest's orders".[4] If we are to feel the full effect of the Act of Uniformity on the minds of those lately ordained, this fact, that Presbyterian ordination had been intended to replace or continue episcopal ordination, not to deny or repeat it, needs to be pondered.

[1] Of those still alive, all but one of these were ejected in 1660–2, like Wickins himself.

[2] *Register-Booke of the Fourth Classis in the Province of London 1646–59* (Harleian Soc., lxxxii-lxxxiii, 1953), ed. C. E. Surman, 108 f.

[3] Ibid., 33, of William Blackmore. The action of the Classis may be compared with the ordination by the Bishop of Salisbury, John Davenant, of William Barlee, rector of Brockhall, Northants, 1643–88, who had "received only *Licentiam in ordine inceptorum* in the Low Countries", which "went not with them for the *Ordo perfectorum Pastorum*": John Humfrey, *Second Discourse about Reordination* (1662), 138.

[4] *DNB*.

"*Tempora Mutantur, & nos Mutamur in illis* . . ." In 1660 a Quaker thus taunted those who "are now minded (if the Word should be, As you were) to face about again to the owning of that late Episcopal Hierarchy".[1] Dr Bosher has drawn attention to "the fact that the greater part of the old Church was quietly absorbed into the Cromwellian Establishment";[2] and now there was a similarly large acceptance of the fact that times had changed. Convinced Presbyterians, such as those[3] who "in the Name, and by the Appointment" of the Provincial Assembly of London had subscribed *A Vindication of the Presbyteriall-Government* (1650) or *Jus Divinum Ministerii Evangelici . . Proving that a Bishop and Presbyter are all one in Scripture; and that Ordination by Presbyters is most agreeable to the Scripture-Patern* (1654) would, of course, stand firm. After writing that to assert "that Christ hath given the sole Power of Ordination and Jurisdiction unto Bishops" was "groundlesse and unscriptural",[4] they could hardly conform. Nor could John Whitlock, who in 1651, after ordination by the Eighth London Classis, became vicar of St Mary's, Nottingham, "on the understanding that Presbyterian models of church administration were to be adopted".[5] This does not mean, however, that all who had actively participated in classical presbyteries declined to conform or discouraged conformity in others. In 1661 an anonymous youthful writer expressed the wish that the "Classical Divines" had been "but half so forward to vindicate their ordinations, as they

[1] Samuel Fisher, *Rusticus ad Academicos* (1660), ep. to reader.

[2] Op. cit., p. xiv.

[3] I.e. George Walker, Arthur Jackson, Edmund Calamy, Roger Drake, Elidad Blackwell, Samuel Balmford, Allen Geare, Matthew Poole, and John Seabrook: of those still alive, all were ejected in 1660–2, with the possible exception of Seabrook, information concerning whom is lacking.

[4] *Jus Divinum*, pt i, ep. to reader.

[5] *CR*. On Whitlock and Nonconformity in Nottingham, see further my chapter in the 1962 Hibbert Lectures, *The Beginning of Nonconformity 1660–1700*.

were to engage young Scholars to accept them".[1] Still less did all those who had received the Presbyterian ordination formerly current turn nonconformists. "The most (that quickly after were ordained)", Baxter observes, "were but young Students in the Universities, at the time of the change of Church Government, and had never well studied the Point on either side."[2] Of the Wirksworth Classis in Derbyshire about a quarter conformed, and of those ordained by this Classis at least a dozen.[3] William Firth, who was ordained by the Nottingham Classis as late as May 1660, was in episcopal orders by May 1662.

There were many, however, who were not opposed to episcopacy in principle, and who in later years are sometimes found among the Occasional Conformists, who yet could not bring themselves to renounce their own ordination. In the autumn of 1660 Giles Firmin published a book entitled *Presbyterial Ordination Vindicated . . . in Defence of his own Ordination, being questioned, because it was performed by Presbyters;* yet on 14 November he wrote to Baxter of the newly consecrated bishops: "so they will not force mee to owne their power as being of Divine Authority, I will not oppose them & would willinglie live under such a Bishop, if I could, for some Episcopacie I owne".[4] Among those classically ordained Samuel Ogden "was for Communicating with the Establish'd Church Occasionally"; but "Re-ordination . . . he utterly disliked".[5] William Bagshaw was another. He

[1] R.I., *Πρεσβύτερος μετὰ ἐπιθέσεως τῶν χειρῶν τοῦ πρεσβυτηρίου. A Peaceable Enquiry into that Novel Controversie about Reordination* (1661), ep. to reader. Calamy's attribution of this (*Continuation,* 769), with initials transposed, to John Reynolds, who was ejected from Wolverhampton, Staffs, is accepted in the anon. *Memoir of the Life of . . . John Reynolds* (*fils*) (3rd edn, 1735), 10.

[2] *RB* I.ii.§23.

[3] For an analysis yielding these figures, see C. E. Surman, "Presbyterianism under the Commonwealth", in Congreg. Hist. Soc. *Trans.,* xv.4 and xvi.1 (April 1948 and 1949).

[4] D.W.L. MSS. 59.4.206.

[5] Calamy, *Continuation,* 194, 196, with (190f) his certificate of ordination by seven ministers of the classical presbytery of Wirksworth.

"several Years attended the Publick Worship in his Parish-Church"; but he was "Perswaded that no Power on Earth could cancel his Authority, and disannul his Obligation to Preach the Gospel".[1] For these men, and many besides, voice was given by John Howe, the ejected vicar of Great Torrington, Devon. Howe had been ordained by Charles Herle (rector of Winwick, Lancashire, and one of the twenty-one divines authorized by Parliament to ordain within the county), and by Herle's assistants in the chapelries of the parish; and "he would often say that this Mr Herle was a Primitive Bishop; and . . . he thought few in modern Times had so truly primitive an Ordination as he". For himself, he worked steadily for unity among Christians. He was received into membership by a Congregational church in Oxford, and was present with the Independents at the Savoy when they issued their *Declaration* in 1658; he was also on terms of personal friendship with more than one bishop in England and Ireland. Yet when after his ejection the bishop of Exeter, Seth Ward, asked him, "What hurt is there in being twice Ordained?"

> Hurt, my Lord, says Mr Howe to him; the Thought is shocking; it hurts my Understanding; it is an absurdity: For nothing can have two Beginnings. I am sure, said he, I am a Minister of Christ . . . and I can't begin again to be a Minister.[2]

Many ministers saw the issues less clearly than Howe did. The diaries of John Pinney and Philip Henry illustrate their perplexity.[3] Pinney had been ordained by five ministers of the First London Presbytery in November 1648[4] and since the following April had held the living of Broadwindsor,

[1] Calamy, *Account*, 542.

[2] Edmund Calamy, "Life of Mr John Howe", prefixed to Howe's *Works* (1724), i. 4,13.

[3] See also Calamy, *Account*, 173–8, for an agonizing "Soliloquy", drawn up between May and August 1662, by John Oldfield, rector of Carsington, Derbyshire.

[4] See *Letters of John Pinney 1679–99* (1939), ed. G. F. Nuttall, app. 1, for the certificate of ordination.

Dorset, from which Thomas Fuller was sequestered. The fact that by an exceptional act of goodwill Fuller had ceded his legal title to Pinney did not make the decision easier. On 24 August 1662 Pinney did not conform; but no successor was instituted till the next January.[1] In the intervening months he wavered. First, "I went to the Bp. 4 tymes about ordin. and Lukes day rec. ord's of him". "Godly people" he comments, "much offended for my going to the Bp. and ordin." His own uneasiness over his action is clear from the following entry: "I obtained ord^{rs} politiqly not intentionally to conforme which was some trouble to me esp. the subscript. that I gave and had some intention to renounce it publiqly." What he calls "the tempt. to conforme" he sets out thus:

1. Profit. putting a family from debt.
2. the tryumph of sectaryes on my outing.
3. the stifnes of the Bp. of Sarū to out me.
4. Feare of future distrusting God.

"No man perswaded me to conforme," he notes, "but all deswaded me;"[2] and in the end he did not.

Philip Henry had been ordained in 1657 to the charge of Worthenbury, in the detached portion of Flintshire, by five ministers of the Fourth Shropshire Classis, and has left in his diary full particulars of his "lengthy but rather superficial" examination by the Classis as well as of the ordination ceremonies.[3] Throughout 1661 we have a lively account of his uncertainty whether or not to conform: "his main objec-

[1] I.e. 1662/3 (cf. *Letters*, 126), not 1661/2, as *CR*.

[2] *Letters*, 125.

[3] *Diaries and Letters* (1882), ed. M. H. Lee, 34–9; the comment is Gordon's, in *DNB*. Not all would call Henry "one of the world's great Diarists" (Thomas Richards, *Religious Developments in Wales 1654–1662* [1923], 161); but a scholarly edition of his numerous and dispersed MSS. (some of which are preserved in the Congregational Library and in the library of New College, London, which also possesses J. B. Williams's own grangerized copy of his edition [1825] of Matthew Henry's *Life* of Philip Henry) is much needed; Lee's work is ill arranged and inefficiently annotated, and does not include all passages from the diaries printed by Williams.

tion was reordination".[1] Some of his neighbours, like Pinney, were prepared to obtain episcopal orders. "Mr Richard Taylor return'd from London," Henry notes in January 1661, "where he was ordayn'd by Dr Sanderson Bishop of Lincoln"; and in September, "Mr Taylor restor'd to Holt by ye Bp who barkes not bec. hee cannot bite."[2] In August "Mr Bruce, after great professions, and high expressions to ye contrary, I heare is reordayned, hath subscrib'd & reads—wherefore let him that thinkes he stands, take heed lest he fall."[3]

In 1658 Worthenbury, previously a curacy in the parish of Bangor Monachorum *al.* Iscoed, had been declared a new parish, with Henry as incumbent; but at the Restoration the *status quo antea* had been resumed, and Henry became curate to the rector, Robert Fogg.[4] In February 1661 the sequestered rector, Henry Bridgeman,[5] now Dean of Chester, sought to persuade Henry to conform, "telling mee, else my prefermt was gone and what? are you wiser than the King & Bishops, but God grant I may never bee left to consult with flesh and bloud in such matters". Three days later, "Ministers met at Hanmer, to discourse about the lawfulness of re-ordination. Mr Orl. Fogg re-ordayn'd, as for mysf I am at present of the mind it ought not to bee, the former being sufficient, lord shew us what thou wouldst have us to doe."[6] In March Henry makes the entry: "Contests about the liturgy, an ever-lasting bone of contention, till remov'd or mended." In June Bridgeman "promised never to remove mee till the law remov'd mee"; but there were "strong reports, I should not

[1] A. Gordon, in *DNB*.

[2] Op. cit., 74, 96; Taylor was duly ejected a year later (Calamy, *Account*, 716).

[3] 94.

[4] Cf. *DNB*, s.v. Henry; for Robert Fogg, see *CR*.

[5] For Bridgeman, later Bishop of Sodor and Man, see *DNB*.

[6] 78; Orlando Fogg, who, as rector of Overton, Flintshire, had signed Henry's ordination certificate, conformed and succeeded his brother Laurence (p. 159, n. 2, above) as rector of Hawarden, Flintshire: see *CR*, s.v. Robert Fogg, his father.

bee suffred to preach to-day, but I did, & no disturbance, blessed bee God, who hath my enemyes in a chain". Next month Bridgeman "told mee, I must speedily conform or there would bee no staying at Worthenb. lord, shew mee w^{t} thou wilt have mee to doe, for I am afraid of nothing but sin". In August Henry notes: "One Sabbaths liberty more, ô: how good is the lord"; "wee are in doubt what to doe in poynt of conformity, lord, say unto us, this or that is the way, & wee will walk in it"; and "Common-prayer tendered, God knowes how loth I am to goe off my station, but I must not sin agt. my conscience." In September "they took ye Cushion frome mee but ye Pulpit was left, blessed be God". The end came in October, when Henry preached "Farewel-sermons—Text Phil. 1.27 my desire was to profit rather y^{en} to affect." On 3 November his successor, Richard Hilton, "preacht, well—read Com. Pr. which was bad, bury'd after ye mode which was worse".[1] Despite this expression of disapproval, Henry thereafter regularly attended service at parish churches, though "he forebore communicating simply on the ground of the kneeling posture".[2]

An exceptionally tortuous course was taken by John Humfrey, the vicar of Frome, Somerset, who had been ordained by "a Classis of Presbyters"[3] in 1649. In 1660 the Bishop of Bath and Wells, William Piers, not only "pressed him to renew his Ordination"[4] but invited him to share in the ordination of others; and he accepted episcopal orders, without subscription. "It was no sooner over than he was uneasy." By way of answering his own scruples he published in 1661 *The Question of Re-ordination, whether, and how, a minister ordained by the presbytery, may take ordination also by the bishop?* His uneasiness, however, increased, together with a sense of

[1] 80, 88 ff, 92 f, 99. For Hilton, who from 1662 till his death in 1706 was vicar of the neighbouring parish of Hanmer, see *Al. Ox.*

[2] *DNB.*

[3] Calamy, *Account,* 616 ("Classe Praesbyterorum": *Second Discourse,* 110).

[4] Ibid. ("ordinationem meam instaurare . . . hortabatur": *Second Discourse,* 106).

indignation at "the absurdity of the Form us'd, which runs back again to Deaconship, where there was already an higher order";[1] till what he calls his "double garment" of ordination became "like a heavy Rugg upon my bed in the Summer, that to be under it makes me sweat, and I cannot well go to my rest till I have fairly justled it off again".[2] He accordingly went to the bishop's registrar, read him a declaration of his decision to "retract, revoke, renounce, and reject"[3] his action, tore up his deacon's orders in the registrar's presence and threw them in the fire. His priest's orders he retained, not knowing "whether they might not save me the enjoying my Ministry".[4]

Meanwhile, his book had called forth three replies.[5] In *A Second Discourse about Re-ordination* (1662) Humfrey made it clear that while he could no longer justify his own acceptance of episcopal orders, he did not hold reordination, "simply consider'd",[6] to be unlawful and was not convinced by the arguments advanced to prove it so. "From a *non solet*, to a *non licet*, is a *non sequitur*."[7] After his ejection, however, he tore up his priest's orders also, "threw one Part into the Flames, and wrapp'd up the other Part in a Letter to the Bishop", which he concluded with these words:

> when the Men of this Generation do make our first Orders by the Presbytery to be void and null, to the Scandal of so many

[1] Ibid., 617 ("formae incongruitate . . . cuius causa ad Diaconatum veluti ἀφ' ἵππου εἰς ὄνον (ut loquuntur) descenditur": *Second Discourse*, 111).

[2] *Second Discourse*, 96.

[3] Calamy, *Account*, 617 ("retracto, revoco, abdico, abrenuncio, derelinquo, procul abjicio": *Second Discourse*, 111).

[4] Ibid., 619.

[5] I.e. R.A. (identified by Anthony Wood with Henry Hickman but now identified with Humfrey's neighbour at Batcombe, Richard Alleine), *χειροθεσία τοῦ πρεσβυτηρίου, or a Letter to a Friend* (1661), which has a Latin dedication to Humfrey and an appendix in answer to his book; Zachary Crofton, *A Serious Review of Presbyters Reordination by Bishops* (1661); and R.I., *A Peaceable Enquiry* (1661: see p. 176, n. 1, above).

[6] Calamy, *Account*, 620.

[7] *Second Discourse*, 35.

Ministers at home, and Churches abroad, let these second Orders of theirs be rendred by me accordingly, null, void, cancell'd . . .[1]

It was to resolve, or to forestall, the uncertainties which afflicted such ministers as Humfrey, Henry, and Pinney[2] that Richard Baxter made his stand as early as May 1662; and to Baxter we may now return.

Baxter had no need to seek episcopal orders, for he already had them: deacon's orders certainly,[3] and he never suggests that he lacked priest's orders, nor was the matter raised when he was offered the see of Hereford. In any case, he could have accepted priest's orders without scruple, for he had not received presbyteral ordination in the interim. "He clung to his churchmanship; holding that Bishops were the proper ordainers",[4] and, as he says himself, "being known to be for moderate Episcopacy".[5] To call Baxter a Presbyterian, as many do, is to fly in the face of his reiterated repudiation of "the odious name".[6] Connotation changes, and those who have borne the name for three centuries may now properly claim it through usage, irrespective of their present discipline; but in 1662 many ministers were staunch supporters of Presbyterian discipline, and this was never true of Baxter. "It was Episcopacy it self", he writes, which the bishops at the Savoy refused; "we pleaded not at all with

[1] Calamy, *Account*, 619 f. Humfrey lived till 1719, when he was 98 years of age, having outlived all the other ministers ejected in 1660–2 save Nathan Denton, formerly vicar of Bolton-upon-Dearne, Yorkshire, "the Picture of an old Puritan", who died in October 1720.

[2] Matthew Jenkins, who as vicar of Gresford, Denbighshire, had signed Henry's ordination certificate (p. 178, above), was "silenced" at Gresford but conformed; in 1662 he was ejected from the perpetual curacy of Shotwick, Cheshire, but later he conformed again and became perpetual curate of Stoke, Cheshire: see T. Richards, *Religious Developments in Wales*, 503.

[3] The certificate, dated 23 December 1638, is preserved at D.W.L.: see *Baxter Treatises* (1959), ed. Roger Thomas, 5a.

[4] A. Gordon, in his edn of *Cheshire Classis Minutes*, 157.

[5] *RB* I.ii.§120.

[6] *RB* I.ii.§242.

them for Presbytery, unless a Moderate Episcopacy be Presbytery." "The Presbyterian Cause was never spoken for . . . Never did we write or speak a word . . . for any one thing which is proper to Presbytery." "We never put up one Petition for Presbytery, but pleaded for Primitive Episcopacy."[1] Nor did Baxter consider himself exceptional in this. Most Nonconformists "of my Acquaintance", he writes, "are for the lawfulness of some stated Episcopacy . . . but they are all agreed that the English Diocesan Frame of Government . . . is unlawful".[2]

With respect to the ceremonies, Baxter had never used the sign of the cross in baptism or worn the surplice; "yet could I not have justified the forsaking of my Ministry for it".[3] Similarly, though unable to justify kneeling at the Lord's Supper, "I did never hitherto, to my remembrance, refuse to give the Sacrament to any one, meerly because they would not take it Sitting or Standing"; "Yea, if I could not otherwise Communicate with the Church in the Sacrament, I would take it kneeling my self."[4]

Again, "a Form of Prayer and Liturgy I judged to be lawful, and in some Cases Lawfully imposed".[5] "I was not of their Mind who charged the Common-Prayer with false Doctrine, or Idolatry, or false Worship in the Matter or Substance, nor that took it to be a Worship which a Christian might not lawfully join in, when he had not Liberty and Ability for better."[6] "My ordinary Communion should be with a Church that used the Common Prayer, rather than with none, or with a worse."[7] Thus neither ceremonies nor

[1] *RB* I.ii.§§96, 113, 242.

[2] *RB* I.ii.§311; cf.I.ii.§23: "most (that ever I could meet with) were against the *Jus Divinum* of Lay Elders, and for the moderate Primitive Episcopacy . . . as well as myself".

[3] *RB* I.i.§19.

[4] *RB* I.ii.§33 (pp. 159, 158), in a letter of 2 February 1655(/6) to Sir Ralph Clare.

[5] *RB* I.i.§19.

[6] *RB* I.ii.§174.

[7] *RB* I.ii.§433.

liturgy, in themselves, made it impossible for Baxter to conform. Nor did the requirement to repudiate the Solemn League and Covenant; for not only had he not taken this himself, he had "kept the Town and Parish of Kiderminster" from taking it, "yea, the most of Worcestershire besides".[1]

Why, then did Baxter not conform? The answer is twofold. It may begin to appear if we note first how he reacted on two other occasions. In 1660, when Clarendon offered him the see of Hereford, he gave this remarkable reason for declining: "it will very much disable me from an effectual promoting of the Churches Peace".[2] In 1669, when in correspondence with John Owen about "a Concord between the Independents and Presbyterians", he wrote of "the Creed, as Expounded in the 4 First Councils, called General": "I can readily subscribe my self, but it's better let them all alone, and not to be so fond of one onely Engine, which hath torn the Church for about 1200 Years."[3] Baxter is one and the same throughout. The considerations which made him unwilling to be a diocesan bishop also made him unwilling, later, to be the pastor of a congregation formed in separation from the Established Church. Conversely, the considerations which in 1672 led him to decline a licence to preach in any category more sectarian than that of nonconformist were those which, first, made him a nonconformist. His nonconformity was, essentially, for the sake of the Church's unity and of others' liberty.

"You could not (except a Catholick Christian) have trulier called me", Baxter wrote later, in his *Third Defence of the Cause of Peace* (1681), "than an Episcopal-Presbyterian-Independent."[4] In 1662 his purpose was thus to hold the door open: open (one might say) for the Church of South India, save that in that Church there are ministers who have fastened on those who come after them what they decline for themselves, whereas Baxter declined to impose on his

[1] *RB* I.i.§100. [2] *RB* I.ii.§123.
[3] *RB* III.i.§§141, 143 (pp. 61, 65). [4] Pt i., p. 110.

contemporaries the episcopal orders which he possessed himself. To him, imposition on the consciences of others, whether or not he shared their scruples, was of the same nature, and as abhorrent, as the "Independent separating rigour".[1] "Charity (or Christian Love) and Unity", he once wrote, "are the great vital Graces of the Christian Church";[2] and "whoever be the Sect-Masters, it is notorious, That the Prelates (tho' not they only) are the Sect-makers".[3] To a separatist he wrote: "I will never join with them that have but one Form in Christ's School";[4] and in effect this is also what he said to the bishops at the Savoy. When Morley and Piers "told me, that it was strange I should make such a stir for other Mens Liberty to forbear kneeling in the act of Receiving when I profest my self to take it to be lawful: I told them that they might perceive then, that I argued not from Interest and Opinion; but from Charity, and for Love and Peace".[5] It was not a mere retort. The whole long story of the Savoy Conference, and of his own part in it, Baxter concludes thus: "I thought it a Cause that I could comfortably suffer for; and should as willingly be a Martyr for Charity as for Faith".[6]

At the time, a nonconformity so broadly based was almost as difficult for nonconformists to comprehend as for conformists. By ourselves, perhaps, it can be better understood. For William Greenhill it was a doctrine of Holy Scripture which precluded conformity to the ceremonies. For John Owen a doctrine of the Holy Spirit precluded use of the liturgy. For John Howe a doctrine of grace precluded reordination: of grace not only as received at ordination but as manifest in a ministry of many years. It is still possible to ground nonconformity in any one, or in more than one, of these doctrines; but what made Baxter a nonconformist was precisely the

[1] *RB* II.i.§103. [2] *RB* app. IV, p. 73. [3] *RB* III. i.§99.

[4] *RB* app. III, p. 62, in a letter of 29 September 1658 to Thomas Lambe.

[5] *RB* I.ii.§212. [6] *RB* I.ii.§236.

"burning desire after the peace and unity of the churches"[1] which to an ecumenical age makes him attractive, accompanied as this was by an equally burning desire "that Christian Lenity be used to all truly Conscientious Dissenters".[2]

In 1691, the year of Baxter's death, a young man named William Bilby came up to Queens' College, Cambridge, fortified with a number of Baxter's books. These he soon locked up in his box to prevent the derision of "ye atheisticall schollars", who "spake of ye Revd. Mr Baxter & his works with ye greatest scorn and contempt, tho' one said yt he only was ye man of sense among all ye ejected ministry". Later that year Bilby was ordained by the Bishop of Lincoln, Thomas Barlow, and became curate of Little Saxham, Suffolk. The preaching of "Godly dissenting ministers", however, made him "long to be in their condicion"; and in 1693, at Sawley, Derbyshire, he was discharged by the incumbent for holding "meetings on weekdays for Repetitions and prayers". The following passage from his diary[3] for that year suggests that he had read Baxter with understanding. It may also recall some of the issues we noticed earlier.

> yt which I disliked in ye church or faction rather of England was:

[1] See D.W.L. MSS. 59.6.94 for a letter of 5 February 1652(/3) to John Durie: "God hath possessed my heart with such a burning desire after the peace & unity of the churches that I cannot forget it, or lay it by. I feele a supernaturall power forceing my strongest zeale & thoughts that way; & I am afraide under pretence of reconciling to frame an Engine for perpetuall divisions by giveing away the only rule & center of reconcilement & unity & so leaving it unpossible; for I know the Devills last way of undoing is by overdoing, & when it fits his turne, he will seeme more orthodoxe & zealous against error than Christ himselfe".

[2] *RB* III.i.§256 (p. 113), in a letter of 15 December 1673 to the Earl of Orrery.

[3] For a transcript (now D.W.L. MSS. 12.62) of this diary, the MS. of which is preserved at the Nottingham Subscription Library, Angel Street, Nottingham, I am indebted to the Rev. C. G. Bolam, minister of High Pavement Church, Nottingham. I have expanded contractions.

1. uncharitableness . . . I think ye imposers are schismaticks & not ye dissenters . . . I see no warrant for a set of Church officers yt ye Scripture never mentions and ye power of imposing is to me as great as ye power of inventing. . . .

forms of prayer do not suit all Cases. ye lawfulness of using them I deny not, but . . . to say that men can pray no otherwise without nonsense & blasphemy is to cast a blott upon ye reformation. . . . Ever since uniformity, forms & a Liturgy has been cryed up ye Spirit of prayer & preaching has been cryed down & ridiculed.

2. I dislike their buryal service to be used promiscuously . . .

3. Most of their Canons I dislike for ye same reasons yt Mr Baxter has laid down. . . .

But all humble moderate men of ye church of England I admire and love and am ready to give ym ye right hand of fellowship, not censuring ym for yt which I approve not of myself.

In 1694 Bilby settled at Gedney, Lincolnshire, then described as "a very heathenish place . . . desirous of a minister".[1] "Here I cast off ye fetters of Conformity & walked at liberty."

[1] *Freedom after Ejection*, 71.

4

COMPREHENSION AND INDULGENCE

ROGER THOMAS

THE alternative confronting the Church of England at the Restoration was not comprehension or indulgence but coercion or toleration. Only if toleration had been chosen would the further question have arisen whether that toleration should be exercised within the Church (comprehension), making it more truly catholic, or outside the Church (indulgence)—always a second best, if you intend the Church to be, like the State, an inclusive body.

On this at least the two largest parties, the Presbyterians and the restored Churchmen, were in agreement, that they both wanted a single established Church, not a multiplicity of sects: separatism was foreign to the aspirations of either. In the eyes of both parties separatism meant either a bid for ascendancy, a usurpation, or the beginning of a degeneration into a chaotic multiplicity of sects. Rome was hated not primarily as a false religion, but as a threat of foreign domination or an ecclesiastical usurpation. Puritanism was hated by Churchmen partly because it had ousted the Church and taken its place, and partly because, having done so, it degenerated into the apparent disorder of the Interregnum.

As is extremely well known, the measures taken to reach a Restoration Settlement resulted in no settlement at all; a large body of Puritans was in open revolt, led by Richard Baxter.[1] And soon what to-day would be called civil disobedience began to be practised in the form of meetings for worship held outside the Church. In a sense the history of comprehension can only begin as the story of efforts to retrace the false steps taken in 1662, when there had come into

[1] When the Act of Uniformity was passed on 19 May 1662, Baxter gave over preaching (on a legal quibble) to let authority know where he stood and to "let all Ministers in England understand in time, whether I intended to Conform or not" (*RB* I.ii.§278). Clarendon lost his patience at this and told Baxter "he might preach if he would, but he gave off because he was proud and factious" (Bosher 258 n).

being this large body of dissidents, to be won back again, if possible, to the Church they had left. Indeed the word comprehension itself only came into use in this sense at about this time with the new situation that had arisen as a consequence of the Ejection.[1] Previously "indulgence" had had to do duty for granting liberty of conscience either inside or outside the Church. Thus when Charles issued his Declaration from Breda in April 1660, promising "a liberty to tender consciences" and expressing his readiness "to consent to such an Act of Parliament . . . for the granting of that indulgence", it is not plain whether the promised indulgence aimed at comprehension or toleration or both.[2] Certainly when he introduced his proposed "Declaration concerning Ecclesiastical Affairs" (called the Worcester House Declaration, from the place where it was debated) in September 1660 with a reference to the Declaration from Breda, it did not seem any inconsistency that its main provisions were for comprehension of Puritans within an established Church.

Although there is thus a sense in which the story of comprehension begins with 1667, there is also a sense in which it must begin with the Worcester House Declaration in the autumn of 1660, the first and in many ways the most effective attempt at comprehension made between the Restoration and the Revolution. Indeed the story of those troubled thirty years may be said to begin and end with Worcester House. At the Restoration it marked the high-water mark of mutual concessions. At the Revolution the last Bill for comprehension ever to come before Parliament would look

[1] The earliest reference to comprehension in this sense in *OED* is 1668. An earlier use of the word is to be found in a letter of 1663, where the writer has to explain its meaning (Congreg. Hist. Soc. *Trans.* ix. 280 f). For changes in public opinion see F. Bate, *The Declaration of Indulgence 1672* (1908), 53.

[2] Declaration from Breda: C. A. Swainson, *The Parliamentary History of the Act of Uniformity* (1875), 4; *EHD* viii.57.

back nostalgically to Worcester House as the one real hope of union between Churchmen and Dissenters.

The Worcester House conference took place at a time when the returned Churchmen still felt insecurely restored; when the reasonableness of the Convention Parliament of 1660 had not given way to the bitter animosity of the Cavalier Parliament of 1661; when Presbyterians and Anglicans could be made to meet on near-equal terms, each side endeavouring to secure as much and to concede as little as circumstances and hard bargaining would allow. The Declaration, as first drafted by Hyde, conceded little that would considerably have altered the character of the Church of England. It granted that no bishop would ordain or exercise jurisdiction without the advice of presbyters forming the cathedral chapters; that confirmations should take place with the advice of the parish minister; that obsolete words and expressions in the Book of Common Prayer should be reviewed and that some controverted ceremonies, etc., should be made optional pending the calling of a national synod.[1] The Presbyterians, called to a conference at Worcester House, the Chancellor's residence, tried to give these terms some stiffening. They wanted disciplinary jurisdiction by the bishop and ordinations to be exercised only with the consent of presbyters and not merely with their advice. This was not granted, but they did win the concession that an equal number of elected presbyters should act with the chapters in giving the bishop "advice and assistance". In the matter of confirmations the Puritans gained the important point that the consent of the local minister should be required, that no one should be admitted to communion until he had made a credible profession of his faith, and that the local minister should be empowered to exclude from communion scandalous offenders; provision was also made for appeals from his

[1] Text (of Draft, 4 September 1660): *RB* I.ii.§105 (pp. 259–64). Text (of Declaration, as issued): *LJ* ix.179–82; *EHD* vii.365–70. Cf. *RB* I.ii.§107 (pp. 275 f).

decisions. They were granted the important point that an equal number of divines from either side should review the liturgy, the specific reference merely to the omission of obsolete expressions being dropped, thus widening the terms of reference. They would also have had a clause inserted against the reordination of those not episcopally ordained, but this they could not obtain. It will be seen that episcopal authority remained intact and that the Presbyterians' only substantial gain was in the matter of discipline at the parish level. The bishop retained his jurisdiction while the parish minister continued to rule his flock. Baxter welcomed the Declaration when it appeared, because to his mind parish discipline was vital, and he had feared that less would have been granted.[1]

Needless to say, some Churchmen thought that the Declaration conceded far too much, so that when the Presbyterians sought to have it given parliamentary sanction, they caused some consternation; Charles did nothing to stand by his Declaration or prevent Court influence from being used to defeat the measure in the Commons. His inaction was a piece of "negligence", as Pepys would have called it, which later he would be unable to retrieve. The mood and the moment for compromise soon passed. More power fell into the hands of the restored Churchmen. The election of the Cavalier House of Commons in the following year brought in men of harder outlook bent on wiping out the years since 1640 and enforcing a rigid conformity to the old Prayer Book and the old Church. The bishops, divided between Laudian claims on the one hand and claims for some Puritan latitude on the other, took refuge in the Commons' policy of the *status quo ante* and gave both Laudians and Presbyterians in effect the same answer to "order all in the old method".[2] The Commons added severities to their Bill of

[1] *RB* I.ii.§115. For a fuller discussion of the Worcester House concessions, see above, pp. 66 foll.

[2] Bosher 246; James Parker, *An Introduction to the History of the . . . Book of Common Prayer* (1877), p. ccxxii.

Conformity and neither King nor chancellor could achieve any modification that would have given a little elbow-room in which to exercise some judicious mercy in the spirit of the Declaration from Breda.[1] When the Act was passed Clarendon twice sought to frame a declaration by which some of those who scrupled conformity on the hard terms enforced by the Act might have been let in on easier terms, but he had to give way before the wrath of Sheldon who imperiously refused to have any tampering with a settlement now settled. A later declaration at Christmas 1662 was brought to nothing by opposition in the Commons when a new session opened in February 1663.[2] A Bill brought into the Lords in the same session with the same end of a limited indulgence to be exercised by the King likewise came to nothing,[3] and the Commons, unchecked, pursued their coercive measures against Nonconformity in the Conventicle Act —the Dutch called it "an Act for suppressing the worship of God"—of 1664 and the Five Miles Act of the following year.[4]

For a number of reasons the year 1667 was a favourable year for an attempt to undo the mischief done by these repressive measures. The Plague of 1665 and the Fire of London the following year had made a twofold impression on men's minds. They were apt to be read as divine judgments, and the heroic picture of Nonconformist ministers, although proscribed, continuing to serve the people in the plague-ridden city tended to create for them a favourable public opinion.[5] By contrast the reputation of the clergy suffered: "those two dreadfull callamities separated Ministers and

[1] C. A. Swainson, op. cit., 33, 44 f; G. R. Abernathy, Jr, "Clarendon and the Declaration of Indulgence", in *JEH* xi.59–64.

[2] 26 December 1662. Text: *EHD* viii.371–4. Cf. Bosher 270.

[3] February 1663. Text: W. D. Christie, *Life of Anthony Ashley Cooper* (1871), i. pp. lxxix ff (app. 6). Cf. *Bulletin* of the Institute of Historical Research, xxxii (1959), 183.

[4] Bate 45.

[5] E.g. [John Humfrey,] *Proposition for the Safety and Happiness of the Kingdom* (1667), 5.

people, not only in place, but Affection".[1] Although some of the clergy had continued to serve in the stricken city, it did not redound to their credit, perhaps because the number that fled was more taken note of.[2] Another misfortune that tended to make 1667 a favourable year was the trade depression. It would be too much to say that the trade of the country was in the hands of the Dissenters, but their major strength lay in the trading community, and from many quarters there were hints, tendentious no doubt but none the less effective, that persecution was having a depressing effect on trade.

This was also the year which had seen the disgrace of Clarendon. Whatever connection he may, or may not, have had with the famous "Code" that bears his name, his fall might well be a signal for reversing penal measures against Nonconformists that were becoming as unpopular as their supposed author. The appointment of Sir Orlando Bridgeman as Lord Keeper to replace Clarendon was equally welcome. A disgruntled commentator from Chester recorded that "the people are transported with joy upon the Lord Keeper's instalment into the ministry, and the Presbyterians big with expectation that their idol gods, their factious ministers, should be tolerated to prate in public".[3] Pepys too reports that "the Nonconformists are mighty high, and their meetings frequented and connived at; and they do expect to have their day now soon; for my Lord Buckingham is a declared friend of them, and even of the Quakers".[4]

We soon hear of efforts on behalf of the Nonconformists. Early in September a newsletter could report that "An

[1] Congreg. Hist. Soc. *Trans.*, iii.203, from B.M. Stowe MS. 186. Cf. *CSPD 1671*, 581.

[2] *RB* III.i.§6; John Worthington's *Diary*, ii.185 (Chetham Soc., Orig. Ser. 36) gives the names of clergy who continued to serve in the city.

[3] *CSPD 1667*, 457 (11 September 1667).

[4] Samuel Pepys, *Diary*, ed. H. B. Wheatley (1905), vii.228 f (21 December 1667).

Act is said to be preparing, against the meeting of Parliament [on 10 October] dispensing with the Act of Uniformity, and clearly against the Bishops' government".[1] A Bill was in fact prepared by Sir Robert Atkyns, whose sympathies are sufficiently indicated by the fact that he was later made Chief Baron of the Exchequer by William III. Thomas Barlow, afterwards Bishop of Lincoln, to whom we owe our knowledge of the contents, calls it the "Comprehensive Bill"; a word with a new meaning had come into the language. The main points of the Bill were, in words mostly borrowed from Barlow, that "Men only ordained by presbyters should be admitted to liveings"; in other words there was to be no reordination. The promoters of the Bill "would . . . have the word consent left out of the forme of subscription, and say only they assent". "They would not be tyed to read Common Prayer themselves, soe they provide one to do it." "They should subscribe the doctrine (not discipline) of the Christian faith." (The reference here is to the Elizabethan Act, 13 Eliz. cap. 12, which at this time was apparently held to waive the 34th, 35th, 36th, and part of the 20th Articles, the 36th being the only Article referring to bishops. This shortened form of the Articles had already found a place in the abortive Bill in the House of Lords in 1663, and it would recur on many subsequent occasions.) Kneeling at the Sacrament, the use of the cross in Baptism, and wearing the surplice were to be made optional and renunciation of the Solemn League and Covenant, as required in the Act of Uniformity, was to be laid aside.[2] The most obvious characteristic of this proposed measure is

[1] *CSPD 1667*, 437.

[2] Text: Herbert Thorndike, *Theological Works*, v (1854) 302 f, from a MS. by Thomas Barlow in Bodleian Library (traced by Mr J. W. H. Nankivell) as B. 14, 15 Linc. See Norman Sykes, *From Sheldon to Secker* (1959), 72 n. Other comments by Barlow in what follows are quoted from the same MS., for a sight of which I am indebted to the Bodleian Library, Oxford. Much, but not all, of this MS. is quoted in Thorndike's *Works*, v.301–8.

its optimism: it might even be said that it was a flagrant example of "too far and too fast". The provision that a minister need not himself read Common Prayer was chiefly intended to allow Congregationals, who were not ordinarily regarded as capable of being comprehended within the Church, to accept the measure.[1]

It was assigned to Colonel Birch, a man of rugged eloquence and a Presbyterian, to introduce the measure into the House of Commons. But, as Barlow reports, "it was never brought into the House though Col. Birch intended it, and once faintly offered it but (despairing of success) sat down". It was evident that something was already known of what he was going to propose. Conservative opinion was alarmed, and Colonel Birch thought it better not to risk a rebuff.

Alarmed though they were, even conservatives felt that some concessions might have to be made and that it might be better to offer less radical concessions of their own. Barlow had his information about the Atkyns Bill by 19 November. About the same time the Lord Keeper, Bridgeman, was employing Sir John Baber (whom we shall meet again in like employment hereafter), "to use his industry to get information what would satisfy the Presbyterians". Sir John consulted Thomas Manton, accounted the leader of the Presbyterians, and he, in January 1668, wrote to Baxter.[2] Baxter was under no illusions about such tentatives. Asked what would satisfy, he pointed out that there were "degrees of satisfaction". "1. If they will take in all Orthodox, Peaceable, Worthy Ministers, the Terms must be the larger. 2. If they will take in but the greater part, somewhat less and harder Terms may do it."[3]

A series of conferences took place between John Wilkins, soon to be Bishop of Chester, and Hezekiah Burton, the Lord Keeper's chaplain, on the one hand and the Presby-

[1] *RB* III.i.§256 (pp. 113, 130 f).

[2] *RB* III.i.§62; D.W.L. MSS. 59.11. 214–15.

[3] *RB* III.i.§62.

terians Thomas Manton, William Bates, and Richard Baxter on the other. The discussions were based on proposals drawn up by Wilkins.[1] He had realized that wide toleration within the Church, such as the Atkyns Bill proposed, would stand small chance of success. He had therefore separated the two questions of tolerating Independents and other Separatists outside the Church and comprehending Presbyterians inside, and had drawn up distinct sets of proposals for comprehension and for indulgence. When the three Presbyterians found themselves confronted with this ingenious cutting of the Gordian knot, they held that they must confine their attention to comprehension, and left it to Baxter to acquaint Dr John Owen "with the substance of the business" so that the Independents could discuss the indulgence proposals and not complain of neglect.[2]

In the proposals for comprehension, instead of sacrificing any of the Thirty-nine Articles, Wilkins proposed a simple "declaration approving of the doctrine, worship and government" of the Established Church; he was willing that kneeling at the Sacrament, the cross in Baptism, and bowing at the name of Jesus should be "left indifferent or . . . taken away", and even favoured a recommendation that only in the event of a review of the liturgy and canons should there be an undertaking constantly to read the liturgy. Baxter saw to it that considerable attention was paid to the liturgy and canons there and then, with considerable effect upon the final outcome. But the greatest difficulty arose over a formula for the admission to the Church of those who had presbyteral but not episcopal ordination. The mildly worded form proposed by Wilkins, "Take thou Authority to Preach the Word of God and to Minister the Sacraments in any Congregation of the Church of England . . .", smacked too much of reordination for Baxter; only after considerable

[1] Wilkins proposals: Text: *RB* III.i.§66; *Baxter Treatises: a Catalogue* (1959), ed. R. Thomas, 13.

[2] *RB* III.i.§67; D.W.L. MSS. 59.2.273.

disagreement about a compromise was the difficulty resolved by the insertion of the word "legal", making the formula run "Take thou legal authority, etc."—a recommendation of Sir Matthew Hale, to whom as Lord Chief Baron was assigned the task of framing the complicated terms of the agreement into a Parliamentary Bill, which had to include, besides the points already mentioned, reference to many individual reforms in liturgy and canons.[1]

While these negotiations were proceeding, Dr Owen and the Congregational brethren had not been idle. Even before he had been notified by Baxter of the Wilkins proposals, Owen may have obtained the goodwill of the Duke of Buckingham for promoting a Toleration Bill in Parliament. Owen and his friends ignored the Wilkins proposals for indulgence. Instead, they prepared separate proposals of their own which followed closely on the lines of the *Humble Petition and Advice* of 1657 and which proposed liberty of worship for those who were strictly orthodox while denying it to Papists and those who could be listed as blasphemous or licentious.[2] By contrast the Wilkins proposals for indulgence say nothing about orthodoxy, with which Owen's proposals were almost wholly concerned, but, as originally drafted, require the registration of teachers and members of congregations, exclude the indulged from public office (while making them subject to fines for offices of burden), and see to it that they do not escape the payment of public dues to the parish. There was nothing in them to exclude Roman Catholics from sharing in the indulgence.[3]

How long the negotiations between Wilkins and the Presbyterians took is not known, but it is unlikely that the final agreement was ready by the time that Parliament met on 10 February, though something of their nature may have

[1] Wilkins proposals in their final form: Text: H. Thorndike, *Theol. Works*, v. 304 f, from Bodleian MS. B. 14, 15 Linc.

[2] Text: H. Thorndike, *Theol. Works*, v.308.

[3] Text: *RB* III.i.§66.

leaked out by then. The Congregational proposals, on the other hand, may very well have been ready by that date; certainly Barlow had a copy of them only a few days later, on 20 February. In Durham, too, a few days after the opening of Parliament, there was a report that "the Duke of Buckingham is the great favourite and his cabal are Major Wildman, Dr Owen and the rest of the fraternity, so that some say we are carried in Oliver's basket. The Act of Comprehension, which the Lord Keeper promotes, will destroy the Act of Uniformity, for it will dispense with cross, surplice and ring in marriage."[1] This is a garbled version; we get something like the truth in Barlow's report that "The Bill they intend against that day [the opening of Parliament] was onely the King's Declaration from Breda which they desired might be put into an Act", which clearly points to the Owen and Buckingham proposals. When Parliament met, Barlow continues, "the King came to the House and in his speech desired a supply of money, and that they would find some way to unite his subjects in matter of Religion (this was said in favour of the Comprehension Bill), but the Commons that morning (before the King came to the House) upon relation of the insolent carryage and conventicles of non-conformists and sectaries in each county, voted the King should be desired (not to give indulgence but) to send out a proclamation to put the laws against the non-conformists into execution". The *Journals* of the House confirm this vote.[2] Pepys adds the lurid detail that "it was moved"—he does not say that it was carried—"that, if any people had a mind to bring any new laws into the House about religion, they might come, as a proposer of new laws did in Athens, with ropes about their necks".[3] It is clear that what nettled

[1] *CSPD 1667–8*, 238 (18 February 1667/8).

[2] *CJ* ix. 44 (10 February 1667/8). In this chapter, references to the *Journals of the House of Commons* (*CJ*) and to the *Journals of the House of Lords* (*LJ*) will normally only be given where there is no reference in the text to the date of the proceedings referred to.

[3] Pepys, *Diary* vii. 292 (10 February 1667/8).

the Commons chiefly was the "insolent carriage" of proposing wide motions of toleration such as those made by the Independents, not a Bill for comprehension, which might indeed go hand in hand with a stricter control of conventicles. It is equally clear, on the other hand, that the reference in the King's speech was to the Wilkins proposals for comprehension. But the noticeable difference in tone between the King's speech and the Commons' debate made it look as if the Commons had gone out of their way to anticipate and veto the King's proposal before it was made.[1]

Be that as it may, the Commons held to their point and the King was obliged, after further pressure, to issue on 10 March a proclamation to enforce the laws against conventicles, a surrender that made Pepys speak of "a negligent prince and a mad parliament".[2] The Commons went ahead also with a new and severer Conventicle Bill to replace the Act of 1664, which would expire later in the year.[3] Increased Dissenting activity in many parts of the country doubtless contributed to this severity. How far it may adversely have affected the prospects of the Wilkins proposals for comprehension is another matter.

When the passage in the King's speech relating to comprehension came to be considered in the Commons on 8 April, the House was not wholly hostile and it was moved "that his Majesty be desired to send for such persons as he shall think fit, to make proposals to him, in order to uniting his Protestant subjects". Although this was lost by 176 votes to 70, a desultory debate followed on concessions that might be made, such as removing the requirement of "assent and consent" and the abjuration of the Solemn League and Covenant and remitting some of the ceremonies objected

[1] *RB* III.i.§81; John Milward, *Diary*, ed. Caroline Robbins (1938), 179 (6 February 1667/8); Burnet, *HOT* i.468 (=i.260).

[2] Pepys, *Diary* viii.1 (1 May 1668).

[3] According to Pepys (*Diary* viii. 74) the 1664 Conventicle Act expired on 11 August 1668.

to.[1] It does not seem therefore that comprehension aroused anything like the antagonism that indulgence had done. Nevertheless the adverse vote closed the door against the Wilkins proposals, and its size may reflect something of the rancour felt against indulgence.

It is probable that until this adverse vote on 8 April it was still hoped that the Wilkins proposals would get a hearing, for in the proposals for indulgence a noticeable alteration was made. This was the insertion of a clause exacting a payment of from 40*s.* to 10*s.* a year from each head of a family claiming indulgence and from 8*s.* to 2*s.* from others, the money so raised being assigned to the building of churches in London.[2] The similarity between this and a clause in the savage Bill against conventicles then going forward in the Commons strongly suggests an endeavour to make the Wilkins proposals more acceptable to a House madly set upon its furious and unpopular Conventicle Bill. But the Wilkins Bill never got a hearing even with this drastic alteration.

Towards the end of the Session Pepys notes that the King had a "great opportunity of making himself popular by stopping this Act against Conventicles", and when the Session ended, on 9 May, he detailed the various Bills that received the royal assent and noted with a certain complacent glee "the Bill against Conventicles being none of them".[3]

The Session had ended without the Conventicle Act, but it had ended, too, without any progress towards either indulgence or comprehension. Baxter put the blame for this failure upon the "prelates"; Manton, on the other hand, saw Dr John Owen, the foremost of the Independents, as the villain of the piece. Doubtless the Wilkins proposals would

[1] John Milward, *Diary*, 248 f (8 April 1668) and 214–22 (11 March 1668); Andrew Marvell, *Poems and Letters*, ed. H. M. Margoliouth (1927), ii. 71; A. Grey, *Debates* (1763), i.126–32; *CJ* ix.77. Milward and Marvell give the vote as 167 to 70; *CJ* and Grey as 176 to 70.

[2] H. Thorndike, *Theol. Works*, v.305.

[3] Pepys, *Diary* viii.3 (3 May 1668), 9 (9 May 1668).

never have gone through with the goodwill of the bishops; certainly George Morley, Baxter's old adversary, now Bishop of Winchester, would strenuously have opposed them. So too would Archbishop Sheldon. But differences amongst the Dissenters themselves may have contributed to the outcome. Manton certainly thought so and in a letter to Baxter of 26 September [1668] complained that "the comprehension thought of by some and endeavoured by our friends in Court was wholly frustrated by Dr Owen's proposal of a toleration which was entertained and carried on by other persons, and those opposite to them who had of their own inclination interested themselves in the business of comprehension for our sakes".[1]

It would have been better if more had been done to coordinate the two points of view beforehand. It was something like this that Dr Owen now proposed belatedly, though his purpose was rather different from a simple coordination. It reveals somewhat unexpected divisions amongst the Presbyterians. Owen paid Manton a visit to defend himself against aspersions that had been cast upon him by Manton for his part in promoting indulgence. He took with him a prominent Presbyterian, Samuel Annesley. Owen did not deny the most material point, that he opposed comprehension, and said quite bluntly: "Comprehension would neither do the King's business nor ours". To convince Manton of this would seem to have been the real object of his visit, for he proposed the holding of a small meeting when, in the words of Manton to Baxter, "the matter to be debated" should be "whether the comprehension should be propounded by us [i.e. Manton, Baxter, and their friends], but expressly asserting that this should not be handled as a difference between us and the Independents but between us and our [Presbyterian] brethren". It becomes clear now why Owen had taken Samuel Annesley with him. Ever since the passing of the Five Mile Act two parties had been forming

[1] D.W.L. MSS. 59.2.273.

within English Presbyterianism, the one prepared to go all the lengths they conscientiously could to fall in with the Church, and the other, of which Annesley was becoming the acknowledged head, prepared to go with the Independents at least in this: that they no longer desired or saw any hope in comprehension, and sought solely to secure an adequate toleration outside the Established Church.[1]

Baxter had seen this drift towards Independency equally clearly and had resented it. His words are characteristically pungent:

> I think I ought to give Posterity notice, that by the Prelatist's (*sic*) malice, and unreasonable implacable Violence, Independency and Separation got greater advantages, against Presbytery, and all setled accidental extrinsick order and means of Concord, than ever it had in these Kingdoms since the World began. . . . And Presbyterians were forced to forbear all Exercise of their way: they durst not meet together (Synodically) unless in a Goal. . . . So that their Congregations were, through necessity, just of Independent and Separating Shape, and outward Practice, though not upon the same Principles. . . .[2]

It is not hard to see why Owen thought comprehension would not do the Dissenters' business. It would be hard to think of a scheme of comprehension in which the Independents would have been comfortable; and Owen clearly believed that eventually the Presbyterians would have to take the same road. But why comprehension would not do the King's business he does not say. The King's business might have been, as it would have been with Shaftesbury, that indulgence would make for peace and a revival of trade. But if that was the King's business, it is clear that the Wilkins proposals for comprehension and indulgence would have done the work equally well. Doubtless part of the objection to these proposals was that they would have strengthened the Church at the expense of the sects by drawing into the

[1] *RB* III.i.§21.

[2] *RB* III.i.§96. Cf. *CSPD 1671*, 496 (21 September 1671), and Philip Henry, *Diary*, ed. M. H. Lee (1882), p. 250.

Church the Presbyterians, the largest of the Dissenting bodies. Owen might dislike this, but why should the King? But this Owen was careful not to say. There is but one key that fits the lock: the King's business was emancipation of Roman Catholics. Sir John Baber had intimated as much when the Wilkins discussions were first mooted,[1] and the Wilkins proposals for indulgence were so drawn that the Roman Catholics could well have crept in under an umbrella ostensibly intended for others. Owen was careful not to say anything of this, and indeed his own proposals for toleration were so drawn as specifically to exclude Papists. But the irony of the situation was not lost upon observers. Baxter sums it up with some asperity: "The Papists must have the Liberty of exercising their Religion". For various reasons the State, the Bishops, and the Papists "must not be seen" in the business. "Therefore it must be done by the Nonconformists. The Presbyterians are sour and will not. The Independent Leaders are for the doing it, but they dare not say so, for fear of becoming odious with the Presbyterians, Parliament and People."[2] The King's Roman Catholic inclinations would continue to bedevil the hopes of comprehension.

Owen proved a good prophet when he said that the King's business would be done by indulgence. We must not attempt to pursue the ups and downs of the debate behind the scenes even if the information were available with which to do it. Sheldon's alarm at the resurgence of Nonconformity led him in 1669 to gather statistics to impress Parliament with the need for resolute action.[3] His success lay in a new Conventicle Act in 1670, though it is noticeable as a sign of the changing climate of opinion that its provisions were hotly contested and the Lords were able to soften some of its severer terms.[4]

[1] *RB* III.i.§62. [2] *RB* III.i.§86.

[3] G. Lyon Turner, *Original Records of Early Nonconformity* (1911–14), iii.72 f.

[4] Bate 64–7.

Before the session had opened, Manton thought that he saw new hopes for a move in the direction of comprehension, but found that Baxter held back.[1] A year later, Baxter himself was writing to conforming ministers urging upon them the importance of comprehension.[2] In the interval between Manton's renewed interest and Baxter's the situation had radically changed and the chances of comprehension were sinking. Perhaps Baxter had sensed a change that was to become painfully apparent only later.

Be that as it may, the change was principally the outcome of the Secret Treaty of Dover, into which Charles had entered in June 1670, and by which he had given his pledge to Louis XIV to support the French in a war with the Dutch and at some convenient date to declare himself a Roman Catholic. Both these pledges contributed to the King's interest in indulgence to the exclusion of comprehension or coercion. Comprehension of Dissenters by itself could be of no service to Roman Catholics, whereas in an indulgence they could be given a useful if not unduly prominent share. In pledging himself to a war with the Dutch the King knew, or was soon to know, that such a war was going to be very unpopular with the trading community from which the Dissenters were chiefly drawn, especially in London where their greatest strength lay. To quieten the Dissenters the grant of indulgence might be a quick and effective bribe.

It is not until 1671 that we come upon definite signs that the mind of the Government was working in this direction. Then at the beginning of September we hear that "several from the King from time to time have met with Dr Owen".[3] We know what measures Owen would support. Soon afterwards we hear of Court agents reporting to Sir Joseph Williamson (Arlington's assistant at the Home Office) on

[1] D.W.L. MSS. 59.4.204 (Baxter to Manton, 17 February [1669/70]); 59.6.108 (Baxter to Manton, 25 February [1669/70]).

[2] *RB* III.i.§189.

[3] *CSPD 1671*, 264 (1 September 1671).

the outlook amongst the Dissenters. Not very surprisingly Williamson's chief difficulties lay in reconciling the two factions amongst the Presbyterians whom he christened "Dons" and "Ducklings": the Dons, our old friends Manton, Bates, Baxter, and others, the old-fashioned Presbyterians still hoping for comprehension and bitterly opposed to being used as stalking-horses for Popery; the Ducklings, the younger and more virulent Presbyterians, of whom Annesley was the leader, who wanted nothing better than a wide toleration outside the Church, shared with the Independents and if need be with Papists too.[1] On 21 September Williamson notes ruefully that "if the Savoy business [i.e. comprehension] had taken effect, there had not been a fanatic in England". As things were, however, "the people grow more fanatic; all the Presbyterians are growing to Independents and so must the teachers".[2] He also notes a rapprochement between Arlington and Shaftesbury, and as Shaftesbury had recently drawn up a report in favour of indulgence it is easy to see which way the wind was blowing.[3] On 2 November he notes ruefully that "the fanatics have no agreement among themselves".[4] Then on 9 November we hear from various sources of deputations both from the Dons and from the Ducklings separately received by the King. Sir John Baber "introduced Dr Manton and some with him [Dons]; Mr Ennis [Innes or Inness] a Scotch Non-conformist, by Sir Robert Murray introduced, Mr Whittakers, Dr Annesley, Mr Watson, and Mr Vincent's [Ducklings]". The King told them "he was sensible of their straits and would endeavour their enlargement. . . . He said he would not willingly be persecuted himself for his own religion, so neither did he like to persecute others for theirs." "He hoped erelong to stand on his own legs, and then they should see how much

[1] *CSPD 1671–2*, 28 (13 December 1671).

[2] *CSPD 1671*, 496 (21 September 1671).

[3] W. D. Christie, *Life of . . . Shaftesbury*, ii. pp. v-xi (app. 1).

[4] *CSPD 1671*, 554 (2 November 1671).

he was against it."[1] Later, on 13 December, Williamson is still in difficulties "begetting a better understanding between these Presbyterian ministers, who have been estranged to one another of late", and the Ducklings, "being led to the King, gave great jealousy to" the Dons.[2]

Inevitably it was the Ducklings who were gaining ground and whose policy found favour at Court. The upshot was the famous Declaration of Indulgence in March 1672, issued on the eve of the King's shameful war with the Dutch.[3] The Roman Catholics, as Baxter learnt without surprise, had their share in the toleration. By whatever intrigues it had been achieved, even the Dons (Baxter doubtless excepted) had been brought to accept indulgence instead of comprehension, though their reluctance and hesitations are shown by the sequel. On 28 March the "Nonconformist ministers thanked the King; in the morning Dr Owen, Griffiths, Palmer [Independents]; in the afternoon, Manton, Bates, Jacombe, Seyman [Seaman]" (all Presbyterians and all Dons).[4] Dr Owen had no qualms about addressing, and the form of his address is known.[5] Not so the Dons, and the form of their address is not known; they suffered from indecision right up to the last minute, so that "when they could not come to Agreement about their Form, the Lord Arlington Introduced them to a verbal Extemporate Thanksgiving, and so", says Baxter, "their Difference was ended as to that".[6]

The reluctance of these Presbyterians lay not only in their disappointment that there was no comprehension but in their unwillingness to acquiesce in the doubtful legality of the King's assumed power to dispense with laws passed in

[1] *RB* III.i.§191; Philip Henry, *Diary*, 243; *CSPD 1671*, 562 (11 November 1671).

[2] *CSPD 1671–2*, 28 f (13 December 1671).

[3] Declaration of Indulgence: Text: *EHD* viii.287 f.

[4] *CSPD 1671–2*, 609 (28 March 1672).

[5] Text: *Gentleman's Magazine* (1761), 253.

[6] *RB* III.i.§214.

Parliament and the fear that the end was not their good but the promotion of Popery. By accepting licences under the Indulgence and still more by returning thanks they were in danger of compromising their principles. "The sectarian chiefs", as the Venetian Secretary in England noted in a dispatch home, "scandalously maintain that it is a weakness on the part of the nonconformists to thank the King for his grant of liberty of conscience, as they thereby approve the authority he thus arrogates to himself, in violation of the oath taken by him to observe the laws." This was on 10 June. He also notes that "one and all" suspect "the king of an intention to revive Popery as they call the Roman Catholic Religion". They also saw in this the hand of the Duke of York, the King's brother and heir to the throne. As a consequence it was noted that the Presbyterians were "preparing for a coalition with the bishops for self defence", hints that foreshadow coming events.[1]

For the moment, however, it was indulgence triumphant, with hopes of comprehension receding farther and farther into the background. Presbyterians and Independents alike, all over the country, hastened to take out their licences—even Baxter, though somewhat tardily in October.[2] Philip Henry's comment, away in Shropshire, was "the Presbyterians glad, the Independents very glad, the Papists triumphant".[3] No wonder that Stillingfleet, writing in 1680, dated the Presbyterian separation from the granting of the famous Indulgence;[4] though, as we have seen, the conversion of some of the Presbyterians slowly into separatists like the Independents can be dated back to the formation of Williamson's Ducklings about the time of the Five Miles Act, when they divided over the question of submitting to the requirements of that Act. The lapsing of the first Conventicle Act,

[1] *CSP Ven. 1671–2*, 225 (10 June 1672).

[2] F. J. Powicke, *Reverend Richard Baxter under the Cross* (1927), 71 f.

[3] Philip Henry, *Diary*, ed. Lee, 250.

[4] E. Stillingfleet, *Unreasonableness of Separation* (1681), p. xxiii.

also, in August 1668, saw many of them emerging into the light of day as leaders of separatist congregations, while the new Conventicle Act of 1670 forced into prominent attention many new-model Presbyterians ready to battle out their separation with or without the connivance of the authorities, like any other separatists.

The Indulgence may have set the seal on the separation though it did not create it. Though its benefits were seized with alacrity, it gave little satisfaction. The Indulgence was seen as a deceitful means of promoting the Popish interests of the King and the Duke of York. Moreover the war with the Dutch was going badly and a party was forming that would certainly make trouble when Parliament met. It would put up a staunch fight against any insidious Popish advances, and, given Presbyterian support, which was readily forthcoming, it would promise Dissenters a liberty as great as any obtained under the Indulgence and might even find means for a modest measure of comprehension. This would have the merit of being a liberty constitutionally sanctioned by Parliament and not dependent on the pleasure and doubtful prerogative of the King.[1]

Parliament was not allowed to meet until the King was once again desperate for money. When it finally had to meet, on 4 February 1673, the King was clearly in for a very rough passage. The Commons promptly resolved on a petition to the King to revoke his Indulgence and with it they coupled a resolve to introduce a Bill for the ease of Dissenters.[2] They made it plain that there would be no money until the Declaration was cancelled. Twist and turn as he might, the King had to give way and on 8 March he surrendered ignominiously and cancelled the Declaration. Even then it was still no money until suspected Roman Catholics near the throne, notably the Duke of York and

[1] K. H. D. Haley, *William of Orange and the English Opposition, 1672–4* (1953), 93–6.

[2] *CJ* ix.251, 253 (10 and 14 February 1672/3).

Clifford, were driven from office by the passing of the Test Act, which amongst other provisions exacted the taking of the Sacrament in the Church of England: a provision which the Presbyterians supported, for it had no terrors for them as it had for the Roman Catholics.

Unluckily the Commons did not take the same precaution to secure the safe passage of their "Bill for the Ease of His Majesty's Protestant Subjects, Dissenters from the Church of England". The heads of this Bill had been introduced into the Commons on 27 February after a committee of the whole House had met on several occasions to consider what should go into it. As originally drafted the main provision was that freedom from penalties and permission to worship in their own way should be granted if ministers presented themselves before two Justices of the Peace, took the oaths of supremacy and obedience, declared their assent to those of the Thirty-nine Articles that were concerned with doctrine (13 Eliz. cap. 12), and made a declaration that it was not lawful to take up arms against the King. Liberty thus obtained had to be confirmed at the next quarter-sessions. Amongst other provisions two parts of the Act of Uniformity were to be repealed: the clause enforcing assent and consent to the Prayer Book, and the part clause requiring, with the abjuration of the Solemn League and Covenant, the assertion that it was an unlawful oath for other people.[1] In making the Act of Uniformity by these concessions a little less burdensome, it made comprehension of Presbyterians within the Church a little easier.

This Bill, given a first reading on 6 March, was sent up to the Lords after a third reading on 19 March. It came back from the Lords on Good Friday, 28 March: the King had already announced his intention to adjourn the session before Easter, that is to say before 30 March. It returned with a number of amendments, most of which the Commons

[1] Heads of Bill: *CJ* ix.259. Text: Bodleian Library MSS. Tanner, 43. foll. 192–4.

found unpalatable. The most drastic amendment proposed to replace the main provision of the Bill by a power put into the hands of the King to issue licences for indulging Dissenters.[1] This was not only a nicely calculated affront to the Commons, who had just compelled the King to cancel his Indulgence because they disapproved of his dispensing power; a much more serious objection was that it gave the King *carte blanche* to issue dispensations in such a way that Roman Catholics might benefit. This of course was not explicitly stated, but the Commons were quick to perceive the snake in the grass.[2]

The next twenty-four hours after the Commons received the Bill back on 28 March were filled with feverish activity in a last-minute attempt to come to some agreement between the two Houses. But the Lords were obdurate and after a morning (Saturday 29 March) spent in fruitless conference, the Commons met once more to decide whether to acknowledge that half a loaf, and that of black bread, was better than no bread at all, and so get the Bill, though woefully mangled, through before the adjournment. Even this much could not be voted upon without a debate, which gave those who had never liked the measure the opportunity to try and talk it out. At length candles were called for. Whether they should be granted was, as customarily, put to the vote. Candles were refused, which had much the same effect as in our day applying the guillotine. The debate had to be wound up. The Lords' amendments were to be voted on one by one. They had just begun on the first amendment: "The question being put, To agree with the Lords in their first amendment;——" (The record breaks off.) Black Rod was standing at the door. The King was waiting in another place to adjourn the session. The faithful Commons must file out to the Bar of the House of Lords to be adjourned until 20 October.[3] The Bill was dead.

[1] Text: Bodleian Library MSS. Tanner, 43. foll. 189–90.

[2] *CJ* ix.279 f (28 March); *LJ* xiii.579 f (29 March).

[3] There is a strong presumption that the Lords' amendments were going to be accepted. A report from a later date expressly asserts as

The Commons had come within minutes of a momentous decision. On the same Saturday night that saw the Bill talked out, Lord Conway was writing in a letter reporting the debacle:

> The Parliament is to-night adjourned till 20 Oct. . . . but the bill for the Dissenters is not passed, the Lords and Commons having disputed several points until it was too late, so that the Presbyterians are left without either law or declaration, and will, it may be, have time and reason enough to repent their fierceness against the King.[1]

Although the Indulgence had been cancelled, ministers and meetings still had their licences. But also the Conventicle Act was still on the Statute Book, and magistrates who refused to put its provisions into operation could be mulcted in a hundred-pound fine. No wonder Sir Joseph Williamson received applications from magistrates for guidance in this Gilbertian situation. No wonder too that an attempt was made in his office to draw up general instructions advising magistrates to follow the London example of giving Dissenters as little disturbance as possible.[2] For some reason it was thought inadvisable to issue any such instructions, and so the next two years remained a period of piebald persecution, which, as Baxter summed it up, left the Dissenters "to the Storm of all their severe Laws, which some Country Justices rigorously executed, but the most forbore".[3]

Churchmen were for the most part relieved that the Commons' Bill had failed, but some of them were uneasy and sensed that matters could not rest as they were. Perhaps Bishop Morley's reaction was not untypical when he wrote

---

much (Morrice MS. Q, 155 f; cf. A. Grey, *Debates* [1763], ii. 180). Technically, as the session was only adjourned, the Bill could have been taken up again when the session was resumed, but it never was.

[1] *CSPD 1673*, 101.

[2] *CSPD 1673*, 367 (13 June); Bate 133–8. Cf. letter of the Earl of Anglesey, *CSPD 1680–1*, 45 f.

[3] *RB* III.i.§230. Cf. I. G. Philip, "Letters of Edmund Bohun" (Congreg. Hist. Soc. *Trans.*, xviii.125–30); *CSPD 1673–5*, 532, 551.

that he "was very glad . . . that the aforesaid Bill miscarried, which would have been an establishment of schism by a law, and that would have been much worse than any connivance, nay than any toleration can be by the king's dispensation and declaration only".[1] The Lords' amendments had shown something like the same reaction. As in 1667, however, the failure of a radical measure left a vacuum, and there were Churchmen who felt that it must somehow be filled lest worse befall. Morley certainly thought so, and, as on the earlier occasion, an effort was made to sound Baxter on the possibility of a compromise. Late in 1673 the Earl of Orrery approached Baxter with a request to draw up briefly terms that would satisfy the Nonconformists "so far as to unite us all against Popery". Baxter was understandably despondent when he heard that Morley was one of the chief movers and went out of his way to tell the Earl that "were but Dr Stillingfleet, Dr Tillotson, or any such moderate Men appointed to consult with two or three of us, on the safe and needful terms of Concord, we should agree in a Week's time".[2] Nevertheless he did what was asked and sent his proposals. Later he received them back with adverse comments scribbled in the margins, which he easily recognized as in the hand of Morley. As Baxter put it, they made him "see that all his Professions for *Abatement*, and *Concord*, were deceitful Snares, and that he intended no such thing at all".[3]

Despite this unfruitful outcome, Morley was not discouraged. Early in 1674 there was a move to bring in a Bill on similar lines to that which had been lost in 1673.[4] Morley is

[1] Norman Sykes, *From Sheldon to Secker* (1959), 78, from Tanner MS. 42. fol. 7.

[2] *RB* III.i.§256.

[3] Ibid. If Morley's incomprehension was characteristic of the man, so too was Baxter's rejoinder. Although he had no "hopes of Agreement with the Author", he argumentatively answered his comments one by one in a document that runs to twenty-seven closely printed folio pages (ibid., pp. 113–40).

[4] *RB* III.i.§257.

credited with having prevented its introduction. Instead he framed a measure of his own, which he called "an Act for composing differences in religion and inviting sober and peaceably minded Dissenters into the service of the Church".[1] All it did was to repeal the same two requirements of the Act of Uniformity as were to have been repealed in the 1673 Bill, namely those concerning assent and consent to the Book of Common Prayer and the renunciation of the Covenant.[2] Morley's Bill was introduced into the House of Lords, where it received a first reading on 13 February and a second reading on the 19th. It was down for the committee stage on the 25th, but Parliament was precipitately prorogued on the 24th. The slaughter of this innocent seems not to have been greatly regretted, certainly not by Baxter, whose verdict was that it "would have been but a Cunning Snare to make us more remediless and do no good".[3]

In the manoeuvrings that preceded the Parliamentary Session that opened on 13 April 1675 there appeared another example of the now familiar pattern of a radical measure on the Dissenters' behalf countered by an attempt to come to terms with the Presbyterians who still hoped for comprehension. The radical measure on this occasion was planned by the Roman Catholic Duke of York, who perhaps as much as anyone had suffered from the vacillation and weakness of the Crown. Charles had capitulated to Parliament over the Indulgence that gave some measure of freedom to Roman Catholics as well as to Dissenters. By the Test Act the King's chief minister had been driven from office and the Duke of York himself had been driven from both his seat on the Privy Council and his post at the Admiralty; and now his right to the succession was being challenged because he was a Roman Catholic. The Duke probably thought, as Shaftes-

[1] Text (in part): H.M.C., 9th Report, House of Lords Papers, ii.44 (no. 170).

[2] The printer of the *Reliquiae* (*RB* III.i.§257 [p. 140]) has made this into "Renunciation of the Government"!

[3] *RB* III.i.§257.

bury had thought, that the King should not have surrendered over the Indulgence, but he could see, too, that the opposition in the Commons had gained strength from the adherence of the very people who had stood to gain most from the Indulgence—the Dissenters. They were a power to be reckoned with. Like the King, he may have believed that they outnumbered the Churchmen; perhaps amongst moneyed men in London they did.[1] At all events the Duke appreciated that they could be powerful allies and formulated the policy of enlisting Dissenting support. Once won over, such support might secure his succession to the throne and might even so far defeat the Test Act as to restore him to his post at the Admiralty and his seat on the Council.[2] In return he would persuade the King to issue a new Declaration of Indulgence and dissolve Parliament in the expectation that new elections would bring in men more favourable to toleration, and in the assurance that in any case the anti-Popery opposition would be deprived of Dissenting support.[3]

The furthest the Duke got with this promising policy was to persuade the King to issue a pardon to Dissenters in Bristol where the bishop, the embittered Guy Carleton, had been making trouble.[4] About the same time we hear of a report that "the Presbyterians . . . are gaining ground and tomorrow their leader will present a petition to the duke for a general pardon for all transgressions in matters of religion. The Independents also petition to be included in this pardon and the one who is to draw up the proclamation tells me that he hopes so to extend it that in many cases it may be interpreted in favour of the Catholics. If the King agrees to grant this favour he will bargain with the Presbyterians and

[1] *CSP Ven. 1673–5*, 354, 367; *EHD* viii. 412; H.M.C., 11th. Report, app., part 14.

[2] *CSP Ven. 1673–5*, 316.

[3] *CSP Ven. 1673–5*, 243, 327; A. Browning, *Thomas Osborne, Earl of Danby* (1951), i.150; H.M.C. Portland Papers, iii.348 (4 January 1657).

[4] *CSP Ven. 1673–5*, 324, 326 f: *Records of . . . Broadmead, Bristol* (Hanserd Knollys Soc., 1847), 214 foll.

Independents that they will oppose all innovations and leave the question of the succession at rest."[1]

The pardon to Bristol Dissenters and the talk of a petition and a new Indulgence was in November and December 1674. The next we hear is, at the end of December, that the proclamation is being postponed.[2] The reason was that Thomas Osborne, Earl of Danby—a staunch Churchman, who had succeeded the Roman Catholic Clifford as the King's chief adviser—when he heard of the Duke's scheme, warned Charles to be very wary. On his advice, at the end of October, the King had invited certain of the bishops to London to advise him on the religious question.[3] "With the remedy in the hands of the bishops themselves, the blame will fall on them", wrote one observer.[4] So when we hear late in December that the proclamation designed by the Duke for Indulgence was being postponed, the reason given was that it was best to await the report soon to be issued by the bishops. If the Duke's scheme had no other result, it stimulated the bishops to delay their report no longer. Their hardest words were for the Roman Catholics, four clauses being devoted to them against one on the Dissenters.[5] They asked for no new legislation, but only that existing legislation should be put into force; so too in the case of the Dissenters, but in addition they demanded that the King should assert that "his licences were long since recalled and that they have no authority or encouragement from him". It was cold comfort to the Duke and his schemes that a significant little note was appended that the King would be glad if "some

[1] *CSP Ven. 1673–5*, 318 f (7 December [=27 November] 1674). It was noticed in Dissenting pamphlets of the time that there was an unusual readiness for toleration of Roman Catholics (E. Stillingfleet, *Unreasonableness of Separation* [1681], p. xxv).

[2] *CSP Ven. 1673–5*, 331 (4 January 1675 [= 24 December 1674]).

[3] A. Browning, *Thomas Osborne*, i.147.

[4] *CSP Ven. 1673–5*, 317.

[5] *CSP Ven.* 337 (11 [=1] January 1675), 354 (8 February [=29 January] 1675); *CSPD 1673–5*, 548 ff.

little door of hope to dissenting Protestants . . . could be found out".[1]

Whether under the stimulus of this clause or for more sinister reasons, and soon after orders had been given in accordance with the bishops' advice in February, Bishops Ward and Morley, "the turbulent Salisbury and his follower Winchester",[2] who had been two of the episcopal advisers, set Tillotson and Stillingfleet on discovering what acceptable terms of union could be reached with the Presbyterians. Morley, if he would make few concessions, was not above taking a hint: the emissaries were the same as Baxter had suggested in his letter to the Earl of Orrery. The Presbyterians drawn into the discussions were certain of the "Dons", Bates, Manton, Baxter, and Matthew Poole. Before the discussions had gone very far, Manton was out of them, being a fugitive from the new orders issued by the King in obedience to the bishops, and Baxter himself had been trotted up and down the town in a coach all the long day by a constable and an informer in search of a magistrate to give judgement on him under the same orders. Remarkable to relate, not one single London magistrate could be found at home.[3]

The discussions themselves were conducted on the basis of a "form of an Healing Act" drawn up by Baxter in advance. Alterations were debated and a modified draft found general agreement. The temperate hand of the Lord Chief Justice, Sir Matthew Hale, may be suspected in the drafting. It contains some sensible proposals and indeed reaches a high-water mark among such efforts.[4] It begins with a simple declaration of assent to the doctrine and sacraments of the

[1] *CSPD 1673–5*, 551.

[2] *CSP Ven.* 357 f. Text of Orders: *London Gazette*, 4–8 February, 15–18 February 1674/5.

[3] *RB* III.i.§§283, 282; H.M.C. Portland Papers, iii.349. I am indebted to Mr I. G. Philip for drawing my attention to a paper (Bodleian MSS. Carte, 77. foll. 578–9, also foll. 633–4) giving Justices instructions how to evade the requirements of the Conventicle Act.

[4] Text: *RB* III.i.§288 (pp. 158 ff) (=D.W.L. MSS. 59.13.165).

Church of England and a remarkable substitute for the renunciation of the Solemn League and Covenant. An incumbent is not obliged to read the liturgy invariably or in its entirety but must be frequently present when it is read. Surplice, cross in baptism, kneeling at Communion are not to be enforced, nor are readings from the Apocrypha nor certain parts of the burial service, and parents are not obliged to provide godparents. The question of reordination is solved by a written licence for those not episcopally ordained, but there is an express provision that "each party shall be left to judge as they see cause" whether "this or that which he now received, shall be taken as his ordination". Express allowance is made that family prayer, no matter how many neighbours are present, shall not be condemned as a conventicle. Finally, for indulgence, there are provisions for those "who conform not so much as is required to the established ministry". Under certain conditions these shall "be so far tolerated . . . as His Majesty, with the advice of his Parliament or Council, shall from time to time find consistent with the peace and safety of his kingdoms"—a remarkably near approach to the limited dispensing power that was to have been accorded to the King by the Lords' amendments to the ill-starred Bill of 1673. There is also, rather as an afterthought, a provision to prevent preaching against the Church or the Government.

Morley was out of town when agreement was reached on these proposals and there is no indication that he showed any subsequent interest in them; it would have been surprising if he had, for he must have known that he would have found quite unacceptable any terms that Baxter could be expected to agree to. Ward showed little interest save to reject the proposals. So Tillotson was left to explain to Baxter that "several things could not be obtained" and that though Bishop Ward had "promised to appoint a time of Meeting", he had "not heard from him since".[1] The rather ugly truth

[1] *RB* III.i.§287: letter of Tillotson, dated 11 April 1675.

has to be admitted that, so far as the two bishops were concerned, the discussions had served their turn no matter what the outcome. By exposing, if not indeed provoking, disunity amongst those supposed to be the Duke's united supporters, the bishops had attained their purpose.[1]

There have been those who believed that it had always been one of the objects of the Court to play upon the differences amongst the Nonconformists and keep them disunited. It is unlikely, if only because hitherto it had needed no Machiavellian machinations to achieve the inevitable. But, as Baxter had foreseen, the continued alienation from the Church served only to reinforce the trend of Presbyterians to become Independents in everything but name and theory, a trend that gave the Duke wide support for his policy. We can be quite certain that Baxter and his friends had never lent themselves to the Duke's scheme, but we may wonder how other Nonconformists looked upon the way in which Baxter and his friends had been made to play into the hands of the bishops; for the bishops had successfully played off the "Dons", with their continuing if often disappointed hopes of comprehension, against the Independents and "Ducklings" to their mutual disadvantage. We may believe that the lesson went home, for two things stand out clear in later events. Within a few years a determined effort was made by the Nonconformist laity of London to weld Presbyterians and Independents into one Nonconformist body so as to eliminate future discord; and the next time that comprehension was raised as a serious political issue, its reception by Nonconformists was so remarkably cool as to alarm even moderate and benevolent Churchmen.

Later in 1675 the Duke of Buckingham promoted an Indulgence Bill in the Lords with much the same purpose as

[1] That rumours were running round the town, that negotiations on comprehension had ended by the bishops' "offering to abandon the entire ceremonial of the Church" (*CSP Ven. 1673–5*, 358, 363), only helped to show that Dissenters were not solidly behind the Duke of York.

the 1673 Bill. But after obtaining leave to bring in his Bill no more was heard of it.[1] Indeed the time for such a measure had gone by. The King's policy of the preceding half of his reign had changed radically and permanently. As Lord Conway put it, "I found that all their measures were alter'd since last I saw him [Danby], that King and Duke were resolved to keep up Parliament, to raise the old Cavaleers, and the Church party and to sacrifice Papists and Presbyterians".[2] Danby had carried his King captive into the arms of a receptive Church, and for the rest of his reign the King would make no more efforts for the relief of Nonconformists. Not until Danby himself fell into disgrace would there be any opening for comprehension or indulgence and then the initiative would come not from the Court but from the country.

The next attempt at comprehension and indulgence came in the wake of the Popish Plot, the dissolution of the long Cavalier Parliament, and the fall of Danby. The period leading up to these events had been marked by growing apprehensions of the nefarious activities of Papists, who were manifestly not being repressed whatever the bishops' advice might have been. The obvious connivance of Roman Catholics did not go unnoticed. By contrast the period was also remarkable for the frequent though sporadic persecution of Dissenters by self-appointed guardians of the law, encouraged and even employed by those in ecclesiastical high quarters. In the curious guerrilla warfare that ensued the Dissenters showed considerable ingenuity in turning the tables on their pursuers. The Conventicle Act depended for its effectiveness on the use of informers; and, if an informer so much as tripped in some particular in his accusation, he

[1] Text (Abbreviated): H.M.C., 9th Report, Lords, ii.68; *The Duke of Buckingham's speech in the House of Lords moving for leave to bring in a Bill for Indulgence to Protestant Dissenters, November 16 1675* (1675); A. A. Cooper, *Two Speeches* (1675).

[2] Camden Soc. 3rd Series, xxiv (1913), Essex Papers, 1.

might find himself charged with perjury, and then it would be the informer and not his victim who found himself in gaol.[1] Confronted with such discouragements in attacking Dissenters the pursuers resorted more and more to certain old Elizabethan statutes that imposed penalties, including heavy fines, for non-attendance at church. To add to the irony, these statutes made it plain in the preamble that they were aimed at Popish Recusants (against whom they were rarely used); but this went for nothing, for, as Burnet observed, "all persons who came not to church, and did not receive the sacrament once a year, were within the letter of the law".[2]

The outcome of the explosion against Popery and against Danby was a sequence of three short-lived Parliaments in 1679, 1680, and 1681, the last, at Oxford, being dissolved after being allowed to sit for only a week. If the first preoccupation of these Parliaments was to hunt down the perpetrators of the "Plot" and to pass a Bill to exclude the Duke of York from the succession, emancipation of the Dissenters came a close second, though it was only in the 1680 Short Parliament that this became apparent. With it began the Whig-Dissenting alliance that was to last a century and more. So little did Charles like the look of this second Short Parliament, elected in the summer of 1679, that he did all he could to prevent its sitting for business. Only after seven prorogations was it allowed to sit at all, in the autumn of 1680. Even when it did sit, its most diligent efforts were to be frustrated at every turn. As one correspondent put it to a friend, "The House has started many hares, but catcht very few."[3]

That the old tormented questions of comprehension and indulgence would be agitated again was becoming evident in the spring and summer of 1680.[4] And so, when Parliament

[1] See p. 219, n. 3, above.

[2] Burnet, *HOT* ii.279 (=i.495).

[3] H.M.C., 7th Report, 496 (25 November 1680).

[4] E. Stillingfleet, *Mischief of Separation*, [May] 1680; *CSPD 1680–1*, 45 (Earl of Anglesey's letter to Mayor of Gloucester).

at last met on 21 October, it was not many days before several measures were tabled for the benefit of Dissenters. There were eventually four. In the Lords, as early as 8 November, there was discussion on liberating Dissenters from the abuse of those old Elizabethan statutes directed against Popish Recusants but actually turned against Dissenters. As a result a "Bill for distinguishing Protestant Dissenters from Popish Recusants" was read a first time in the Lords on 9 December.[1] It went to the Commons after its third reading on 3 January, too late, however, to pass into law, since Charles cut short the life of his second Short Parliament abruptly on 10 January. The Bill was one of the many "hares not catcht".

Meanwhile in the Commons an attack was made upon "a severe act passed in the end of Queen Elizabeth's reign, when she was highly provoked with the seditious behaviour of the Puritans, by which those who did not conform to the Church were required to abjure the kingdom under the pain of death".[2] The Commons appointed a committee to consider this Act (35 Eliz. cap. 1) on 6 November. A Bill for its repeal, read for the first time on 23 November, was read a third time two days later and sent to the Lords, where it received its third reading on 5 December with certain amendments which the Commons agreed to on the 17th. This Bill at least should have reached the statute book, for it passed both Houses in good time to have received the royal assent, but it too was to be one of the "hares not catcht", and that for the most scandalous of reasons. Few have ever believed that it was a mere venial error on the part of Secretary Jenkins that this Bill was somehow missing when the King came to give his assent to Bills passed during the Session.[3]

[1] Text: H.M.C., 11th Report, pt 2, Lords, 203 f, (no. 289, 20 November 1680).

[2] Burnet, *HOT* ii.278 (= i.494); H.M.C., 11th Report, pt 2, Lords, 214 (no. 305, 26 November 1680).

[3] W. D. Christie, *Life of . . . Shaftesbury*, ii. pp. cxii-cxv (app. 6); H.M.C., 11th Report, pt 2, 269 (no. 386, 21 March 1681).

These two Bills were not the only, nor indeed the most important, hares started on behalf of the Dissenters. There was a determined effort to pass a measure for comprehension. On 3 November the Commons appointed a committee to prepare such a Bill. Several members of the committee were Dissenters, and it was doubtless from one of them, possibly Sir John Maynard, that Roger Morrice, one of the silenced Presbyterians and one of the "Dons", to whose diary of public events we shall on a number of occasions be indebted, received the information that he records on 6 November that "The Bill for uniting his Majesties Protestant subjects (as it will be offered to the House by the Committee if it be seasonable to offer anything of that nature) is like to be wonderfully good".[1] Presumably Baxter had heard something of what was afoot, for a few days later, on 9 November, he wrote a letter to Sir Edward Harley enclosing a draft of a Bill of his own.[2] He was evidently not so sanguine as his friend Roger Morrice that what laymen and amateurs had produced would be so "wonderfully good". Nor was his the only other attempt at a Bill; the mood of reconciliation affected the bishops or some of them—or was it that they too dreaded the amateur lay approach and thought (as on some previous occasions) that a too radical measure might have to be countered by something that they considered more appropriate and less drastic? Be that as it may, a few days after Baxter's letter to Harley, the newly appointed Bishop of St Asaph, William Lloyd, approached the Presbyterian John Howe on the subject. They met at the house of John Tillotson, and the bishop put the time-honoured question to Howe, "What he thought would satisfy the Nonconformists, that so they might be taken into the Church". After some discussion on parochial reformation,

> At length they agreed upon a meeting the next Night, at seven a Clock, at Dr Stillingfleet's, the Dean of St Pauls. Mr

[1] Morrice MS. Q, 274. The names of the Commons' Committee are printed in *CJ* ix. 645.

[2] Text: *RB* App. 9, 131.

Howe proposed to bring Mr Baxter along with him; but the Bishop would by no means allow of it. Then he propos'd to bring Dr Bates, and was answer'd, that no Man could be more proper. Accordingly Dr Bates and Mr Howe went at seven in the Evening to Dr Stillingfleet's, as had been appointed the day before. The Dean had provided a very handsome Treat, but they found not the Company they expected. They waited till eight, till nine, till near ten a Clock; but the Bishop neither came, nor sent, nor took any notice of the matter afterwards. And that very night [15 November], as they heard the next Morning, the Bill of Exclusion was thrown out of the House of Peers, by a majority of thirty Voices [actually 63 to 30], fourteen of which were Bishops. And after this, there was no further occasion for any talk of Comprehension.[1]

This may be near enough the truth if it relates simply to a measure to be introduced with episcopal blessing in the House of Lords. But in fact, so far from the loss of the Exclusion Bill on 15 November putting an end to talk of comprehension, serious discussion of a measure in the Commons was then only just beginning. It was on 18 November, three days after the Lords' rejection of Exclusion, that the committee appointed by the Commons on 3 November agreed on the heads of their proposed Bill.[2] It would seem that some of the committee were not content to limit their proposals to comprehension; they insisted also on proposals for indulgence, which is not surprising when we notice that Independents were prominent members of the Committee. Permission was sought and obtained in the Commons on 24 November to prepare two Bills instead of one, a Bill for comprehension and a Bill for indulgence. Both Bills received a first reading on 16 December.[3]

By the Comprehension Bill subscription was required to "the Articles of Religion mentioned in the Statute made in

[1] Edmund Calamy, *Memoirs of the Life of . . . John Howe* (1724), 72 f.

[2] Edmund Calamy, *Abridgement of Mr Baxter's History*, (2nd edn 1713), i.350.

[3] Text (with shorthand additions): D.W.L. MSS. 59.11.266–8. Cf. Morrice MS. P, 288; H.M.C. Beaufort, etc. (12th Report, pt ix), 100 f.

the Thirteenth year of the Reign of Queen Elizabeth, excepting only the Thirty-fourth, Thirty-fifth and Thirty-sixth Articles. And also except these words in the Twentieth Article (viz.). The Church hath power to Decree Rites and ceremonies, and Authority in controversies of faith". Those ordained by presbyters between 1644 and 1660 are accepted without reordination. The declarations in the Act of Uniformity not to take arms against the King, giving assent and consent to the Liturgy, and abjuring the Solemn League and Covenant are repealed. The oaths of Supremacy and Allegiance are required, as also the declaration against Popery from the second Test Act (of 1678), but the oath of canonical obedience is waived. A black gown and not the surplice is to be worn except in cathedrals and King's chapels. The sign of the cross in baptism becomes optional both for minister and parents. Godparents are not required. Kneeling is not to be enforced at communion. The parallel measure for indulgence[1] exempted from the penalties of a series of Acts from the reigns of Elizabeth and James I all those who subscribed the same 35 articles of religion as were required in the Bill for comprehension (one half-article less in the case of Baptists). As with the other measure, the oaths of Supremacy and Allegiance were required as also the declaration against Popery. In addition, there were provisions to prevent Dissenters from escaping tithes and other dues, and they had to find deputies for the duties of churchwarden. They were not to conduct worship behind locked doors. Exemption from penalties was specified for Dissenting schoolmasters as well as for ministers and people. As originally drafted there was a provision to cover the needs of those (i.e. Quakers) who had scruples against taking oaths, but this provision was apparently struck out at the first reading of the Bill.[2]

[1] Text: *A collection of the substance of severall speeches . . . relating to the horrid Popish Plot* (1681), pp. 16–20. I am indebted to Mr Henry Horwitz of St Antony's College, Oxford, for locating this copy of the text (B.M. England. Parliament. H. of C. Proceedings. Gen. Collections).

[2] Morrice MS. Q, 286.

What would have been the fate of these two Bills if they had ever reached the Lords we cannot know, but we can guess that they would have been hotly debated, for Stillingfleet published a book on the eve of the second reading debate, in the preface of which he directed criticism against some of the provisions in the two Bills.[1] Though he had no objection to a subscription limited to the Articles of Religion in the case of indulgence, he strongly objected to any such reduced subscription in the case of comprehension, on the ground that it set up two classes of Churchmen. Rather than tamper with subscription to the Book of Common Prayer, he would prefer to see a careful revision in which passages that might be open to exception were amended. In the controversy over the surplice and the ceremonies he was willing to make adequate concessions. It is not too big a guess to see in these criticisms the lines that debate would have taken in the House of Lords. To indulgence Stillingfleet was wholly unsympathetic. He had during the year been in the controversy with the Dissenters over the need for Protestant unity in face of the Popish menace, and his main point had been that toleration would permit endless separations and divisions when what was needed above all was unity. If some measure of indulgence there had to be, he would make the terms a stiff deterrent. Some of his proposals were that the indulged should be incapacitated from holding office; they should pay twelve pence a Sunday for the privilege of worshipping in their own way, and they should be debarred from training up scholars, so that they should be prevented from using education to perpetuate the schism.[2] No wonder Burnet could say of him that "he went into the humours of that high sort of people beyond what became him, perhaps beyond his own sense of things", a comment which suggests

[1] E. Stillingfleet, *Unreasonableness of Separation* (1681 [but actually published about the middle of December 1680]), pp. lxxxii-xciii. Cf. Thomas Birch, *Life of . . . John Tillotson* (1752), 86: "The Bishops thought this too much, and the Dissenters too little".

[2] E. Stillingfleet, op. cit., pp. lxxxv-lxxxviii.

that Stillingfleet's strictures fairly represent the mind of the dominant element in the Church at the time.[1]

If that was the mind of the Church, what of the Dissenters? It will have been noticed that it was from within the committee appointed by the Commons that a move was made to introduce a Bill for indulgence as well as a Bill for comprehension. And there is a report that "the Bill of Indulgence was so well attended by an industrious Member of the House, that nothing was wanting to the Compleating of it; but the Bill for Comprehension, being drawn up by Gentlemen that did not, and could not fully understand the Scruples of the Nonconformists [presumably Anglican laymen], was both imperfect and neglected".[2] Of the Nonconformists on the committee the Independents were evidently in the ascendant. Moreover during the years between 1675 and 1680 terms for uniting Presbyterians and Independents into one body had been drawn up and union had almost been achieved.[3] For Independents and Presbyterians, thus united, comprehension would have nothing to commend it, and it is easy to see why the Comprehension Bill "was looked after very sorrily".[4] The lessons of 1675 had not gone unheeded. There was, however, a remnant of Presbyterians who regretted this neglect, and who, if they had had their chance and been represented on the Commons' committee, would have attempted to make improvements in the proposals for comprehension. They could not be satisfied with a provision against reordination that stopped short at 1660. Nor could they be satisfied with a too rigid subscription to the surviving Articles of Religion without any loopholes for those who had doubts about some of them, such as the Calvinist Seventeenth Article which Arminians among the Nonconformists might scruple. And finally they were dissatisfied that

[1] Burnet, *HOT* i.336 (= i.189).

[2] [John Humfrey,] *King William's Toleration* (1689), 10.

[3] "*An Essay of Accommodation*", ed. R. Thomas (1957); *An earlier version of an* "*Essay of Accommodation*", ed. R. Thomas (1960).

[4] [George Jones,] *The Samaritan* (1682), 114.

the Bill did nothing to secure parochial discipline.[1] But it was only belatedly that they raised their voices. What at the time drew attention was the complete Nonconformist indifference to comprehension, and this was greeted by Churchmen with shocked surprise. Thus Morrice could report that "all that I have heard of who desire comprehension, desire Indulgence also for others, though multitudes desire indulgence that most fervently oppose comprehension. This begets great misunderstandings".[2] "Misunderstandings" was too mild a term. Churchmen were not only startled, they thought they had cause for alarm, an alarm which was reflected in Burnet's assertion that the Nonconformists "hoped they were so near carrying all before them, that they despised comprehension".[3] The spectre of the 1640s and a new civil war loomed large. No doubt there were some ready to foment such alarm.

Perhaps Charles too was not sorry to see an anti-Puritan phobia replacing an anti-Popish phobia. At all events he dissolved his second hated Short Parliament with alacrity on 18 January 1681. Writs for a new Parliament were issued promptly in the hope that the reaction already setting in would bring different men into Parliament. To further the good work, the new Parliament was to meet in Oxford, as far away as possible from the Whig influences of London. But the new Parliament proved no better than its predecessor; it was determinedly Whig.

The third Short Parliament met in March. Charles endured it for only a week. But even in that short space of time, with much other business on hand, the Commons found time to reintroduce the repeal of 35 Eliz. cap. 1, and to inquire narrowly into the reasons for the King's failure to give it the royal assent in January. They found time, too (whatever

[1] Ibid., 115–19, 124.

[2] Morrice MS. Q, 288 (30 December 1680). Cf. [John Humfrey,] *Answer to Dr Stillingfleet's sermon* (1680), 26.

[3] Burnet, *HOT* ii.279 (= i.495).

the lukewarmness of Dissenters), to reintroduce the Comprehension Bill. Daniel Finch, one of the promoters of the Bill, not being able to be present at the opening of the Session, wrote to Sir Edward Harley, asking him to bring the Bill into the new Parliament,[1] which he did on 26 March, though it was revived only to die almost immediately with the dissolution on 28 March.

So many hares not catcht! But in 1689, after the Revolution, some at least of them would be catcht: for the Indulgence Bill of 1680 became substantially, and to a large extent verbally, the Toleration Act of 1689. The 1680 Comprehension Bill, also, became the basis of comprehension measures of 1689 in both Lords and Commons, though the ancestry of the Lords' Bill of 1689 would be hardly recognizable because of modifications clearly adumbrated in Stillingfleet's criticisms of the 1680 measure.

But in 1681 these events lay still a long way in the future, and the immediate result of the King's power to dissolve Parliament with impunity and to finish his reign without recourse to any check from that quarter was that Dissenters had to pay the penalty for their support of the Whig interest. As John Howe put it in 1689, looking back at the three short Exclusion Parliaments, the Dissenters "every where so entirely and unanimously fell in with the sober Part of the Nation, in the Choice of such Persons for the three Parliaments . . . as . . . did most generously assert the Liberties of the Nation, and the Protestant Religion. Which alone . . . drew upon us, soon after the Dissolution of the last of those Parliaments, that dreadful Storm of Persecution, that destroyed not a small Number of Lives in Goals, and ruin'd Multitudes of Families".[2] It was the turn once more of coercion.

In the years of Charles II's abject surrender to the Tories

[1] D.W.L. MSS. 59.11.266: a shorthand note giving particulars of Daniel Finch's letter to Harley. Cf. *CJ* ix.711.

[2] John Howe, *Case of the Protestant Dissenters,* repr. in Calamy, *Abridgement* i.433.

that ended his reign, a few lone voices might be raised in warning of dangers ahead. A sermon of Tillotson might bemoan that "our religion and liberty in all human probability would expire with" his reign, but few took any heed.[1] When James succeeded his brother in 1685, Church and State seemed lulled into the quiescence of a fools' paradise. James promised to support the Church; the persecution of Dissenters went on; the futile Monmouth Rebellion only afforded excuse for greater severities against them. Parliament voted the new King revenues enough to make him independent of Parliament for the rest of his reign. But though so many refused to see it, the situation was changed, and that radically. James ended the sittings of his first (and only) Parliament in the first year of his reign as soon as it refused to look on quietly while he dispensed with the Test Act in order to officer the army with Roman Catholics. To make matters more difficult for any complacent spirits, Louis XIV served James one of the scurviest tricks that ever one friendly monarch served another. James had been little more than six months on his throne when Louis advertised to the world the perfidy of a Roman Catholic monarch by revoking the irrevocable Edict of Nantes, by which he himself, as well as his forebears, had pledged toleration to French Protestants. He had long been untrue to his promise, but the final act of revocation was perfidy so glaring that it demanded as the only possible inference that the word of an absolute Roman Catholic monarch was worthless. How could any English Protestant trust Roman Catholic James after that? The endless stream of Protestant exiles, fleeing from France to every Protestant country in Europe, saw to it that the inescapable inference was driven home. The London coffee-houses buzzed with the news of each fresh turn in the French persecution, and letters to friends in the country bulged with the news of each new atrocity and of the arrival of each fresh batch of fugitives.

[1] *CSPD 1683*, i.40 (2 February 1683).

It was obtuse folly in James not to see the obvious; it was even greater obtuseness, when, at a later date, having decided upon an Edict of Nantes of his own, and having issued his Declaration for Liberty of Conscience, he promised to find some means of making it irrevocable.[1] To invite so damaging a comparison in so blatant a fashion was nothing short of insulting the intelligence of his subjects. Early in his reign the consequences became apparent. The ink was hardly dry on the Revocation of the Edict of Nantes when we first hear of a club of anti-Popery writers drawn from the clergy of London. Prominent amongst those "who understood each other" in this were Deans Tillotson, Patrick, and Stillingfleet and Drs Tenison and Fowler, who all play a prominent part in the last efforts to arrive at a comprehension of Dissenters within the Church.[2] The Popish-Protestant controversy rose to heights unknown before. The pamphlet warfare grew to an enormous literature.[3] We can imagine the King's rising irritation at the all too attentive swarm of preachers and pamphleteers and at the Church that harboured them. Patience was not one of his most signal virtues.

The year 1686 was not very old before James seems to have realized that he would either have to subdue the Church or be subdued by it. He revived the old, dangerous policy of 1672—indulgence to Dissenters, both Protestant and Roman Catholic—in which Charles had burnt his fingers and learnt his lesson. It was to revive, too, his own projected policy of 1674, in which the same was to be attempted again, had not Charles and his wary ministers thwarted it by transferring allegiance to the bishops and the Church. In subduing the Church and promoting the Roman Catholic interest he needed allies. He could count on a few obsequious clergy

[1] H.M.C., Downshire, 243; Morrice MS. Q, 89.

[2] Morrice MS. P, 491 (7 November 1685).

[3] The catalogue of tracts for and against Popery of the period, edited by Thomas Jones, runs to two volumes of the Chetham Society publications (O.S. 48, 64).

here and there; he might reckon on some support from the Anglican theory of passive obedience. But that would not carry him very far. What better ally could he have than the Dissenters? They were but a minority, though in London their ministers might outnumber the clergy; but what made them count for more than their numbers was their wealth. If they could be won over, he was home. And he had one trump card: the Church of England, or its official representatives, had played Louis XIV to the Dissenters ever since 1660. From the spring of 1686, splitting the Church and enlisting the support of Dissenters became the King's settled policy. And forgetting nothing if he learnt nothing, he doubtless remembered that some of the Dissenters had in 1674 been ready to countenance toleration of Roman Catholics.

To begin with, James felt his way carefully. His first move was, as in 1674, to exert the dangerous dispensing power in a few isolated cases.[1] He also sought out judges to give a favourable ruling on its use.[2] Then he pressed on to somewhat more extensive measures. Towards the end of 1686 he set up a licensing office in London where a Dissenter might buy a dispensation for himself and family for fifty shillings.[3] What is remarkable is that many Dissenters—the more politically conscious of them—in spite of the relief offered, regarded the King's every move with considerable suspicion. Though the licensing office was open in November, by the end of the following February only some Baptists had taken out licences and reopened their meeting houses publicly.[4] The trend of the King's intentions were sufficiently obvious and as a result moderate Churchmen became alarmed not only at the encouragement given to Popery by a Popish king but at the threat that his blandishments might carry the

[1] David Ogg, *England in the reigns of James II and William III* (1955), 180 (10 March 1686); Morrice MS. P, 563 (10 July 1686); cf. also a case at Abingdon (24 July 1686), 584, 615, etc.

[2] *EHD* viii.83.

[3] Unitarian Hist. Soc. *Trans.*, xii.41.

[4] Morrice MS. Q, 74.

Dissenters over to his side. It is not surprising therefore that we begin to hear persistent rumours of moves towards a rapprochement between Church and Dissent.[1]

Soon, however, the system of licences of November 1686 was swallowed up in the general indulgence of April 1687 when James issued his Declaration for the Liberty of Conscience.[2] The way of reconciliation between Church and Dissent was thereby made harder. The King's policy was beginning to show results, but for full success it was required that the Dissenters should enrol under the King's banner by waving addresses of thanks. Once again the more politically conscious Dissenters hung back. On 9 April Morrice could write: "I do not hear that any but some Anabaptists in London that petitioned for Licences have yet or are resolved to returne his Majesty theire express thanks."[3] On 14 April the Baptists came forward with their address, but one of John Ellis' friends wrote to him on the 19th: "Some Dissenters address the king by way of thanks; Quakers . . . Anabaptists . . . gave florid thanks yesterday. . . . The Presbyterians will not do it."[4] But he was wrong. James was not to be satisfied with so little; our old friend, Sir John Baber, was set to work to stimulate addresses, and soon speculation as to his success was becoming the talk of the town. On the 23rd Morrice had heard a jocular surmise to this effect.

> A noble Peere comeing to the Earl of Sunderland thus exprest himselfe, Here is a pleasant world, I saw Pen goeing out at one door [of the Palace] with his Quakers, and Sir John Baber comeing in at the other door with the head of the Presbyterians, and the head of the Independents at another.[5]

It was only too near the mark. On the same day Morrice reports that two or three Presbyterian ministers, headed by

[1] Morrice MS. Q, 84, 86.

[2] Text: *EHD* viii.295 f.

[3] Morrice MS. Q, 90.

[4] *London Gazette*, 14–18 April 1687; John Ellis, *The Ellis Correspondence*, ed. G. A. Ellis (1829), i.274.

[5] Morrice MS. Q, 102.

Vincent Alsop (who had ulterior motives for gratitude because of a pardon desired for his son), had determined on addressing, "though many others of their own persuasion differed utterly from them".[1] This move seems to have stimulated some other Presbyterian ministers to prepare a more official address. And the next that we hear from Morrice is that

> on Thursday last [28th], at the King's Levy there was an Address presented . . . by Mr Hurst, Mr Veal, Mr Oakes, Mr Rosewell, Mr. Slater, And 4 more ministers subscribed it, but Dr Annesley could not go to present it, because he useth not to stir abrode, and I believe subscribed it not. It was agreed on and signed at his house. Mr Baxter, Dr Bates and severall others I am most acquainted with have not been consulted in this matter.[2]

Samuel Annesley's name makes it clear that we are once again introduced to the split amongst the Presbyterians between Dons and Ducklings. Next came William Penn and the Quakers with their address. And then, on Saturday, at last came Alsop's threatened address, presented by "3 gentlemen, 3 citizens and 3 ministers" on behalf of "the Inhabitants of the city and liberty of Westminster".[3] Alsop supplemented the address with a short speech, and His Majesty "shewed them extraordinary respect by his frequent moving of his hat to them and by the bowing of his body at the end of every passage".

> Immediately after this the Independents (who would address singly by themselves, and not jointly with others) Mr Baker [? Barker] Mr Cockayne, Mr Godman, Mr Loaves [Loeffs], Mr Collins, Mr Lobb, Mr Faldo, and two others who presented it, nine in number, all ministers and signed by about 140 laymen.[4]

The faithful *London Gazette*, which had been singularly neglectful of news about Huguenots fleeing from France,

[1] Ibid.
[2] Ibid., 112 f.
[3] Ibid., 114 f.
[4] Ibid., 115.

printed these addresses in full and many more from all over the country where the same general pattern of addressing was followed.

In London it was well known that Baxter and his associates had not co-operated in any of the addresses presented. Baxter in particular was "charged with great ingratitude" for he had only a little while before been released from prison by the King's pardon.[1] Sir John Baber was sent for to take him to task. In his reply, amongst a number of somewhat ironical excuses, Baxter let fall one that must have given deep offence. It was this:

> I have these 35 years made love, concord and peace the main study of my life; and I dare not violate it causelessly with the body of conforming clergy. And I have not skill enough to draw up an address that shall neither displease his Majesty nor them.[2]

On receipt of this Sir John had another errand to undertake, and his conversation with Baxter showed that it was this reference to concord with the clergy that had above all rankled. Baxter was hard put to it to be polite and yet adhere to his point.[3] In the swift deterioration of the situation that was to mark the remainder of the reign, this determined stand of Baxter and the Dons was to take on considerable significance. Since 1668 the Dons had been steadily losing ground, but their integrity at this juncture was to give them in the coming months a restored prestige and a renewed influence.

It was not only the Dons who would not address; the King could get no thanks from the London clergy. It may seem odd that he should have expected it, but there were subservient bishops willing to engineer an address. They found, however, that the London clergy were "drunk with the

[1] Ibid., 176 (22 October 1687).

[2] D.W.L. MSS. 59.5.40–1.

[3] Ibid., 59.1.110. Cf. Powicke ii.167 f, where the sequence of the two letters should be reversed.

feares of Popery", as one of them angrily put it, and there was no address.[1] Thanks a King might solicit, but could not command. Next year he would seek his revenge.

The climax was to come in the summer of 1688. It would seem that the King sought a deliberate clash of arms with the Church. Its sullen opposition or that of some of its members was obvious enough, but left everything unsettled. James wanted a settlement. The brilliant manoeuvre by which he intended to force the Church to show its hand, or rather exhibit its divisions, may have been invented by Stephen Lobb, a Congregational minister. He and William Penn, the Quaker, were amongst the King's most attentive courtiers. Late in April the King reissued his Declaration of the previous year.[2] It seemed a pointless act and left people guessing what the purpose could be. They were soon to learn. A week later they had some inkling what was afoot, when by an Order in Council of 4 May the King directed that his Declaration should be read in all the churches, in London on the last two Sundays in May, and in the rest of the country on the first two Sundays in June.[3] It was a clever ruse. The previous year the clergy had been able to avoid any open clash of loyalties by the simple expedient of doing nothing. By the new order they were forced to a decision and their manifest disunity put them in a quandary. The best part of a fortnight, between the publication of the order and the Sunday when the Declaration had to be read, was taken up in fevered attempts to reach agreement what to do. Archbishop Sancroft was willing to make a stand only if the London clergy were unanimous in refusing to read. Some of the London clergy were for refusing because they hated indulgence to Dissenters. Others, like Tillotson and his friends, had no wish to alienate the Dissenters, but were against reading because to do so was to countenance the use

[1] Morrice MS. Q, 102, 106, 107, 114.

[2] Text: *EHD* viii. 399 f.

[3] Text: *EHD* viii. 83.

of the royal dispensing power and its use on behalf of Popery. In those few days of incessant debate agreement not to read was reached only when the opinion of Dissenters had been sought and their support for not reading had been secured. It was then that the famous formula was hammered out, beginning that the clergy were not averse to publishing the Declaration "for any want of due tenderness towards the Dissenters". It was not until the Thursday evening before the appointed Sunday that Dean Patrick could at last report the required agreement to the archbishop. Most of Friday was taken up in settling the terms of a petition based on the agreement signed by the clergy, and it was not till late the same evening that seven bishops had audience of the King and handed him their petition. James had heard that something was afoot, but he had been told that the petition would be against toleration for Dissenters, an outcome that would have been most propitious for his plan of driving a wedge between Churchmen and the Dissenters. What then was his dismay as he read a petition befriending the Dissenters and challenging his right to dispense with the laws? The ground had suddenly gone from under his feet and he was left floundering, furious, and foolish, hurling threats at these meek but offensive bishops. The same night a somewhat garbled report of the meeting and the petition had been printed "and was so bawled and roared through the streets by the hawkers that people rose out of their beds to buy it".[1]

With the stirring events that followed the momentous presentation of the petition, the bishops before the Council, the bishops committed to the Tower, their release and trial, the all-night sitting of the jury, and finally their acquittal we are not here concerned. The bonfires that greeted their release from the Tower were as nothing to the rejoicing at their final victory. But the real victory went to Deans

[1] R. Thomas, "The Seven Bishops and their Petition", in *JEH* xii.56–70.

Tillotson, Patrick, Stillingfleet, and their friends and to the Dissenters, Baxter, Bates, Howe, Griffiths, and others.[1] They had brought about concord and peace between the Nonconformists and conforming clergy. The three deans and their friends had won over the archbishop and the other petitioning bishops to a serious determination to foster comprehension, while Baxter and his friends were able to bring about an extraordinary degree of unanimity amongst the Dissenters.

Achievement of that unanimity had not been easy. Soon after the presentation of the petition Sir John Baber had been present at a meeting of Dissenters that became legendary in later times. They had been called together to consider the presentation of an address of thanks for the King's renewal of his Declaration and they were told "that His Majesty waited in his closet, and would not stir from thence till an account was brought him of their proceedings". The Dons now came into their own. Although there were present several who had addressed the year before and who were doubtless ready to do so again, the argument went against them and the address was refused. The King waiting "in his closet" had to take the rebuff as best he could.[2] For him it was a more serious defeat than the acquittal of the seven bishops which still lay six weeks ahead. A few days afterwards the papal nuncio was writing home in his report on 1 June: "the whole church espouses the cause of the bishops. There is no reasonable expectation of a division among the Anglicans, and our hopes from the Nonconformists are vanished".[3]

Hardly had the bonfires of rejoicing at the acquittal of the

[1] George Griffiths had been secretary of the conference of Independents at the Savoy in 1658. His name at this time proves that Stephen Lobb was by no means representative of the Independents. The action of Sir John Shorter, an Independent, when he was made Lord Mayor of London, the previous autumn, in refusing to avail himself of the King's suspension of the Test and Corporation Acts, tells the same tale (Morrice MS. Q, 189–90, 196).

[2] Morrice MS. Q, 263, 269; Daniel Williams, *Practical discourses* (1738), p. x; Edmund Calamy, *Memoirs of . . . John Howe* (1724), 134 f.

[3] *JEH* xii. 69 (translated from the Italian).

bishops burned low before evidence begins to accumulate of the Church's new-found purpose and policy of "due tenderness to the Dissenters". In July we hear that "the Archbishop and the clergy of London . . . have had several conferences with the chiefs of the Dissenting ministers, in order to agree such points of ceremonies as are indifferent between them, and to take such measures for what is to be proposed about religion in the next Parliament".[1] The heads of these measures have been identified by Brother George Every in Francis Lee's *Life* (1718) of Kettlewell, though in that work assigned to an impossible date after the Revolution.[2] The government of bishops was to be retained, but "the terms of communion" were to "be as large as was consistent with the constitution of a National Church". The Liturgy and Articles were in substance to be unchanged, but the Liturgy was to be reviewed and a new book of canons prepared and such alterations made as might probably bring in the Dissenters. There was also to be a new, less exceptionable, subscription "to this purpose: I, A.B., do approve the Articles and Liturgy, and Government, of the Church of England, as by Law Established; and will conform myself thereto". Those who still dissented in spite of these concessions were to have "publick Places allowed them", but the names of both teachers and people were to be registered, with annual revisions, and they were to "fine moderately for Offices of Burden". The Kettlewell paper may have been no more than personal notes taken at various meetings, but it fairly represents the accord that was being achieved in July. Then, or a little later, much detailed preparatory work of revision of the liturgy was undertaken by the archbishop, Patrick, Tenison, and perhaps some others in readiness for the promised meeting of James's second Parliament in November.[3]

[1] *Ellis Correspondence*, ii. 63; G. Every, *The High Church Party 1688–1718* (1956), 22.

[2] Text; G. Every, *The High Church Party*, 22 f, 41 f; Francis Lee, *Memoirs of the Life of Mr John Kettlewell* (1718), 392–5.

[3] Norman Sykes, *From Sheldon to Secker* (1959), 84 f.

But there was no Parliament in November; in November came William of Orange and the Revolution.

The petition, trial, and acquittal of the seven bishops had been a mine that exploded beneath the King's policy and shattered it irretrievably. But before the new purpose of Church and Dissent in mutual understanding could work itself out into any settled concord, a second mine exploded beneath the first and shattered not only the King's policy but his throne, and with it, ultimately, the concord between Church and Dissent. William landed on 5 November. By Christmas James was gone over the water. A convention Parliament met on 22 January. On 6 February, after a long wrangle, the Lords bowed before the fury of all the pent-up resentment in Whiggish breasts and concurred with the Commons that James (whether he knew it or not) had "abdicated", "and that the throne was thereby vacant". Some people improved on English grammar; James had *been* abdicated, they said.[1] "I think this", wrote the Earl of Clarendon, son of Charles II's first chancellor, "was the most dismal day I ever saw in my life. God help us: we are certainly a miserable, undone people."[2] To Roger Morrice, however, "This was a very joyful vote", though he went on to lament the size of the Tory minority in the Commons, especially as "it will sound ill abrode".[3] Sancroft and most of the petitioning bishops could have echoed from their hearts Clarendon's desponding sentiments. The momentary unanimity in the face of the Popish danger was dissolving. The country was once more dividing along the old party lines, and the hopes of comprehension were dimmed.

The decision of 6 February meant that James would be supplanted as King by William III. Sancroft and his friends

[1] Morrice MS. Q, 536.

[2] Henry Hyde, *Correspondence of Henry Hyde, Earl of Clarendon . . . with the Diary of Lord Clarendon from 1687 to 1690*, ed. S.W. Singer (1828), ii.262 (6 February 1688/9).

[3] Morrice MS. Q, 459.

had done all that they could to stave off that decision. Early in January a number of them had met. Their original intention had been to negotiate (or persuade William to negotiate) with James for his return to the throne.[1] But there was vehement opposition to this, notably from the Bishop of St Asaph, and before the meetings had proceeded very far, the Bishop of Ely was lamenting to Sancroft in a letter, "We came home from Lambeth, four bishops in my coach, and we could not but deplore our case, that we should disagree in anything, and such a thing as the world must needs observe".[2] The non-juring schism had virtually begun. Before the end of the month William Sherlock, Sancroft's mouthpiece and pamphleteer, published a *Letter to a Member of the Convention*, attacking the move to put William on the throne in place of James. On the opening page we read: "The *Dissenter* is very busie to undermine the Church, and the *Commonwealth Man* to subvert the Monarchy, and *the Lord have Mercy upon us all*". A little further on we read:

> Those of the Church of *England* are very glad to get rid of Popery, but they will not be contented to part with their Church into the Bargain, for this would be as bad as they could have suffered under Popery. The several Sects of Dissenters are glad to be rid of Popery also; but now they expect glorious Days for themselves, and what they expect God Almighty knows, for I am confident they don't know themselves.[3]

Such sentiments from such quarters were no good omen for concord or comprehension.

Those who had carried the day for comprehension when the seven bishops presented their petition still pursued the policy they had been promised; but when one of them, Thomas Tenison, pressed Sancroft on the point, on the eve of the meeting of bishops in January, Sancroft hedged with the excuse that "without a commission from the king"—he

[1] Ibid., 424.
[2] Clarendon, *Corresp.* ii.507.
[3] *Seventh Collection of Papers* (1689), 19, 23.

meant, of course, James II—"it was highly penal to enter into church matters", and followed this up with almost the same unpromising language that Sherlock was to use in his pamphlet: "He believed the Dissenters would never agree among themselves with what concessions they would be satisfied".[1]

Within a few days, while the bishops were still meeting early in January, Baxter, Bates, and Howe were also meeting to decide "what was fit to be offered about Church matters for themselves and those of their persuasion, and other dissenting Protestants. They thought many particulars in the Uxbridge Treaty [debated in 1645] fit to be offered".[2] This meant that they were going back beyond the Worcester House agreement of 1660 and demanding "that the bishops shall exercise no Act of Jurisdiction or Ordination without the consent and counsel of the Presbyters".[3] This was one of the chief concessions they had tried to obtain at Worcester House, and it had then been refused. In the same mood of assurance, William Bates could use language, in addresses to William and Mary on 28 February, calculated to send a cold shudder down the spine of any good episcopalian. For comprehension he sought nothing less than "the terms of union wherein all the Reformed Churches agree".[4] It would clearly be a case of no compromise on reordination or unlimited episcopacy. No wonder that Burnet could sum it up later in a letter to Limborch in Holland: "It happens as so often falls out that while the Nonconformists, hoping for more, despise the offers made them, the stricter Conformists are equally convinced that the terms are too generous".[5] It was natural that, with a Dutch king of the Reformed

[1] Clarendon, *Corresp.* ii.240; G. Every, *The High Church Party*, 24.

[2] Morrice MS. Q, 423 f.

[3] *Historical Collections*, ed. John Rushworth, 3rd pt, vol. ii (1693) 872 f.

[4] Address presented by about a hundred ministers on 28 February 1689. Text: Calamy, *Abridgement* i.425.

[5] T. E. S. Clarke and H. C. Foxcroft, *Life of Gilbert Burnet* (1907), 276 (24 July 1689).

Religion on the throne, the Dissenters should have high hopes. Bates's reference to terms of union in which all the Reformed Churches agree was not only a well-turned compliment to a Dutch king; there is evidence that in this the Dissenters had the ear of the King and his sympathy. It was common talk that "the Prince upon his arrival, seemed more inclined to the presbyterians than to members of the church; which startled the clergy".[1] It aroused their resentment.

There were nevertheless Churchmen who were not influenced by such antipathies. "The Bishops had their last great meeting . . . at Ely House" on 14 January.[2] Later on the same day another meeting of a very different character was held at the house of Dr Stillingfleet, attended by William Lloyd (Bishop of St Asaph), Tillotson, Patrick, John Sharp (afterwards Archbishop of York), and Tenison, "to consult about such concessions as might bring in dissenters to our communion". They agreed "that a bill should be prepared to be offered by the bishops", and they "drew up the matter of it in ten or eleven heads".[3] The outcome was that the Earl of Nottingham prepared a Bill, under the title of "An Act for uniting Their Majesties Protestant Subjects".[4] Leave was given in the Lords on 27 February to introduce such a measure. It received its first reading on 11 March. The Bill, though based on the 1680 measure, was very much altered. The chief modifications look back to the Wilkins proposals of 1668 and to the Worcester House Declaration of 1660, which is specifically mentioned. Thus, instead of a repeal of part of the Act of Uniformity as in 1680, we now have a

[1] John Reresby, *Memoirs* (ed. 1904), 327.

[2] Morrice MS. Q, 430.

[3] Simon Patrick, *Works*, ed. A. Taylor (1858), 516 f. A paper containing what are almost certainly the ten heads referred to has been identified by Mr H. Horwitz of St Antony's College, Oxford, as Nottingham University MS. Portland 2322.

[4] Text: H.M.C., 12th Report, appendix, pt 6, Lords, 1689–90 (1889), 49–52 (no. 32).

declaration approving the doctrine, worship, and government of the Church of England, as in the Wilkins proposals, and, instead of accepting presbyterian ordinations prior to 1660, the Wilkins expedient is adopted of supplementary ordination for those not episcopally ordained. The most important provision in the Bill is an express reference to the Worcester House Declaration of 1660 and reforms governing admission to confirmation and to ordination. For this and other purposes the Bill asks for a Royal Commission "to make such alterations in the liturgy and reformation of the Canons and Ecclesiastical Courts as may conduce to the establishment of the Church in peace and tranquillity, and to present such alterations and reformations to the Parliament".[1] Doubtless one reason for the Commission was to leave room for all the preparatory work on the liturgy done by Sancroft and others the previous year. As in 1680, concessions are granted in the use of the surplice, the sign of the cross in baptism, the provision of godparents, and kneeling at communion.

Also, as in 1680, there was to be a measure for indulgence to meet the needs of Independents, Baptists, Quakers, and all others who could not accept comprehension. For this purpose Nottingham revived the 1680 Bill, making certain minor modifications and necessary changes and a number of additions, chiefly to include exemptions from the penalties of certain laws which in 1680 had been the subject of separate legislation. Under the title of "An Act for exempting Their Majesties Protestant Subjects, dissenting from the Church of England, from the Penalties of certain Laws", the Bill was read a first time in the Lords on 28 February.[2] Both Comprehension and Indulgence Bills received their second readings on 14 March, and both were assigned to the same peers for the committee stage.

[1] Ibid.

[2] Text (of Statute): *EHD* viii.400–3. For amendments, etc., see H.M.C., 12th Report, pt 6, Lords, 34–6 (no. 19).

In February Morrice had bemoaned the size of the Tory minority on the abdication question. In March, on the religious question, the two sides were, in the words of Sir John Reresby, "almost equally matched, and sometimes one carried a vote in both houses, and sometimes the other".[1] On 14 March the Comprehension and Indulgence Bills received their second reading; two days later we hear of the Devil Tavern Club, so named from the fact that the Devil Tavern was the meeting-place of a large number of members of Parliament, not confined to Tories, but all pledged to the defence of the Church of England.[2] Reresby's remark was that "indeed it was high time for her sons to exert themselves".[3] Indeed it was—from their point of view. The new King's sympathies with the Dissenters were known. William Bates had addressed him on a Church of England remodelled on the lines of the Reformed Churches on the Continent. In Scotland the Presbyterians were carrying everything before them. In London the entrenched position of the Church was being attacked from every side. So the Devil Tavern Club prepared to fight. In the Commons a vote to repeal the Corporation Act of 1660 was defeated; so too was an effort to have the sacramental test taken out of the Test Act.

Meanwhile, in the Lords, nearly every concession in the Comprehension Bill was attacked in committee, and in several cases amendments were carried. One withdrew the concession on kneeling at communion. Another struck out the whole clause on ordination. Yet another required that the Royal Commission should report not only to Parliament but to Convocation also.[4] Early in March Nottingham had

[1] John Reresby, *Memoirs* (ed. 1904), 352.

[2] Morrice MS. Q, 505, 542; R, 106.

[3] John Reresby, *Memoirs* (ed. 1904), 351. Cf. H.M.C., 11th Report, app., part 7, 32.

[4] H.M.C., 12th Report, pt 6, Lords, 49–52. The concession on kneeling was restored on the report stage, by Burnet's efforts and the casting vote.

submitted his proposals to Stillingfleet, who in a letter of 8 March had commented that without a Convocation "our clergy will hardly come into it, and such a Convocation is at present impracticable". He had evidently approved of the proposal to refer to a Commission the detailed work of revising the Liturgy and Canons, as well he might, remembering his criticisms of 1680, but thought that six weeks, which Nottingham must have mentioned, was too short a time for the work. "I rather think the whole Summer will be little enough for it." He therefore wanted the Commission to report "to another Parliament, when a Convocation may sitt to approve what is done".[1] Accordingly the amendment to make the Commission report to a Convocation comes as no surprise.

There were finally two other amendments, on the report stage on 4 April and at the third reading on 8 April, of rather opposite tendency. One was a change in the wording of the declaration to be taken by ministers, for which Burnet must be given credit. Instead of "I approve of the doctrine and worship and government of the Church of England", the wording was altered to read: "I submit to the present constitution of the Church of England; I acknowledge that the doctrine of it contains in it all things necessary to salvation, and I will conform myself to the worship and government thereof . . ."[2] This was certainly an easier formula for a conscientious Churchman or a Dissenter to subscribe. It said all that was necessary, and, in view of detailed changes in the liturgy and canons which the Royal Commission was expected to advise later, no one was required to "approve" what the Commission was clearly expected to disapprove. The other change was less benevolent. It was a proviso added at the very last minute before the third reading was taken.[3] Its purpose was to put a stop

[1] H.M.C., Finch, ii.194.
[2] H.M.C., 12th Report, pt 6, Lords, 50.
[3] Text of this proviso: Morrice MS. O. viii(3).

to a practice that was later to be notorious as occasional conformity. Under the Test and Corporation Acts communion in the Church of England was required as a qualification for office. The new proviso disqualified anyone who had so qualified but who subsequently attended a Dissenting meeting for worship. It was in substance the Occasional Conformity Act which the Tories of a later date succeeded in carrying in 1712, towards the end of the reign of Queen Anne. For practical purposes it would have disabled Independents, Baptists and Quakers—anyone who refused the proposed comprehension—from holding office.

The Bill was read a third time on 8 April and went to the Commons. Meanwhile complaints from the Dissenters had been growing louder. When the terms of Nottingham's Comprehension Bill were first known, Morrice grumbled that it fell far short of what Nottingham himself had promoted in 1680 when he was plain Mr Daniel Finch. It only made matters worse that the Bill was made less acceptable during its passage through the Lords. Criticism led to a counter-move, and on 1 April the Commons appointed a committee "to prepare a Bill of Comprehension".[1] The appointment of such a committee at such a time is no mean measure of Whig disgust at the proceedings in the Lords, a conclusion that is confirmed by the contents of the Bill that the committee prepared and presented with great speed a week later on 8 April.[2] Like the Lords' Bill it was based on the Bill of 1680, but there the similarity ends, for the few changes from 1680 are in a radical direction. On the great stumbling-block of reordination the Commons' Bill was calculated to outrage much Anglican opinion by accepting, as sufficient for orders in the Church of England, ordination "according to the course used in any Reformed churches", and this was no mere concession covering presbyterian ordinations for the time past. It was a Dutch–

[1] *CJ* x. 74, where also the names of the committee are given.
[2] Text: Morrice MS. O. viii(1).

Dissenting victory with a vengeance. On the matter of Prayer Book revision we find ourselves back in 1667 with the Atkyns Bill: an incumbent is not obliged to read Common Prayer himself if he has a curate to do it as and when required. For the rest there is little change from 1680.

The first reading of this Bill on 8 April resulted in a long and acrimonious debate. When it was proposed to adjourn the debate for a fortnight, one member interrupted to move that it be adjourned till doomsday. In fact it was given a first reading, and the second reading was appointed for the following Thursday week. The debate had gone on so long that the Lords' Comprehension Bill, received during the debate, had to wait for a first reading until the following day, when it too was appointed to be read a second time on the following Thursday week. But doomsday would have been nearer the mark, for neither Bill was ever called again. On the 9th there was a great meeting at the Devil Tavern, when a political bargain was struck that if the Whigs would drop the Comprehension Bills and concur in asking for a Convocation instead, the Tories would concur in allowing the Indulgence Bill to go through.[1] The terms of the bargain were incorporated in an address to the King, agreed to by both Houses. In it they asked that he would be graciously pleased to issue out writs for calling a Convocation "to be advised with in Ecclesiastical Matters" and assuring him that it was their intention "to proceed to the Consideration of giving Ease to Protestant Dissenters".[2] William's reply conceded a Convocation but pointedly reminded them of their promise of ease to Dissenters.[3] Burnet was more emphatic. He and Halifax were angry at the Devil Tavern bargain. "To call a Convocation", said Burnet, "would be the utter Ruin of the Comprehension Scheme."[4] There can be little doubt that that was precisely what was intended.

[1] G. Every, *The High Church Party*, 35; K. Feiling, *History of the Tory Party, 1640–1714* (1924), 265.

[2] *CJ* x.86.

[3] *CJ* x.97.

[4] John Reresby, *Memoirs* (1734), 344.

The King's reply was on 20 April. Two days earlier, the Lords had given a third reading to the Indulgence Bill. In Committee the Bill had lost the clause granting exemption from penalties to Nonconformist schoolmasters, a change for the worse that echoes Stillingfleet's narrow interpretation of toleration in 1680 and foreshadows recurrent attempts later to interfere with Dissenting schools and academies until George II (or Walpole) made it plain to the courts in the case of Doddridge's Academy that pettifogging persecution of this sort must stop. It was not until 15 May, nearly a month after receiving it, that the Commons gave the Bill a second reading. The delay may have been due to pressure of business, but other explanations are possible. Two days later the Bill received a third reading, and then, after a conference with the Lords about sundry amendments, it rapidly received the royal assent on 27 May. On the passing of the Bill, Morrice comments: "Certain it is the Devil Tavern Club did call for it and did promote the passing of it. *Nota.* And it's as certain they do now heartily repent they have past it, and if it were not past they would stop it." Which is perhaps no more than sober truth.[1]

The rest of the story may be briefly dismissed. If William had done nothing else, he had forced through the Indulgence Bill, better known as the Toleration Act; he was willing to promote comprehension too, if that could be achieved. In June he had a conversation with John Howe on the subject of a "Comprehension Act" when he raised the question "what clauses must be in it to make it answer its end". Howe raised specifically the question of reordination and argued that under Elizabeth ordination by presbyters had been allowed. The King could see no reason why they should

[1] Morrice MS. Q, 558. Amendments to the Bill: H.M.C., 12th Report, pt 6, Lords, 34 ff (no. 19). The Commons set on foot an alternative Indulgence Bill to that in the Lords (Morrice MS. Q, 557). Mr H. Horwitz informs me that B.M. Harleian MS. 1237, no. 7, 41–7 appears to be a draft of this Bill.

not "grant all now that they did then".[1] How serious he was in the matter was shown by the sequel. The Lords had gone on record in the Bill strangled by the Devil Tavern Club as desiring a Royal Commission to advise on liturgical and other reforms. Though the Bill had not been passed, the King went out of his way to appoint the Commission. From the point of view of comprehension the Commission did its work well and quickly. That the more virulent of the High Church members boycotted the proceedings may have assisted the work both in speed and quality. Though the Commission never reached the canons, it had virtually completed its work on the liturgy in the six weeks from 3 October to 18 November. It then felt obliged to discontinue its meetings because the promised Convocation was on the point of meeting.[2] To take but one example of the Commission's work, the solution of the vexed problem of re-ordination was to allow conditional ordination for the time past: "Receive the Holy Ghost for the office and work of Priest . . . if thou hast not been already ordain'd", and it is expressly stated that those so ordained should have "the freedom of their own Thoughts concerning their former Ordinations".[3]

But nothing came of the Commission's work. The elections for Convocation produced a Lower House resembling the Devil Tavern Club and justifying Burnet's fears that "to call a convocation would be the utter ruin of the comprehension scheme". As Edward Fowler, soon to be Bishop of Gloucester, put it to his friend Roger Morrice, "Convocation was like to be exceeding bad, so he desired that it might either be so bad that it would grant nothing considerable, or so good that

[1] Morrice MS. Q, 574 f, referring to an interpretation of 13 Eliz. cap. 12. Cf. G. Every, *The High Church Party*, 40.

[2] *Alterations in the Book of Common Prayer, prepared by the Royal Commissioners, for the revision of the liturgy, in 1689* (House of Commons, 1854: cmd 283), 94–108; G. Every, *The High Church Party*, 43–56.

[3] *Alterations in the Book of Common Prayer* (1854), 86.

it would grant enough, which he praied for, but did not hope".[1] His more desponding desire was fully realized.

Baxter, preaching at Charterhouse Square, "prayed for ... a blessed effect of convocation, that all ministers might have a sound mind and quiet disposition, and for a reconciling of all differences, that party nor sect be never heard any more among Protestants". But he who had made concord the main study of his life had now to confess that "both regular clergy and dissenters despise him".[2] Tillotson, Patrick, Tenison, Fowler, Bishops Burnet, Lloyd, Compton, who had striven manfully to honour the pledges and purposes of the previous year, in desponding mood might have been tempted to make a like confession. For when, after some delay over a defective mandate, the two Houses of Convocation proceeded to business, the Lower House quarrelled with the Upper over the terms of an address of thanks to the King, and eventually, having agreed on a chilly dilute address, and having attended the King with it on 12 December, they promptly adjourned until 24 January; and, when 24 January came, they were speedily dissolved with Parliament.[3] And after that neither King nor anyone else wanted to see any more of Convocations for a very long time to come. Comprehension was dead. The Ejection became more firmly established than at Black Bartholomew Day in far-off 1662.

[1] Morrice MS. Q, 648 (9 November 1689).

[2] D. Maclean, *London at worship 1689–1690* (1929), 16, 11.

[3] Thomas Lathbury, *History of the Convocation* (1853), 325–33; [Thomas Long,] *Vox cleri* (1690), 59–72.

5

TOLERATION AND ESTABLISHMENT: 1

A Historical Outline

ERNEST A. PAYNE

IN his shrewd and attractive study *Britain and the British People* (1942), Sir Ernest Barker argued that the religious key is the one which unlocks most doors of English life. "Apart from any question of their relative numerical strength," he wrote, "it may be said that the general relations, the general balance, and the general interaction of Anglicanism and Nonconformity have been a cardinal factor in English life and development for over three centuries."[1] Professor G. M. Trevelyan has some of the same facts in mind when he says that "from the Restoration to the latter years of the Nineteenth Century, the continuity of the two parties in English politics was very largely due to the two-party system in religious observance, popularly known as Church and Chapel".[2] To the existence in this country of two bodies of reformed religion—that is, of non-Roman Catholic religion—almost equal in strength, Sir Ernest Barker traced the development here of parliamentary democracy; a system of political parties such as parliamentary democracy needs; characteristic national activities, such as education, largely determined by religious factors; the idea of the limited State within which voluntary associations have their own sphere; and the avoidance of the bitter class divisions that have appeared in certain other lands.

These are large claims. That a strong case can be made for them, no one familiar with English history from 1662 onwards would deny. It is important, however, not to oversimplify matters. Though the two political parties may have arisen in the latter half of the seventeenth century as a result of religious difference—the Whigs allied to the Nonconformists and the Tories to the Anglicans, and though for the next 250 years the Whigs (and their Liberal successors) drew support from Nonconformity in all its social gradations,

[1] Op. cit., 24.

[2] *An Autobiography* (1949), 198.

while the Tories (and Conservatives) could count on the votes of Anglicans of all classes, yet many other factors besides specifically religious ones separated the two political parties and the two religious groups. Moreover, there was rarely and on few issues a clear-cut and complete division between Anglicans and Nonconformists. Both communities were subject to internal stresses and contained those of differing opinions. The relationships between Church and Chapel from 1689 to 1910 make a chequered story. With whichever side one's inherited or initial sympathies and prejudices lie, there is much in that story that cannot be looked upon with pride. There was considerable mutual provocation and misunderstanding. But though neither side can now be entirely happy about the past, it furnishes abundant evidence of loyalty to convictions and fervent partisanship. In the course of the years some notable figures have emerged to take their place in the annals of the Church Universal. In the end Anglicans and Nonconformists have come to accept and respect one another and now co-operate in the search for the manifestation of a deeper Christian unity.

The events of nearly two and a quarter centuries have here to be outlined. The period may conveniently be divided into five parts: (1) from the passing of the Toleration Act in 1689 to the defeat of the Young Pretender in 1745; (2) from 1745 to 1791, when cries of "Down with the Dissenters" were heard in the streets of both Birmingham and London; (3) from 1791 to 1829, by which time the Test and Corporation Acts had been repealed and the Catholic Emancipation Act passed; (4) from 1829 to 1871, when at long last religious tests were abolished at the Universities of Oxford and Cambridge; and (5) from 1871 to 1910, the year of the World Missionary Conference at Edinburgh and the beginning of the modern Ecumenical Movement.

The Toleration Act of 1689 brought to an end the persecution to which Nonconformists had been subject at intervals and in periods of varying intensity since the Restoration. Writing more than a century and a half later, Macaulay ranked it as "among those great statutes which are epochs in our constitutional history"[1] and this remains true. The Act guarantees freedom of worship to those who dissent from the forms and ceremonies of the Church of England. But the toleration immediately granted was of a distinctly limited kind. All Nonconformist preachers and teachers had still to subscribe to the Anglican Articles of Religion, except the 34th, 35th, and 36th, that is those dealing with the tradition of the Church, the public reading of the second Book of Homilies, and episcopal ordination (Baptists being allowed to except also part of the 27th Article, and Quakers being exempted from taking an oath). Roman Catholics and any who denied the doctrine of the Trinity were excluded from the benefits of the Act. The laws compelling attendance at some place of worship remained in force. The Test and Corporation Acts were not repealed, so that public office was restricted to communicants with the Church of England.

So far as doctrine was concerned, Nonconformists in general had no desire at the time for any wider freedom, though a number had begun to question the principle of subscription to creeds. What was unexpected, and what goes some way to justify the statement of Macaulay that "of all the Acts that have ever been passed by Parliament, the Toleration Act is perhaps that which most strikingly illustrates the peculiar vices and the peculiar excellencies of English legislation",[2] is the fact that a Comprehension Bill introduced at the same time, and widely regarded as its natural, if not essential, complement, was not proceeded with. The Comprehension Bill was entitled "An Act for uniting their Majesties' Protestant subjects". It had the support of the new King and of Tillotson, soon to be made Archbishop of Canterbury, Tenison, who became his successor, and Gilbert

[1] *History of England* (Everyman edn), ii.282.
[2] Op. cit., ii.278.

Burnet, the new Bishop of Salisbury. A commission of Anglican bishops and clergy, including these three, prepared a revised Book of Common Prayer which, had it been adopted, would, in the judgement of Edmund Calamy, "have bro't in two-thirds of the Dissenters".[1]

When Convocation met, the bishops showed themselves in favour of conciliation. The Lower House, however, was not ready even to consider the scheme. Had comprehension proposals accompanied the Toleration Act, English history—secular and religious—would have been very different. The Presbyterians and most of the Independents would almost certainly have entered the new National Church. "The strength of English Protestant Dissent would have been broken"[2]—temporarily, at least. Few but Baptists and Quakers would have remained outside the Establishment, and one is tempted to speculate whether that more inclusive body might not have been able to retain within it the new life of Methodism.

The comprehension proposals failed. Nonconformists had to be content with "an official claim to a second-class status".[3] The Presbyterians accepted the fact that they were tolerated Dissenters. Their London ministers drew up "Heads of Agreement" with the Congregationalists and joined in the building of meeting-houses, a policy they had hesitated to embark upon while there was any chance that they might be again worshipping in the parish churches. The older generation of Nonconformist leaders passed to their reward. Bunyan had died in 1688. Baxter, Fox, and Hanserd Knollys all died in 1691. Baxter's papers, issued by Matthew Sylvester in 1696, became the basis six years later of young Calamy's first attempt at a popular statement and defence of the case for Nonconformity, with biographical details of the ministers ejected in 1662.

[1] *An Abridgment of Mr. Baxter's History of his Life and Times* (1702), 655.
[2] H. S. Skeats, *History of the Free Churches of England* (1891 edn), 119.
[3] G. R. Cragg, *The Church and the Age of Reason* (1960), 134.

The development of a common attitude and ethos was furthered by the hostility shown to Dissenters by Queen Anne and those whom she appointed to office. It soon appeared that such liberties as Nonconformists possessed under the Toleration Act might be taken away. The Protestant Dissenting ministers in the cities of London and Westminster and the vicinity formed themselves in 1702 into a committee of the Three Denominations, Presbyterian, Independent, and Baptist, the latter being for the first time accepted on an equality with the others. The popular excitement which accompanied the scurrilous sermons of Henry Sacheverell, the attempts to stop "occasional conformity", the attacks on the Nonconformist Academies, and the terms of the Schism Bill of 1714 (which would have become law but for the death of the Queen) all indicate a rather desperate attempt to damage what there was obviously now little hope of suppressing or reclaiming. It was only natural that the Dissenters should support the House of Hanover, since the return of the Stuarts might well mean further penal legislation.

In considering the relationship of Anglicans and Nonconformists, the practice of occasional conformity requires careful scrutiny. So long as the Test Act remained on the statute book, all those appointed to public office, civil or military, were required, in addition to taking the oaths of allegiance and supremacy, to "receive the Sacrament of the Lord's Supper, according to the usage of the Church of England, within three months after his or their admittances in or receiving their said authority and employment, in some public church, upon some Lord's day". From the date of the passing of the Act in 1673, there were some who were ready for the sake of office and without any sincere religious conviction to take the sacrament. After the failure of the comprehension proposals, a number of prominent and public-spirited Nonconformists, like Sir Thomas Abney, one-time Lord Mayor and Member for the City of London, were occasional conformists. Daniel Defoe might call it "playing Bo-peep with God Almighty", but within the Church of England Archbishop Tenison and Bishop Burnet, and outside it men such as John Howe and Edmund Calamy, were ready to defend the practice. Few Baptists conformed in this manner, for in general they objected in more radical fashion than did the Presbyterians and Independents to a State Church. In 1742–3 a London Baptist church, after consulting all the London Baptist ministers, expelled one of its members who took communion at an Anglican church in order to become a Common Councillor. But that was at the time when the Corporation had begun its shameless policy of appointing Nonconformists as sheriffs in the hope that they might refuse office and be fined. When, in 1781, Cowper wrote scornfully about making the sacrament "an office-key, a pick-lock to a place", the Test Act was held in general contempt, though it remained the law of the land for nearly another half-century.

"Occasional conformity" might and did, sometimes at least, have deeper and more religious roots. "Look on all particular Churches as members of the universal . . . ", said Richard Baxter, "and chuse the best thou canst for thy ordinary communion. . . . But deny not occasional communion with any (though accused by others) further than they force thee to sin, or than they separate from Christ."[1] The tradition of Owen, Baxter, and Howe was never entirely forgotten.

The early decades of the eighteenth century were not an easy or attractive period so far as English religion was concerned. During the reign of George I a good many Dissenters joined the Church of England. On the other hand, certain Anglican historians have suggested that the Toleration Act, for all its merits, was responsible for an increasing laxity among parishioners, who were able to excuse themselves for non-attendance at church by declaring themselves Dissenters. The years 1730 to 1750 have been described as "the

[1] *Search for the English Schismatick* (1681), 44.

most depressing twenty years in English Christianity in the eighteenth century".[1] Moral standards were low: but these were the years when, in spite of the prevalence of Deism, William Law and Joseph Butler published their justly famous works, Isaac Watts and Philip Doddridge were influential among the Dissenters, and Daniel Neal produced his famous *History of the Puritans*. At the close of the preface to his first volume, dated 1 February 1731/2, Neal exhorts Protestant Nonconformists to gratitude that they have been delivered from "the Yoke of Oppression" and are "secure of their Civil and Religious Liberties". He goes on: "And may Protestants of all Persuasions improve in the Knowledge and Love of the Truth, and in Sentiments of Christian Charity and Forbearance towards each other, that being at Peace among themselves, they may with greater Success bend their united Forces against the common Enemies of Christianity!"

How far were ideas of an altered religious settlement cherished? Had Neal in mind anything more than co-operation against unbelief and immorality by two separately organized groups? It is difficult to say. Isaac Watts greatly strengthened the customary pattern of worship in Nonconformist meeting-houses by his paraphrases and hymns. He also argued, in his *Humble Attempt towards the Revival of Practical Religion among Christians* (1731), that the principles and practices of the Dissenters were more favourable to the growth of piety than were those of so-called Churchmen, and followed this up with an *Essay on Civil Power in Things Sacred* (1739), which condemned any National Church as unscriptural. Bunyan had made Christian say to By-Ends: "If you will go with us, you must go against wind and tide . . . you must also own Religion in his rags, as well as when in his silver slippers." Many of the Dissenting churches formed in the decades immediately after the Toleration Act soon dwindled to small groups of little social standing, and were often faction-ridden. At the same time, in the

[1] J. H. Colligan, *Eighteenth Century Nonconformity* (1915), 90.

metropolis and in a number of other towns the meeting-houses were supported by the trading and professional classes. The Dissenting Academies provided a more varied and useful education than did Oxford and Cambridge. There was being built up by the writings of men such as Watts and Michaijah Towgood, the Presbyterian, a tradition that sought not comprehension but the disestablishment of the Church of England.

Doddridge differed from Watts on the matter of establishment. A civil establishment of religion, combined with its compulsory support, was not, in his mind, contrary to the laws of justice and equity; if sufficiently broadly based, it could serve the best interests both of religion and society. The lead which Doddridge and other Dissenting ministers and laymen gave in support of the throne at the time of the rebellion of the Young Pretender in 1745 was rewarded with a special Act of Indemnity for those who, contrary to the provisions of the Test Act, had accepted commissions. In 1748, after conversation with Samuel Chandler, a well-known London Presbyterian divine, the Bishops of Norwich and Salisbury approached the new Archbishop of Canterbury, Thomas Herring, and suggested a fresh effort at comprehension based on an attempt to put the Anglican Articles in scriptural phraseology. The archbishop is said to have expressed interest and sympathy. Nothing further came of the proposal and Chandler was criticized by some of his fellow-ministers. Shortly afterwards, however, Doddridge visited Herring and suggested to him the possibility of "a Sort of a Medium between the present State and that of a perfect Coalition", namely "to permit the Clergy to officiate among us if desired" with "a Counterpart of permitting Dissenting ministers occasionally to officiate in Churches".[1] Again the archbishop is said to have replied sympathetically, but nothing more happened.

[1] New College, London, Doddridge MSS., i.102 (letter of 4 Aug. 1748).

Anglicans and Nonconformists alike had had much of their zeal sapped by the Deism which was intellectually popular. A century had passed since George Fox journeyed through the country starting one of the great revival movements in English religion, and even his followers had become restrained and inbred. The time was ripe for another incoming tide of religious interest and power. It began unexpectedly within the Church of England and within a few decades had transformed the ecclesiastical situation in this country.

The story of the rise and spread of Methodism and its relation to the Church of England has been often told. To the day of his death John Wesley claimed to be a loyal son of the Church. But the Nonconformity of the Restoration period had provided the early religious background of both his parents and, if he inherited from them the proverbial zeal of the convert, he no doubt also inherited a streak of independence and rebelliousness. His grandfather, the Reverend John Westley, was among the Dorset ejected ministers and was several times imprisoned for unlawful preaching. His father, the Reverend Samuel Wesley, after being at the Newington Dissenting Academy, conformed in 1683 in order to enter Exeter College, Oxford. His mother's father, Dr Samuel Annesley, was also among the ejected ministers and for thirty years or more was regarded as one of the leading London Presbyterian divines. Both his grandfathers died before John Wesley was born. He came of stock which had deserted Dissent and it is not without significance, perhaps, that in the years immediately after John's birth his father, Samuel Wesley, was engaged in a vigorous pamphlet attack on Dissenters and Dissenting Academies.

The intense young man owed his final spiritual release to the Moravians and to some words of Luther. What happened in Aldersgate Street in May 1738 coincided almost exactly with the appearance of the fourth and final volume of Daniel Neal's *History of the Puritans*. Nine years later, in the spring of 1747, Wesley, while visiting the Methodist societies in the north of England, "snatched a few hours to read *The History of the Puritans*". His comment is interesting:

> I stand in amaze: First, at the execrable spirit of persecution, which drove those venerable men out of the Church, and with which Queen Elizabeth's clergy were as deeply tinctured as ever Queen Mary's were. Secondly, at the weakness of those holy confessors, many of whom spent so much of their time and strength in disputing about surplices and hoods, or kneeling at the Lord's Supper.[1]

Though at one time, as he himself said, "so tenacious of every point relating to decency and order",[2] Wesley had long since ceased to be interested in such things. He had become an evangelist, determined to preach everywhere and anywhere "the glad tidings of salvation". His friend, George Whitefield, had persuaded him to the "strange way of preaching in the fields", but the societies Wesley organized were originally intended to be auxiliaries to the normal ministrations of the parish churches. "Are we not then Dissenters?" it was asked at a conference of sympathetic clergymen and lay preachers held in August 1766, by which time opposition of many different kinds had shown itself. The answer given was:

> We are irregular. 1. By calling sinners to repentance, in all places of God's dominion. 2. By frequently using extemporary prayer. Yet we are not Dissenters in the only sense which our law acknowledges: namely, persons who believe it is sinful to attend the service of the Church: for we do attend it at all opportunities. We will not, dare not separate from the Church.... We are not Seceders, nor do we bear any resemblance to them. We set out upon quite opposite principles.... They begin everywhere with shewing their hearers, how fallen the Church and ministers are. We begin everywhere, with shewing our hearers how fallen they are themselves.[3]

[1] *Journal*, ed. N. Curnock (standard edn, 1938), 13 March 1747.
[2] Ibid., 31 March 1739.
[3] *Minutes of the Methodist Conferences*, i (1812) 57.

Though hardly fair to the Dissenters, this statement indicates Wesley's own intention. A number of clergymen welcomed his efforts and caught something of his enthusiasm. Thomas Adam in Lincolnshire, Grimshaw at Haworth, Samuel Walker in and around Truro, Romaine, chaplain to Lady Huntingdon, John Berridge of Everton, Henry Venn in Huddersfield, and John Newton, first in Olney and then in London, set the pattern of a new type of ministry and became the precursors of the Evangelical party in the Church of England.

Most parish priests, however, resented Wesley's itinerant evangelism and they were supported in this by the episcopate. Joseph Butler, who was Bishop of Bristol in 1739, said to Wesley: "You have no business here; you are not commissioned to preach in this diocese. Therefore I advise you to go hence".[1] Lavington, Bishop of Exeter, called Wesley's followers "a dangerous and presumptuous Sect" animated with an "Enthusiastic and Fanatical Spirit".[2] Inevitably the breach widened when the Methodist lay preachers began to administer the sacraments (1760); when Whitefield's associate, the Countess of Huntingdon, was driven to register the chapels she had built as Dissenting meeting-houses (1781); when Wesley set apart Thomas Coke as superintendent of a mission to America and ordained two presbyters to assist him (1784); and when, at length, in 1787, Wesley registered his own preaching-rooms and, in spite of the opposition of his brother, Charles, ordained a number of preachers.

A new group had established itself in English religious life, separated from the Church of England and with certain features in common with Dissent, yet not easily nor at once assimilated to it. Wesley repudiated the idea that he was a Dissenter: the Dissenters were by no means sure they approved of Wesley. Most of them were Calvinists in theology

[1] See Curnock's note in Wesley's *Journal*, ii.256, n. 1.

[2] *Enthusiasm of Methodists and Papists Compared* (1749), pref.

and he was an Arminian. They were not, however, uninfluenced by the revival of evangelical interest and activity. Whitefield's zeal had been quickened by his contacts in America with Jonathan Edwards, a Congregationalist, who combined missionary zeal with a stern Calvinism which he defended with much intellectual acuteness. Whitefield, though an ordained clergyman of the Church of England, was often welcomed by the Dissenters. The chapels which he and the Countess of Huntingdon established became closely associated with the older Dissenting bodies. The writings of Jonathan Edwards prepared the way for a reformulation of Calvinism: this found particular expression among the Baptists, and its impact may be seen by comparing the writings of John Gill (1697–1771) and John Brine (1703–65) with Abraham Booth's *Reign of Grace* (1768), Robert Hall's *Help to Zion's Travellers* (1781), and Andrew Fuller's *The Gospel Worthy of All Acceptation* (1784).

Both the Church of England and the older Nonconformity had to meet another challenge besides that of the Methodists. It came from those growingly critical of subscription to creeds. Arian and Socinian views of the Person of Christ had long circulated in England and had found representatives in all the religious bodies, but principally among the Presbyterians and the General Baptists. Richard Price and Joseph Priestley were outstanding figures among the "Rational Dissenters", with reputations in public affairs—the one in politics and economics, the other in chemistry. Both were Presbyterian ministers, the product of Dissenting Academies. Both moved far from the Calvinism in which they were brought up. The first public move against subscription came, however, from within the Church of England. In 1771 Archdeacon Francis Blackburne, a Yorkshire clergyman, organized a petition against the signing of the Thirty-nine Articles by the clergy. The petition was actively supported by Theophilus Lindsey, the vicar of Catterick, Yorkshire, who resigned his charge, came to London, and opened what became in time the first Unitarian chapel. Blackburne's petition gained no official encouragement, but Nonconformists realized that, had it succeeded, they might have been left as the only group compelled to sign the Articles. The proposal to substitute a declaration regarding the Scriptures was opposed in the House of Lords by the Archbishop of York and most of the bishops, but drew from the Earl of Chatham a notable defence of Dissenters. Not all of the latter pressed their cause very vigorously at this time, for there were fears of the growth both of Romanism and Unitarianism. Subscription had come to be accepted as more or less a formality. In 1779 an amended declaration secured approval, and was followed by a Catholic Relief Act which led to the Gordon Riots. These were no credit to Lord George Gordon or the Protestant Associations which supported him.

Nonconformists of all types found themselves increasingly opposed to George III and his Tory ministers. "The dissenters are all for us", wrote Benjamin Franklin just before the outbreak of the War of American Independence.[1] That John Wesley sided with the Government against the colonists was another sign that he was not aligning himself with the traditional political attitudes of Nonconformity. The main body of opposition to Lord North's policy came, it is said, from the large trading towns and the Dissenting Churches. The hundredth anniversary of the "Glorious Revolution" of 1688 was approaching, and it was felt by many that it was high time that the Test Act was repealed. The passing of annual Indemnity Acts to protect offenders against the letter of the law only emphasized the humiliating position in which Nonconformists were placed. Attempts at Parliamentary action were made in 1787, 1789, and 1790, but even with the support of Charles James Fox they failed. Pitt and even Wilberforce voted for the retention of the Test Act,

[1] *Memoirs of . . . Benjamin Franklin* (2nd edn, 1818), ed. W. T. Franklin, iii.372 (letter of 7 July 1773 to T. Cushing).

hinting darkly that the next demand might be for exemption from church rates or even the disestablishment of the Church. Richard Price, in November 1789, in his eloquent sermon on "The Love of our Country", looked back to the Toleration Act but also across the Channel to what had recently occurred in France. In the words of Wordsworth, Price

> . . . from the pulpit zealously maintained
> The cause of Christ and civil liberty
> As one, and moving to one glorious end.

But feeling soon changed when what was happening in Paris became more widely known. In Birmingham in July 1791 Priestley's house was wrecked and nearly all his books, papers, and apparatus destroyed by a mob crying "Down with the Dissenters!", "Church and King!" In many other parts of the country Nonconformists found themselves ostracized or attacked. The improvement of their legal position, which had seemed so near, was postponed for more than a generation.

The next forty years saw further dramatic changes in the religious scene. Almost all the Nonconformist bodies grew considerably in size and influence, Methodism taking its place among them. The Test and Corporation Acts were repealed and, with the approval and support of Nonconformists, the main disabilities under which Roman Catholics laboured were removed. These last steps were taken under the patronage of members of the royal family and as a result of a reluctant surrender on the part of bishops in the House of Lords. On many issues, the Established Church and Dissenters stood over against one another in embattled array. But a new form of voluntary individual co-operation began. This was the age of societies, formed for a variety of religious and philanthropic purposes. Those influenced by the different phases of the Evangelical Revival found it possible to work together on behalf of a number of causes. Cutting across the traditional divisions between Churchmen and Dissenters, or between High and Low Churchmen, there appeared a new division between the enemies and the professors of what was called "vital godliness".

One of the earliest of the societies which drew support from members of many different denominations was that formed in 1785 to promote Sunday Schools of the kind started by Robert Raikes in Gloucester. Two years later, on the initiative of the Quakers, a united committee began a campaign against the slave trade. To begin with, official support came chiefly from Quakers and Baptists, but before long Beilby Porteus, Bishop of London, spoke out in favour of the committee, William Wilberforce became its parliamentary leader, and the aged John Wesley announced a public sermon in Bristol "upon (what is now the general topic) Slavery".[1] Within a few years the modern overseas missionary movement was launched, the Particular Baptist Society for the Propagation of the Gospel amongst the Heathen (1792) receiving financial help from a number of evangelical Anglicans and being followed by the formation in London of The Missionary Society (1795), a body without specific ecclesiastical affiliation. Even when Anglicans, Methodists, and Scottish Presbyterians had started their own missionary societies, there was a general feeling of unity in a great cause, and from 1813 to 1855 *The Missionary Register* chronicled the work of all the societies.

The Religious Tract Society (1799) and the British and Foreign Bible Society (1804) were founded by the same group of friends. The committee of the Bible Society should consist, it was decided, of an equal number of Churchmen and Dissenters, its three secretaries being one an Anglican, one a Nonconformist, and one a Lutheran. For a dozen years or more there was controversy among Anglicans as to whether it was right or expedient for Churchmen and Dissenters to unite in circulating the Scriptures and whether

[1] *Journal*, 3 March 1788.

under any circumstances the latter should be circulated without the Prayer Book. Here, as at other points, the Evangelicals gradually won the day. What the new fellowship across ecclesiastical boundaries meant to those who shared in it is vividly illustrated in an account of the meeting of the Norwich auxiliary of the Bible Society in 1811, which was followed by a party at Earlham Hall, the home of John Gurney, the Quaker. "We had a vast party at Earlham," wrote his son, "and a remarkable day, a perfectly harmonious mixture of High Church, Low Church, Lutheran, Baptist, Quaker! It was a time which seemed to pull down all barriers of distinction, and to melt us all into one common Christianity."[1] "Now of a truth", said Joseph Hughes—a Baptist, who became one of the secretaries of the Bible Society—"I perceive that God is no respecter of persons, but that in every age and nation those who fear Him and work righteousness are accepted of Him."[2]

These and a number of other societies owed much to the group of friends connected with Clapham—the Clapham Sect, as they came to be called—Henry Thornton, William Wilberforce, Charles Grant, Lord Teignmouth, Granville Sharp, Zachary Macaulay, and James Stephen. They formed a remarkable galaxy of talent, experience, and religious zeal, and, though all of them devoted Anglicans, were ready to co-operate with and aid Dissenters. They owed much to the Clapham rector, John Venn (son of Henry Venn of Huddersfield), and to the aged John Newton, who both in Olney and in London included many Nonconformists among his friends. Charles Simeon and Isaac Milner, in Cambridge, and Hannah More were among those who collaborated with them. Wilberforce's *Practical View of Christianity*, published in 1797, represented the general standpoint of them all. In this widely circulated volume, Wilberforce warmly commended the "masterly defence of the

[1] A. J. C. Hare, *The Gurneys of Earlham* (1895), i.230.
[2] Ibid., 231.

doctrines of Christianity" by Andrew Fuller, the Baptist. Of no less significance was the eulogy of Thomas Robinson, the Evangelical vicar of St Mary's, Leicester, uttered by the great Dissenting preacher, Robert Hall. "The change which Baxter accomplished at Kidderminster", said Hall, "*he* effected at Leicester."[1] In a few rare instances certain of the Anglican Evangelicals were prepared to sit down at the Lord's Table with those of other traditions, less rarely with members of the Established Church of Scotland. Instances are also recorded in the cases of William Wilberforce, Hannah More, and Claudius Buchanan—though the action was sometimes challenged.

As already indicated, this growing fraternization did not meet with immediate or general approval. The unsectarian schools started by the Royal Lancastrian Institution for Promoting the Education of the Poor (1808) were the subject of violent attack on the ground that they endangered the influence of the Established Church. The rival National School Society (1811) made attendance at a parish church and instruction in the liturgy and catechism compulsory. The year this latter society was formed, Viscount Sidmouth expressed concern at the increase in the number of meeting-houses and Dissenting ministers and proposed that the provisions of the Toleration Act be more stringently enforced. A flood of petitions to Parliament from all parts of the country caused the rejection without a division of Sidmouth's Bill. He had, however, correctly noted the considerable increase in the number of Nonconformist churches. The older Dissenting bodies, as well as Methodism, showed themselves better able to cope with the increase and shift of population which accompanied the Industrial Revolution. It is estimated that, in the early years of the nineteenth century, out of a total population of about ten million, some two million were Nonconformists. R. F. Wearmouth, who has made careful and detailed studies of Methodism, shows

[1] Robert Hall, *Works*, ed. O. Gregory (1832), iv.289.

that it made its greatest advances at the time when and in the places where the population showed the largest increases.[1] But Hensley Henson was right in noting that the Methodist preachers and those of the Baptists and Congregationalists often had the field to themselves. "We were not Dissenters", said a well-known miners' leader of a later generation; "there was nothing for us to dissent from."[2] Writing of "Cobbett's England" and "the mass of unregarded humanity in the factories and mines", G. M. Trevelyan says that "no one but the Nonconformist minister was their friend".[3] This is not altogether fair, but the measure of truth in it provides a clue to the growing power of Nonconformity during the era of Napoleon and the Industrial Revolution. As a result full civil rights were demanded with renewed confidence and militancy.

After the failure of Lord Sidmouth's attack there was formed in London a Protestant Society for the Protection of Religious Liberty, which set itself to secure the repeal of a number of the objectionable penal laws. Since 1732 a body of laymen known as the Protestant Dissenting Deputies had kept a watchful eye on any infringements of the existing rights of Dissenters. They had been active at the time of the exactions of the City Corporation and when earlier attempts were made to secure the repeal of the Test Act. The Deputies joined with the ministers of the Three Denominations in supporting the efforts of the Protestant Society, and in 1812 the Conventicle and the Five Miles Acts were repealed, while a clause was inserted in the Charter of the East India Company, which gave missionaries the right of passage to India and protection when there. The following year the statute was repealed which made it blasphemy to deny the doctrine of the Trinity: Unitarians thus secured recognition. Though isolated voices were raised

[1] *Methodism and the Common People* (1945), 182.
[2] H. H. Henson, *Retrospect of an Unimportant Life*, ii (1943) 80.
[3] *English Social History* (1944), 476.

against all these measures, they were acceptable to the general body of opinion both in Parliament and the country. In 1828, with virtually no responsible opposition, the Test and Corporation Acts were repealed, and in the next year the Catholic Emancipation Act placed Roman Catholics in the same position as Nonconformists.

H. S. Skeats[1] suggests that the willingness of the leaders of the Church of England to see certain of these old statutes disappear was the result of some kind of bargain by which Nonconformists on their part agreed not to oppose an increase in Queen Anne's Bounty, the fund established in 1704 for the augmentation of the livings of the poorer Anglican clergy, from which, since 1777, loans had been made for the building and repair of parsonage houses. The truth would seem to be that the removal of legislation which made Nonconformists only "half-citizens" came as a result of the increase in the numbers and vigour of the Nonconformist bodies, among which the Methodists had now to be reckoned, and as a result also of improved relationships among all those influenced by the revival movements of the eighteenth century.

The next forty years proved a more troubled period than might have been anticipated. G. M. Young in his *Portrait of an Age* speaks of a "state of stable equilibrium which the political advance of the middle classes, the Oxford Movement, and the growth of the Wesleyans destroyed".[2] If "stable equilibrium" suggests too quiet a state for the actual relationships existing between the Church and Dissent at the beginning of the nineteenth century, the new factors to which attention is drawn were certainly powerful and disturbing ones.

The Duke of Sussex presided in June 1828 over a banquet to celebrate the repeal of the Test and Corporation Acts. Three months earlier, John Henry Newman had become

[1] Op. cit., 454 f.

[2] 1960 edn, 65.

vicar of St Mary's, Oxford. There was about to be an upsurge of new life within the Church of England, very different from either Evangelicalism or the broad and somewhat rationalistic attitude which characterized not a few. Sir Ernest Barker described the Oxford Movement as "at once an opposition to nonconformity and an expression of nonconformity".[1] It sought to assert the Catholic element in the Church, in opposition to the Protestant, and at the same time opposed the State control of the Church and even challenged the official leadership. The movement provoked opposition within the Church and a sharply unsympathetic, even hostile, reaction from Nonconformists. It encouraged the latter to press not only for full religious equality and the ending of a number of privileges still attaching to members of the Church of England, but also for the disestablishment of the Church.

Bad times had brought much hardship and poverty in the towns. There was widespread agitation for an extension of the franchise and the sweeping away of much that was corrupt and effete. What appeared to be the slow acceptance by the bishops in the House of Lords, and by the clergy generally, of the need for parliamentary and municipal reform increased the eagerness with which most Nonconformists supported the agitation and then went on to campaign against rates levied for the upkeep of the fabric of parish churches, against the regulations governing marriages and burials, and against the restrictions of degrees at Oxford and Cambridge Universities to professed Anglicans. The Religious Freedom Society took up these causes in 1839. Before long there was an Evangelical Voluntary Church Association and in 1844 an Anti-State Church Society, which later became, as the Liberation Society, the main channel through which Nonconformists conducted political agitation for thirty years or more. Writing in 1839, an able young Baptist minister named Joseph Angus, who later

[1] *Britain and the British People*, 90.

became one of the most restrained and respected Nonconformist scholars and leaders of his day, prophesied that twenty years was the "utmost limit"[1] before the public establishment and endowment of religion would be ended and Church and State be completely separated.

That things did not work out in this way was due partly to the substantial internal reforms which the Church of England itself carried out and partly to the quickened spiritual life which the Oxford Movement brought to many parishes. It was due also to the fact that the Liberal party, though always eager for Nonconformist support and ready to undertake the disestablishment of the Church in Ireland—and later in Wales—never committed itself to the more difficult and controversial cause of English disestablishment. Initially the chances of success seemed considerably increased by the Disruption (1843) in the Church of Scotland, of which Thomas Chalmers was the central figure, and by the formation of the Evangelical Alliance (1846), which formally linked together Churchmen and Dissenters of the same theological and religious outlook. But a number of new factors soon complicated these relationships. The sharp controversies over the education clauses of Sir James Graham's Factory Bill of 1843—which, if passed, would certainly have placed elementary education largely in the hands of the clergy of the Church of England—and over the increased state grant to the Roman Catholic College of Maynooth showed how difficult it was for evangelical Churchmen and evangelical Dissenters always to see eye to eye on public questions. The results of the Religious Census of 1851, made public two years later, indicated how strong Nonconformity had become. So far as worshippers were concerned, Churchmen and Dissenters appeared to be in the proportion of 52 to 48; but more than a third of the population able to attend public worship when the census was taken had not done so and, had any large number of them, in the towns, wished to, there would have been no accommodation for them.

[1] *The Voluntary System* (1839), 207.

The census coincided with the re-establishment of the Roman Catholic hierarchy in Britain. Some 253,000 attendances at Roman Catholic services were recorded on the Census Sunday, but the Catholic population at the time has been estimated as nearer 680,000.[1] John Henry Newman had been received into the Roman Church in 1845 and Henry Manning followed him in 1851. The cry of "No Popery" was again raised, but an Ecclesiastical Titles Bill, hastily passed through Parliament by Lord John Russell, proved a dead letter. The implications of toleration were accepted by the great majority of the citizens, though few foresaw that in the century that followed 1850 the number of English priests of the Roman obedience would increase more than eightfold and their churches and public chapels more than threefold.

The main tensions in English religion continued to be those concerned with the claims of Dissenters and those within the general body of Evangelicals. When in 1862 the bicentenary of the Act of Uniformity and the Great Ejection was celebrated by Nonconformists in a somewhat truculent manner, it could not but provoke protests. Shortly afterwards, the most famous Nonconformist preacher of the day, C. H. Spurgeon, touched off a controversy, which lost him many friends, by denouncing Anglican Evangelicals who subscribed to the doctrine of baptismal regeneration. Spurgeon withdrew from the Evangelical Alliance and caused considerable disappointment to Lord Shaftesbury, who was always anxious to bring the leaders of the Churches together. Thomas Binney, of the King's Weigh House, was another Dissenting preacher who was frequently involved in public controversy. Lord Shaftesbury had difficulties with his fellow-Anglicans, particularly in connection with the evangelistic services he arranged in London when the results of the 1851 census were known, in the leadership of which Nonconformist ministers participated.

[1] See P. Hughes, in *The English Catholics 1850–1950* (1950), ed. G. A. Beck, 45.

In this atmosphere, and with the changes and chances of Victorian politics, Nonconformist grievances were only slowly redressed. The Marriage and Registration Acts of 1836 and 1856 did much to remove a number of difficulties. They served to protect from question marriages conducted by Nonconformist ministers, though a registrar had to be present. Church rates were not abolished until 1868. Three years later religious tests for office in Oxford and Cambridge at length disappeared. None of these changes came without a long and arduous struggle and even in 1871 the burial laws remained unaltered and caused frequent local scandals.

The period from 1829 to 1871 had proved a turbulent one, but beneath the troubled surface of ecclesiastical affairs some significant trends may be noticed. The Methodists had continued to grow in numbers, though the main body—the Wesleyan—had in 1857 suffered another substantial secession. The Baptists and the Congregationalists had both created nation-wide unions to link together their autonomous local churches, and these unions had begun to be effective central agencies. The Unitarians were losing some of the vigour and influence they had had in the early decades of the century. A number of Presbyterian congregations, which had formerly looked to Scotland, had become the nucleus of the new Presbyterian Church of England. A number of other smaller bodies had come into existence, of which the Plymouth Brethren were destined to be the most influential. Methodists, Baptists, Congregationalists, and Presbyterians all had substantial overseas missions, as had the Church of England, though its missionary awakening had come somewhat later and had been relatively less enthusiastic. In all the Nonconformist bodies there were some who deprecated the zeal and methods of the "Political Dissenters" whom Edward Miall led. Among both Anglicans and Nonconformists there were a few who realized that whatever the result of conflict over legal issues, and whatever the temptations to provocative action on either side, deeper questions would one day have to be faced.

As early as 1834 A. P. Stanley, whose father became Bishop of Norwich and who was himself later a notable Dean of Westminster, expressed his regret that Dissenters were not admitted to Oxford and Cambridge and prepared a scheme for admitting as far as possible all English Christians to the Established Church. In 1843 Thomas Chalmers made an eloquent plea for Christian union, his slogan being "Co-operation now, and this with a view, as soon as may be, to incorporation afterwards". Chalmers hoped that the Presbyterian system might reconcile episcopacy and congregationalism, and regretted that the Evangelical Alliance was formed on an individual and not a church basis. The leaders of the Churches did not very often meet, save those who supported the Bible Society and the Evangelical Alliance. In 1857 the Archbishop of Canterbury (John Sumner) invited two or three Nonconformists to Lambeth Palace and was attacked for encouraging "Spurgeonism in the Church". The same year A. C. Tait, then Bishop of London and later Archbishop of Canterbury, administered communion to delegates to an international Y.M.C.A. conference in London, in spite of public criticism in advance.

Tait was a liberal-minded man whose general attitude to the question of church relations has been compared to that of Archbishop Tillotson at the close of the seventeenth century. He was frequently criticized by High Churchmen, but gained the increasing confidence of Nonconformists by his friendliness and integrity. Nor was he without supporters in his own Church, among whom Henry Alford, Dean of Canterbury from 1857 to 1871, played an important part. "Nothing is more strongly impressed on my mind, when I look over the religious state of England," said Alford (in an address in 1867, afterwards printed in *The Contemporary Review*, of which he was editor), "than that we, who are members of her Established Church, have need to face the whole important question of our relations to Nonconformists, with a view to a re-adjustment, in the light of the Christian conscience, of our words and our acts respecting them."[1] Private meetings followed both in Canterbury and London, which did much to draw together Churchmen and Nonconformists. The part played in this process by Dean Stanley was an important one. His willingness to have the remains of David Livingstone interred in Westminster Abbey and to have placed there memorials of John and Charles Wesley, as well as the help he gave in representations to the Emperor of Russia in regard to the persecution of Baptists, did much to counteract the suspicions and acerbities that were all too frequent in the middle years of the nineteenth century.

The co-operation of Anglican and Free Church scholars in the preparation of the Revised Version of the Bible must be regarded as one of the most significant and influential events in the chequered story of church relations in this country. Within a few months of the decision in 1870 that such a version should be prepared, it was decided that Nonconformist scholars should be invited to share in it. In the end three Scottish Presbyterians, two Baptists, and one Congregationalist were members of the Old Testament company, while three Scottish Presbyterians, one Baptist, one Congregationalist, one Methodist, and one Unitarian were members of the New Testament company. Dean Stanley invited all the participants to a Communion Service in Henry VII's Chapel. The holding of this service, and more particularly the presence at it of Dr Vance Smith, the Unitarian, brought sharp protests from certain quarters, but F. J. A. Hort regarded it as "the beginning of a new period in Church history"[2] and what occurred had the support of J. B. Lightfoot (later Bishop of Durham) and B. F. Westcott (his successor in that see). The Revised New Testament appeared in 1881, the Old Testament in 1885. The contribution

[1] *Essays and Addresses* (1869), 65.

[2] A. F. Hort, *Life and Letters of F. J. A. Hort* (1896), ii.139.

of the Nonconformist scholars was no small one and the fifteen years of close collaboration played an important part in building up mutual respect and confidence.

The preparation of the Revised Version was not completed until well into the fifth and final period under review. While the scholars were at work, the visits to England of D. L. Moody and I. D. Sankey introduced to the churches of this country, particularly the Methodist and Baptist churches, new and quickening revivalist influences from America. These were years of growing controversy over biblical criticism and over the doctrine of the Atonement. The Anglican Church had had to face some of these issues as early as 1860, when *Essays and Reviews* appeared, and later when Bishop Colenso attacked the Mosaic authorship of the Pentateuch. The other Churches were not seriously involved until the Robertson Smith case in Scotland (1876–81), difficulties within the Congregational Union in 1877–8, and the more spectacular Down Grade controversy among Baptists, which led Spurgeon in 1887 to withdraw from the Baptist Union. Discussion of the application to the Bible of methods of scientific study, and the revolution in thinking demanded by the work of Darwin and Huxley, cut across the traditional ecclesiastical divisions. Every Church had its liberals and its conservatives. It is significant that none of the Churches was at denominational level split on these issues. Local and temporary embarrassments there were in plenty, but by and large all the Churches found the new ways of thought acceptable. In the process there was further cross-fertilization in the field of scholarship. Nonconformists recognized their debt to the great Anglican biblical and patristic scholars: Anglican scholars, on their part, welcomed the establishment in Oxford in 1886 of Mansfield College, and were soon ready to collaborate with Free Churchmen in establishing a theological faculty in London University.

The Church of England was much troubled during these years by the growth of ritualistic practices. A Public Worship

Regulation Act, promoted by Archbishop Tait in 1874, proved largely a dead letter. The Liberation Society thought the time ripe for a new campaign for disestablishment and prepared a blueprint with proposals dealing with compensation and with the disposal of both buildings and surplus property. But the Liberal party, to which the Society looked for help, was led by Gladstone, and no one appeared able or willing to take up the mantle of Edward Miall. Developments of a different kind were in process and gradually provided a new and wider setting to the whole problem of Anglican–Free Church relations.

The first Lambeth Conference of bishops of the Anglican Communion took place in 1867, but was solely concerned with domestic issues. The second, in 1878, considered the relations of the Church of England with the Moravians and the Old Catholics. The third, in 1888, prompted by a declaration of the General Convention of the Protestant Episcopal Church in the United States, adopted what has come to be called the Lambeth Quadrilateral as "a basis on which approach may be, under God's blessing, made towards Home Reunion". The Quadrilateral specified the Holy Scriptures, the Apostles' and Nicene Creeds, the Sacraments of Baptism and the Supper of the Lord, and "the Historic Episcopate, locally adapted in the methods of its administration to the varying needs of the nations and peoples called of God into the unity of His Church". After the Conference Archbishop Benson invited the Free Churches to confer as to "what steps can be taken, either towards corporate reunion, or towards such relations as may prepare the way for fuller organic unity hereafter". The initial response was not very encouraging, but the Free Churches were challenged by the invitation to clearer thinking about their own convictions and principles, to closer unity among themselves and to greater awareness of their position as world-wide communions. The General Presbyterian Alliance had been founded in 1877 and in 1881 the first Methodist

Ecumenical Conference had been held. An International Congregational Council met in 1891. Baptists were somewhat slower in this field, but when in 1905 the Baptist World Alliance was formed, it was clear that Baptists were to be one of the largest and most vocal of the world confessional bodies.

No less important for the British scene were new relationships between the Free Churches. In 1886 the Baptist Union and the Congregational Union, both bodies of growing strength, had held a joint session. There was some talk in 1890 of a world organization embracing both denominations. In 1892 a Free Church Congress was held in Manchester—the third Church Congress of the Anglicans had been held there as early as 1863—and from it there developed in 1896 a National Council of the Evangelical Free Churches, with a formal constitution and a full-time organizing secretary. Many saw this movement as a step towards a United Free Church. To some it heralded the long-delayed triumph of Nonconformists over the Establishment. In the minds of Charles Berry, a Congregationalist, and Hugh Price Hughes, a Methodist, the movement had a deeper significance. They not only summoned Nonconformists to take a fuller part in the religious life of the land and to be active in united evangelism; they also pleaded for a more considered and consistent churchmanship. A comment by Dr Elliott-Binns is apposite:

> This discovery by Nonconformity of the Catholic Church . . . saved it from lapsing into a barren individuality. Had it been content to face the twentieth century with the merely negative policy of the Liberation Society, disendowment and disestablishment, its fate might well have been that of the Liberal Party with which politically it was so closely involved. The vision and power of a number of great statesmen and prophets . . . enabled them to rise above the limitations of their heritage into a clearer air.[1]

[1] *Religion in the Victorian Era* (1936), 488 f; cf. E. K. H. Jordan, *Free Church Unity* (1956), ch. 3.

This was not easily or at once accomplished, however. Indeed it cannot be said to have been yet accomplished. The National Free Church Council had hardly been formed, with a supporting network of local councils, before renewed controversy in the field of national education diverted its energies into public agitation, as R. W. Dale of Birmingham, one of the greatest of Victorian Nonconformists, had feared might happen. The struggle over the Balfour Education Act, with the Passive Resistance movement which followed its passing, did no great credit to any of the parties concerned. In Parliament and in the constituencies it appeared as a conflict not only between Conservative and Liberal, but also between Church and Chapel. Wild men on both sides made reasonable compromise very difficult. Most Nonconformists were buoyed up by the hope that victory at the polls in 1906 would secure the abolition of the dual system in education and, further, the disestablishment of the Church in Wales as a step towards disestablishment in England. With so many members of the Government men of Nonconformist background and upbringing and so many Nonconformist M.P.s, such hopes appeared to have substance in them.

The politics of the period delayed the fulfilment of these hopes. The war of 1914–18 was to destroy them, or at any rate to postpone their fulfilment to a much more distant time and to very different circumstances. The last of the substantial grievances suffered by Nonconformists disappeared with the Burials Act of 1880. By the turn of the century, they could claim full equality with Anglicans, save for the advantages in public life—and no mean ones they remained—provided by the latter's State connection. An increasing number of boys and girls from Free Church homes were reaching the Universities, and other Free Churchmen besides Congregationalists were determined to establish theological colleges in Oxford and Cambridge. It is idle, though fascinating, to speculate whether a United Free Church might have been established in the first decade of the twentieth century but for the education controversy, and to wonder what might have happened to church relations had there been no war in 1914.

What, as can now be seen, was destined to determine the ecclesiastical and religious events of an era and of more than one continent was the World Missionary Conference held in Edinburgh in the summer of 1910. This would not have taken place but for earlier conference and co-operation by the various missionary societies. It owed much, also, to the Student Volunteer Missionary Union, formed in America in 1886, and to the World's Student Christian Federation, which came into existence at a conference in Sweden in 1895. A new generation began to appear, its members knowing and trusting one another in a manner denied to their predecessors. Not unnaturally they were somewhat impatient about "Old, unhappy, far-off things and battles long ago", whether of 1662 or 1862. They found it difficult at first to appreciate the hesitation shown by the Archbishop of Canterbury (Randall Davidson) as to his attendance at the Edinburgh Conference and the suspicious approach to one another of a number of the representatives. However, the Conference proved a remarkable occasion, the fountain-head of many ecumenical streams. The Commission on Co-operation and the Promotion of Unity reported that "the ideal which is present to the minds of the great majority of missionaries is" that it is "the aim of all missionary work to plant in each non-Christian nation one undivided Church of Christ".

If so, and whether the delegates realized it or not, they were presenting the Churches of Britain, divided since the seventeenth century, with an inescapable challenge regarding their own relationships, a challenge the more difficult to meet since during the past three hundred years the blessing of God has rested upon them, if not with "undistinguishing regard"—to borrow Charles Wesley's phrase—at least without exclusiveness. But it should be noted that though the Churches came a long way between 1689 and 1910, they never in that period really faced together the issues that separated them in 1662, namely the nature of the Church and the unity and order that may truly be said to be part of the divine intention. As Daniel Jenkins has remarked, "There has been little proper theological controversy about the nature of the Church and of God's ordinance for it since 1662".[1]

[1] *The Nature of Catholicity* (1942), 8.

6

TOLERATION AND ESTABLISHMENT: 2

Studies in a Relationship

EDWARD CARPENTER

POLITICS is the art of the possible, and the most that well-wishers of the Dissenters could hope to achieve—and liberal opinion came reluctantly and realistically to recognize this—was a Toleration Act (1689), which tolerated Dissent but did no more. Under its terms Dissenters could meet in buildings duly licensed, but their exclusion from Parliament was maintained under the Test Act and also from the Universities of Oxford and Cambridge. To secure more extensive privileges (or rights?) they must practise occasional conformity: but the difficulty during the next thirty years, particularly during the reaction under Queen Anne, was to keep this loophole open, not to advance beyond it.

Yet it was not only pressing political needs which led to the Toleration Act of 1689. The tumultuous history of England for the last hundred years had slowly engendered a more critical attitude towards religious affairs, of which John Locke (1632–1704) is the best and most influential exponent. If his more technical philosophical thought runs counter to ordinary common sense, his political thinking seemed to sum up what most intelligent and not over-zealous Englishmen had learnt as a result of the painful religious upheavals of the preceding century. Advanced opinion, represented by such as Chillingworth, the Cambridge Platonists, and (more extreme) Lord Herbert of Cherbury, had already shown signs of growing weary of divine decrees and infallible dogma, all of which helped to make the life of men in society disturbed and fratricidal. Was it not possible, they asked, to find a reasonable religion upon which all men of goodwill could agree: a version of Christianity which would bring together rather than divide and separate?

To such and kindred questions John Locke believed that he had hit upon a simple and quite uncomplicated answer. "Young man," said a worthy old gentleman to Francis

Blackburne (1705–87) when he went up to St Catharine's College, "let the first book thou readest at Cambridge, be Locke upon government."[1] Certainly no treatise was more powerfully formative of an age or, paradoxically, more clearly evoked by it. As Locke saw it, there was an absolute and clear-cut distinction between Church and State. The latter existed solely to promote civil interests—that is, in general, to maintain life, liberty, and property. To this end, and only to promote this end, it possessed, and had a duty to use, a coercive jurisdiction. The Church, on the other hand, was a voluntary society concerned with that aspect of life which requires "an inward and full persuasion of the mind". It existed to promote the worship of God and thereby to secure for its members "a certain expectation of eternal life". Hence it follows that force, which is proper to the State and capable of being used to serve the ends for which it exists, is wholly improper in the Church and in fact quite unable to secure those "inward aims which are alone its concern".

As to the nature of this "voluntary society", Locke is again equally definite, and he is not particularly interested in, nor sympathetic towards, a great deal of contemporary religious controversy. To those who asserted that there could be no true Church without a bishop or a presbyter, he replied with asperity, and in the spirit of Chillingworth, that nothing could be demanded except "such things as the Holy Spirit in the Scriptures has required"—and that is a profession of the Lordship of Christ. What mattered was not a "true Church", but the salvation of souls: and he (John Locke) was content to rely upon the promise, "Where two or three are gathered together in my name, there am I in the midst of them". It follows, therefore, that though Christians may be required to suffer persecution, they may never persecute: and the only punishment the Church can rightly inflict is exclusion from its own membership. From such

[1] Francis Blackburne, *Works* (Cambridge, 1805), p. iv, n*. The reference is to John Locke's *A Letter concerning Toleration* (1689).

general principles, Locke affirmed with authority: "The toleration of those that differ from others in matters of religion is so agreeable to the Gospel of Jesus Christ, and to the genuine reason of mankind that it seems monstrous for men to be so blind as not to perceive the necessity and advantage of it, in so clear a light."

What, however, was transparently clear to the lucid mind of the refined Whig philosopher did not (unfortunately) shine with so self-evident a light to Churchmen who lacked some of his sweet reasonableness. But there can be no doubt as to the influence of Locke upon his contemporaries, an influence which was felt increasingly as the years went on: nor that the willingness to tolerate after 1689 owed a great deal to his calm reflection upon events. His political philosophy may well have been somewhat superficial, but after a century of profound and bloody debate its essential message was much needed. Many Churchmen and Dissenters were wise enough to learn it.

The Act of Toleration, whatever its limitation from the Dissenters' point of view, certainly created a new situation. For one thing, it made it much more difficult for churchwardens to check absentees from public worship. This was, of course, not part of its intention, for the Act in no way affected the Englishman's legal duty, under the Act of Uniformity, to attend to his religious obligations on Sundays. Indeed it expressly stated "that all the laws made and provided for the frequenting of Divine Service on the Lord's Day, commonly called Sunday, shall be still enforced and executed against all persons that offend against the said laws, except such persons come to some congregation or assembly of religious worship allowed or permitted by this Act".[1] The fine for absenteeism was a shilling—no mean sum in those days.

The fact, however, became apparent that it was now much more difficult to enforce the law (it was never, of course, completely enforced): and Henry Compton, Bishop of

[1] Wm. & Mary, c. 5, s. 16.

London, in a conference he held with his clergy (1689–91) on "how they ought to behave under a Toleration", pointed out that to ensure attendance at divine worship on Sunday, Church of England and Dissent must now work together in the parishes. If they did not co-operate, recalcitrant parishioners would slip through the fingers of both. He therefore urged his clergy to cultivate friendly relations with the Nonconformists so that together they could see that the law was obeyed: though he later complained bitterly that in this matter he had been much misunderstood "as if he designed to disturb and interrupt that repose which the law had given the Dissenters". If both parties would respect the other's rights under the Act, Compton said, then it would "render charity triumphant over division . . . and make us of one spirit tho' of different minds".[1]

It is unlikely, however, that all the bishop's clergy found this advice congenial. Many of them felt an understandable, if none the less regrettable, sense of irritation at this new tolerated status which the Dissenters had come to occupy, the more so as under the halcyon days of Queen Anne's patronage Stuart and monarchical oppression seemed but a remote memory. To be fair to some of these clergy, the new situation meant a great psychological adjustment which they did not at first find it easy to make. Convinced Whigs such as Tenison, Archbishop of Canterbury, and Wake, his successor at Lambeth, bent their energies (unsuccessfully) to prevent the breaking out of any religious controversy which was likely to disturb the *status quo* and to unleash old passions. The leaders of the rank and file of the clergy, however, who had in the main returned to their traditional Toryism, and who were beguiled by the irresponsible but forceful leadership of Francis Atterbury (1662–1732), struggled through their representatives both in Convocation and in Parliament to prevent the Dissenters from taking

[1] *The Bishop of London's Eighth Letter to his Clergy upon a Conference how they ought to behave themselves under a Toleration* (1692).

advantage of Occasional Conformity to get round the Test Act. So strong was this Tory pressure that a Bill to this effect successfully passed through the House of Commons in the first session of Anne's first Parliament, but was thrown out by the bishops and Whigs in the Lords. It was introduced again in 1703 and 1704 with the same result, Thomas Tenison on the latter occasion, in spite of his gout, speaking against the Bill in the following forthright terms:

> I think the Practice of Occasional Conformity, as used by the Dissenters, so far from deserving the Title of a vile Hypocrisy, that I think it the Duty of all moderate Dissenters upon their own Principles to do it. I think that however it may be disapproved by some rigid Dissenters, it ought to be encourag'd by all good Church-Men, as a likely Means to bring them over. The employing Persons of a different Religion from the Establish'd has been preached in all Countries where Liberty of Conscience has been allow'd. That we have gone further already in excluding Dissenters than any other Country has done. That whatever Reasons there were to apprehend our Religion in Danger from the Papists, when the Test Act was made, yet there does not seem the least Danger to it from the Dissenters now: But on the other Hand, I can see very plain Inconveniences from this Bill at present. As it is brought in this last Time indeed, they have added a Preamble, that though it was put in the First Edition of the Bill, was left out in the Second, viz. That the Act for Toleration should always be kept Inviolable. But the Toleration Act being to take away all the Penalties that a Man might incurr by going to a separate Congregation, and the Occasional Conformity Bill being to lay new Penalties upon those that do it, how they can say, that this is not, in it self, a Violation of the other, I cannot very easily comprehend; . . . At a Time that the Protestant Dissenters, (however they may be in the Wrong by separating from us) yet are heartily united with us against the common Foes to our Religion and Government. What Advantage those, who are in earnest for defending these Things, can have, by lessening the Number of such as are firmly united in the common Cause, I cannot for my Life imagine . . .[1]

[1] *Memoirs of the Life and Times of . . . Thomas Tennison* (2nd edn [1715]), 103 f.

The Tories had yet, however, to reach the zenith of their power, and a Bill against Occasional Conformity finally became law (at the time of the Sacheverell scare) in 1711. Nor was this all. In 1714 there was passed the notorious Schism Act, under which no man was allowed to teach publicly or privately without first signing a declaration of conformity, which required him to have received the sacrament for a year previously according to the rites of the Church of England. Both Acts, fortunately, were repealed in 1719.

In Convocation during the reign of Anne the prevailing temper of the Lower House, till this ecclesiastical assembly was suppressed in 1717, was equally hostile to any assertion of Dissenting claims. Rather the interests of its members ran in a contrary direction. They found it more congenial, for example, to draw up a form for receiving Dissenters into the Church of England: and there was also a strong move (and as a consequence a heated pamphlet warfare) to declare lay baptism (i.e. baptism by non-episcopally ordained ministers or laity) "invalid"—"a Doctrine", so William Talbot, Bishop of Oxford, declared, "that do's at once Unchristian all the Reform'd Churches abroad, even those Blessed Martyrs among them, who have been Baptiz'd in their own Blood, laid down their Lives for the Gospel, and glorified God by their Deaths".[1] In the latter controversy the weight of scholarship—principally that of Joseph Bingham (1668–1723)—was able to foil the attempt.

This attack on the status of Dissenters by one section, and that the most vocal section, of the Church of England, was both serious and regrettable. It was also the more deplorable because Occasional Conformity was not in fact a practice exclusively inspired by the Test Act: it had been resorted to by some of the most eminent of the Dissenters, both Presbyterian and Independent (including Baxter and Bates), long before the Test Act was thought of—that is, since St Bar-

[1] Quoted [Roger Laurence], *The Bishop of Oxford's Charge Consider'd* (1712), 46.

tholomew's Day 1662. Such men communicated at Church of England altars for no political purpose whatsoever, and even suffered the embarrassment of being condemned for so doing by the more rigorous members of their own communions. The hostility of many extreme High Church clergy to this practice was, moreover, of recent origin ("but of late") and it reflected internal stresses within the Anglican Church itself—the tension between Whig and Tory, between Latitudinarian and High Church, between the Upper and Lower Houses of Convocation. In fairness to some of these high Anglicans, it must be allowed that such bigotry had its counterpart in the Dissenting camp, particularly at the parochial level, and that the story of expropriation during the Commonwealth was still remembered with great emotion.

But it would certainly not be a complete picture of the ecclesiastical scene, during the reign of Queen Anne, if it were viewed solely through the eyes of members of Parliament or of vocal clerics in Convocation, though the polemics in which these indulged undoubtedly had their influence upon relations between Church and Dissent in the parishes. Evelyn's diary shows that an occasional sermon against the Dissenters was part of a vicar's armoury and was expected of him. There were, however, many clergy and laity of the Church of England whose main concern was to combat the ignorance and lax morality of their age, seen in sexual licence and the profanation of the Lord's Day. These came to regard the Dissenters as their allies in an endeavour to secure reform. From such concern there sprang, at the close of the seventeenth century, various Societies for the Reformation of Manners which were almost exclusively Anglican in origin. The greatest of these was the Society for Promoting Christian Knowledge, founded in 1699 through the initiative of Thomas Bray.

From the beginning, this Society determined to shun divisive religious controversy and to promote a common

Protestant Christianity. Henry Newman, its indefatigable American secretary, enunciated its policy as follows: "The Society have purposely declined (as foreign to promote Christian knowledge) to concern themselves with the controversy between the Established Church and Dissenters, except in the instance . . . of defending infant baptism, the common result of disputes among Protestants being rather a lessening of charity than conviction of truth."[1] In pursuance of this intention, the Society steadily refused to publish literature which was polemical in tone (except towards Roman Catholics), and the author of a pamphlet entitled *The Duty of Public Worship Prov'd* was informed that it was not suitable for the instruction of children, since it could "lead them into controversies which might beget in them an uncharitable opinion of other Protestant Churches".[2] Even an episcopal author was discreetly told that his work was unacceptable for the same reason.

The Society adopted a similarly sensible attitude in its relations to those Charity Schools which it did so much to establish and to support, the increase in the number of which was such a striking feature of the early years of the eighteenth century. Religious debate was again rigorously avoided, with the happy result that "Dissenters sent their children to them and subscribed to them, sometimes more liberally than Churchpeople".[3] In maintaining this enlightened policy, however, the Society encountered a great deal of opposition, and had to engage in a hard struggle. In many a parish, where a high church Anglican parson secured control of the Charity School, a very real problem could result. Zealous Whigs began to suspect that such schools often became hotbeds of Jacobite sedition, and that their teachers "very indiscreetly fell at railing at the Dissenters".[4] There was

[1] Henry Newman to the Rev. Mr Paley, Leeds, 27 May 1727 (S.P.C.K. CS 2/18): quoted L. W. Cowie, *Henry Newman, An American in London 1708–43* (1956), 64.

[2] Ibid. [3] Ibid., 84.

[4] Christ Church, Oxford, Wake MSS., Arch. W. Epist. 15: quoted Cowie, op. cit., 85.

indeed a measure of truth in such charges, though they were often greatly exaggerated, and the words of Dr Isaac Watts, himself no mean educationist, were in part well-founded: "The Children were brought up in too many of these Schools in Principles of Disaffection to the present Government, in a bigoted Zeal for the word *Church*, and with a violent enmity, and a malicious Spirit of Persecution against all whom they were taught to call *Presbyterians*, though from many of their Hands they received their Bread and Clothing. It was Time then for the *Dissenters* to withdraw that Charity which was so abused."[1]

The controversy—there were over a thousand schools in 1713, educating some twenty thousand children—began to assume large proportions, so much so that Edmund Gibson, Bishop of London, feared lest the whole fruitful experiment should collapse. The Society, at headquarters, remained firm in its intention not to antagonize Nonconformists, and, when in 1717 a Charity School in Monmouth elected a Dissenter as master, it refused to interfere, though it tactfully sent him "a packet of books proper for his instruction as a Christian".[2] Edmund Gibson, a life-long friend of the educational movement, decided in 1723 to give a charge to the masters and mistresses of the Charity Schools "within the bills of mortality", in which address he earnestly pleaded with them to teach loyalty to the throne, and to cultivate co-operative relations with Dissenters. His words seem to have had some effect—the charge was published—and slowly across the years the problem disappeared.

Even the most convinced liberal opinion in the Church of England at the beginning of the eighteenth century, represented in such as Tenison and Wake, never contemplated that official relations with Dissent in England could be on

[1] Isaac Watts, *Essay towards the encouragement of Charity Schools* (1728), 13.

[2] Newman to Rowland Cotton, 2 July 1717 (S.P.C.K. CS 2/6): quoted Cowie, op. cit., 91.

the same footing as those between the Church of England and the Protestant Churches on the Continent. The latter had seceded from the corrupt Church of Rome; the former from the reformed Church of England. Caroline divines were divided as to whether Anglicans ought to receive the sacrament from the hands of ministers of the Reformed Churches abroad, and in return to welcome them to Anglican altars in this country. But the main stream of the English tradition, from John Cosin and Jeremy Taylor through to William Wake, took the more liberal and accommodating view. Of Peter Gunning (1614–84) his chaplain wrote: "There is not one setled Church, established by publick Authority, that he is not at Concord withall, and holds Christian Communion, and would actually embrace, and receive to his Prayers and Sacraments, and count as Members of the same Mystical Body, whereof Christ is the Head, . . ."[1]

The phrase "established by publick Authority" is, of course, the operative one. It was the same point which Archbishop Wake made in a letter to William Beauvoir, Chaplain to the British Ambassador in Paris:

> The scheme that seems to me most likely to prevail is, to agree in the independence, as to all matters of authority, of every national church on any others; of their right to determine all matters that arise within themselves; . . . and for points of doctrine, to agree as far as possible in all articles of any moment (as in effect we either already do or easily may); and for other matters to allow a difference, till God shall bring us to a union in those also. Only one thing should be provided for: to purge out of the public offices of the church all such things as hinder a perfect communion in the service of the church, so that whenever any come from us to them, or from them to us, we may all join together in prayers and in the Holy Sacraments with each other.[2]

[1] William Saywell, *Evangelical and Catholic Unity* (1682), 300.

[2] Lambeth Palace MSS., Wake-Beauvoir letters, XXI (letter of 18 Nov. 1718), quoted N. Sykes, *William Wake Archbishop of Canterbury 1657–1737* (Cambridge, 1957), i.277. This passage was referred to in a debate in Convocation on 2 March 1859.

The English Church at the Reformation had accepted (in practice) the principle of *cujus regio ejus religio*: and it was against this principle that Dissent had offended. In this respect, to quote from the Bishop of Winchester in Convocation nearly two hundred years later (1887):

> The very principle of Dissent is a denial of the principle of the English Reformation.... The Dissenters have a totally different principle—namely, that for very slight differences of opinion you may separate from a great national Church, and that any body of men that like may set up a new Church of their own ... however well intentioned the Clergy may be who wish to join in public worship in the chapels of our Nonconformist brethren, the doing so is untrue to the principles of the English Reformation.[1]

It was this position that Henry Compton tried to establish in a correspondence with a number of distinguished French and Swiss Protestants,[2] all of whom frankly confessed that if they were living in England they would certainly subscribe to the Established Church—that is, they would be conformists. Monsieur de l'Angle wrote that "it is without doubt the duty of all the Reformed of your Realm, to keep themselves inseparably united to the Church"; and Monsieur Claude that "to imagine that we cannot with a good Conscience be present at Assemblies, but onely when we do fully and generally approve of all things in them, it is certainly not to know neither the use of charity nor the law of christian society".[3] It was according to the same principle of reformed national Churches that Archbishop Tenison, in the debates in the House of Lords in 1707 in connection with the Act of Union with Scotland, was able to say with complete conviction that "he had no scruple against ratifying, approving and confirming it within the bounds of Scotland [since] he thought that the narrow notions of all the Churches had been their

[1] *The Chronicle of Convocation*, 12 May 1887.

[2] They were Etienne le Moyne, Jean Maximilien de l'Angle, and Jean Claude.

[3] Edward Stillingfleet, *The Unreasonableness of Separation* (1681), 421, 446.

ruin and he believed the Church of Scotland to be as true a Protestant Church as the Church of England though he could not say it was so perfect".[1] A common protestantism was more important than a common episcopacy. True it is that some high church Anglicans opposed Archbishop Tenison in the House of Lords in the Act of Union debate: and that the Earl of Nottingham, acting as their self-appointed spokesman, expressed his bemusement that the same Parliament could recognize the establishment of a non-episcopal Church in one kingdom and yet maintain an episcopal Church in another. It seemed to him to make theology a branch of geography![2]

Yet though Tenison took this view in respect of Presbyterianism in Scotland, he did not for a moment envisage any two-way traffic in relations between the Established Church and Dissent at home in England. He would welcome the occasional conformist at an Anglican altar: but he would not expect to go to communion with him, though he would have been happy to receive communion at the hands of reformed ministers abroad.[3]

Yet interchange of worship was not quite the same thing as the enjoyment of full civic rights, and Dissenters were beginning to make this distinction. The principle *cujus regio ejus religio* was an adaptation to new circumstances by the Reformers of an older medieval ideal: but the process of adaptation had weakened its authority. Toleration of Dissenters was itself a violation of the principle, and the Whigs having gone so far as to grant this in the Act of 1689, it was not logically easy for them (as opposed to High Churchmen) to stop short of conferring upon Dissenters full civic rights. If

[1] *State-Papers and Letters addressed to William Carstares*, ed. J. McCormick (Edinburgh, 1774), 760.

[2] It is worth noting that by the Act of Union the 16 peers representing Scotland in the House of Lords and the 45 commoners in the Lower House were exempted from the English sacramental tests.

[3] The existence of an episcopal Church in Scotland made matters a little more complicated in practice.

pressed, such men as Tenison would probably have taken a purely practical view, namely that, given the divisions within the Church of England, toleration with occasional conformity was the best immediate solution. As it was, he preferred not to discuss the matter, and in his latter years, in view of extreme pressure from militant high church Anglicanism, his one concern was to avoid controversy. Very wisely, he prevented the proposed terms of the comprehension of 1689 from being made public: "as one side would upbraid their brethren for having given up so much; while the other would justify their non-conformity, because these concessions were too little, or, however not yet pass'd into a law".[1]

Certainly it would have been difficult to justify the exclusion of Dissenters from public office in terms of the politico-theological philosophy of John Locke: and even more difficult in the logical working-out of his ideas by Benjamin Hoadly (1676–1761).

Hoadly strongly supported the Dissenters in their occasional conformity but did his best (in his *Persuasive to Lay Communion*) to encourage them to re-enter the Church of England by advocating that the latter be made as acceptable to them as possible. His sermon on *The Nature of the Kingdom, or Church, of Christ* (1717) sparked off the Bangorian controversy, which led to a vast pamphlet warfare and generated a great deal of heat. "In the Affairs of Conscience and Eternal Salvation...", Hoadly said, Christ hath "left behind Him, no visible, humane Authority; ..."[2] Thus in one short sentence he sought to explode the claims of a thousand years! The distinction between Church and State is absolute, he affirmed, and the State may only exclude from full civic rights in order to protect itself, as in the case of Roman Catholics who support a foreign power, or of atheists who undermine the principles on which government rests. The Test and Corporation Acts must therefore be repealed.

[1] Thomas Birch, *Life of ... John Tillotson* (1752), 191.
[2] Op. cit., 11.

One of Hoadly's chief opponents in the Bangorian controversy was Thomas Sherlock (1678–1761), an intelligent High Churchman who enjoys the unique distinction of having declined both the archbishopric of York and that of Canterbury. Sherlock rejected the basic presuppositions on which Locke's whole philosophy of the State was built and in much of his thinking he anticipated the views of Edmund Burke. In Sherlock's eyes, society was a much more delicate and living organism than Locke's logical analysis would seem to suggest: and in his *Vindication of the Corporation and Test Acts* he began by declining to make any clear-cut distinction between Church and State. The life of the one was bound up in the life of the other, and the history of both, since the Reformation, showed only too plainly that when the Church was overturned the State also was plunged into anarchy—or was submitted to dictatorship. Was there any guarantee, he asked, that if Dissenters were now admitted to offices of trust they would behave differently? Was it not still necessary to protect the mass of the nation from the enthusiasm of the few? To talk of the profanation of the sacrament in that it was required as a test for civic office was simply not true. In fact receiving the sacrament was *not* the qualification for office under the Act, but simply the *proof* of such a qualification. "These men", he observed caustically, "are not *made* wicked by the Law; but *being* wicked, they *abuse* as well the *Law* of their *Countrey*, as the *Institution* of the *Gospel*."[1] In a letter written some years later to Dr Philip Doddridge, Sherlock said: "The Act of Toleration was designed with no other view than to ease the *conscience* of those who *could not conform*."[2]

Sherlock's and Hoadly's views assume two different attitudes towards the nature of Church and State and of their

[1] Op. cit. (2nd edn 1718), 19. Such an argument would, of course, logically preclude Occasional Conformity.

[2] Philip Doddridge, *Correspondence and Diary*, ed. J. D. Humphreys, v (1831) 199 (letter of 11 May 1751).

mutual relations. Hoadly is at his weakest when he pushes his logic too far: Sherlock in his appeal to history, for England in the early eighteenth century was not the England of the Commonwealth. The Tory in Sherlock stands in protest against the liberal-secular State which was in process of emerging, and which for all practical purposes was to become neutral in respect of religion. Hoadly, on the other hand, stands for an essentially secular order, in which, when it is fully worked out, Christian and non-Christian, religionist and non-religionist, will find their place in a common citizenship in response to a common national idea.

By and large an understood relationship between Anglican and Dissenter[1] was now beginning to grow up. It could be disturbed by a difficult incumbent or an aggressive minister—and tithes, particularly in respect of the Quakers, might always break up the peace of a village. William Cole, vicar of Bletchley, Buckinghamshire, found it difficult not to feel a constant irritation when in the presence of Dissenters, and particularly resented it when any of them referred to "when he was at College".[2] On the other hand Mr Millar, vicar of Harlow, Essex, a "very mild, benevolent man", was often seen walking "arm in arm" with the Dissenting minister settled in his parish.[3] Dr Samuel Johnson, that staunch Churchman, said of Isaac Watts's biographer: "I took to Dr Gibbons.... I shall be glad to see him. Tell him, if he'll call on me, and dawdle over a dish of tea in an afternoon, I shall take it kind."[4] The Dissenter was fast beginning to establish himself as an accepted and familiar ingredient in the English scene, both religious and social. He had already a venerable history behind him. Customary relations with his neighbour were springing up, and in an age of deistical

[1] I am not here including Methodism in Dissent.

[2] William Cole, *Bletchley Diary*, ed. F. G. Stokes (1931), 102.

[3] William Jones, *Diary*, ed. O. F. Christie (1929), 262 f.

[4] *Boswell's Life of Johnson*, ed. G. B. Hill & L. F. Powell (Oxford), iv (1934) 126.

religion it was being increasingly felt that Church and Dissent were ultimately standing for the same thing. Even that stout Tory, Thomas Sherlock, mellowed by the passing of the years, felt it not improper to observe to Dr Philip Doddridge: "Whatever points of difference there are between us, yet I trust that we are united in a hearty zeal for spreading the knowledge of the gospel, and for reforming the lives and manners of the people according to it."[1] He would not have written like this earlier. Responsible people were much more concerned with raising the general level of individual and corporate morality, with preventing the excesses of gin drinking and the sexual promiscuity of the upper classes, than with the niceties of religious dispute.

If the rise of Methodism in the middle years of the century made life more difficult for many an Anglican incumbent, as Archbishop Herring's visitational returns suggest, it tended to make him feel more at home with the longer established and not so enthusiastic Dissenter. The latter had seceded much earlier, beyond the memory of living men: he took his nonconformity for granted and had become much more respectable with the passage of years. When the *St James's Chronicle* printed the following doggerel in September 1773, most readers must have regarded it as faintly ridiculous:

Then shall Dissenters acquire
The Thing of all Things (Heaven knows)
After which they as warmly aspire
A stroke at our Creeds and our Laws.
Then shall we inactive be found
When by rage puritanical full-blown
Our Church is pull'd down to the ground
And our Monarch depos'd from his Throne.[2]

It is surely significant that Parson Woodforde, in his long, delightful, and gastronomic diary, makes hardly any querulous references to Dissenters: though it is clear that even his

[1] P. Doddridge, *Correspondence and Diary*, v.153 (letter of 24 March 1750).

[2] *St James's Chronicle*, 25 September 1773.

accommodating temperament found the Methodists a little trying from time to time.

This same general picture is borne out in the detailed visitational returns of the diocese of Canterbury for the years 1758, when Thomas Secker was archbishop, and 1788, in the time of John Moore. It is quite clear from the temper of the returns, made by innumerable parish priests in both town and country (principally the former), that neither Dissent nor, for that matter, Methodism constituted a really serious problem. True, there are many references to meeting-houses duly licensed: to families of Independents, Presbyterians, Methodists, and (less frequently) of Quakers. Often it is specifically stated of Methodists or Dissenters that they "come to Church regularly", sometimes with an addition in respect of the latter "except on Sacrament Sunday". There was a fairly large number of Nonconformists in the city of Canterbury in 1758, but relations between them and the various incumbents seem to have been easy. The vicar of St Andrew's returned that he thought of late years sectaries were fewer, "owing to the moderation with which they have been treated". In the parish of St Mildred the rector, Theodore Delafaye,[1] wrote that "there are 3 or 4 presbyterian families but they scruple not to attend the Church service, whenever their own is intermitted". The one Methodist family in the parish also "constantly attend divine service on the Lord's Day and the Sacrament of the Lord's Supper whenever administered". In another parish there were some thirteen families of Anabaptists, but the incumbent notes that they attend church once a month. It is interesting to find that the rector of Little Birchhill made a convert of an Anabaptist at the age of 90: and that the rector of St Mary's, Canterbury, felt that he must inform the archbishop of a congregation of Methodists of "the lower sort" which was meeting regularly in the Palace![2]

[1] Probably of Huguenot descent.

[2] Visitational Returns for the Diocese of Canterbury, 1758 (Lambeth Palace Library).

It is not so much the details of the returns which are significant, as the spirit in which the returns were made. They do not suggest angry and frustrated men. The same story is in essentials told in Archbishop Herring's Visitational Returns for the diocese of York (1743), except that relations with Methodists seem to be somewhat more difficult.

It is perhaps understandable that many Anglicans did not know how to deal with the novel kind of Dissent which they found in Methodism, so near to the Church of England and yet so far. Even Parson Woodforde, as we have seen, whom no one could accuse of being awkwardly zealous, felt a faint irritation at its existence, though the irritation was soon forgotten. A more extreme case is that of John Skinner[1], a devoted, zealous, but irascible clergyman who was rector of Camerton in Somerset from 1800 till he blew his brains out in a wood close to the rectory in 1839.

It is clear from his diary that Skinner found the Methodists a source of unsettlement in his half-rural, half-industrial parish. He resented their building a new meeting-house; their presence at the bedside of the dying; their lack of deference to his office. He would accost them in the street and engage them in argument. Once he asked two Methodists whether it was possible for uninstructed persons to preach, only to receive the reply that "there was no reason that the colliers should be despised if they had the gift of God to perform his commandments". To John Skinner, Wesley was an "unprincipled adventurer", and he asked in his diary: "Is it the same thing to attend the crude, undigested effusion of a cobbler, or a collier, under the name of prayer, as the beautiful service of our Liturgy? Is it the same thing to have a Minister resident amongst them to visit the sick, advise the ignorant and relieve the afflicted, or to contribute at the Meeting House to a needy adventurer, who himself is greedy of the dole extorted from the hard hands of mechanics?"[2]

[1] *The Journal of a Somerset Rector*, ed. G. A. Coombes and R. Bax (1930).

[2] Ibid., 24.

This is miserable stuff; and it was to be expected that the Methodists in Camerton ceased to attend their parish church, except occasionally to flock in for a funeral. Yet, deep down, Skinner could not but realize the solid worth of some of these men, for he writes regretfully that they "could be very useful to the clergy" if they were not "hurried away by feeling and fancy". No one knew better "the private lives and dispositions of the poorest workers".

Skinner was a prejudiced, bad-tempered man; and his parish, unlike Woodforde's, included a pocket of industrial workers, mainly miners. But he was also a dedicated and zealous man, anxious to do the best for his parishioners. What happened in Camerton doubtless occurred elsewhere: and many a sincere and zealous incumbent, perhaps in his heart of hearts conscious of failure, vented his frustrations upon the Methodists. It was likely to be the Skinners rather than the Woodfordes who found relations difficult. Perhaps there were more of the latter than the former.

Indeed, some incumbents agreed with the Dissenters in regarding subscription to the Thirty-nine Articles as an intolerable burden. The concern of such Anglicans, however, in wishing to secure a measure of relaxation, was not so much to meet the scruples of the Dissenters—though they might certainly benefit—as to preserve their own intellectual integrity. For example, in 1749 John Jones, vicar of the troublesome parish of Alconbury, Huntingdonshire, published *Free and Candid Disquisitions relating to the Church of England*, in which he proposed a number of modifications in the Prayer Book services, in both form and ritual, which would go a long way to meet the scruples of Latitudinarians and indeed of Dissenters. This little book was read in manuscript by Francis Blackburne (1705–87), vicar of Richmond, Yorkshire, who, though he thought it "too milky", yet rallied to the support of the author in *An Apology*, followed by *Pillars of Priestcraft and Orthodoxy Shaken.* In this latter work Blackburne argued against the casuistry which enabled people to subscribe to the Thirty-nine Articles with mental reservations and a loose interpretation. For himself he determined never to subscribe again. Blackburne's best-known book, written many years before it was published in 1766, was *The Confessional: or a Full and Free Enquiry into the Right, Utility and Success of establishing Confessions of Faith and Doctrine in Protestant Churches*. In this exposition, Blackburne accepts in its entirety the argument of Chillingworth that the Bible is "the Religion of Protestants", and from this concludes that a simple and direct profession of belief in the Scriptures as the Word of God is the sole pledge which ought to be demanded of Protestant pastors. History showed how harmful to the cause of true religion was the imposition of confessional tests.

Blackburne's book led to a spate of pamphlets; and, more practically, to a meeting in the Feathers Tavern in London in 1772, at which two hundred enthusiastic persons signed a petition urging Parliament to give effect to Blackburne's proposals. The petition was eventually debated in the House of Commons, where it was thrown out after an eloquent speech against it by Edmund Burke.

Blackburne, who was near to being a Unitarian, must not be thought of in this context as representing a majority of his brethren in the Church of England: but the rationalistic approach to theology was typical of his age, and it did not lend itself to arguing a case for the exclusion of Dissenters from University and Parliament.[1] There can be little doubt that many members of the Church of England were unhappy about such a denial and felt that it needed justification. Two examples of such questioning may be quoted from the works of Warburton and Paley.

Dr William Warburton (1698–1779), Bishop of Gloucester, who has been described as a "mass of ill-digested learning", handles the subject in his *The Alliance between Church and*

[1] From 1727 annual Indemnity Acts allowed Dissenters to hold municipal, civil, and military office.

State (1736). He accepts, in essentials, the position of John Locke, agreeing that there is a clear-cut distinction between Church and State, the former having as its aim truth, the latter utility. Through the "original compact" or alliance between the two, the Church is enabled to serve the State, and the State, in return, to protect the Church. This demands, in practice, a national religion which necessitates a Test Act when there are competing religious patterns within the one State. To place all religions on an equal level would be to break the original alliance, and anyhow would be found unworkable.

But how is the one national or established religion to be chosen? This is a nice question but its nicety flies above Warburton's head. His answer (in the spirit of Thomas Hobbes) is simple—the choice must fall on the most powerful sect; though he leaves himself a loophole of escape from the charge of naked utilitarianism by adding "where there is an equality in other points". "Truth", it must be charitably understood, is one of those points, but how is the "true Church" to be established when represented by a minority group? Anyhow, who determines what *is* true? The fact is, of course, that Warburton is arguing to justify an existing situation, and though he writes in terms of universal principles it is the England of his own day that he has in mind. Thus he maintains that to establish Episcopacy in England and Presbyterianism in Scotland is perfectly right and proper.

If it is the case (as I suspect) that Warburton is not very happy about the disabilities to which Dissenters were subjected, this is even more true of Archdeacon William Paley (1743–1805), the famous author of the *Evidences*, though our concern here is with his *The Principles of Moral and Political Philosophy* (1785).[1] One of Paley's distinguishing characteristics is his extraordinary clarity and frankness—the latter virtue making some of his ideas appear rather shocking to Christians in our own day.

[1] Book 6, ch. 10: "Of Religious Establishments and Toleration".

Paley admits, at the outset, that establishment is no necessary part of Christianity, but simply a means of promoting it. The authority of a church establishment therefore depends on its utility, whether it is the best means in a given situation of communicating (and preserving) "religious knowledge". What may be asserted in general terms is that, if it is to do this, there must be a clergy, a legal provision for them, and in practice the preferring of one sect to another, since it is unlikely that sects will work together if they are all on a level. There are obvious dangers, Paley admits, in making such a preference. If too rigorously maintained, it can stifle intellectual curiosity, coerce the conscience, prove inimical to liberty, and be continued, in respect of particular sects, long after the necessity for it is past. Such a restriction can only be justified when the test laid down is absolutely minimal and "subject to constant review". One thing is quite certain. It is idle to base the preference on the discovering of a church order supposedly laid down in the Gospels as valid for all time. The episcopate developed simply out of the exigencies of a particular age. Its continuance depends on whether it is found to be equally necessary in another. For himself Paley believed that it still had a value in eighteenth-century England, and for three reasons: (1) it helps to secure "tranquillity and subordination" amongst the clergy; (2) it corresponds "with the gradations of rank in civil life"; (3) "the same fund produces more effect, both as an allurement to men of talents to enter into the church, and as a stimulus to the industry of those who are already in it, when distributed into prizes of different value, than when divided into equal shares".

Such a thoroughgoing utilitarian approach, Paley realizes, raises many problems, not least the position of Dissent within the Establishment. He sees no difficulty, however, in the civil magistrate's "interfering in matters of religion", though he recognizes that some oppose this on the grounds that it is a private affair between God and a man's conscience. "There is nothing in the nature of religion, as *such*," he writes, "which exempts it from the authority of the legislator, when the safety and welfare of the community requires his interposition." This at first seems a departure from Locke, but it is in fact only a quibble about words. The acts of the civil power cannot, of course, affect a man's eternal salvation, though the same civil power may deprive him of liberty, even of life. Quite obviously religion affects the whole of existence, corporate as well as individual, so that if religion is not at times subject to civic control there would be no civil government at all. "Religious liberty is like civil liberty, not an immunity from restraint, but the being restrained by no law, but what in a greater degree conduces to the public welfare."

Subject to such overriding necessity, toleration is both just and expedient, particularly in that it promotes truth, the highest value which religion can seek after. Can such overriding necessity still be pleaded as an excuse for excluding any citizens in 1785 from public office? Paley replies that this is a practical question, since some religious principles might be incompatible with the "necessary functions of civil government"—e.g. a profession of community of goods with the existence of private property; or Quaker peace principles with the needs of defence. Apart from the latter (Quakers), Paley goes on to say that he cannot find a single tenet held by the Dissenters which disqualifies from State office, particularly since it cannot reasonably be held that *mere* "discordancy" disqualifies. "I perceive no reason", he writes deliberately, "why men of different religious persuasions may not sit upon the same bench, deliberate in the same council, or fight in the same ranks, as well as men of various or opposite opinions upon any controverted topic of natural philosophy, history, or ethics."

Test laws, therefore, ought to be imposed only where there are two religions contending for supremacy, in which case the way to secure peace might be by establishing the one and excluding the other: or, more reasonably, when "some disaffection to the subsisting government happens to be connected with some religious distinctions". Here the State is not concerned with a man's faith but with his politics, and a religious test is imposed only because no other test is possible. It must be withdrawn the moment the political danger ceases.

No one could legitimately maintain that the Dissenters in 1785 constituted such a menace, and Paley's judgement would seem to be (by the implications of his own logic) that the imposition of disabilities upon them could not be justified. "The wisest and safest system which a state can adopt", he writes, is "a comprehensive national religion, guarded by a few articles of peace and conformity . . .; and with a *complete* toleration of all dissenters from the established church, without any other limitation or exception, than what arises from the conjunction of dangerous political dispositions with certain religious tenets."

If Paley could write like this in the eighteenth century and have a great deal of responsible opinion behind him, why was it that the Test Act remained on the statute book till 1828, and the exclusion of Dissenters from degrees at Oxford and Cambridge remained effective till the second half of the nineteenth century? The answer is to be found in the history of the intervening years. It would be interesting, but certainly idle, to speculate what might have happened in the relations between the Church of England and Dissent, had there been no bloody French Revolution and no aggressive Napoleon. Perhaps without this bogey both the complete emancipation of Nonconformity and much-needed reform within the Church of England would have come much earlier. As it was, the excited cry of triumph with which Dr Priestley and the young Wordsworth greeted the fall of the Bastille was offset by the impassioned eloquence of Edmund Burke, who in the course of his Irish rhetoric achieved the seemingly impossible feat of creating a mystique around the eighteenth-century Church of England, caught up as it was in pluralism and non-residence. Certainly his philosophy of the State was more subtle and much more profound than the atomistic Whig tradition of Locke, Hoadly, and Paley: but his native capacity to romanticize was as much a snare to him as the temptation to rationalize was to the Whigs. "We know," writes Burke in his *Reflections on the Revolution in France* (1790), "and what is better we feel inwardly, that religion is the basis of civil society, and the source of all good and of all comfort." Thus he will have nothing to do with an absolute distinction between Church and State, or with an "original alliance" between them. Church and State are one and indivisible; and the Establishment, against which Priestley and Price complained in the petitions of the Unitarians received by the House of Commons on 11 May 1782, was really "a great national benefit, a great public blessing". So it came about, *mirabile dictu*, that Burke's insight into the organic nature of society and the complex of reason and emotion which go into the making of it, made him see in the inadequate Church of England a great and precious bulwark against the forces of godless revolution. "We must venerate", he said, "where we cannot comprehend": which implied, in practice, that to disturb the Establishment in any way might well open the floodgates to the onrush of anarchy and violence.

In taking this view, Burke was articulating the feelings of the ruling classes in England, and later of those who were disillusioned by what had happened in France. The retreat of such as William Wordsworth from the lyrical outburst of "Bliss was it in that dawn to be alive" to joining the volunteers and becoming a regular churchgoer was symptomatic of a general temper of mind. The result was, almost for a generation, to sap the vitality of liberal opinion, and to transfer crusading ardour to the radicals. The Peterloo massacre and the Six Acts were the unthinking reaction of the Government to the new pressures. Yet fear of revolution could not permanently halt the course of reform. The fact that the Test and Corporation Acts (though mitigated by the annual Acts of Indemnity) were still on the statute book was felt by liberal men to be an affront, and in 1828 they were repealed.

The repeal was an open if long-delayed recognition that membership of the Church of England could no longer be required for full membership of the nation: and indeed that, if the Establishment were to be maintained, this could only be secured by recognizing a fundamentally changed situation, implicit since 1689. No longer could Establishment confer unique political status. Yet the repeal of the Test and Corporation Acts, perhaps inevitably, led to a rallying of those minority and conservative forces which opposed the new secularism and stood for the reinstatement of an older ideal. An indication of this nostalgia is to be found in the republication in 1826 of Thomas Sherlock's *Vindication of the Corporation and Test Acts* and in an article published some time earlier in the *Quarterly Review* where the author writes:

> If a discussion of this subject should be brought on, we have one request to make. It is, that no member of the legislature will give a suffrage on the question, without previously perusing a small tract of Bishop Sherlock on this subject, a tract first drawn up in the Bangorian controversy. . . . We care not if everything be read over and over again that was ever written against the test laws; but shall be amply satisfied if only this small treatise be read in their defence. Let a plain understanding, biassed by no prejudices, be brought to the discussion, and we shall have no fears as to the result.[1]

Whether it was that not enough people read the pamphlet cannot be known: but certainly the repeal of the Test Act passed through Parliament. The truth is, of course, that Sherlock's pamphlet was based upon presuppositions, going right back into the Middle Ages, which were no longer

[1] ii (1809) 309.

acceptable, and which anyhow were quite incapable of being implemented in the England of the nineteenth century. Also the historic appeal to what happened during the Commonwealth had become ridiculous. Even Pusey half recognized this fact and saw in the Test Act the expression of a sordid Erastianism, so much so that he described it as both in its means and in its end "a disgrace and deterrent to religion".[1] Yet at the same time he suspected that anti-Church bias was the mainspring of the demand for its abolition. Parliamentary opposition to repeal came more from those who venerated the Establishment as such and were opposed on principle to change of any kind.

The effects of the repeal of the Test Act on the psychology and attitudes of the Dissenters, if they were not immediately dramatic, were none the less profound. The end of Occasional Conformity and Acts of Indemnity was an invitation to campaign against other grievances which were still very real. The rise of "the Nonconformist conscience" and of "the dissidence of Dissent" was bound to have repercussions in the relations of Anglicans to Nonconformists; the more so as something was happening within the Church of England itself which was to upset the older balance.

The Evangelical Revival within the Church of England, though powerful in its impact, affected only a small number of Anglican clergy. By and large the eighteenth-century pattern, with its High, Broad, and Latitudinarian clergy, with its scandalous absenteeism, pluralities, and gross inefficiency, lingered well on into the next century. Such abuses became an understandable object of attack in an age of utilitarianism.

It is one of the great paradoxes of English church history that the *Ecclesia Anglicana* was in fact saved by a strange combination, that is by reforms in its organization carried through by the Parliament following the Reform Bill of 1832 and also by the passionate devotion of men who were moved

[1] H. P. Liddon, *Life of Edward Bouverie Pusey* (4th edn, 1894), i.133.

to protest against the nature of these reforms because of the secular spirit in which they were carried through.

The particular way in which Parliament tackled this problem of much-needed overhaul—that is, by the establishment of a supreme ecclesiastical court in the Privy Council; by the setting up of the Ecclesiastical Commission; by the reduction of the Irish sees; by the restriction of pluralities—was bound to lead to a general discussion of the nature of the Church, and hence of its position *vis-à-vis* the Dissenters. Interesting as a contributor to this debate is Thomas Arnold, who stood four-square for a national and comprehensive Christian establishment which would consecrate and direct the rising national energy. Such a Church would include all Dissenters except Roman Catholics, Quakers, and Unitarians, the first two because Arnold believed their systems incompatible with a national Church, the latter because they were not fully Christian. Arnold's ideal was the theocracy of the Old Testament or, in more recent years, the pattern which the Reformers had hoped to establish in the reign of Edward VI. "Civil society", he wrote in *Principles of Church Reform*,

> aims at the highest happiness of man according to the measure of its knowledge. Religious society aims at it truly and really, because it has obtained a complete knowledge of it. Impart then to civil society the knowledge of religious society, and the objects of both will be not only in intention but in fact the same. In other words, religious society is only civil society fully enlightened: the State in its highest perfection becomes the Church.[1]

Arnold's basic thesis is a curious restatement in a new guise of the medieval ideal: it betrays a nostalgia for the past, and an extraordinary lack of awareness of the movement of ideas in the present. It fails also, in fact, to do justice to a genuine horror of an establishment, such as is rooted in the Dissenting position. A comprehensive Church along Arnold's lines could

[1] Op. cit. (4th edn, 1833), 105.

be an object of thought: but it was quite impossible to establish it in the nineteenth century. The drift of contemporary society was in an entirely contrary direction. Arnold was mistaken again in supposing that the Christian religion *was* the unifying factor in the rising national states of the day, though its dynamic had undoubtedly contributed to the feeling after that unity.

Equally insistent on the vital place of a national Christianity, embodied in a national Church, was Frederick Denison Maurice, though his more theological approach led him finally nearer to the position of the leaders of the Oxford Movement than to Arnold. He found the principle of unity in the nation embedded in "the God-given principles, constituting the ordinances of the Catholic Church"; and he therefore deplored the contemporary slackness of thought which regarded "all opinions ... to be indifferently true"[1]. The final question for everyman was simply: "*Is* there a principle of order?"—which in a theological context becomes "Is there a Catholic Church?"

Here Maurice, in contrast with Dissent, saw in the continuance of episcopacy the "witness of something beside mere individual [i.e. voluntary] association". True, all sects had value in their affirmations, rather than in their denials, and all of them, consciously or unconsciously, were seeking after the order for which the Catholic Church stands. A true Church will necessarily seek to realize itself in the life and forms of the nation: and its desire, together with its ability, to do this will constitute the measure of its catholicity. Concerning the nexus between Church and State, Maurice wrote in language reminiscent of Burke: "I do think that it requires something far deeper and more subtle than any such measures, to destroy a union which has cemented itself by no human contrivances and which exists in the very nature of things." Methodism, in Maurice's eyes, was "essentially extra-national". It was "the effort to establish

[1] F. D. Maurice, *The Kingdom of Christ*, ed. A. R. Vidler (1958), i.13.

a powerful government in the heart of a nation, which at no point shall impinge upon, or come into contact with, the government of the nation".[1]

This is not the place to indulge in a critique of Maurice's theological position, or to ask how far he was affected by the full flood of nineteenth-century nationalism. His personal relations with Dissenters were friendly and he worked with and alongside a great many of them in his "Christian Socialism": but theologically he saw Dissent as needing to find and fulfil itself in Catholic Christianity. In education, however, Maurice had a horror of handing instruction over to the State, and he accordingly wished to leave it in denominational hands.

F. D. Maurice regarded himself essentially as a theologian, and it was precisely this claim which Newman, Pusey, and Keble made for themselves and saw as constituting their right to speak. To them the Oxford Movement represented the reassertion by the Church of England of her rightful place as part of the One Holy Catholic and Apostolic Church—a Church which had a history going back to the days of Christ and a life quite independent of Acts of Parliament and state politics. Such a Church was visible here on earth and men were either within it or outside it. Newman had no doubts in his own mind that Dissenters were outside it, though he was, in charity, willing to recognize that "if they know no better, God, we trust, will accept them as he did the Shunamite. I wish, with all my heart, that they partook the full blessings of the Church; but all my wishing cannot change God's appointments".[2] In another sermon he took the opportunity of saying that "there is not a dissenter living, but, inasmuch and so far as he dissents, is in a sin".[3]

Newman's view, as expressed in pulpit and tract, was

[1] Ibid., ii.312; i.145.

[2] J. H. Newman, *Parochial and Plain Sermons* (1877 edn), iii.231.

[3] Ibid., iii.202.

extreme and logical: Keble's, though more pastoral, was in essence the same. When the Oxford Movement left the universities and invaded the parishes, it was almost bound to make its influence felt liturgically—in vestments, crosses, and candles. But by encouraging parochial clergy to be far more Church-conscious, to be more aware of themselves as priests with specialized functions, it widened the gulf between the incumbent and the Dissenting minister—and it did this at a time when political Dissent was emerging and beginning to feel its strength. The first citadels of Anglicanism to be attacked, though it was Anglicans within the city who began the assault, were the Universities.

Oxford and Cambridge, at the time of the Reform Bill of 1832, were still preserves of the Church of England. True, the absolute barrier was sometimes lifted for Dissenters in the case of Cambridge, though they could not take their degree because of the need to subscribe at the time of graduation: but at Oxford all undergraduates had to assent to the Thirty-nine Articles and to communicate once a term. It was to be expected, against the background of secular reform, that this ecclesiastical monopoly would be the target of bitter attack, and that determined efforts would be made to get rid of it. In 1834, sixty-three resident members of the Cambridge Senate petitioned Parliament for the abolition of all religious tests, except for degrees in divinity, and a Bill towards this end passed through the Commons with a large majority. Strenuous in support of abolition was R. D. Hampden (1793–1868), later Bishop of Hereford, whose *Observations on Religious Dissent* argued with great skill against the Tests on two grounds: first, that the Thirty-nine Articles were fallible human inventions and it was therefore quite unfair to expect young men to give their assent to them; and secondly, that the Articles were in fact simply employed in this context for the purpose of excluding Dissenters. Petitions against the Bill were dispatched to London from those concerned with teaching and discipline; from the Convocation of Oxford University; and even from the parents and guardians of undergraduates. When the Bill was thrown out by the House of Lords on 1 August 1834, those of more liberal views determined to carry on with the struggle. On 10 November the Heads of Houses at Oxford decided by a majority of one to introduce a measure into Convocation to abolish subscription, and to replace it by some mild and eirenical formula. Newman and Keble were still earnest in their opposition. Pusey, in a letter to Gladstone, had pointed out the lamentable results in Cambridge which had already resulted from allowing young men of "unsound faith" into the University,[1] where they had lowered the general tone of the debating society. Newman's attitude was equally uncomplicated. It was one thing to admit Dissenters into a secular Parliament: quite another to introduce them into Universities whose overriding purpose was to educate priests and to promote sacred studies. The Universities were sacrosanct as part of the life of the Catholic Church. "The admission of Dissenters would be a repeal, not of one, but of all our statutes",[2] he remarked.

The forces of reaction proved too strong and in May 1835, when the vote was taken, and Hurrell Froude made a dramatic appearance in Oxford, the proposed change in subscription was defeated by an overwhelming majority. As a result of this opposition Dissenters (and Roman Catholics) had to wait till 1854 before they could take bachelors' degrees at Oxford (1856 at Cambridge). It was fortunate that University College, London, had received its charter in 1836. In 1871 Gladstone's Universities Tests Act excluded religious tests before admission to all degrees (except degrees in divinity) and to lay academic offices.

In the parish, the areas of possible friction in the first half

[1] Liddon, op. cit., i.294.

[2] *Letters and Correspondence of John Henry Newman*, ed. Anne Mozley (1891), ii.38.

of the nineteenth century were only too evident. First, there was the vexed question of church rates—a thorny problem always liable to generate emotion, which became linked with politics at a national level. The imposition of a rate for the repair of a church was at the mercy of a local vote in the vestry, where Dissenters had as much right as Churchmen, though they were, of course, usually in a minority. Several of the great cities ceased to levy rates during the political campaigns of the 1830s, and in most industrial parishes the rate could no longer be enforced after 1853. Many Churchmen valued its maintenance, nevertheless, because in nearly all the country parishes the rate was paid without controversy or hardship; it was widely regarded as improbable that a little country village, with a poor population, would be able to repair its church if forced to rely upon subscriptions; and in Parliament Conservatives steadily and perilously argued that public contributions were necessary to the whole idea of establishment. Some Dissenters, especially Methodists, preferred the rate on the ground that they then possessed an irrefutable status in their parish churches.

But the incidence of the rate in divided towns like Birmingham or Manchester or Leicester or Nottingham was calamitous for the relation of Church and Dissent. On the one hand the manner of its imposition—by a popular vote at a public meeting—might have been designed to produce the maximum irritation to both sides, and led to sacrilegious and tumultuous scenes in churches. On the other hand the defence of the rate identified the Church of England with the Conservative party, and the assault upon it encouraged the Dissenters to pursue a policy of cultivating political interest and to abominate the Establishment. Its abolition at last, after numerous unsuccessful attempts, in an Act of 1868 introduced by Gladstone, afforded a much-needed relief from vexatious strife in the parishes.

A second cause of friction concerned the right to conduct services of burial in the parish churchyard. Legally the churchyard was the freehold of the incumbent; before the introduction of cemeteries it was often the only place of burial, and zealously did many incumbents guard it. By Peel's Act of 1836 marriages were permitted in Dissenting chapels but over his own churchyard the parish priest still presided with almost undiminished sovereignty. What he was prepared to allow the Dissenter to do depended on local relationships—and often on the churchmanship of the parson. The anxieties of Lee Warner, incumbent of Tarrant Gunville in Dorset and Beckley in Sussex, show vividly the possibility of strife, misunderstanding, and even of broils, to which the situation could give rise. Often after he finished the committal at the graveside, another service began. The Dissenters on their part felt that it was a cruel injustice that they should be denied the privilege of laying one of their own flock to rest with such prayers and commendation as they saw fit.

Once again it was the principle of establishment which Anglicans felt to be at stake: or to take a rather lower view, it was this principle which some of them used (perhaps unconsciously) to retain privilege and authority. Disraeli took the view, in the debate on Morgan's Burial Bill (1870), that since many Dissenters refused to pay Church Rates they thereby acknowledged that both church and churchyard belonged to Churchmen.[1] This logically must mean that they were prepared to accept such conditions as were laid down. Many Anglican clergymen felt that this was a matter on which they must take a firm line. It was agreed that it would be wrong to allow Dissenters a right to hold services inside the church, and sometimes it seemed not easy to distinguish between church and churchyard. It was suggested that if Dissenters wanted to conduct their own services at the graveside, they should create public cemeteries and not try to use those of the Church. The argument, though intel-

[1] G. E. Buckle and W. F. Monypenny, *The Life of Benjamin Disraeli* (1920), v.252.

ligible, failed to do justice to the sentiments of the Dissenter whose parents and grandparents had also been buried in that graveyard, and whose outlook towards Anglican clergy had much changed since those grandparents had been peaceably buried by one of them. The extremism of the attack, especially of the Liberation Society where hot-headed orators occasionally demanded a public right not only to the graveyard but to the church building itself, naturally made the resistance more emotional and intransigent. In 1861 the Lower House of Convocation in the province of Canterbury passed a resolution requesting the bishops "to take such measures as may seem best to prevent a bill now before Parliament, having for its object to allow persons not in communion with the Church of England to officiate in our churchyards, from becoming law".[1] It did not become law; and the struggle went on until 1880, when with the approval of many sane Churchmen and with 16,000 petitioning against it, relief was finally given in Selborne's Burial Laws Amendment Act.

It was the question of education, however, which continued to be, for the greater part of the century, a constant cause of division, and which led to a determined effort on the part of the Dissenters to break the privileged position of the Church of England. A brief discussion of the struggle must suffice.

Obvious historical causes had determined that the voluntary system which obtained up to, and beyond, the Reform Bill of 1832 was in substantial part under the aegis of the Church of England, and this applied to ancient foundations as well as to the more recent Charity Schools. It was only during the nineteenth century, when the increasing entry of the State into matters educational coincided with the growth of Nonconformity as a political interest, that the controversy developed which was to waste energies, to hold up the development of English education, and sometimes to disturb the peace of small villages.

[1] *The Chronicle of Convocation*, 27 February 1861.

The new interest of the State undoubtedly caused a great deal of heart-burning amongst the more rigid clergy, for after 1839 government grants were accompanied by government inspection and the beginning of a measure of control. Indeed on 14 February 1865 Archdeacon Denison, most fiery of High Churchmen of the older school, initiated a debate in the Lower House of Convocation expressing concern at the stipulations made by the Committee of the Council of Education in their grants to the National Society. In a similar debate the next year the archdeacon affirmed that if a government inspector came into his parish he would throw him in the pond.[1]

In the early days of the century many Nonconformists were equally suspicious on principle of state intervention, and strongly resented that so much government money should be spent on Church of England schools. They successfully resisted the compulsory educational clauses of Graham's Factory Bill of 1843. Yet in demanding a voluntary system the Dissenters were acutely aware of being caught on the horns of a dilemma. Since their own community was scattered and numerically small, particularly in outlying rural areas, they were forced to recognize that this would mean attendance at Church of England schools. The alternative seemed to be, and reluctantly—as, for example, in the case of that most persistent of political Nonconformists, Edward Miall (1809–81)—they were converted to it, a state system.

Moreover, as the century went on, both Dissenters and Anglicans were forced to recognize that the vast educational requirements of an enfranchised proletariat had outgrown, and in fact could not be met by, an unaided voluntary system. The paramount need was to build more schools and to get more children into them.

It was reckoned in 1869 that 1,300,000 children were in state-aided schools: that one million were in non-grant-aided, non-inspected schools: and that two million children

[1] *The Chronicle of Convocation*, 8 February 1866.

went nowhere.[1] Englishmen began to feel a sense of shame at such an unsatisfactory position, the more so as it was commonly said that the triumph of North America in the Civil War was due to the "common school" and the Prussian victory over Austria at Sadowa to the elementary school. In 1870 Forster's Education Act attempted to combine the existing voluntary system with a state system. In areas where the existing (denominational) schools were believed to be adequate, nothing was to be done; but elsewhere elementary schools were established at the expense of the exchequer and the rates. No pupil was to be required to attend religious worship or instruction (or anti-religious instruction) if his parents objected, and this applied to the denominational schools also. Under the Act the state grant to denominational schools was doubled: but an endeavour was made to meet the conscientious scruples of Dissenters by the "timetable clause". So far as the board schools were concerned, the famous Cowper-Temple clause provided that "no catechism or religious formulary which is distinctive of any particular denomination shall be taught in the school". It was even possible for a board school to forbid religious instruction altogether.

The Nonconformists, on the whole, under the forceful leadership of Dale of Birmingham and Miall, regarded the Act as far too lenient to church schools and (as such) a great triumph for the Church of England. They were bitterly disappointed, as a consequence, with Mr Gladstone. "We respect Mr Forster," protested Dale, "we honour Mr Gladstone, but we are determined that England shall not again be cursed with the bitterness and strife from which we had hoped that we had for ever escaped, by the abolition of the church rate." He was greatly dismayed, he confessed, "that his government should be erecting new difficulties in the way of religious equality".[2] Miall protested to the Grand

[1] John Morley, *Life of William Ewart Gladstone* (1903), ii.302 n.
[2] Ibid., ii.304 f.

Old Man personally, doubtless more in sorrow than in anger. By the Act, he complained, Mr Gladstone had brought the Liberal party through the valley of humiliation, and he added: "Once bit, twice shy. We can't stand this sort of thing much longer."[1] John Bright, that indefatigable champion of radical causes, described the Education Act as "the worst Act passed by any liberal parliament since 1832".[2] The Nonconformists had now come down definitely on the side of a comprehensive state system which showed no preference to any one religious body. There can be no question that their acute disappointment led to "refrigeration and estrangement" between the Liberal party and themselves and that this had its effect upon Gladstone's fortunes in the election of 1874.

The resentment aroused in these matters of church rates, burials, and education convinced Dissenters that it was the Establishment, and the protective psychology which it engendered, that were the cause of all the trouble. In this conclusion the leading political Dissenters, Bright, Dale, and Miall, all concurred. In 1841 Miall established the weekly radical paper *The Nonconformist*, with the settled intention of producing a school of aggressive politicians. If justice was to be done to Dissent, he saw the need for it to cultivate a political interest, and he came to recognize in Mr Gladstone the great hope of doing this.

Superficially, no prospect could have seemed less promising, but Miall knew his man, and it is probably true to say that Gladstone did more to encourage and sustain the Dissenting community (from outside Dissent) than any other single person during the nineteenth century. He believed the Dissenters to have been unjustly treated: and his own deeply religious sense enabled him to be sensitive to other people's cherished convictions, though they might differ from his own. If persuasion could not prevail, he was prepared to use Parliament to secure justice. Yet in championing Dissent

[1] Ibid., 305. [2] Ibid.

he never compromised his own conscience, and in the various disestablishment debates in the House of Commons he regularly spoke against the motion. In 1873, after such an instance, Dr Allon, editor of the *British Quarterly Review* and a much respected Dissenter, wrote a letter of mild protest which evoked from Gladstone the reply that Nonconformists had "shown me great kindness and indulgence".[1]

Nor were his relations with them purely of a formal or political nature. He was on friendly and personal terms with many of their most distinguished leaders, whom he used to meet regularly at the house of Newman Hall—Binney, Allon, White, Baldwin Brown, Reynolds, and Dale. So suggestible did he seem that Newman Hall began to believe that the "free church theory" would win its way by a gradual and general acceptance. Indeed one Dissenter observed to Gladstone in 1864 that "many dissenters would enter the church whatever their theory about establishment, if such slight modifications were made as would allow them to do so conscientiously".[2] Such hopes were, of course, wildly optimistic, and much more realistic was the sobering reflection made to him by another Nonconformist that "there were many ideas in the Prayer Book which cannot be admitted by any one".[3] Yet it is an eloquent tribute to the concern which Gladstone genuinely felt that he was held in such high esteem by so many Dissenters, and was on one occasion asked to lay the foundation-stone of a chapel. On 15 April 1878 Dr Allon wrote to him:

> The kind of intercourse that you have kindly permitted with nonconformists, has helped more consciously to identify them with movements of national life, and to diminish the stern feeling of almost defiant witness-bearing that was strong a generation or two ago. It is something gained if ecclesiastical and political differences can be debated within a common circle of social confidence and identity. . . . Their confidence in you has made them amenable to your lead in respect of

[1] Ibid., ii.458. [2] Ibid., ii.134. [3] Ibid., i.135.

methods and movements needing the guidance of political insight and experience.[1]

In 1852 something happened in the Church of England which was eventually to shift the discussion of relations between Anglicanism and Dissent away from the social and the political fields to the more specifically theological. It may yet prove more difficult to solve the latter than the former. In that year, owing largely to the initiative of Bishop Wilberforce, the Canterbury Convocation was revived, as a sitting assembly, after a virtual suppression of nearly a hundred and fifty years. This meant that the Church of England had once more a public platform on which to discuss its own and the nation's affairs: and that at least some of the frustrations which silence had engendered could be dispelled in the light of common day. Public debate of this kind, however, increased the temptation to stand behind entrenched positions.

In part, the revival arose out of a greater awareness by the Church of itself as a religious society in its own right, and of its differentiation from the State. In one sense, this might seem to remove it further from Dissent: but many earnest Churchmen, who had so often smarted under the gibe that the Church of England was a parliamentary creation, felt that this recovery of synodical government, and through it of a greater self-discipline, would at least remove one stumbling-block in the way of the more conciliatory Dissenter. At the same time, in rediscovering this awareness of itself, the Church of England in Convocation felt a quickened concern for those Christians who lived their lives outside it. The story of this concern, though the results of it were not spectacular—indeed, in my judgement, disappointing—is yet worth telling.[2]

Upon its assembling, almost the first act of business by

[1] Ibid.

[2] The following narrative is taken from the official *Chronicle of Convocation*.

Convocation was to place on record that it met "in the earnest hope and trust that all the deliberations of the synod may tend, under God's blessing, to the removal of mutual misunderstandings . . . and may prepare the way for gathering to the bosom of the Church those who are now not of her communion". The effect of this pronouncement was to encourage a meeting of Churchmen and Dissenters at St James's Church, Westminster, on 6 December 1855. There was a great deal of exploratory discussion, but the general feeling of the Anglicans present was that "the minds of those who are separate from us were not then prepared to entertain the question of reunion". When these deliberations are placed against the background of the political and social *milieu* to which reference has been made earlier, this is not surprising. The Dissenter doubtless felt that he must establish his own position and rights before he thought of absorption into another, if parent, communion.

Yet interest was now growing and on 15 April 1856 John Lonsdale, Bishop of Lichfield, brought before Convocation a petition signed by a number of clergy and laity and entrusted to him by the Reverend Ernest Hawkins, Secretary of the Society for the Propagation of the Gospel. The petitioners, it said, "laying to heart the great dangers we are in by our unhappy divisions, and earnestly desiring a closer union among Christians", had asked themselves in particular what it was that impeded the Wesleyan Methodists from returning to the Church of England. There were, in their opinion, four obstacles: (1) the impression that the Church of England was not sufficiently careful concerning her selection of clergy; (2) that the Church of England formally disapproved of class meetings; (3) that episcopal ordination of Wesleyan ministers imposed a period of three years' silence before ordination; and (4) that the Church of England in its desire for reunion was seeking temporal power and patronage.

The petitioners then went on to suggest that the Wesleyans ought to be reassured in respect of these matters, and that the possibility of reunion would be increased (1) if Methodists communicated only at their parish church, and (2) if those Wesleyan ministers 'of one mind with the Church' sought episcopal ordination. The document ended: "Your petitioners therefore humbly pray, that your two Houses will be pleased to take the premises into your serious consideration, and to advise upon such measures as to you may seem most expedient, for bringing about a restoration of the Wesleyan Methodists to the communion of the Church of England."

The ensuing debate was somewhat disappointing, and betrayed too much of that ecclesiastical complacency which is not always helpful. The Bishop of St David's remarked that it was an "extraordinary petition" and that he, for one, could not accept the "insinuations" which it contained: while Henry Phillpotts, Bishop of Exeter, in characteristic militant mood, observed that, though it was in part due to the apathy of the Church of England that the Methodists had seceded, yet there was no need to go about "begging" them to return.

> All he wanted was, that they should acknowledge their error, and express a wish to be delivered from it. That must be accompanied with a feeling that their error was a sin. The Church ought to be very cautious how it received them until they indicated some sense of the condition in which they must be regarded by every faithful member of the Church. They were in a state of schism, and therefore a state of sin; but he would anxiously encourage any proposition by which they could be fairly admitted.

We are not surprised (it has an all too familiar ring about it) that the petition was ordered "to lie on the table".

The matter, however, was not allowed to rest, and on 2 March 1860 the Reverend F. C. Massingberd[1] proposed in Convocation that the faithful be urged to pray "for the reunion of the divided members of Christ's Body". The proliferation of sects, he said, could not be regarded as other than harmful, for to mention only one of its evils it was injurious to all missionary enterprise. The responsibility for

[1] He had already made efforts to debate this on two former occasions.

such division must be shared equally by Churchmen and Dissenters. In the past, two methods had been employed to secure union but both had failed—coercion, which was wrong in principle; comprehension, which disturbed the consciences of many already within the Church. The best way, he felt sure, was through a truly national Church, and all congregations should be urged to use the prayer for unity from the accession service.

Reunion obviously constituted a great preoccupation in the sixties of the last century, and much serious thought was given to it. An indication of this may be seen in two small books published by Anglican incumbents, *Hints on Christian Union* by John Paul and *A Scheme for the Restoration of Dissenters to the Church* by C. Robinson. The Church Congress at Wolverhampton in 1867 also devoted one of its sessions to "The Best Means of bringing Non-Conformists into Union with the Church".[1]

At this latter gathering, Lord Lyttelton introduced the subject in a rambling speech which covered a good deal of ground. Religious dissent was a sin, he said, but since Christianity was committed to a definite credal statement it was not enough simply to be friends and to agree to differ. Yet the Church of England might consider doing certain things to encourage Dissenters to return, which he listed as follows: (1) The Church of England must recover its internal liberty. (2) The phraseology of the Athanasian Creed might be changed and the damnatory clauses be removed. (3) The emphasis on regeneration in the service of Baptism should be changed; as also (4) the promises of godparents. (5) The Thirty-nine Articles should contain something on "inspiration". (6) The section on the sacraments might be extended. (7) In the eleventh Article, the word "only" should be omitted (i.e. in connection with justification by faith); and (8) the Articles as a whole be revised and made less technical and academic; and (9) a new translation of the Bible should be undertaken.

[1] See *Report of the Church Congress, 1867* (Wolverhampton), 40–72.

Lord Lyttelton's paper was followed by a shorter one from the Reverend George Venables, who endeavoured, as he thought, to strike a more practical note. Reunion was possible, he said, but the first step was for the Church of England to put its own house in order, and at the same time to ask itself why the Dissenters went out. The Methodists wanted "spirit-tual counsel and brotherly communion", which they found in their class meetings. The Independents, disgusted at pluralism and the abuse of patronage, decided to ordain their own men. Unfortunately the Dissenters, "in the eagerness of their pursuit after a seemingly lost truth, have forgotten the preciousness of Unity; and hugging their acquired and perhaps valuable treasure with inordinate zeal, they have lost other treasures of yet greater value". Venables realized that the Church of England had nothing to offer the responsible lay person comparable with the class meeting: and he suggested that the solution might be to revive an effective diaconate together with some of the older lay offices. "The Church", he quoted, "has the organic life and constitution, but Dissenters have the congregational and adaptive energy." With great gusto, he affirmed that no one could be "so sanguine as to think it probable that England's millions will ever come to believe that the worship of God has been as fully attained as you yourselves desire, by participating in services beginning seven hundred and thirty times . . . with one or more of but eleven verses of Holy Scripture and 'Dearly beloved Brethren' ".[1]

In the general discussion which followed the papers a great deal was said as to the need for additional services, a well-worn subject which Convocation had often debated at

[1] An interesting comment on such views is to be found in the visitational returns made to William Thomson when he became Archbishop of York in 1862. Dissent in his diocese was extremely strong. The vicar of Moss reported that all his parishioners were Methodists; in another parish 300 out of 360 were Dissenters: and the vicar of Weaverthorpe regretted that the former "friendly feeling" of the Methodists towards the Church was replaced by "a hostile and aggressive spirit". One of

length. Not very much that was new, it must be admitted, emerged. One member of the Congress, speaking for the Dissenters' point of view, argued that in the main they were kept from the Church of England by an inherited feeling that there was more scope for individual lay effort in their own communion: and by a deep conviction that the Church of England's standing as a national Church was radically wrong. One speaker, W. R. Clark, vicar of Taunton, thought that the Dissenters were better served if the Church was truly the Church than if it compromised.

One practical result, however, did come out of the Congress, for it led to the formation of a "Committee of Association of Laity and Clergy for the Promotion of Re-Union of Christians at Home". The committee, which consisted in the main of London clergy, was soon at work and a petition was presented to Convocation in 1870 suggesting that some of the clauses in the Athanasian Creed might be changed. Convocation, however, preferred to appoint its own "Committee for Home Reunion of the divided members of Christ's Body", which presented a Report on 3 May of the same year.

This lengthy document first reviewed the history of former and unsuccessful attempts at comprehension, both before and after the Revolution of 1688; and then went on to ask what steps might at present be undertaken. The committee was not prepared, it said, to advise any alteration in existing formularies, at least for the present, though there might subsequently be concessions "in a spirit of love and unity", if negotiations with the Dissenters were to begin. But there

---

the reasons for this, so many incumbents reported (the quotation is from the vicar of Ellerton), was that many people "had a marked desire after a more exciting mode of worship than the beautiful and scriptural liturgy of the Church of England". See H. Kirk-Smith, *William Thomson, Archbishop of York* (1958). In the East Riding, so a correspondent wrote in the *Church Times*, "Church is altogether tame after the religious exercises to which they (i.e. Methodists) are accustomed".

should be more regular prayers for unity in the Church: and the advantages of union pointed out. If any overtures to a particular nonconforming body were to be made, then these had better begin with the Methodists. "It is sufficiently apparent that no such overtures would now be entertained which should not leave the existing institutions of the body, its chapels, its property, and its general system, as they are, or nearly so."[1]

Realistically recognizing this situation, the Report went on, tentatively it is true,[2] to suggest a penetration of Anglicanism into Methodism, or conversely a taking-up of Methodism into Anglicanism. This was to be done without immediately blurring the distinctions between them. The proposals were that

1. Certain Methodist ministers, approved by their own Conference, should be admitted by bishops of the Church of England to the diaconate and priesthood;
2. Methodist chapels should be licensed for the celebration of Holy Communion at the request of the Conference; and
3. Bishops of the Church of England might consecrate one or two leading ministers as suffragan bishops, so long as they promised not to continue the succession.

The first step would be for an approach to be made to the President of the Methodist Conference, "expressive of the earnest desire for union which it has pleased God to awaken in so many hearts", inviting the Conference at the same time to mutual prayer and assuring it that any response on its part would be thankfully and cordially welcomed. Perhaps, later on, the Report said, similar approaches might be made to other nonconforming bodies, particularly since "a great part of the objections" of Nonconformists were not matters

[1] The Report is to be found as an appendix to *The Chronicle of Convocation* (1870).

[2] "There have not been wanting those among ourselves . . ."

of doctrine but had to do with "the supposed subjection of the Church [of England] to the State"—an objection which the recovery of synodical government ought to go some way to remove.

The debate which took place in Convocation on 7 and 8 July did not measure up to the challenge implicit in the practical proposals which the Report contained. Those who spoke preferred to talk in general terms without grappling with any immediate practical issues. There were, of course, the inevitable speeches breathing goodwill: and variations around the perpetual theme of the Methodists' dislike of the State connection. Both Dr Stanley, Dean of Westminster, and Bishop Mackenzie drew attention to the great social gulf which made many Nonconformists think of the Church of England as the preserve of the gentry and their dependants. Mackenzie, who was Bishop Suffragan of Nottingham, was optimistic that Methodism would soon be absorbed into the Church of England, and claimed that eight hundred Anglican clergy were sons of Methodists. Perhaps the most valuable contribution came from Dr Fraser, who in the spirit of F. D. Maurice reminded Convocation that the Methodists essentially stood for three very positive things: (1) the Kingship of Christ against any claim of Crown or Parliament; (2) individual piety and a corrective discipline; and (3) the rights of minorities in respect of conscience. The words of another speaker in the debate are perhaps worth quoting: "There is no one system of Christianity, no one system of religion, except absolute atheism, which does not contain in it some germ of truth; and it is by taking the truth that people hold and enlarging upon that, not shocking their prejudices wantonly, that you may hope to regain them by treating them with tenderness and Christian love."

Certainly there was no lack of admirable sentiments, but the debate ended very much where it had begun, except that it was decided to add a prayer for unity to the prayers said daily in Convocation. A suggestion that the heads of the Methodist Conference should be informed of this decision was withdrawn.

These debates in Convocation and Church Congress bear witness to the impact of the Oxford Movement as well as to the Evangelical Revival. They also show signs of that liberalism which expressed itself within the Church of England in "Open Communion" and in the clergy's acceptance of invitations to preach in Nonconformist churches. So much was the latter the case that on 9 February 1887 Canon Hole (a great rose-grower, later Dean of Rochester) proposed in the Lower House of Convocation

> that their Lordships the Bishops be respectfully requested to take such steps as may be in their power to prohibit and to suppress an innovation which is becoming a great scandal in the eyes of many devout churchpeople, and is detrimental, in consequence, to the spread of true religion.

Canon Hole argued his case with energy, pointing out that there were two hundred and twenty-three Christian sects and that it was the solemn duty of the Anglican priest to drive away strange doctrine and not to encourage it. The motion which was finally passed by the Lower House, while "acknowledging the charitable motives and intentions of those who accept the invitations", yet went on to add that such acceptances tended "to hinder rather than promote the unity of Christian people", were "detrimental to the spread of true religion", and were "a great scandal in the eyes of many devout Churchpeople". It therefore urged the bishops "to take such steps as may be in their power to prohibit and suppress this innovation". This resolution was debated in the Upper House on 12 May, when the bishops agreed to use their "authority and influence" with the clergy to this end.

These debates show signs of a hardening of theological attitude towards the Dissenters: but this did not mean that the question of reunion was one which Convocation could neglect to explore, particularly as the Home Reunion Society under its indefatigable and evangelically-minded chairman, Lord Nelson, often endeavoured to prod it into action. Thus on 2 March 1888 Canon Medd proposed in the Lower House that a joint committee be appointed

> to consider and, from time to time, to report on the relations existing between the Church and the separated communities, especially in this country; and generally to make any suggestions as to the means which might tend, by God's blessing, to the furtherance of the union, especially among English-speaking Christians, of all who hold the essentials of the Christian faith.

In introducing this motion Canon Medd spoke with genuine feeling. Disunion at home, he said, meant "waste of energy, waste of money, waste of time, waste of temper, and, worse than waste, the actual misdirection of Christian energies against each other". The Church of England must be prepared to admit its own shortcomings, in particular that it had "not preached the Gospel to the poor, who, even after all these centuries of Christianity, lie to a great extent outside our Church system". A joint committee, if set up, would by its very existence call attention to the need for reunion: and so far as the Dissenters were concerned "an attitude of conciliation" would meet with a ready response.

The resolution produced a debate in which some shrewd things were said. Canon Bernard, for example, thought that there was now much greater cohesion among the Nonconformist bodies themselves, and that this sense of unity had replaced the principle of Dissent as the rallying ground for their corporate life. It fell to the lot of Canon Bright to bring the discussion (as he thought) down to earth. What, in fact, was the committee to do? Was it to convert individual Dissenters, or win over whole Communions? If the latter, must it not be recognized that Dissent was, at the moment, moving further away from the Church of England? The resolution, in a slightly amended form, was carried (2 March 1888), and the committee was accordingly set up. Before it reported, however, certain events had taken place.

First there was the meeting of the Lambeth Conference in 1888, which, in its famous Quadrilateral, laid down the Anglican norm as to the characteristics of the Catholic Church of Christ.[1] The effect of this pronouncement, embodied in a letter to all Christian people, was to transfer interest in the discussion of the mutual relations of the Church of England to Dissent away from their purely historical, social, and political context to the far more debatable areas of theology and Church order. This change was immediately apparent in the reaction of many leading Nonconformists to the Lambeth Letter.

Secondly there took place, in 1889, the notable Langham Street Conference at which leading Anglicans and Congregationalists entered into friendly and informal discussions of a highly theological character under the chairmanship of Lord Nelson. These centred upon the nature of the Church, Sacraments, and Ministry; and it was clear that the differences on these subjects were "wide and deep". As a consequence little progress was made, except that the Anglicans allowed that prevenient grace could be active in the adult prior to the grace of baptism.[2]

The committee appointed some three years earlier reported to Convocation in 1891, by which time the atmosphere had noticeably changed. Speakers in the debate launched into deep theological waters, though Archdeacon Kaye declared that he himself was a little reluctant to regard the divisions between the Church of England and Noncon-

[1] These were the acceptance of (1) the Scriptures; (2) the Apostles' and the Nicene Creed; (3) the two Sacraments ordained by Christ; (4) the historic episcopate. In the *Encyclical Letter* (1888), 15, it is stated: "We lay down conditions on which such inter-communion is, in our opinion, and according to our conviction possible. For however we may long to embrace those now alienated from us, so that the ideal of one flock under one Shepherd may be realised, we must not be unfaithful stewards of the great deposit entrusted to us. We cannot desert our position either as to faith or discipline."

[2] Similar conferences were held by the Bishop of Lichfield and the Bishop of Truro.

formity as both "deep and wide", as suggested by the Dean of Worcester. Indeed he was prepared to regard the threefold ministry as an "apostolical institution" rather than a "divinely appointed constitution"—a distinction which, so Canon Bright alleged, did not cease to make the differences "deep and wide". Archdeacon Farrar expressed his exasperation by retorting that if Nonconformists were not members of the Church of England, they were certainly members of the Church of Christ. After much debate, the following resolution was passed. Its tone is not optimistic of immediate progress:

> In view of the evident differences between the Church and the Nonconformists respecting the words 'Church', 'Sacraments', and 'Ordination' which are both grave and practical, it is desirable to call into larger use the whole force of intercessory prayer for the reunion of Christians in England.

There the matter rested for the time being so far as Convocation was concerned, though as the century drew to its close the difference in attitude between what may be described (for want of a better word) as the high Anglican school and the more liberal school in the Church of England became increasingly noticeable. This may be seen in the contrast between Canon A. J. Mason's dogmatic statement that the Nonconformist bodies "form no part of the Church of Christ but occupy (even when unintentionally) a position of rivalry and antagonism towards it"[1] and a speech made by Dr Hensley Henson when in July 1903 he proposed in Convocation:

> That in view of the widely felt desire for the union of Christians and the mischievous consequences of existing religious divisions, the President be respectfully requested to direct the appointment of a Joint Committee to investigate and report on the obligation of the Church of England to the whole body of baptized persons.

[1] A. J. Mason, *The Faith of the Gospel* (3rd edn 1892), 240.

In the course of his speech Dr Henson remarked that much had happened since Convocation had last debated this question of inter-church relations. Some thirty years ago, he said, most members of Convocation were of the opinion that Nonconformists, by and large, were anxious for reunion: now, however, the "Free Churches" were moving closer to each other, and in the process were beginning to constitute a great federation. Anglicans must therefore take account of (1) the permanence and indeed the expansion of non-episcopal Christianity; (2) the quiet growth of co-operation between Christian Churches in social and missionary work which has required "a revision of ecclesiastical relations [and] ... led men irresistibly to a larger fellowship than their ecclesiastical systems permitted". Also it had done this "precisely in proportion to their detachment from official responsibility for these systems"; (3) the practical failure of denominationalism as evidenced in the great work of William Booth, the founder of the Salvation Army. To call such Christians schismatics is "obviously offensive and not less obviously absurd. Yet in their formal ecclesiastical relations the Church treated them as schismatics."

After a very short debate Dr Henson had his way. The motion was carried and the committee appointed. That little progress was subsequently made showed the resistant nature of the theological problems involved. But at least the turn of the century seemed to show that, except in the realms of education and the Principality of Wales, the classical Victorian irritants were fading into the memory.

Historical memories, however, can be powerful, and may be powerful without always being fully conscious.

7

TOWARDS CHARITY AND UNDERSTANDING: 1

The Ecumenical Background

OLIVER. S. TOMKINS

TO measure charity is beyond human capacity, and even to assess understanding is rash. But the historian of church relations in England since 1662 can at least point to certain objective facts in the past fifty years which have no parallel in earlier decades or even centuries.

The most obvious for our present purpose is that there exists to-day a *structure* of inter-church co-operation which is completely new. In past centuries there have often been sporadic attempts to restore the unity of Christendom or to promote friendlier relations between its divided parts. The story since the Reformation has been told with great comprehensiveness in *A History of the Ecumenical Movement*, edited by the late Ruth Rouse and Bishop Stephen Neill.[1] Here is gathered together in one volume information spread wide over many detailed treatises. Here is told the story of the abortive attempts to reunite Eastern and Western Christendom at the Council of Florence in the mid fifteenth century, and the many attempts during the fermenting Reformation century, 1517 to 1618, to heal the breaches which rapidly grew up between different Reformed Churches; of such interesting figures in England as John Durie (1595–1680) and Archbishop Wake (1657–1727), whose efforts were so ambitious and so fruitless. But the last fifty years has seen the creation of a permanent organization, supported by the common consent of different Christian bodies.

The Missionary Conference at Edinburgh in 1910 is often referred to as the watershed of the modern Ecumenical Movement. The metaphor of a watershed is used advisedly, but it must not be thought that Edinburgh was a fresh spring rising from the bare ground. It was the meeting-place of streams already flowing as well as the source of new developments. Dr K. S. Latourette points out that

[1] *A History of the Ecumenical Movement, 1517–1948* (1954).

international gatherings for the furtherance of missions had already been held, those in London in 1878 and 1888 and in New York in 1900 being especially notable.[1] The last gathering was called, significantly, the Ecumenical Missionary Conference "because the plan of campaign which it proposes covers the whole area of the inhabited world". Attendance at these international gatherings was progressively larger. The late Dr Tatlow in his history of the Student Christian Movement revealed in some detail how he and his colleagues used the existing confidence in the S.C.M. to persuade "high church" Anglicans such as Bishops E. S. Talbot, Gore, and Montgomery to participate in the Edinburgh Conference.[2] The conference was predominantly Protestant. It was never proposed that Roman Catholic missions should be represented and the Eastern Orthodox were not invited, although at that date (and until 1918) there was a considerable Russian Orthodox mission in the Far East. But the range of invitations was wider than to any previous gathering. Dr Latourette thus describes the new features of its composition:

> The Conference was composed of official delegates from missionary societies. To at least two of the earlier conferences, those of 1888 and 1900, representatives had been appointed by various missionary organizations, but they were also open to any who might care to come. Indeed, the sponsors of the Ecumenical Missionary Conference of 1900 had rejoiced that thousands had been in attendance. By contrast, the membership of the Edinburgh Conference was limited to those delegated by their respective organizations (except for some places reserved for special nominations by the Executive Committee). Only societies which actually had missionaries at work abroad were eligible, and representation was in proportion to the share of each in the missionary enterprise, as measured in financial giving. Since many of the societies were the official agencies of their respective denominations, the Conference was more nearly a body authorized to speak for the Churches than

[1] *HEM* 353–62.

[2] *The Story of the Student Christian Movement* (1933), 404–11.

any of the gatherings which had preceded it. It included many who were church-minded. Yet it was still a conference of societies and not a council of Churches.

Not all missionary societies were invited. Only those were included which were operating among non-Christian peoples. Efforts to win Christians from one form of the Faith to another—as by some American denominations on the continent of Europe, or among the ancient Churches in the Near East, or among the Roman Catholics of Latin America—were not to be in the purview of the gathering. Missions whose purpose it was to hold to the Faith emigrants from Europe to other lands were not included. These limitations seemed to be advisable, if the Conference was to be sharply focused and not widely scattered in its objectives. They made it possible for the German societies, sensitive about Methodist and Baptist missions in Germany, to send representatives; and for Anglo-Catholics, who looked askance at missions by Protestants among peoples of other Christian traditions than their own, to come to the Conference. The narrowing of the scope of the Conference to missions among non-Christian peoples made it possible to bring in a larger number of societies and a greater variety of ecclesiastical and theological convictions than had been represented in any previous gathering. Largely because of the influences which issued from Edinburgh 1910, the ecumenical movement became widely inclusive.[1]

There were only seventeen native members of what were later called "the younger Churches", but the prominent part they were given in the programme—for example, in giving the public addresses—showed that the responsible officers of the Conference recognized the key part they played and presaged.

The Conference was prepared for by months of preliminary study. Here may be seen the handiwork of J. H. Oldham who, by the time he came to prepare for the Life and Work Conference at Oxford in 1937, had developed this technique to perfection. And it was a favourite saying of the Chairman of the Conference, Dr John R. Mott, that "you should organize as though there were no such thing as

[1] *HEM* 357.

prayer and pray as though there were no such thing as organization". The range of the Conference's business and purpose may be gleaned from the topics of its eight commissions. They were (1) Carrying the Gospel to all the Non-Christian World; (2) The Church in the Mission Field; (3) Education in relation to Non-Christian Religions; (4) The Missionary Message in relation to Non-Christian Religions; (5) The Preparation of Missionaries; (6) The Home Base of Missions; (7) Missions and Governments; and (8) Co-operation and the Promotion of Unity.

As one re-reads the contemporary and subsequent accounts of the Conference, two positive consequences stand out.

First: It marks the beginning of continuous, organized Christian co-operation. The Conference passed only one resolution: to appoint a Continuation Committee with a whole-time secretary. Hitherto there had been many *ad hoc* Christian gatherings, though on a somewhat restricted Protestant front. After Edinburgh there was brought into being an official organ of continuing consultation and co-operation so that busy delegates, returning to their several responsibilities in their several Churches, were not to be allowed to let the work of the conference simply recede into a memory; they were to be kept in continuing contact. It is impossible to estimate the significance for future ecumenical work of the fact that the first whole-time secretary was Dr J. H. Oldham. Subsequent generations have had ample opportunity to recognize the unusual combination of gifts in that quiet, slight figure: his *Devotional Diary* affords a glimpse of the deep resources of hidden spirituality which are the secret of his influence. Added to that, he showed a wisdom which always picked out the important issue from a mass of material, a gift for enlisting the co-operation of first-class minds, and a rigorous standard which refused to accept anything but the best in Christian work. He always resisted the fatal tendency in Church circles to suppose that pious goodwill may be a substitute for accurate knowledge or technical competence. All this combined to ensure that the first experiment in continuous Christian co-operation, shortly to be embodied in the International Missionary Council, set a high standard which, if it has not always since been attained, afforded an example which cannot be ignored.

Secondly: It marks the beginning of work for Christian Unity on a wider basis. Paradoxically, the fact that doctrinal questions were excluded from discussion (largely on the insistence of the high Anglicans) revealed the necessity for those issues to be faced and on the widest possible basis. The story has often been told of how Charles Brent, Bishop of the Philippines, saw at Edinburgh a new vision of the unity of the Church which led to the foundation of the Faith and Order movement.[1] From its beginning Faith and Order made a determined attempt to be all-inclusive. It succeeded with the Orthodox; it failed with the Church of Rome when, in 1919, Benedict XV declined to take any part in the proposed meetings, though he expressed the hope that the movement would be blessed by God in its own sphere—an attitude which has been consistently adopted by succeeding Popes. From 1920 onwards, when the organization of Faith and Order could be resumed after the First World War, the Edinburgh vision of "world evangelization" has been accompanied by patient, persistent work for Christian unity. The integration of the International Missionary Council with the World Council of Churches is but the recognition, in organization, of the connection between "mission" and "unity" which was inherent from the beginning.

The theological content of the Faith and Order Movement for unity is a matter to which we shall return later in this chapter. Here we are only concerned with the establishing of the movement as part of a continuing structure in relations between the Churches.

The explorations consequent upon the initial resolution

[1] E.g. in *HEM*, 405 foll.

sponsored by Bishop Manning and Bishop Brent in the General Convention of the Protestant Episcopal Church in America in 1910 were followed by a long period of careful and personal cultivation of the potential co-operators in other Churches. It was not before a meeting representing Orthodox, Anglican, and Protestant Churches, held in Geneva in 1920, that the structure began to take firm shape. The first manifestation of the new movement was at Lausanne in 1927, where the first world conference on Faith and Order was held in order "to draw churches out of isolation into conference". The Lausanne Conference had something of a honeymoon air, for the delegates had scarcely expected to discover the depth of fundamental Christian unity which was there revealed. Under the enthusiastic chairmanship of Bishop Brent, the delegates were less conscious of the long heritage of separation of their Churches from one another than of the heart-warming discovery that a common faith in Christ goes deep.

Lausanne inaugurated the Faith and Order method of work which has remained basic to this day. A large and representative conference of appointed church delegates divides into a number of commissions on selected topics in order, through discussion, to register the degree of agreement and, with equal honesty, the degree of disagreement which exists upon the topic. A conference report registers these agreements and disagreements, and a continuation committee is appointed to decide which topics demand further study. The continuation committee appoints the requisite number of international theological Study Commissions which, by the exchange of papers and by occasional meetings, prepare reports for another representative gathering. At the resulting conference the topics prepared in the smaller groups are again subject to discussion in a wider forum, issues of agreement and disagreement are clarified, and the topics for further discussion defined.

The second world conference on Faith and Order, at

Edinburgh in 1937, carried this process further. At this stage it was proposed to form a World Council of Churches, which was envisaged as the fusing together of the two independent streams of the Faith and Order Movement and the Life and Work Movement. When the World Council of Churches was eventually formed, the Commission on Faith and Order came into it as one of the constituent parts, and, within the structure of the World Council, Faith and Order has continued to operate in its distinctive way.

The third world conference on Faith and Order was held at Lund in 1952, where specific topics were again assigned for continuing discussion. These—"Christ and His Church", "Worship", "The Tradition and our traditions", together with a study of the non-theological factors focused upon the fact of "Institutionalism"—are at the present moment being considered by a number of theological commissions.

Meanwhile the Life and Work Movement had been growing up under the inspiration of Nathan Söderblom, Archbishop of Uppsala. It had taken as its *motif* "Theology divides but Service unites". The hope was that Churches, which could only run into difficulties in their discussion of doctrinal questions, would find themselves immediately in close fellowship on the Christian approach to ethical matters. The Stockholm Conference of 1926 was the first gathering under this banner. The second, at Oxford in 1937, is perhaps still unique in the thoroughness and range of its preparatory studies, which were organized with characteristic care for high standards by Dr J. H. Oldham. Its central theme, "Church, Community, and State", was dictated by the fact that in the 1930s the great challenge to the Christian Church in many parts of the world came from various kinds of totalitarian state. This had brought about a sharper awareness of the separate entity, and the mutual relations, of the Christian Church as a society claiming supernatural sanctions, the nation as a modern political form now reaching extremes of totalitarian organization, and the entity best described by the German word *Volk*, intimately related to but not identifiable with either the Church or the nation.

Both at Oxford and at Edinburgh in 1937 the proposal was made that these two movements should merge to form a World Council of Churches, continuing the work of them both. The suggestion was not without its opponents; in England the opposition was led by the redoubtable A. C. Headlam, Bishop of Gloucester. But in spite of misgivings in some quarters the idea was carried, and William Temple seemed to be the natural leader of the move forward. He was chairman of a committee, representing both the previous movements, set up to devise a detailed plan. This Provisional Committee was interrupted in its work by the outbreak of war in 1939, though not before significant beginnings had been made. Dr W. A. Visser 't Hooft, until then General Secretary of the World's Student Christian Federation, had already been nominated as General Secretary of the new Council, and from the wartime isolation of Geneva he was able to maintain sufficient communication between the separate Churches to give a real sense of unbroken Christian community throughout the strains of war. George Bell (Bishop of Chichester), Marc Boegner (President of the Reformed Church in France), Eivind Berggrav (Primate of Norway), and Dietrich Bonhoeffer and others in Germany managed from time to time to exchange personal messages by devious routes. The whole story, which has not yet been published in full, would be a fascinating one.

When at last the Provisional Committee was able to hold its first post-war meeting at Geneva in 1946, there was a remarkable service in the Cathedral of St Pierre. Three preachers bore testimony, one after another, to what the war had taught them about unbroken fellowship in Christ. Each of them had spent a good deal of time in prison. Martin Niemöller spoke first. He told how, when he was finally arrested and taken to prison, his old father had said to him, "Be of good cheer, my son. Remember that there will be Christians praying for you from Greenland to the Pacific Islands"; and how that knowledge, in the eight years that followed, some of them in solitary confinement, had kept him not merely sane but joyful. The second preacher was a Chinese who had been imprisoned in Japanese-occupied Shanghai throughout the Sino-Japanese war. He told how, occasionally, his Japanese gaoler had been found to be a fellow-Christian and, when they discovered it, they would kneel in prayer together in his cell; that fellowship in Christ had conquered the forces that kept them apart. The third speaker was Eivind Berggrav, the splendid Primate of Norway who, for his part in leading the Christian resistance, had been kept under house-arrest in the forest. He told how one day the old man who brought the rations to his cottage whispered through the window, when the guards were not looking, "My old woman and I were listening to the B.B.C. last night, and we heard the Archbishop of Canterbury pray for you by name." Berggrav concluded: "God has been saying to us Christians, in these war years, 'My Christians, you are one.'" In that spirit the World Council was born.

Thus when the World Council of Churches held its First Assembly at Amsterdam in 1948 it was on the crest of a wave of conviction that such a continuing organ was a spiritual necessity. From the beginning it was made clear that here was both an organ for continuing every form of inter-church co-operation and service to mankind, and at the same time (exhibiting the heritage it had incorporated from Faith and Order) a forum in which the Churches were to continue to seek the meaning of the unity of the Church as a goal which lies beyond co-operation.

The small international chaplaincy to prisoners of war, which in war-time had already become a means of expressing Christian fellowship across the frontiers of warfare, rapidly developed first into "Christian reconstruction in Europe"—a programme for inter-church aid in restoring church life where it had suffered the ravages of war—and later into the present extensive programme of Inter-Church Aid and Service to Refugees, which, in terms of money and man-power, represents by far the biggest element in the programme of the World Council.

By the time the World Council held its Second Assembly at Evanston, near Chicago, it was beginning to be accepted as part of the permanent scenery of Christendom. Previously the Ecumenical Movement had tended to be regarded as the hobby of a comparatively small group, viewed with suspicion by some and unknown to most. At Evanston an almost intolerable glare of publicity enveloped the delegates. This discomfort, and even the distortion of proper business which it involved, was the price that had to be paid for bringing home to general Christian awareness in the United States this new phenomenon. It was inevitable that America, with its vast variety of Christian denominations participating in the Council and its vast wealth in a poverty-stricken post-war world, should carry the greater part of the financial burden, though from the beginning every effort was made to see that all the participating Churches took their fair share of the load in accordance with their capacity.

Meanwhile the International Missionary Council, founded after Edinburgh 1910 with John R. Mott as its Chairman and J. H. Oldham as its Secretary, had continued to develop along somewhat similar but parallel lines. This was an international organization not so much of Churches as of missionary societies and the national Christian Councils of the younger Churches in Asia and Africa. At the Third Assembly of the World Council of Churches at New Delhi, in the winter of 1961, the natural development of the Ecumenical Movement came to fulfilment when the International Missionary Council merged with the World Council of Churches, to provide one over-arching and permanent ecumenical organization to be the forum in which all aspects of the

Churches' common concern were freely to be discussed and forwarded.

Thus the modern Ecumenical Movement is the intertwining, slowly but inevitably over a period of more than forty years, of the three separate strands which have been in it from the beginning. The three great themes of the New Delhi Assembly, under the general heading of "Jesus Christ, the Light of the World", were Witness, Service, and Unity, representing the International Missionary Council, the Life and Work Movement, and the Faith and Order Movement, though now seen as of necessity belonging to one another. This is the brief history of how the present structure of inter-church co-operation and the pursuit of unity has reached its present form. We have spoken of the structure in its world-wide aspect but it has been paralleled by comparable national development. In Great Britain the British Council of Churches, which was formally constituted under the chairmanship of William Temple in 1942, reflects the same pattern at national level. But this is to look at the matter only in terms of the developing structure itself. We must now look at some of the forces in the larger world outside which were making this development possible, if not inevitable.

Most obvious is the fact that the contemporary world has become "one world" as never before in its history. No part of the world can remain unaffected by great happenings in any other part. The Christian Churches are necessarily affected by the new technical changes, which have transformed the consciousness of mankind. Yet the vision of a world-wide Church is not, in itself, a modern phenomenon. It has been implicit from the very beginning in the notion of the catholicity of the Church. It is the distinctive glory, as well as the distinctive difficulty, of the Roman Catholic conception of Christendom that it always conceives of itself as a world-wide empire. Even in Protestant Christianity the idea of international contact and co-operation is no new thing. William Carey, writing from Calcutta in May 1806 to Andrew Fuller, Secretary of the Baptist Missionary Society, saw this vision:

> The Cape of Good Hope is now in the hands of the English; should it continue so, would it not be possible to have a general association of all denominations of Christians, from the four quarters of the world, kept there once in about ten years? I earnestly recommend this plan, let the first meeting be in the year 1810, or 1812 at furthest. I have no doubt but it would be attended with very important effects; we could understand one another better, and more entirely enter into one another's views by two hours conversation than by two or three years epistolary correspondence.[1]

When the Ecumenical Movement began to take shape in the twentieth century it was because technical achievements were making such visions realizable. No doubt there was in Christian minds in the 1920s something of the international optimism which provided a secular ideal for the great protagonists of the League of Nations. But it is significant that the international Christian ideal does not appear to have shared in the widespread disillusionment that followed the failure of the League of Nations. It was never merely an idealized vision, but contained the tougher ingredient of faith in a universal God, so that when, after the end of the Second World War, international and world-wide Christian organization took its fresh form, it was probably less indebted to secular impulses than had been the earlier pioneers in the years following the First World War. Of course it still remained true that contemporary political divisions reflected themselves in Christian quarters. The sharp divisions of the world into the Communist and the non-Communist camps was inevitably reflected in the limited relationships possible between Christians on either side of the Iron Curtain. In 1948 a gathering of Orthodox Churches called together by

[1] See Ruth Rouse, "William Carey's 'Pleasing Dream'", in *International Review of Missions,* April 1949, 181–92. The original letter is preserved in the vestry of St Mary's Baptist Church, Norwich. Cf. *HEM* 355, n. 2.

the Patriarch of Moscow denounced the World Council of Churches as simply a piece of western ideology. To some extent the Christian Church in its outward relationships must remain dependent upon the changing winds of political expediency, though in the World Council of Churches, as in many other Christian circles, the division between "East" and "West" has never been willingly accepted, and every attempt was made, and is still made, to transcend its limitations. At New Delhi in 1961 the Russian, Bulgarian, Rumanian, and Polish Orthodox Churches became members of the World Council.

The basic fact remains that a world-wide Christian conscience, which had always been implicit in the very idea of the Church from early centuries, became technically possible in the twentieth century in a way which had never been true before. A striking analogy is provided by the Reformation emphasis upon the importance of the Bible being accessible to every Christian believer—an insight which could only be practically realized when the roughly contemporary discovery of printing made it possible for the Bible to be distributed in unlimited quantity.

There are of course dangers in a romantic internationalism at the political level and a romantic ecumenism in the life of the Church. It is possible, in dreaming of a world-wide and international community, to take refuge from facing the realities of one's actual neighbours. G. K. Chesterton once remarked: "I find it easy to love the Eskimos because I have never seen an Eskimo, but I find it hard to love my neighbour who plays the piano over my head too late at night." In somewhat the same way there is a temptation for Christians to entertain sentiments of confraternity towards Christians in distant parts of the world which can too easily be a substitute for really meeting face to face fellow-Christians in the dissenting chapel down the street or in the parish church on the green. To be aware of temptations may be to go part of the way to overcoming them.

At a deeper level the awareness by Christians of one another across confessional divisions has been increased by the common realization that the Christian community is a minority movement in the world. One of the striking differences between the atmosphere of the Edinburgh Conference of 1910 and more recent missionary thinking might be designated as awareness of the end of the Constantinian era of church history. It was assumed at Edinburgh 1910 that the function of "Christian Governments" throughout the world was to foster and favour the development of the Christian mission. To a large extent it was unconsciously assumed that Europe and North America constituted a Christian civilization serving as the home base for a missionary enterprise going out to the heathen in Asia and Africa. Two world wars and innumerable revolutions have brought home the realization that we no longer live in the era which began with Constantine's "Edict of Milan". The whole magnificent concept of Christendom, which may be dated from the crowning of Charlemagne in 800 A.D., dominated the western world in its fundamental thinking for a thousand years. Even the Churches of the Reformation which quarrelled with the Roman Catholic version of Christendom never relinquished their conception that they were part of a Christian culture.

It is difficult to describe without exaggeration the present situation of western Christendom. Any such description must reckon with the phenomenal strength of organized Christianity, for example in the United States of America, where recent figures show that 63.4% of the American people are enrolled in active church membership. This is in itself a difficult fact to assess because, when church membership is part of social conformity, it is hard to measure the true influence of the Church in society. Even in Europe, with the admittedly weaker hold which church membership has in both Catholic and Protestant countries, it is misleading to speak too simply of Europe as a mission field, as the

Catholic Church in France so vigorously did in the book *France, Pays de Mission.* It is still true that there is a profound difference between a culture which has been moulded by Christian influences and one which has never known them. In the United Kingdom one of the most difficult pastoral problems which confronts the contemporary Christian Churches is to know how far the widespread residual Christianity is an ally or an enemy of a true appreciation of the Gospel.

But when all the necessary qualifications have been made, it still remains true that the Ecumenical Movement has been accelerated by the awareness of all Christians that they constitute a minority movement in the world, whether in the face of a sometimes dramatic decline of active church membership in western lands or in the face of an equally dramatic resurgence of ancient religions in Asia. This whole resurgence has to be seen in the light of the emerging into power of the peoples of Asia, Africa, and Latin America.

In spite of what has just been said about the old-fashioned attitude of the Edinburgh Conference towards Christian governments and their paternal protection of foreign missions, the Christian movement has for long been aware of the great significance of these non-western countries. Spectators of the Ecumenical Movement—as for example, certain Roman Catholics—have sometimes thought that the younger Churches were given an undue prominence in its life and thought. Certainly one can detect a touch of ambiguity in this deference to the opinion of the younger Churches, somewhat comparable to the ambiguity that underlines deference to the opinions of "Youth". It is a characteristic of societies which are conscious of their own failure, and have to some extent lost their nerve, to pay great attention to the opinions of the young. On the other hand, it is a healthy phenomenon to pay such attention, because even the most secure and successful society will eventually be in the hands of those who are at the moment the younger generation. Their ideas are important in any circumstances because, however much they may be "suppled by time and tamed", they will eventually have ideas which are not quite the same as those of their fathers.

The same ambiguity underlies the attention of the Ecumenical Movement to the voice of the younger Churches. In part it was due to the bad conscience which the western Churches have for having planted a divided Church in the mission field. They preached a Gospel of the reconciliation of men to God, but preached it in an open or hidden rivalry with each other. The Churches of the western world were reproduced in the younger Churches in a bewildering pattern, to which both national and confessional divisions contributed. The younger Churches were not slow to find that battles fought long ago in the western world had little meaning for them. Controversies which had bitterly divided sincere men in the west no longer had the same cogency. It remains true that differences of principle remain differences of principle in any setting, and that diverse answers to the same big theological questions have still to be found. But voices from the younger Churches were insistent to remind the west that the divisions which they had inherited were not of their own creation and had not the same power over them. Furthermore, in this divided state they faced, as a tiny minority, the overwhelming odds of the great classical religions of the east or the emotionally powerful claims of more primitive and animistic faiths.

The dialogue between the younger Churches and the older Churches of the missionary-sending areas brought home to the Christian conscience, before it was acutely realized by western politicians, the profound significance of the changing balance of power in the world. It is the most significant fact of our time, and it is developing with breath-taking speed.

It provides the context in which the resurgence of the old religions is to be seen. A great deal has been written in commentary upon this undoubted fact. In part, it has been provoked by the success of Christian missions. They have introduced into the east conceptions of life and service which the older religions have imitated. In part, the resurgence is an aspect of newly-found nationalism, whether it be in the refined and sophisticated forms of Islam, the reformed Hinduism of Dr Radhakrishnan, or the self-conscious Buddhism of independent Ceylon; or even, on another plane, in the crude and repulsive revivals of primitive religion in such movements as Mau Mau. At a deeper level than mere nationalism is the need to give cultural depth to a newly conscious national life. The moral failure of the west, with its two world wars in a generation, has stimulated the old cultures of the east to find, in their traditional religions, a more sufficient basis for human living. Buddhism is openly claiming to-day to offer mankind the only road to peace. And beneath even the need for cultural depth is a widely-felt need for psychic security. We are accustomed in our own society to hear appeals for religious renewal as a bulwark against delinquency, sexual immorality, social disintegration, and so forth; but all over the world old landmarks are being swept away, old securities undermined. It is therefore not surprising that wherever religious resources of any kind are to be found, those who care for the health of society should appeal to them, whether those resources are in Christianity or in Islam, Buddhism, Hinduism, or Shinto. It is an appeal which no one who cares for the flowering of the human spirit dare despise. Its challenge to Christianity is—for that very reason—the more penetrating.

Confronted by this change in balance of power and with a greater sense of the urgent need for unity in the face of overwhelming odds, the whole Ecumenical Movement has been stimulated in its impulse towards Christian unity. Steady pressure has come from the younger Churches. It was only to be expected that the most radical experiment in a united Church should come from India. From its beginnings at the

Tranquebar Conference, the movement which led up to the Church of South India was fundamentally Christian in its apprehension of the imperative to unity lying within the Gospel itself. But it was spurred on by its awareness of the need for a united Christian testimony in order to make any impression upon the indigenous faiths of India. The story is well known of how Bishop Azariah testified that his whole approach to Christian unity was transformed by the experience of a group of Indians who were deterred from conversion to Christian faith by the realization that the unity which, to some extent at least, they enjoyed within the religion of Hinduism would be lost when they had to confront the choice between a variety of competing Christian Churches, one of which they would have to join if they became Christian. The advanced state of preparation for unity in North India and Ceylon carries the same story further.

It is clear that only in proportion as Churches in the west are also dominated by a sense of urgency to bear a united missionary testimony will they overcome the various forms of inertia and prejudice which prevent them from being "one, that the world may believe".

Finally, amidst all these external pressures, we must note the greatest single revolution within Christian thinking in the course of this century. The Church has come to occupy a central place in all theological thinking. Within this awareness there has developed a body of biblical interpretation and of systematic theology concerned to elaborate what is now seen to be the central theme of the Bible itself—a salvation-history which God carries out through his people. In England one of the decisive influences was undoubtedly Edwyn Clement Hoskyns, whose teaching at Cambridge produced a generation of students who accepted his fundamental thesis that "the primary duty of the Christian is to understand the biblical language", in the sense that only by entering into the whole way of thinking of the New Testament writers can we understand the Gospel. And this is no merely Anglican phenomenon, for at Cambridge also was that most influential teacher C. H. Dodd, a Congregational scholar, whose New Testament work is firmly grounded in an awareness of the Church as the believing community.

It is therefore not surprising that in recent years a great volume of theological writing has been concerned with the doctrine of the Church. Two successive Faith and Order conferences have seen the nature of the Church as the most central theme for common study, and this preoccupation is reflected in a volume of writing from every part of Christendom concerned with the exposition of the Church as the believing community and the vehicle of God's salvation of mankind.

8

TOWARDS CHARITY AND UNDERSTANDING: 2

In England

JOHN HUXTABLE

IF church relations in England have improved as much as they demonstrably have, even when due allowance has been made for remaining pockets of bigotry, it may properly be asked: Why have they not improved still further? Why have the Churches made such slow progress towards unity? The Methodists in England have been united since 1932, and almost all the Presbyterians in Scotland joined the newly constituted Church of Scotland in 1929. Most notable among many unions overseas are the United Church of Canada (1925) and the Church of South India (1947). The latter is the first to include with ex-Anglicans a number of non-episcopalians. Why has there been no corresponding broadly-based reunion in England? To put the question in another form, what obstacles remain to be overcome before all our professed longings for Christian unity can be fulfilled in this land?

Not least among these obstacles is the plain fact that ecclesiastical habits are hard to change, nor are ever changed unless enough people care enough about an issue to expound its importance and to work for its accomplishment with such enthusiasm and wisdom as to convince their fellows. At the present, the ecumenically-minded in each communion are relatively few, and they have by no means persuaded the mass of Christian folk that the unity of all Christian people in this country is a desirable, a possible, a necessary ideal. It is indeed not difficult to evoke a great deal of lip-service to the slogan-like notion that our divisions are sinful, and to pass lightly to the theoretical statement that it would be good for them to be healed; it is quite a different matter to bring those who are persuaded thus far even to contemplate actual unity with whatever other Christian body is the nearest neighbour. It is relatively easy to assent to Christian unity as an ideal until it becomes a matter of actually loving the brother we have to meet often, of whose ecclesiastical habits we are by no means enamoured. It would mean learning to put up with extempore prayers or the Book of Common Prayer.

Such natural ecclesiastical inertia might indeed have been largely overcome by now, had it not been for the fact that there are real difficulties to be faced and overcome before all Christians can be gathered into one Church. It will be the not very grateful purpose of the rest of this chapter to record what they are and, in part, to assess their importance.

Not the least of these difficulties are two facts which may be examined before we look at the more profound theological issues which still await solution.

First: it can hardly be denied that to no one has it yet been given to declare the sort of unity which we ought to seek in such terms as all other Christians are prepared to accept. (1) There are those who would be content with a simply "spiritual" unity, and would dismiss all attempts to give such unity a structure and an organization as a superfluity of ecclesiastical naughtiness. This view, which has been given something of a fillip by Emil Brunner's *The Misunderstanding of the Church* (1952), may be sharply criticized because it so stresses the notion of the Church as a fellowship that it overlooks the fact that if the Church exists in history it must have a recognizable structure, and that this structure cannot be a matter of theological indifference any more than it can be left to the chaos of sectarian taste. The nature of the Church's structure ought not to be left to the preference of a group, any more than it should be determined solely by ecclesiastical tradition; it should be as much an expression of the Gospel by which the Church lives as is its worship and preaching. This means that all Christian bodies should constantly be inquiring how far their familiar structures are in fact consonant with the Gospel, and to what extent they need reformation so as to become more conformable with it. (2) Others are wont to declare that the presence of a certain kind of ministry in the Church represents a continuity which guarantees its sacramental life, and that without such a ministry Churches are either irregular or defective or both, having a sacramental life which is uncertainly guaranteed and more a sign of God's uncovenanted mercies than an indication that their church life is pleasing to the Lord Christ. (3) The non-episcopal bodies, on the other hand, have as a rule been indifferent to historical continuity, and have based their thinking about the structure of church life on fidelity to the Word of God. If they believed themselves able to say that such a church order was "agreeable to the Word of God", they have been content; indeed, at times they have been as truculent towards those who stress historic continuity as these have been in deploring the lack of any more manifest guarantee of apostolic succession. (4) Yet again, other and in most cases more recent groups have claimed that the manifest presence and activity of the Holy Spirit is the only valid guarantee that any group is a "real" Church.

It may be argued[1] that all these positions are partially true and that each group needs the others for the completion and enrichment of its ecclesiastical life. The important point, however, is that at present no one has been able to formulate a statement of what should be the marks of the Church in such a way as to convince even a majority of Christians that this represents a church life into which they could obediently and gladly enter, together with those from whom they have so far been separated. To say this is not to disregard or undervalue what has been accomplished in the realm of Faith and Order, nor to underestimate that growth in mutual understanding which has been so happy a feature of church life in this century: it is simply to state what still needs to be done, and to say that we cannot expect much further progress until the objective has been more precisely defined.

Secondly: it is sometimes said that denominational barriers no longer represent the real divisions between Christians;

[1] Cf. J. E. Lesslie Newbigin, *The Household of God* (1953).

and this draws attention to a fact which it is extremely difficult to evaluate. Conservative Evangelicals, for example, are to be found in all the main communions, though they flourish more in some settings than in others; and it is clear that they have more in common with one another than, say, those in the Anglican Communion have with their more "Catholic" fellow-Anglicans. A particular attitude to the Bible and to certain fundamental doctrines is far more important to them and to their fellow-believers in other communions than the particular ecclesiastical tenets of their own communion. It may be noted that as a rule Conservative Evangelicals are opposed to the activities of the World Council of Churches, and take their stand on the conviction that fellowship presupposes theological agreement. Similarly, but usually not so obviously, those who value a more "liberal" approach to theology find themselves having much more in common with like-minded people in other communions than with the more "obscurantist" members of their own. What is of even greater relevance to our theme is the fact that those who support and have been influenced by the Ecumenical Movement have a fellowship with one another which transcends denominational boundaries. They have seen something of the irrelevance of western ecclesiastical divisions in an Asian or an African setting. Usually it is such folk as these who have come to a deeper understanding of the place of the Church in the purpose of God than was common in 1910. They find it no longer possible to think of the Church as an optional extra for gregarious Christians. They see the people of God as integral to the purpose of redemption. This conviction chimes with the whole development of biblical theology: indeed the two insights are very closely related and intertwined. And so in their minds is raised the question: What does God mean the Church to be? It seems clear that none of the Churches wholly fulfils its true vocation, that none of them in separation can be faithful to its calling, and that unity is plainly one of the Church's essential marks. The prevailing emphasis on eschatology has convinced many that what the Church is to be is at least as important for its present life as what it has ever been. Taken all in all, these convictions represent a coherent outlook which has won the adherence of many in various communions, and has given them much more in common with one another than many of them have with such fellow-communicants as lack them. Of these three "trans-denominational" groupings the last is the most relevant to our purpose. The ecumenical enthusiasts represent a conviction which would logically and ultimately lead to the visible reunion of Christ's Church; but the insights upon which their convictions rest, and the passion which they engender in those who have been seized of them, are not at present shared by a majority of churchmen, who are for the most part content to do no more than pay lip-service to the cause of Christian unity, thankful indeed that church relations have improved, and inclined to ask what more can be required than ecclesiastical good manners and continued growth in co-operation. If growth in charity and understanding is to develop into some more visible expression of Christian unity, this majority must be persuaded of its necessity.

It is plain that if the ecumenically uncommitted multitude is to be persuaded of the necessity of Christian unity, two sorts of obstacles must be overcome. Apart from the more strictly theological issues, which will be dealt with later, there are a number of merely ecclesiastical and non-theological factors which call for examination.

Dr C. H. Dodd, in a now famous essay,[1] instanced a number of non-theological factors which impede progress towards Christian unity all the more powerfully for not being always consciously recognized. How many Methodists,

[1] In C. H. Dodd, G. R. Cragg, and J. Ellul, *Social and Cultural Factors in Church Divisions* (1952).

for instance, are held back from closer relations with the parish church because Anglicans are not committed to total abstinence? How much does this affect intercommunion? Some churches permit dancing on church premises; others are not specifically anti-gambling; yet others are more lax about Sunday observance than some of their Christian brethren think right. Apart from such differences concerning matters of personal behaviour, there are even more subtle and perhaps more powerful differences which are rooted in class-consciousness: the Established Church tends to be identified with the "upper classes", while the Methodists and the Salvation Army, for example, are more proletarian; Presbyterians are often said to be more "intellectual" than the more "evangelical" Baptists. All these "beliefs" might upon closer examination be proved either to be entirely false, or, at least, to be only partially true; in their unexamined forms, however, they certainly weigh against whatever more explicit considerations point towards unity. At times those engaged in theological discussion are inclined to dismiss these so-called "non-theological" factors as of relatively little importance, but it is doubtful whether this is a sound judgement: the power of prejudice and unexamined hearsay can, at the parish level, carry far greater weight than the doubtless much sounder conclusions reached around a conference-table.

But, it is sometimes asked—even by those who are quite ready to argue that disunity is sinful and that unity should be sought as urgently as possible—would not any large-scale programme of reunion result in some mammoth ecclesiastical organization? Would not the local congregation count for less and less, and a powerful bureaucratic organization tend to impose on all parts of the newly-formed Church a monolithic uniformity? Such fears are often felt among non-Methodist Free Churchmen in Great Britain, who find their rejoicing in Methodist union considerably qualified by what they take to be the large closely-knit organization which has resulted from bringing together the ex-Wesleyan and other forms of Methodism. It may well be that their apprehensions are mistaken and that Methodists can prove from experience that life in their united community is freer and ampler than it was before; but until that proof has been convincingly conveyed to Baptists and Congregationalists in particular, fear of being a cog in a mammoth ecclesiastical machine will continue to hinder reunion. It is worth noting that such fears are not expressed to anything like the same extent with respect to the Church of England, which is numerically larger than Methodism. This seems to indicate that the problem is less that of size than organization. Although, as everywhere else, there are forces at work within the Church of England to make it more centralized than it is at present, so far, at any rate, the diocesan system has preserved sufficient local autonomy and evoked sufficient local loyalty to enable the parishioner to feel that he belongs to a larger whole and yet not feel that in the larger whole he is lost. The particular facts upon which this illustration rests may be disputed; nevertheless, it will serve to focus one of the major ecclesiastical problems involved in reunion.

Those who feel such difficulties as these, together with those who despair of ever getting the majority of Christians to do more than regard Christian unity as an ideal to be admired but not translated into fact, join forces with those who are still more blatantly content with things as they are, to suggest two possible alternatives to Church union. What about federation? What do we need more than co-operation?

By federation is usually meant an arrangement whereby the member Churches join together for such common purposes as they have agreed upon, without in any way infringing the autonomy of any of them or attempting to bring their theological convictions into any kind of mutual confrontation. The Free Church Federal Council is an excellent example of this sort of church relationship. In this body are united and amalgamated the former Federal Council of the Evangelical Free Churches of England and the National Council of Evangelical Free Churches, together with the National Free Church Women's Council. Its objects are stated thus:

1. to express the essential unity in Christ of the Evangelical Free Churches in England and Wales;
2. to secure their federation on the basis of their common Evangelical faith, each denomination retaining liberty to fulfil its own distinctive witness and mission;
3. to foster their fellowship in worship and work, to co-ordinate their counsels, activities and resources for the evangelization of the people and the extension of Christ's Kingdom in every sphere of life;
4. to maintain the spiritual testimony of the Free Churches, to uphold full religious liberty and to take action when authorized to do so in matters affecting the responsibilities and rights of the federated Churches;
5. to promote fellowship and united action where possible with other branches of the Church throughout the world and in particular the British Council of Churches.

This statement of the objects of the Free Church Federal Council is followed by a doctrinal statement, prefaced by two paragraphs which are significant for our present purpose:

1. The Evangelical Free Churches of England claim and cherish their place as inheritors, along with others, of the historic faith of Christendom, which found expression in the oecumenical creeds of the early and undivided Church; and this declaratory Statement does not profess to be a comprehensive creed, but is a declaration of such truths as, in the circumstances, it seems proper to rehearse and emphasize.
2. It is an essential element in the proposals for federation that each of the federating Churches should preserve its own autonomy as regards faith and practice; this Statement, therefore, is not to be imposed as a disciplinary standard on any of these Churches, nor, on the other hand, does it

> supersede or in any way alter the place of whatever doctrinal standards any of these Churches may maintain in their constitution.[1]

It would be as idle as it would be untrue to suggest that this way of bringing Churches together is valueless, since it provides ample means of fellowship and co-operation both at the national and at more local levels. All this is very much to the good; but as an alternative to actual union, federation is open to severe criticism. It is not the experience of the English Free Churches that they have been brought closer together in the fifty years or so during which they have been federated in the Free Church Federal Council.[2] Recent attempts to promote union between the Free Churches have proved abortive—no doubt for a variety of what were taken to be sufficient reasons, into which it is not our present business to inquire: the simple point is that after so many years of federation the Free Churches are constitutionally as much separated and autonomous as they have ever been. The original intention has been admirably maintained; and it is of interest to note as well that the almost entire inter-communion between these Churches has not led to unity. Federation, however, is open to theological objection at a serious level. If we are right to deduce that it is part of the divine purpose that the very fabric and structure of the Church should declare Christ's power to reconcile those who would otherwise remain in separation; if we are right in believing that in the thought of the New Testament the Great Church is prior to the local church;[3] if the existence of separated groups of Christians in any locality—whatever historical justification for their separation there may have been—mars the witness of the Church and makes it

[1] *The Constitution of the Free Church Federal Council*, 2 f.

[2] See E. K. H. Jordan, *Free Church Unity* (1956), *passim*, especially ch. 16.

[3] Cf. C. H. Dodd's essay, "The Church in the New Testament", in *Essays Congregational and Catholic*, ed. A. Peel (1931).

impossible for it fully to demonstrate Christ's power to reconcile; then the only possible justification for federation would be that it was designed to bring divided communions together with a view to their closer unity. On this understanding of the matter federation as such has no ultimate theological justification whatever: nothing short of the union of all Christian people is a sufficient objective.

The practical value of federation is that it encourages and makes possible a great deal of co-operation; but that such co-operation can happen without federation is exemplified by the existence and work of the British Council of Churches, which is quite self-consciously not a federated body. When it was inaugurated on 23 September 1943, the member Churches came together on the basis of agreed Articles of Amalgamation. The second of these Articles is that the basis of the Council shall be the same as that of the World Council of Churches, namely "a fellowship of churches which accept our Lord Jesus Christ as God and Saviour"; and the third describes the functions of the Council. The first paragraph of this Article says that a main function of the Council shall be to continue the work of the bodies for inter-church co-operation which had come together in the Council; the remainder reads:

2. To facilitate common action by the churches in evangelistic enterprise, in promotion of international friendship, in stimulating a sense of social responsibility, and in guiding the activities of the churches for the welfare of youth.
3. To facilitate such other common action as may later be determined.
4. To promote co-operation in study . . .
5. To assist the growth of oecumenical consciousness in the members of all churches and generally to promote Christian unity[1].

By prosecuting these aims the British Council of Churches has become an increasingly useful instrument of Christian

[1] *Documents on Christian Unity: Third Series, 1930–48*, ed. G. K. A. Bell (1948), 143.

co-operation, and under its aegis the member Churches have undoubtedly increased in mutual understanding. But it becomes more and more clear that the nearer the Churches come to one another in co-operation the more they are driven to ask questions about the reasons for their divisions and the way back to unity. Dr W. A. Visser 't Hooft has recently made an illuminating comment on the Edinburgh Conference of 1910 which is of wider application. At the thirteenth meeting of the Central Committee of the World Council of Churches (St Andrews, 1960), he remarked that a study of the great and lively discussion at Edinburgh about co-operation and the promotion of unity "makes it clear that we wrestle to-day with the same problems in this field as did those who met fifty years ago". While preparations for that conference were being made, a definite pledge was given that "questions affecting the differences of Doctrine and Order between the Christian bodies should not be brought before the conference for discussion and resolution"; and certain missionary bodies made it perfectly clear that only on such conditions would they participate in the conference at all. The fact, however, is that while in those circumstances it would have been perfectly natural for the conference to have confined itself to discussing practical co-operation in missionary service, a great many speakers expressed the conviction that, good as co-operation might be, unity is better; and the need for a conference on the questions "which have been tabooed" was affirmed. Visser 't Hooft comments: "It seems to me a remarkable fact that already at the time of the very first consideration of co-operation in the field of missions two things become so very evident, namely that mission points to unity and that co-operation is not the goal, but a stage on the road to that goal."[1]

Amid such movements towards co-operation there is

[1] *Minutes and Reports* of the Thirteenth Meeting of the Central Committee of the World Council of Churches (Geneva, 1960), 108.

another which is of a more ambiguous character altogether, namely world-confessionalism. As long ago as 1881 the Methodists formed the World Methodist Council; the Alliance of Reformed Churches had already been formed in 1875; and Congregationalists and Baptists formed similar organizations in 1891 and 1905 respectively. These international councils are older than the Ecumenical Movement; they began as natural opportunities for those of a particular religious persuasion to take counsel together on matters of common interest on the widest possible scale. With the advent of the Ecumenical Movement, however, it was inevitable that the question should be asked whether these world confessional groups, as they have come to be called, should continue to function, and, if so, in what ways. The very factors which favoured the growth of the Ecumenical Movement, of course, favoured the growth of these groups as well; and since it was now much easier for international conferences to be arranged and held, these international denominational bodies tended to meet more frequently and to have a more vigorous life. Whereas in earlier days these organizations were staffed entirely by voluntary labour, they now tend to maintain a staff of permanent salaried officials. From the ecumenical point of view it has been most fortunate that *so far* those most prominently identified with these world confessional groups have been deeply involved also in the work of the Ecumenical Movement, and this has demonstrated the evident sincerity of such declarations as have been made that these groups in no way tend to run counter to nor in any way undermine the aims and objects of the World Council of Churches. While all this is to be taken at much more than its face value, these groups are nevertheless a *potential* danger to the Ecumenical Movement. If their leadership were to fall into sectarian hands, a ready-made and fairly powerful organization is in being by which the particular confession could be led away from its ecumenical commitment. Moreover, however ecumenical the intentions of the leaders may be, these organizations represent a cause for which loyalty can be more easily evoked than for more ecumenical purposes. It is easier, because it involves little or no sacrifice, to love the Congregationalist in Australia, whom you are unlikely ever to be called upon to meet, than the Anglo-Catholic or the Quaker in the same town, from whom you ought not to be divided but with whom it costs so much to unite.

In the section of the Lambeth Report of 1958 which deals with Christian Unity and the Church Universal, an attempt is made to regularize the use of the term "intercommunion".[1] The Report suggests that it should be more sharply distinguished from "full communion", and that the two terms should be used to describe two different sets of circumstances. This differs from the usage suggested by the Lund Faith and Order Conference (1952), according to which "full communion" should be used to describe the close relation which exists between Churches of the same denominational or confessional family, such as the Churches of the Anglican Communion or the Orthodox, Lutheran, or Reformed families of Churches. According to the same suggested usage, "intercommunion" should be used to describe varying degrees of relation between Churches of one communion with a Church or Churches of another, e.g. the unrestricted *communio in sacris* which the Provinces and Churches of the Anglican Communion enjoy with the Old Catholic Churches. The Lambeth Fathers, however, hold that while this might be logically a very satisfactory distinction, "there is no distinction so far as spiritual reality is concerned", since "in each case there is unrestricted *communio in sacris*". A different (and probably better) distinction is therefore suggested, as less confusing and more true to reality: "full communion" should be used to describe all cases where a Province or Church of the Anglican Communion by agreement enters into a relation of unrestricted

[1] *The Lambeth Conference* (1958), pt 2, 23.

communio in sacris, including mutual recognition of ministries with another Church; "intercommunion" could then be used "to describe the varying degrees of relation other than full communion, which already exist, or may be established in the future, between Churches of the Anglican family and with others outside the family".

Such attempts to define and regularize the use of the word "intercommunion", whether the Lund or the Lambeth use be preferred, are to be welcomed, since a good deal of confusion of thought has arisen around this word, partly, though by no means wholly, owing to a lack of precise agreement what it should be taken to mean.

The scandal of Christ's people being unable to be at one at the Holy Table is plain for all to see. Free Churchmen are often impatient of Anglican scruples on the point, and find it difficult to see why their own solution of the problem is so unacceptable to the Church of England. It is their habit to welcome at the Lord's Table communicant members of other Churches who desire to be present, and it is by no means infrequent for Baptists, Congregationalists, Methodists, and Presbyterians to join together in a service of Holy Communion according to the manner of one or other of these Churches. So truly does this custom reflect their habit of mind that Free Churchmen have to make a real effort of sympathetic imagination to understand why the episcopal bodies cannot share it. For the Free Churchman, intercommunion presents few, if any, problems, and appears to provide an admirable opportunity for demonstrating to the Church and to the world that unity of spirit which binds the Churches together despite their outward divisions; for the Anglican, the issue is beset with difficulties. If sacramental grace depends on an episcopal ministry in the apostolic succession, if those who communicate should have been confirmed by a bishop in that succession, and if all other ministries and modes of admission to communicant status are either irregular or invalid or both, how can an Anglican consent to or take part in a celebration of the Holy Communion when the validity of it is to him at least uncertain and to participate in it would make nonsense of conscientiously held convictions? Moreover, he might well argue that such a service would pretend a unity which in fact does not yet exist. Such a position can be taken consistently with believing that God honours and blesses the ministries of the non-episcopal bodies, and that such ministries are true ministries within the Universal Church. Nevertheless, the conviction that there is a divinely appointed ministry in the Church which the non-episcopal Churches lack prevents those who hold it from agreeing to intercommunion with such Churches, save in certain clearly specified circumstances —despite the fact that they do not wish to deny that God's grace is in fact given through the sacrament as observed. To decline such intercommunion is not intended to reflect upon the status of the non-episcopal Churches: it is simply to bear witness to certain different convictions about the nature of the Church and its ministry.

Those Anglicans who take such a view, which may perhaps be called post-tractarian, regard intercommunion as a goal to be reached. Others, by no means only non-episcopalians, regard intercommunion as a means by which fuller unity might be reached. These believe that Churches may have *communio in sacris* without being entirely agreed about the ministry, so long as they hold the apostolic faith and order their lives accordingly. Anglicanism in history and at the present time takes two views of this matter, as the late Dr Norman Sykes's book *Old Priest and New Presbyter*[1] makes clear; and to some extent, though for different reasons, a similar ambivalence prevails in Free Church circles. Apart from a limited number of Baptists who retain the practice of closed communion, most Free Churchmen, as we have seen, welcome to the Lord's Table all who are communicant members of any part of the Church; but a number of them

[1] Cambridge, 1956.

now decline such invitations as come to them to receive communion in Anglican churches because they know that to accept would cause affront to the consciences of other Anglicans and also because they have come to share the conviction that intercommunion should be reserved for a time when a greater measure of ecclesiastical agreement and of visible unity has been reached.

Nevertheless, it must also be said that many Free Churchmen believe that the Anglican refusal of intercommunion does in fact imply some sort of adverse judgement on the churchly character of the non-episcopal bodies; protests that this is not so have met with only limited credence. To say of the Church of Scotland, for example, that it is a true part of the Universal Church, despite its non-episcopal character, and at the same time to refuse intercommunion, save in quite exceptional circumstances, is seen by many as taking away with one hand what is given with the other. Such an attitude, however conscientiously held, must be regarded as a major obstacle to reunion in this country, notwithstanding the fact that many who adopt it are very keenly involved in ecumenical activities and are most anxious to serve the cause of unity. Nor was the situation eased at all by the way in which the Lambeth Conference dealt with the Church of South India.

The Lambeth Conference of 1948 felt that certain difficulties arose concerning those bishops, priests, and deacons who had been consecrated or ordained since the formation of the Church of South India in 1947. While ready to declare that "the orders and ministry of the Church of South India are regular and valid so far as regularity and validity can be guaranteed by the 'form and manner' used in consecrating and ordaining", and to agree that the Church of South India had been "most careful to maintain the episcopal succession by the participation of three Anglican Bishops in its first consecration", the conference believed that "form and manner alone are not sufficient to guarantee the character of a ministry", which could only "be substantiated by the faith and practice of the Church itself".[1] The conference was unable to be unanimous about the right way of responding to the new situation thus created by the Church of South India. A majority held that "such bishops, presbyters and deacons" as had been consecrated and ordained since the union "should be acknowledged as true bishops, presbyters and deacons in the Church of Christ and should be accepted as such in every part of the Anglican Communion, subject only to such regulations as are normally made in all such cases by the responsible authorities in each area". Another view, which was held by a substantial minority, was that it was not yet possible to pass such a definite judgement "upon the precise status of such bishops, presbyters and deacons in the Church of Christ or to recommend that they be accepted in the Anglican Communion as bishops, presbyters and deacons". No member wished to condemn or declare invalid the episcopally consecrated or ordained ministry of the Church of South India; and it was recognized that there would be "differences in the attitudes of the Churches, Provinces and Dioceses regarding the status of the bishops, presbyters and deacons of the Church of South India"; but the unanimous hope was expressed that such differences may never be made a ground of condemnation of action taken by any Church, Province or Diocese.[2] The conference looked forward "hopefully and with longing to the day when there shall be full communion between the Church of South India and the Anglican Communion as a whole".[3]

When the Lambeth Conference met again in 1958, it could be recorded that seven Churches or Provinces of the Anglican Communion had taken synodical action with regard to the ministry of the Church of South India. Two of the seven had accorded recognition only to former Anglican

[1] *The Lambeth Conference* (1948), pt 2, 47.
[2] Ibid., pt 1, 39. [3] Ibid., pt 1, 38.

clergy and had permitted them to exercise their ministry within the province concerned, provided they did so in Anglican churches only. Five other Churches in virtually the same form acknowledged the bishops and episcopally ordained presbyters and deacons of the Church of South India to be truly ministers in the Church of God; and another had before it the advice of its Commission on Ecumenical Relations that it need no longer postpone a similarly favourable judgement. These five Churches were reported to have made regulations about the ministrations of the clergy so recognized within their several jurisdictions and thus made possible a limited intercommunion with the Church of South India in the thirty-year interim period. Invitations to the Church of South India clergy to preach were permitted; and four of the Churches allowed the bishops and episcopally ordained clergy to celebrate the Holy Communion in Anglican churches, conditionally upon their willingness to confine their celebrations to Anglican churches while sojourning within the territory of each particular Church. The report of the committee on Church Unity and the Church Universal was received and endorsed by the Lambeth Conference as a whole. It seemed to the bishops that a good many of their earlier misgivings had been or were on the way to being dispelled, and there seemed reason to hope that increasing connection between the Church of South India and the Churches of the Anglican Communion would hasten the day when full communion between them might be possible.

The hesitations which this narrative makes obvious were not unnoticed by the Free Churches in Great Britain and their fellow-churchmen elsewhere. Not everyone was sympathetic with the causes of these hesitations, and all had to draw the reluctant conclusion that the way to intercommunion was neither as easy nor as swift as they had hoped. Indeed, the reserved reception given to the Church of South India by the Anglican Communion as a whole—

particularly the regulation that episcopally ordained ministers of the Church of South India should limit their celebrations of the Holy Communion to the Church of England—made many Free Churchmen wonder what sort of reception would be given to them by the Anglican Communion if they did indeed "take episcopacy into their system", as they were counselled to do by Archbishop Geoffrey Fisher. In a sermon preached before the University of Cambridge in November 1946, almost a year before the actual formation of the Church of South India, Dr Fisher had made this remarkable suggestion, having in mind no doubt the special situation regarding the Church of England and the Free Churches as a result of the Establishment. He suggested a possible way of achieving intercommunion between Anglican and non-episcopal bodies which are sufficiently agreed in the realm of faith through the acceptance by the non-episcopal Churches of the historic episcopate with the functions which traditionally belong to it. The Churches involved would remain distinct Churches: intercommunion, not reunion, was in view. They would remain side by side, though one main barrier between them would have been removed; and each would develop the episcopate and adapt it according to its own particular needs and tradition. Admittedly, several episcopal Churches existing side by side would create a very anomalous position, though it might not be as anomalous as several Churches being out of communion with one another. This sermon was warmly received as yet one more token of that concern for Christian unity which was so conspicuous a feature of Dr Fisher's tenure of the see of Canterbury, although a good deal of the enthusiasm evaporated when intercommunion between the Anglican Churches and the Church of South India was so limited, since that Church seemed as episcopal as the Free Churches in England were ever likely to be in the lifetime of any then alive.

On the basis of this Cambridge sermon, conversations took

place between representatives of the Church of England and the Church of Scotland, and between representatives of the Church of England and the Methodist Church. In 1957 *Relations between Anglican and Presbyterian Churches* made public the result of the former of these conversations, which had turned out to be concerned not simply with the relation of the two National Churches but with "the more fundamental and fruitful subject of the relations between the Episcopalian and Presbyterian systems of Church Order".[1] As such a discussion, this report contains much that is valuable and deserves more serious attention than it has so far received in some quarters; but it was received with a mixture of cool respect and vehement enmity by the Church of Scotland, which seemed in some ways animated at least as much by nationalist as theological and ecclesiastical considerations. A good deal must happen before the word *bishop* has a good odour in Scotland! *Conversations between the Church of England and the Methodist Church* (1958) indicates that useful ground has been already covered, although it is too soon to speak of the final outcome since this is an interim report. The Methodists spoke for their non-episcopal brethren as well as for themselves in saying that

> the one fatal objection to Church reunion would be any requirement of the reordination of its ministers, which would in fact be a denial of Methodism's place in the Catholic Church.... A way forward to that Union of Christendom to which we believe God is calling us now, whose Will is our peace, may lie not through negative judgements on each other's order, but through a positive and creative Act of Unification of Ministries in which each could find an enlargement and self-fulfilment.[2]

In both documents there are excellent statements of the meaning of episcopacy, which, if they were carefully studied, would clear a good many non-episcopal minds of many misconceptions.

[1] Op. cit., foreword. [2] Op. cit., 37.

While such practical results have followed from Archbishop Fisher's sermon at Cambridge, these two reports make plain what several other considerations also suggested, that the archbishop may not have made such an illuminating suggestion as he undoubtedly hoped. Precisely the same considerations are involved whether Anglicans and Free Churchmen are talking about intercommunion or church union: neither, it seems, is to be possible unless in some way the non-episcopalians become episcopal. What is not at present in view is mutual recognition and acceptance, and this because of fundamental disagreement about the nature of the Church and its ministry. To an examination of these divergences we must now turn.

While anything like a complete examination of the discussions and controversies about the nature of the Church and ministry during the present century is not here possible, it is essential to see the scope of the problem and to disclose the difficulties which have prevented a greater degree of unity than has so far been achieved in Great Britain.

One of the most remarkable books on this subject was A. C. Headlam's Bampton Lectures for 1920, *The Doctrine of the Church and Christian Reunion* (1920). It was given a mixed reception at the time of its publication; it had great influence on the historic Lambeth Conference of the year in which it appeared; it still represents one Anglican point of view. So far as his proposals about reunion are outlined in his final chapter, Headlam reduced the matter to great simplicity. He saw the Church as the company of all baptized Christians who believed in Christ; and he had no doubt that it was God's will that all these should be united in one body. It was sin which had broken this unity and prevented it from being displayed. It could be recovered, he believed, on the basis of what has subsequently come to be known as the Lambeth Quadrilateral: the Scriptures of the Old and New Testaments, the Nicene Creed, the two Sacraments of

Baptism and Holy Communion, and the historic episcopate.[1] These four points do not require any agreement about the nature of the Church, which Headlam seems not to have considered to be the fundamental point at issue. He believed that these four points were a sufficient basis for reunion:

> The necessary elements of the Christian faith are few, and it is the right and wise course to insist on them only. If you really mean reunion, it is only possible if you reduce what you demand from others to things which you feel that you can rightly insist on. . . . What the fullest and richest religious life demands is, on the one hand, a firm and simple faith; on the other, the widest intellectual freedom.[2]

Consistently with this, Headlam did not demand any particular interpretation of the creeds and sacraments: "to impose any particular interpretation on the Creed . . . is the same as to put forth a new and additional creed";[3] and what was essential about the sacraments was that we should make clear in our way of celebrating them that we intend to do Christ's will. Much evil, Headlam remarked, had come from trying to define what could not be defined.[4] As for orders, Headlam laid it down that all who appoint their ministers as Christ's "Apostles did with prayer and the laying on of hands, must be held to have valid Sacraments and Orders".[5] "This meant that he was prepared not only to accept the validity of non-episcopal ministries, provided that they were appointed with prayer and the laying on of hands, but also to dispense with reordination in a reunited Church. What was required was a mutual recognition of all orders and the granting of a new commission to all ministers to work under new conditions, with the clear understanding that all future ministers in such a Church should be episcopally ordained".[6] This view was possible for Headlam because

[1] Op. cit., 209, 231, 280.
[2] Ibid., 282.
[3] Ibid., 238.
[4] Ibid., 281.
[5] Ibid., 280.
[6] R. C. D. Jasper, *Arthur Cayley Headlam* (1960), 144 f. The references in the Bampton Lectures are 306, 307; cf. 254, 268, 311.

he did not accept Augustine's theory of the indelibility of orders. He taught that the authority of bishops was held from the Church, and was not inherited by sacramental transmission from the Apostles.[1]

The influence of this teaching on the *Lambeth Appeal to all Christian People* of 1920 is obvious enough. The famous Quadrilateral, which had its origins in the Chicago Convention of the American Episcopal Church in 1886, declared that the visible unity of all Christian people would involve the whole-hearted acceptance of:

> The Holy Scriptures, as the record of God's revelation of Himself to man, and as being the rule and ultimate standard of faith; and the Creed, commonly called Nicene, as the sufficient statement of the Christian Faith, and either it or the Apostles' Creed as the Baptismal Confession of Faith;
>
> The divinely instituted sacraments of Baptism and the Holy Communion, as expressing for all the corporate life of the whole fellowship in and with Christ;
>
> A ministry acknowledged by every part of the Church as possessing not only the inward spiritual call of the Spirit, but also the commission of the Church and the authority of the whole body.[2]

The *Appeal* also asked whether it might not reasonably be an episcopal ministry. "It is not that we call in question for a moment the spiritual reality of the ministries of those communions which do not possess the Episcopate"; nevertheless, it was suggested that the episcopate might well be the best instrument for maintaining unity and continuity in the Church; and it was greatly desired that the office of a bishop should be everywhere exercised "in a representative and constitutional manner". So that reunion might indeed come about, it was thought that the bishops of the present Anglican Communion should accept from the Churches with whom they might be uniting "a form of commission or

[1] Op. cit., 124–33.

[2] Quoted in the form adopted by the Lambeth Conference of 1920, which differs somewhat from the original.

recognition which would commend our ministry to their congregations, as having its place within the one family". "It is our hope", another paragraph adds, "that the same motive would lead ministers who have not received it to accept a commission through episcopal ordination, as obtaining for them a ministry throughout the whole fellowship".[1]

The *Lambeth Appeal* was a generous document, which set a new tone to the discussion of the problems of unity: in that sense, at least, it is a landmark. It shared, however, the weakness of Headlam's position in that, out of anxiety not to define what cannot be defined, it left the door open to dangerous and misleading ambiguity. If Headlam's view of the episcopate had been the only one, it would have been a different matter; but there had been other influences at work besides his, and one of the most powerful of them was personified in Charles Gore, who took a very different view of the whole issue. If the episcopate and orders are so important, why are they so? A great many Anglicans could feel that the *Lambeth Appeal* left too many important issues vague, and Free Churchmen who have been consistently offered the episcopate could be excused for asking precisely what they were being invited to accept. In more than one quarter, then, there were those who were asking for more definition; but definitions are apt to be divisive.

Charles Gore, by any reckoning one of the greatest figures in British Christianity during the present century, had expounded his views in a number of well-known volumes: *The Church and the Ministry* (1888), *Essays in Church Reform* (1889), *Catholicism and Roman Catholicism* (1923). In the first of these works, Gore developed his view that the Church was intended to be a visible society and that this is what should be expected in a fellowship springing out of the incarnation; the notion of apostolic succession corresponds to the incarnation and the sacraments, and is important as a bond of union

[1] *The Lambeth Conference* (1920), 28 f.

of a universal spiritual society, as laying emphasis on men's dependence on God's gifts, and as satisfying the moral needs of those who minister. In spite of variable features, which may have been partly inevitable and beneficial, there have been certain first principles of supreme importance which have been uniformly maintained, which "represent what the Church has continuously believed with reference to the ministry, and consistently acted upon . . . since the middle of the second century down to the period of the Reformation".[1] These principles Gore sets forth thus:

1. that Christ instituted in his Church, by succession from the Apostles, a permanent ministry of truth and grace, "of the word and sacraments", as an indispensable part of her organization and continuous corporate life:
2. that while there are different offices in this ministry, especially an episcopate, a presbyterate, and a diaconate—with functions and mutual relations fundamentally fixed, though containing also variable elements—there belongs to the order of Bishops, and to them alone, the power to perpetuate the ministry in its several grades, by the transmission of the authority received from the Apostles, its original depositaries; so that, as a consequence, no ministry except such as has been received by episcopal ordination can be legitimately or validly exercised in the Church:
3. that the transmission of ministerial authority, or Ordination, is an outward act, of a sacramental character, in which the laying-on of hands, with prayer, is "the visible sign". It will appear also
4. that the Church, without change of principle, and merely by the clearing-up of ideas, came to reckon the effect of ordination as indelible, and to recognize a Priesthood, the ministry of bishops and presbyters, which it conferred.[2]

If these principles are sound, "we must", as Newman says in his first Tract, "necessarily consider none to be *really* ordained who have not *thus* been ordained". Gore did not hesitate to draw this conclusion. Towards the end of

[1] *The Church and the Ministry* (1888), 104.
[2] Ibid., 104 f.

The Church and the Ministry, he states as a clear consequence of his argument that

> the various presbyterian and congregationalist organizations, however venerable on many and different grounds, have, in dispensing with the episcopal successions, violated a fundamental law of the Church's life . . . . Beyond all question they "took to themselves" these powers of ordination, and consequently had them not . . . . It follows then—not that God's grace has not worked, and worked largely, through many an irregular ministry where it was exercised or used in good faith but—that a ministry not episcopally received is invalid, that is to say, falls outside the conditions of covenanted security and cannot justify its existence in terms of the covenant.[1]

To an imagined retort, "How can you suppose that we can accept conclusions which would falsify the prolonged experience we have had in our churches of the systematic action of the grace of God?", Gore would reply: "We do not ask you to deny any spiritual experience of the past or the present. The blame for separations lies, on any fair showing, quite sufficiently with the Church, to make it intelligible that God should have let the action of His grace extend itself widely and freely beyond its covenanted channels".[2] This large admission did not, however, modify his general conclusion.

"The conception of the Church, the apostolic succession, and the Anglican vocation held by Charles Gore had immense influence. It deeply affected, though it did not wholly determine, the Anglican approach towards Christian reunion."[3] For that reason it has been important to consider his position in some detail and to set it against Headlam's; the two represent the poles between which Anglican thinking on this issue has moved ever since. A vast literature could be cited in which the grounds on which either view rests have been gone over, but with no significant change of detail.

If *The Apostolic Ministry* sought to find somewhat new

[1] Ibid., 313. [2] Ibid., 314.

[3] A. M. Ramsey, *From Gore to Temple* (1960), 116.

support for what was virtually Gore's position by the more than dubious device of equating *shaliach* with *apostolos* too precisely, and attempting to prove that the Apostles had the mandate to transmit their apostolate because the *sheluchim* could transmit their office and authority, little of the new foundation survived the undermining blast of T. W. Manson's criticism in *The Church's Ministry*: Gore's version stands the test of examination better than the work of Kenneth Kirk and his colleagues.[1]

Had the Free Churches been more familiar with the ways of thinking characteristic of the writings of either Gore or Headlam, and of the members of the Lambeth Conference, they might have been able to make more vigorous and more fruitful reactions to the claims made and the suggestions offered. Under the stimulus of the Tractarian Movement the Anglican Church had done a good deal of thinking about the nature of the Church and its ministry, by no means all of it favourable to the Tractarian point of view. The Free Churches, on the other hand, had become either more aggressively anti-Romanist or had become so obsessed with the more extreme forms of theological liberalism that it was questioned by many of them whether the Church had any relevance to the Gospel at all: might it be no more than an optional extra for Christians who are gregarious, and the form of its life and ministry a matter of taste or convenience? The fact that one cannot point to volumes by Free Church scholars which compare in weight of scholarship and ecclesiastical statesmanship with those of Gore and Headlam is significant enough: for the first decade or so of our period the best Free Church scholars were occupied with other issues than that of the Church and its ministry and stood aside somewhat from leadership in the Churches, while the leaders either were not scholars at all or did not see that theological issues were deeply involved in their most important tasks. A book which shows how things stood is P. T.

[1] K. E. Kirk (ed.), *The Apostolic Ministry* (1946); T. W. Manson, *The Church's Ministry* (1948).

Forsyth's *Lectures on the Church and the Sacraments*.[1] It is a stinging rebuke to the unchurchly and unbiblical ways in which Free Churchmen of that time were thinking about the Church and its life and worship; at the same time it raises and expounds the issues which Free Churchmen need to raise when Anglican claims are made in the way in which Gore expounded them. To sense from his book the background against which Forsyth wrote is to understand how unprepared the Free Churches were to understand and reply to Gore; nor does Forsyth himself come within sight of answering him in his own terms. He insists that the Church arises from the Gospel, and must be understood in the light of that from which it takes its origin and be seen as rising essentially from it: "we belong to the Church because we belong to Christ". He pleads for Christian unity, thinking that federation might well be a way towards it, declaring that polity is a matter of relative indifference, and rejecting the idea that uniformity of polity was at all necessary for unity. While he also rejects the notion that the Church is an extension of the incarnation, he insists that our thinking about the ministry must be sacramental. Of immediate relevance to our topic is Forsyth's emphasis on three points which have subsequently had great influence upon Free Church thinking. First, he wished to combat a popular misunderstanding of the Church as a voluntary society, which seemed to suggest that in New Testament times "the great Church was composed by the coagulation of a certain number of single Churches, each of which was a Church in its own right". He argues that something very different was in fact the case:

> what the Apostles planted was not Churches but stations of the Church. What the Gospel created was not a crowd of Churches but the one Church in various places. What we have everywhere is the one Church of Christ put down here and there, looking out in Corinth, Ephesus, or Thessalonica . . . . Wherever you went it did not matter, you went to *the one*

[1] Published in 1917; 2nd edn (1947) as *The Church and the Sacraments*.

> *Church* . . . . The localness was a mere matter of convenience . . . . It [i.e. the local Church] had a right to exist only as a living occurrence of the one Church.[1]

In the second place, Forsyth pleads that the work of reformation was not simply an event in the sixteenth and seventeenth centuries, but a continuing task: he thought it doubtful whether the Reformation, so far as it had gone, was sufficient or final, and was certain that "the Reformation itself is in process of being reformed. And that it needs it is shown by the state of those Churches or parties in Churches that claim to have the special guardianship of the evangelical principle, but which have ruined the name of evangelical almost beyond recovery". The principle of this continuing reformation, which purges the Church of what is unchristian and at the same time "makes the sect die to its spirit of separation" is the Gospel: reformation according to the Word of God.[2] Thirdly, Forsyth makes a comment on apostolical succession. He argues that the Apostles could not send out as they had been sent by Christ, and that the ministry is no more the prolongation of the apostolate than the Church is an extension of the incarnation. "The prolongation of the Apostolate and the legatee of its unique authority . . . is the New Testament . . . . The Apostolic succession was at first a succession of truth".[3] This is followed by a series of characteristically caustic comments on the use of such terms as "invalid" and "irregular" to describe Free Church ministries: "there is but one thing that regularises the ministry. It is the gospel and a Church of the gospel."[4] While it may truly be said that Forsyth has not really weighed the value of historic continuity or adequately reckoned its importance in the life of the Church, he recognized two facts about the apostolic succession which are both of great importance. On the one hand, as over against the impatience of some Free Churchmen, he has seen that the doctrine of

[1] Op. cit., 63.
[2] Ibid., 68 f.
[3] Ibid., 129, with n. 1.
[4] Ibid., 131.

apostolic succession raises the right question, even if the usual Catholic answer cannot be regarded as satisfactory. How is the Church in this age to maintain its claim to be identical with the Church in the apostolic age? Unless an adequate answer to that question be found, the Church has lost effective contact with its Founder. Whether, on the other hand, Forsyth's answer to the question is adequate is still debated, and by many Anglicans still denied; but those who most heartily reject it should see in it the typically Free Church belief that a doctrine of succession through office and/or officers is, *by itself and standing alone*, actually or potentially in contradiction to the New Testament conception of grace, and that the whole notion of succession in whatever form it be cherished must, like all else in the Church, come under the judgement of the Gospel. Twenty-five years later these points were taken up in a remarkable book by D. T. Jenkins, *The Nature of Catholicity* (1942), in which what is essentially the same position is stated, with the difference that, much more explicitly than Forsyth, Jenkins seeks to state the Free Church point of view in terms intelligible to Anglicans and within the context of current theological debate.

The relative unpreparedness of the Free Churches to deal with Anglican claims is evident in such responses as they made to the Lambeth Appeal of 1920 and similar approaches in more recent years. It may be that what might have been said had the non-episcopalians been thinking with the same power on these matters would not have been essentially different from what in fact was said: but it might have been said with greater acumen and more impressive depth.

After the Lambeth Conference of 1920 a Joint Conference of Anglicans and Free Churchmen was held, a report of which appeared in May 1922. Among the best known of the Free Church leaders taking part were J. D. Jones (the then Free Church Moderator), A. E. Garvie, John Scott Lidgett,

P. Carnegie Simpson, and J. H. Shakespeare. The main topics of consideration were the nature of the Church, the nature of the ministry, and the place of creeds in a united Church. A considerable measure of agreement was reached, as is set forth in the *Report as Accepted by the Conference*:[1] in particular it was agreed that the episcopate ought to be accepted as such for any possible united Church, though it was explicitly stated that acceptance of episcopal ordination "would not imply the acceptance of any particular theory as to its origin and character, or the disowning of past ministries of Word and Sacrament otherwise received, which have, together with those received by Episcopal Ordination, been used and blessed by the Spirit of God". Moreover, it was agreed that the Nicene Creed should be accepted in such a united Church as a sufficient statement of its corporate faith, on the understanding that this should not be understood as accepting creeds as a complete expression of the Christian Faith or as excluding reasonable liberty of interpretation; they would be accepted as "agreeable to the Word of God contained in the Holy Scriptures". Alongside this recognition of the rightful place of creeds in the life of the Church should go a recognition of the continued presence and teaching of the Holy Spirit within the Body of Christ.

At the annual Assembly of the Evangelical Free Churches of England in September 1922 this report was received with general approval, while certain outstanding difficulties were recognized, among them particularly the status of the existing Free Church ministries, upon which a memorandum was later prepared by the Anglican members of the Joint Conference.[2] This important document recognized the Free Church ministries to be "real ministries of Christ's Word and Sacraments in the Universal Church", and suggested

[1] *Documents on Christian Unity 1920–4*, ed. G. K. A. Bell (1924), 143 ff.

[2] Ibid., 156 ff.

that the terms *valid* and *invalid* should fall out of use, since they seemed to imply a knowledge of the divine will, purpose, and grace "which we do not possess, and which it would be presumption to claim". Nevertheless, it was asserted that "the Anglican Church is bound to secure the authorization of its ministers for its own congregations, and no one could be authorized to exercise his ministry among them who had not been episcopally ordained". This decision was reached not merely out of a desire to maintain a matter of internal discipline, but because it embodied a principle to which the Anglican Church had adhered throughout its history, and because to abandon it would not only minimize the special position which the Anglican Church claims within the Christian Church, but might impair relations with other episcopal Churches in West and East and cause pain and even schism within the Anglican Church itself. This issue was further elucidated in a second statement on the same subject, dated 19 June 1925, when the distinction between "spiritual efficacy" and "due authority" is expounded, and the issue of reordination is explained as ordination *sub conditione*.[1] The Evangelical Free Churches felt bound to reply that there was "little or no prospect of this being accepted by any non-episcopal Church",[2] and insisted that authorization of non-episcopal ministers to serve in any newly formed united Church must be otherwise than by ordination; and the Congregationalists, believing that to say that ministries "possess spiritual reality" is inconsistent with insisting on episcopal ordination, declared that "we should be prepared to welcome some solemn act of mutual recognition; but the proposal of ordination *sub conditione* cannot be accepted by us".[3] These Joint Conferences were suspended in 1925, to be resumed again after the Lambeth Conference of 1930. In 1936 the Joint Conference issued

[1] *Documents on Christian Unity: Second Series*, ed. G. K. A. Bell (1930), 79 ff.

[2] Ibid., 100 f. [3] Ibid., 115.

A Sketch of a United Church, which the Convocation of Canterbury commended to the attention of the Church; and in 1938 there came an *Outline of a Reunion Scheme.*[1] The *Outline* is a thorough and eirenical document, drawn up by Anglican and Free Churchmen together; and it drew from the Free Church Federal Council a lengthy reply in September 1941[2] in which exactly the same points were raised about episcopacy. By this time, however, the world was at war. Afterwards, as we have seen, Archbishop Fisher reopened conversations between the Anglican Communion and the non-episcopal Churches not on the topic of reunion as such, but on intercommunion; and, having perceived, it may be, the difficulty of dealing with the Free Churches as a whole through the Free Church Federal Council, he preferred to consult with each of the non-episcopal Churches separately. He was to find that the change of theme did not bring any change of difficulties: whether the theme be intercommunion or reunion, precisely the same issues are involved.

Less thoughtful enthusiasts for reunion are apt to regard this as a bleak prospect, and are inclined to counsel impatient or even lawless action to further the desired end of closer relations between the Churches; but it would be idle to pretend that the theological issues involved in reunion are not serious, or to pretend that they can be bypassed. There are, however, some signs that serious theological discussion is taking new and hopeful turns. In addition to the continual encounter of participation in the British Council of Churches and the World Council of Churches, through which they come to deeper and deeper mutual understanding, two particular points may be noted. Whereas the conclusion to be drawn from this sketch of the history of church relations in England since 1910 might

[1] *Documents on Christian Unity: Third Series, 1930–48*, ed. G. K. A. Bell (1948), 71 ff.

[2] Ibid., 102 ff.

seem to be that there are two distinct and separate understandings of the Christian Church which are virtually irreconcilable, the significant fact is that neither party to these discussions can conscientiously accept such a conclusion. While the Catholic Anglican affirms his understanding of the nature of the Church and its ministry in such a way as demonstrates the plain impossibility of reunion by slick ecclesiastical joinery, he cannot and does not desire to disown his Free Church brethren: he sees and accepts them as part of the Universal Church. Similarly, the Free Churchman, holding to his Protestant convictions more strongly, because more deeply, than was possible a generation ago, convinced that he must be loyal to the ecclesiastical consequences of justification by faith alone, cannot and does not desire to disown his Anglo-Catholic brethren. So the two apparently self-consistent and mutually exclusive wholes are not what they appear to be, and must each derive from a common source which it is our business to discover and express. It may be that we have already begun to do this in more recent discussions about episcopacy. "Bishop" is now a loaded word, not only north of the Tweed; yet ἐπισκοπή is a feature of the life of every Church, whether it be exercised by an individual, a presbytery, or a local church meeting; and it seems possible that the Churches may learn from one another how to enlarge and enrich what each already in part possesses.

Certainly, if we are to be obedient to the task which Christ has laid upon us of discovering the outward unity which is his will for his Church, we must continue to learn from one another what is Christ's will for the nature of the Church, what each has learned about ἐπισκοπή and pastoral oversight, discipline and authority, so that "the coming Great Church" shall contain the treasures we have severally gathered. If the episcopalians and the non-episcopalians continue to confront one another from prepared positions which neither is ready to modify, we are at a deadlock indeed; but if each is prepared not only to learn from history or from the Churches' achievements hitherto but also to consider what it is Christ's will that his Church should become, then the Holy Spirit will in the end surely bring us to the place where Christ is all in all.

BIBLIOGRAPHICAL EXCURSUS ON WORKS PUBLISHED 1660-1665

GEOFFREY F. NUTTALL

A RECENT survey of the works published during the six years 1660–5 in relation to the restoration of the Church of England and to the beginnings of Nonconformity has revealed that their number was very considerable. By far the most prolific year was 1660, then 1661, and so on with a steady decrease, till in 1665 relatively few pieces appeared. The purpose of the present brief excursus is, with the help of this survey,[1] to draw attention to about a hundred little-known items, reference to few of which has been made in the earlier chapters of this book. The following nine headings have been chosen:

1. Restoration sermons
2. Sequestrations
3. Fanatics and plots
4. Oaths and covenants
5. Ceremonies
6. Prayer and the Prayer Book
7. Episcopacy and ordination
8. Uniformity, conformity, and nonconformity
9. Moderation and peace

1. Restoration Sermons

The restoration of the monarchy in 1660, and therewith of the Church of England, was naturally acclaimed by many preachers. Most but by no means all of these conformed in

[1] For this survey, which was undertaken by representatives of the Baptist, Congregational, Friends', Presbyterian, and Unitarian Historical Societies, together with Dr Williams's Librarian, see *The Beginnings of Nonconformity, 1660–1665: a checklist*, ed. G. F. Nuttall (duplicated, vii + 82 pp. + 38 pp. appendix on Quaker and Anti-Quaker writings, obtainable from Dr Williams's Library, 14 Gordon Square, London W.C.1, 20*s*., with the following primary locations: Dr Williams's Library; the Congregational Library; the Library of the Society of Friends; Lambeth Palace; New College, London; and Sion College).

1662. The obvious title *God save the king* was chosen by Ames Short, vicar of Lyme Regis, who in 1662 was ejected, as well as by Anthony Walker, rector of Fyfield, Essex, who conformed, and by others. Gilbert Sheldon's sermon, *Davids deliverance*, is almost his only published work. Richard Baxter's carries the characteristic title, *Right rejoycing*. Many sermons also were published in which the fidelity of Charles I to the Church of England was recalled with admiration, such as *King Charles I his imitation of Christ*, by J. W., and *The royall martyr*, by W. H. B. Henry Leslie brought out a new edition of his *Martyrdome of King Charles I*. The rector of Little Horsted, Sussex, Nehemiah Beaton, who in 1661 published a sermon entitled *No treason to say, kings are Gods subjects*, was among the ejected a year later.

2. Sequestrations

Walter Bushnell, sequestered vicar of Box, Wiltshire, published a *Narrative of the proceedings of the commissioners . . . for ejecting scandalous and ignorant ministers* (1660) on his own case; to which one of the commissioners, Humphrey Chambers, rector of Pewsey, Wiltshire, who was ejected in 1662, issued an *Answer* (1660). To the *Apology in the behalf of the sequestred clergy* (1660) by Robert Mossom, sequestered curate of Teddington, Middlesex, an anonymous *Plea for ministers in sequestrations* (1660) appeared in reply. An anonymous *Humble caution concerning the danger of removing godly and approved ministers out of sequestrations* (1660) was also published.

3. Fanatics and Plots

In 1660 those whose religious convictions led them to oppose the restoration of the Church of England were quickly identified with those whose political opinions made them dangerous to the restored monarchy: as in the anonymous *Old anabaptists grand plot discovered*; *Mirrour, wherein the rumpers and fanaticks may see their deformity*; and *Phanaticks plot discovered.* In 1661 Venner's rebellion provided additional ground for the identification: as in the anonymous *True discovery of a bloody plot contrived by the phanaticks*; *Semper iidem: or a parallel betwixt the ancient and modern phanatics*; and *Munster paralleld in the late massacres committed by the fifth-monarchists* (copy at Sion College). A *Renuntiation and declaration of the ministers of congregational churches . . . in . . . London: against the late horrid insurrection* (1661), carrying twenty-five signatures, was put out; but the *Brief narrative of that stupendious tragedie late intended to be acted by the satanical saints*, which was published in 1662, was so popular that it was reissued in the following year.

4. Oaths and Covenants

On the oaths of allegiance and supremacy, Theophilus Brabourne wrote *Of the lawfulness of the oath of allegiance* (1661); Philip Nye *The lawfulness of the oath of supremacy* (1662); and the Baptist John Tombes, vicar of Leominster, Herefordshire, who in 1662 was ejected, a succession of pieces, *A serious consideration of the oath of the kings supremacy* (1660); a *Supplement* (1660/1) to this; and *Sepher-sheba, or the oath-book* (1662).

On the perpetuity or abrogation of the Solemn League and Covenant, a protracted controversy was carried on between John Gauden, who was to become Bishop of Worcester, and Zachary Crofton, the ejected curate of St Botolph's, Aldgate, London, whose autobiographical *Defence against the dread of death* (1665) was written in 1662 at a time when he was imprisoned in the Tower of London. When in 1660 Gauden reissued his *Certaine scruples and doubts of conscience about taking the solemne league and covenant* of 1645, Crofton attacked this in *'Ανάληψις, or Saint Peters bonds abide* (1660). Gauden then issued *'Ανάλυσις. The loosing of St Peters bands* (1660), to which Crofton replied in *'Ανάληψις ἀνελήφθη, The fastning of St Peters fetters* (1660). Gauden retorted in *Anti-baal-berith, or . . . a just vindication of Dr Gauden's Analysis*

(1661), to which Crofton replied once more in *Berith-anti-baal* (1661). Outliers in this controversy were the anonymous *Anatomy of Dr Gauden's idolized non-sence and blasphemy in his pretended Analysis* (1660); *The solemn league and covenant discharg'd or St Peters bonds not only loosed but annihilated* (1660), by John Russell, sequestered rector of Chingford, Essex; *Short strictures or animadversions on . . . Mr Croftons Fastning St Peters bonds* (1661), by Thomas Tomkins, conforming Fellow of All Souls, Oxford; the anonymous *Mr Croftons case soberly considered* (1661, copy in Congregational Library), by Hugh Griffith, Henry Hall, James Green, and Thomas Eaton; and *Anti-baal-berith justified* (1662; copy at Regent's Park College, Oxford) by Robert Cressener. Other pieces on this subject included *The solemn league and covenant arraigned and condemned* (1661; copy at Sion College), by Laurence Womock, who became Bishop of St David's; *An abandoning of the Scotish covenant* (1662), by Matthew Wren; and a *Discourse of the nature and obligation of oaths: wherein satisfaction is tendered touching the . . . unlawfulness of . . . the solemn league and covenant* (1662), published anonymously by John Stileman, conforming vicar of Tonbridge, Kent.

5. Ceremonies

Eleazar Duncon, sequestered rector of Haughton-le-Skerne, Co. Durham, published *Of worshipping God towards the altar* (1660). Replies to this were *Altar worship, or bowing to the communion-table* (1661), by Zachary Crofton; and *Bowing towards the altar . . . impleaded as grossely superstitious* (1661), by Daniel Cawdrey, rector of Great Billing, Northamptonshire, who was ejected in 1662. William Wickins, ejected rector of St George's, Southwark, issued *The warrant for bowing at the name Jesus . . . examined* (1660); an anonymous piece, *Several arguments against bowing at the name of Jesus* (1660), also appeared. Among more general works were the anonymous *Modest discourse concerning the ceremonies . . . shewing the unlawfulness of them* (1660); and *Dissertatio de ceremoniis ecclesiae anglicanae, qua usus earum licitus ostenditur* (1661), by George Ritschel, conforming vicar of Hexham, Northumberland.

6. Prayer and the Prayer Book

The conciliatory tone of *A help to prayer and meditation both extempore and by a set forme* (1660), by Zachary Bogan, Fellow of Corpus Christi College, Oxford, breathed an earlier air, for it was written in 1651 and Bogan had died in 1659. Henry Hammond issued *A Vindication of the ancient liturgie of the Church of England* (1660); Nathaniel Hardy, conforming rector of St Dionis Backchurch, London, *The apostolical liturgy revived* (1661); John Durel, who was to become Dean of Windsor, *The liturgy of the Church of England asserted* (1662); and John Barbon, conforming vicar of Dallington, Northumberland, *Λειτουργία θειοτέρα ἐργία: or liturgie a most divine service* (Oxford, 1662). Another Oxford publication was the anonymous *Touching the liturgy or common-prayer-book, certain queries and objections answered, together with a letter to a non-conformist, by a friend to the Church of England* (1661; copy in the Congregational Library), which was probably by the sequestered rector of St Nicholas, Hereford, Clement Barksdale.[1] An anonymous *Defence of the liturgy of the Church of England* (1661) also appeared. On the other side, in addition to the pieces noticed in chapter 3 of this book, were *The common prayer-book unmasked . . . by divers ministers of Gods word* (1660); the Scottish Robert Baillie's *Parallel of the liturgy with the mass-book* (1661); and an anonymous *Position disputing the lawfulnesse of ministers receiving an imposed liturgy* (1663; copy at Sion College). Henry Leslie wrote a *Discourse of praying with the spirit and with the understanding* (1660); and John Bunyan, *I will pray with the spirit* (1663). In *Pulpit-conceptions, popular deceptions* (1662) Laurence Womock attacked what was then termed "conceived prayer".

[1] Cf. Falconer Madan, *Oxford Books*, iii (Oxford, 1931), item 2546; no copy was known to Madan, and this piece is not listed by Donald Wing, *Short-title catalogue*, iii (New York, 1951).

7. Episcopacy and Ordination

To accompany his anonymous *Englands monarchy asserted* (1660), Sir Edmund Peirce put out an anonymous *English episcopacy and liturgy asserted* (1660). An anonymous *Remonstrance to the presbyterians concerning the government established in the Church of England; and a vindication of episcopacy* also appeared in 1660; and *A scholasticall discourse demonstrating . . . the order and jurisdiction of the bishops of the Church of England*, by R.C., in 1663. On the other side, in addition to the pieces noticed in chapter 3 of this book, attention may be drawn to *A serious review of presbyters reordination by bishops* (1661), by Zachary Crofton; and to *The holding the bishop and presbyter equall* (1661), by Luke Cranwell, vicar of St Peter's, Derby, who was ejected in 1662.

8. Uniformity, Conformity and Nonconformity

John Gauden published the anonymous piece, *χάρις καὶ εἰρήνη: or some considerations upon the act of uniformity* (1662; copy at Lambeth Palace). To *The grand case of the present ministry: whether they may lawfully declare and subscribe, as by the late act of uniformity is demanded* (1662), issued anonymously by Francis Fullwood, who in 1660 had become Archdeacon of Totnes, Devon, reply was made in *A short surveigh of The grand case . . . by some conformable non-conformists* (1663), by M(ark) D(own), the ejected rector of St Petrock's, Exeter, and four others; Fullwood retorted with an anonymous *Review of The grand case* (1663). Laurence Womock's *Antidote to cure the calamites* (1663) (*sic*, the reference is to Edmund Calamy) was answered by R.S. in *A word to Dr Womocke* (1663; not listed by Wing, but copy at Sion College); Womock replied with *Conformity re-asserted, in an echo to R.S.* (1664; copies at Sion College and the Congregational Library).

The old non-conformist, touching the book of common-prayer (copy in Dr Williams's Library) appeared anonymously in

1660, and *The judgment of the old nonconformists* anonymously in 1662; but the use in a title of the term "nonconformist" in reference to the Act of Uniformity perhaps appears first in Sir John Birkenhead's anonymous *Cabala: or an impartial account of the non-conformists private designs* (1662); to which the anonymous *Mystery of godlinesse, and no cabala: or a sincere account of the non-conformists conversation* (1663) was a reply. Birkenhead's *Cabala* is to be distinguished from the anonymous *Cabala: or the mystery of conventicles* (1664; copy in the Congregational Library), by David Lloyd, later canon of St Asaph. Thomas Palk, ejected curate of Woodland, Ipplepen, Devon, published *The loyal non-conformist* (1664; not listed by Wing, but copy at Dr Williams's Library); and Robert Wild, ejected rector of Tatenhill, Staffordshire, *The grateful nonconformist* (1665). The anonymous *Sober enquiry about the new oath enjoyned on non-conformists* (1665) was by John Tickell, who had lost his position as one of the ministers in Exeter appointed by the Corporation, but who later conformed and became curate of Barnstaple, Devon.

9. Moderation and Peace

A number of conformist writers sought, with Herbert Thorndike, a *Due way of composing the differences* (1660). William White, conforming rector of Pusey, Berkshire, published *Via ad pacem ecclesiasticam* (Oxoniae, 1660); Martin Blake, sequestered vicar of Barnstaple, Devon, *An earnest plea for peace and moderation* (1661); Edward Stillingfleet, later Bishop of Worcester, *Irenicum: a weapon-salve for the churches wounds* (1661); John Stileman, *Peace-offering: an earnest and passionate intreaty for peace, unity and obedience* (1662); and Alan Carr, conforming rector of West Chiltington, Sussex, *A peaceable moderator: or some plain considerations to give satisfaction to such as stand disaffected to our book of common prayer* (1665). The anonymous *Way to true peace: or a calm, seasonable, and modest word to independents, phanaticks, anabaptists, presbyterians, quakers, papists and fifth monarchists* and the anonymous

Terms of accommodation between those of the episcopall and their brethren of the presbyterian perswasions . . . by a countrey minister both appeared in 1661; *The reformed presbyterian: humbly offering . . . arguments for obedience to the act for uniformity, as the way to unity*, by Richard Lytler, in 1662. Richard Baxter's hopes and aspirations are contained in his *Catholick unity, True catholick*, and *Universal concord* (all 1660). *The moderate independent proposing a word in season to the churches episcopal and presbyterial* (1660; copies at Sion College and the Congregational Library), which was anonymous, stands somewhat alone.

INDEX

INDEX

Virtually all references to seventeenth-century names are included; references to most other names are included only if they occur in the text.

FROM UNIFORMITY TO UNITY
1662-1962

Nuttall, Geoffrey, F. & Chadwick, Owen

DATE DUE

APR 1 6 2008			